TENTH-CENTURY STUDIES

New Minster Charter, BM Cotton Vespasian A.viii, folio 2ᵛ. King Edgar adoring Christ.
By courtesy of the Trustees of the British Museum. Photo: BM.

TENTH–CENTURY STUDIES

Essays in Commemoration of the Millennium
of the Council of Winchester and
Regularis Concordia

Edited with an Introduction
by

DAVID PARSONS

Phillimore

1975

Published by
PHILLIMORE & CO. LTD.
London and Chichester

Head Office: Shopwyke Hall,
Chichester, Sussex, England

ISBN 0 85033 179 X

Thanks are due to the generous help of
The Marc Fitch Fund
and
University of Leicester Research and Education Boards
in enabling this volume to be published

Printed in Great Britain by
UNWIN BROTHERS LIMITED
at The Gresham Press, Old Woking, Surrey

CONTENTS

LIST OF ILLUSTRATIONS

PLATES

TEXT FIGURES

PREFACE

Among the tasks of adult education, at least in its university extra-mural aspect, are those of helping to keep specialists up to date in their own field and *au courant* with developments in related subjects; and of providing a forum for interdisciplinary debate, which is not easy to arrange as frequently as one would wish in other sectors of education. It was with these aims in mind that the University of Leicester Department of Adult Education held a conference in December 1970, to celebrate the millennium of the compilation of *Regularis Concordia*. The conference was an attempt to set *Regularis Concordia* against its ideological and physical background by presenting papers on a wide range of specialist topics covering the fields of church and medieval history, literature and liturgy, art history and archaeology. Thus it gave a conspectus of English affairs in the late tenth century (although with some regrettable but unavoidable omissions) by putting *Regularis Concordia* itself — while it provided the theme and the opportunity for the conference — into perspective.

It is hoped that the title chosen for this publication of the conference papers fairly represents that perspective; that it will attract students and general readers as well as specialists; that they will find the individual chapters a comprehensible introduction to the fields of study which they represent; that it will be apparent in the volume as it was at the conference that there is an essential unity of interest among the specialist contributors (indeed, the notes to their chapters make plain the extent to which they use common material for somewhat different purposes); and that at the same time this publication will give some impression of the great diversity and breadth of interest in late Saxon England and the materials it offers for study.

It is hardly surprising that the various chapters display an equal diversity, not only in their subject matter but also in their length and degree of originality. In some cases, such as Abbot Symons's and Mr Farmer's chapters, much has appeared in print already and what is needed is a résumé of the current state of knowledge. In others, for instance Professor Wickham's and Mr Biddle's, major publications are expected in the near future, and a summary statement seems appropriate in the context of this book. At the other end of the scale, the precise subject of some chapters, like Mr Hohler's, has received little attention so far in print, and the authors have thought it necessary to go into some detail in arguing a case or in making clear the limitations of the material. Amidst all this diversity, though, what has seemed important is that all the papers should appear together, rather than scattered in a wide variety of journals.

With two exceptions this book consists of the papers read at the conference, but they have been amended as a result of discussion when they were delivered and of further study since. Originally there was no paper on the general history of the monastic revival, and Mr Farmer has kindly written his chapter specially for this publication. The conference sadly missed the presence of the late Professor Francis Wormald, who was to have given the paper on manuscript illumination but was unfortunately prevented by illness; Dr Alexander read a paper in his stead, and it is that which appears here. Mr Eric John was also unable to attend, and his place in the programme was taken by Professor Bullough, whose contribution was an entirely independent paper on a rather different topic. Unfortunately it has not proved possible to include a chapter from Mr John.

One of the perplexities facing the editor of a collection of papers such as these is the order in which they should be presented. The inter-relations between them are so complex that the necessarily linear progression of a book cannot hope to do them justice. Perhaps the order is not important. At all events, I hope that that which I have decided upon does not appear too arbitrary or unsatisfactory; I have tried in the introduction to outline the underlying logic of the book as a whole, and to indicate throughout the major points at which the reader might profitably refer to matter in another chapter. These cross-references are given in the margin by means of italic numerals; marginal numbers preceded by 'Plate' or 'Fig.' refer to the illustrations in this volume.

1970 was chosen for the conference since it was a thousand years after the normally accepted 'round figure' date for the writing of *Regularis Concordia*. Abbot Symons argues here for 973 as the date of the Council of Winchester which authorised its production; when this preface was first written it was hoped that these papers would be published in 1973, and thus celebrate the millennium a second time. This intention has been frustrated by difficulties in the printing industry, and further delay was caused by the national three-day week of winter 1973-74.

I am grateful to Mrs Betty Britton and to the clerical staff of my department for help with the typescript; to Mrs Vivienne Robertson, who typed the index; and to Dr Babette Evans, Mr D.H. Farmer, the late Professor H.P.R. Finberg, Professor H.A. Jones, Mr M.M. Rix and Dom Alberic Stacpoole, OSB, for much help, advice and encouragement. My wife called over all the proofs with me, including every item of punctuation (though it is my fault if any errors remain uncorrected), and helped me compile the index; my children Richard and Katharine helped with the final check-sheets. They all have my special thanks.

David Parsons

Leicester, July 1972, revised February 1975.

ACKNOWLEDGMENTS

Permission to reproduce the following illustrations is gratefully acknowledged:

Bayrische Staatsbibliothek, Munich: Plate XXIV*c*.
Bibliothéque municipale, Boulogne-sur-Mer: Plate III.
Biblioteca Apostolica Vaticana: Plate VI*b*.
Bodleian Library, Oxford: Plates IV*b*, V*a*, VI*a*, VII*b*.
Department of the Environment: XX*a*.
Herzog Anton Ulrich-Museum, Brunswick: Plate IX.
Lechmere Collection: Plate XIX.
Museum of Archaeology and Ethnology, Cambridge: Plate XX*c*
Royal Commission on Historical Monuments (England), National Monuments Record: Plates XX*a*, XXII*a*.
St John's College, Oxford: Plate V*b*.
Southampton Museum: Plate XXII*b*.
Trinity College, Cambridge: Plate VII*a*.
Trustees of the British Museum: *frontispiece*; Plates IV*a* and *c*, VIII, X, XI, XII, XIII, XIV, XV, XVI*a*, XVIII, XX*a*, XXIII, XXIV*a* and *b*; Fig. 10.
Victoria and Albert Museum, London: Plate XVII.
Warburg Institute, London: Plates VIII, X, XII, XIV, XV.
Winchester Excavations Committee: Plates II, XXII*c*; Figs. 3-6.

Chapter 1

INTRODUCTION

by David Parsons

Thirteen studies by different authors on aspects of the tenth-century monastic revival are bound collectively to present a picture which seems crowded with problems. This is only to be expected when different forms of evidence are treated more or less independently of each other or when the same evidence is interpreted in several different ways; but there are also difficulties inherent in the evidence itself, which at some points at least is apparently inconsistent or paradoxical. Some of these are stated at the outset by Mr Farmer's chapter, which poses a number *Chap. 2* of basic questions, as any good general survey should, about the nature of the monastic reform movement in tenth-century England. Of these perhaps the most significant is the question of the extent to which the impetus of the revival fell away after the death of the three prime movers, Dunstan, Aethelwold and Oswald. In attempting to assess *see pp.15-18* whether there was a decline, or at least to indicate ways of approaching such an assessment, Mr Farmer suggests that the standards of the reform and the reformers were not particularly high in the first place, *see pp.18-19* and that there was not very much for the eleventh century to live up to. At the beginning of a book celebrating the monastic revival one is faced, then, with the proposition that the event is perhaps less worthy of celebration than has commonly been thought. But the issue is not as clear-cut as that; the chapters which follow present very divergent views of the state of affairs in monastic England at the end of the tenth century. Indeed, Mr Farmer's chapter itself is by no means universally critical of the reform movement; and while it embodies a reaction against the uncritical acclaim which the movement receives in some quarters and at the same time points out some of its limitations, it also draws attention to a number of solid achievements to the credit of the *see pp.10-11* reformers, which outlast the tenth century and, in some cases, the Anglo-Saxon period as a whole. These, however, may perhaps be regarded as political and institutional rather than spiritual and intellectual achievements.

It is in the intellectual sphere that there is most evidence and this gives rise to the greatest differences of opinion among the contributors to this volume. Abbot Symons, quoting the internal evidence of *Regularis Concordia* itself, presents a view of its compilers as men *see pp.45-8* familiar with relevant European texts, who made it their business to seek out and study examples of the best monastic practice at the time. Professor Loyn takes a positive view of the achievements of the next *see pp.99-102* generation in the person of Archbishop Wulfstan who may be credited with a high degree of attainment as a creative homilist and political thinker. Looking at the period through its vernacular literature, Pro- *Chap. 8* fessor Clemoes gives an overwhelming impression of the quality and variety of late Old English prose, and of the accurate and intelligent understanding of a considerable range of Latin sources on the part of Aelfric and other writers; typical of their work is a vigorous use of the homily to disseminate the elements of Christian education among the laity. The picture which emerges from Professor Clemoes's survey is of *see p.108* 'an age of intellectual breadth and clarity' in early medieval terms. In *Chap. 5* contrast to this, Mr Hohler draws attention to the gross mishandling of texts from which material was incorporated into *Regularis Concordia* and other documents; he takes a vastly less flattering view of Wulfstan; he suggests that the reformers' knowledge, even of the Bible, was poor; and he castigates them for their incompetence in Latin. Mr Farmer *see pp.15-16* supports him in his view of the clerics' poor latinity, and points out, too, the indifferent quality of the hagiography of the period; to Mr Hohler it comes as no surprise that it was left to foreign scholars to *see p.72* write the Lives of many of the later Anglo-Saxon saints.

Whatever may be the truth about the intellectual state of late tenth-century England, there is no denying the artistic achievement of its monasteries, and in particular of their scriptoria. Manuscripts from the period of the reform until beyond the Norman Conquest, whether richly illuminated in the full colours of the Winchester and derived styles or enlivened by the related line-drawing styles, are high-quality productions. The brilliance of the Winchester Style spills over into the sculpture, especially the ivory-carving, and into the metalwork of the period; although there is a paucity of some classes of material, enough outstanding pieces have survived to indicate the quality that the craftsmen could achieve. It is not clear, however, to what extent these two crafts are a direct or indirect witness of the monastic revival: how far were the craftsmen in independent, secular employment, and merely called upon by the monasteries to fulfil specific orders? The relation-ship of the manuscripts to the reform is clear: they were written in the monasteries by inmates of the monasteries; but it is less certain, as *see p.184* Professor Cramp says, 'how sculpture was produced and under what patronage'. Metalworking is likely to have been an even more secular craft, despite documentary evidence for saintly craftsmen.

None of this is evidence, however, for the quality of spiritual life and monastic observance. The former is difficult, if not impossible, to gauge, although there are features in the liturgical manuscripts which lead Mr Hohler to talk of 'grimmest superstition'. As far as monastic *see p. 72* observance is concerned, even the apparently fanatical St Aethelwold was prepared to relax the Rule on occasion. Evidence of a more *see p. 71* mundane sort suggests that in other quarters the degree of monasticisation was not high. In his analysis of the signatures on leases in the Worcester archive Professor Sawyer is able to show that changes in the *see pp. 87-93* monastic community at Worcester under Oswald were quite slow, and that the number of members disappearing from the lists of signatories over a thirty-five-year period can be satisfactorily accounted for by natural wastage. At all events, there is nothing in the nature of a 'purge' *see p. 89* which could compare with Aethelwold's drastic treatment of the community at Winchester. There is, of course, nothing wrong with a gradualist policy, but the further evidence from the Worcester leases, that signatories were only infrequently described as 'monk', suggests *see pp. 92-3* that the community was very far from being changed into a completely monastic one. This, together with the accepted fact that Canterbury, too, did not become fully monastic until after the death of Dunstan, while it does not justify the outright condemnation of the whole reform movement as ineffectual, does indicate at the least a serious difference of opinion between Dunstan and Oswald, the moderates, on the one hand, and Aethelwold and his adherents, the radicals, on the other, about the pace and rigour of the reform. It may be that such a breach lay behind the Council of Winchester; *Regularis Concordia* states that its intention was to secure uniformity of practice throughout *see pp. 39-40* England, and this was not necessarily confined to externals. One may perhaps speculate that it had become clear to Aethelwold by the early 970s that Dunstan and Oswald, despite their continental experiences, were committed to taking a soft line and would not follow the example of his Winchester expulsions; and that he persuaded the King to summon the Council with the intention of commanding adherence to the radical party line. He was well placed to exert such influence, since he lived until about this time in the royal palace in Winchester. If such *see p. 133* an interpretation is admissible, then Dunstan's possible absence from *see p. 42* the Council and his apparently slight contribution to the text of *Regularis Concordia* appear in a slightly more sinister light.

There is complete agreement about the importance to the revival of royal support. Several contributors mention in passing the part played by King Alfred as a precursor of the tenth-century reform movement, and it may be that his contribution has been undervalued. It is clear, though, that whatever was achieved around 900, including the new monasteries in Winchester and elsewhere, was due entirely to royal initiative. This continued to be true later in the tenth century. Professor Loyn's study of royal enactments shows, for example, that the King's *see pp.97-8* support was necessary for the enforcement of such obligations as the payment of tithes — a basic necessity for the church. It was even more necessary to ensure the proper endowment of the refounded monasteries, and *Fisher I* gives an idea of the possible hardship caused, and the hostility likely to have been engendered, at all levels of society, by the reallocation of estates in favour of the monasteries. The reforming churchmen needed the King on their side to obtain the charters which would confirm their title to these lands. It is interesting to note the part played by Winchester in the matter of the charters. In his introductory *see pp.84-5* remarks Professor Sawyer reminds us that Dr Chaplais has demolished the old theory that there was a central royal chancery in tenth-century England. I hardly dare, as a non-specialist, to argue with them; but when a large number of the charters, and nearly all the early ones, can be shown to issue from the episcopal scriptorium at Winchester, does this not amount to a near monopoly? And is this not tantamount to a central chancery? It does not indeed mean a *royal* chancery; it is something more insidious. It is a private, sectional scriptorium in a monastery directly under the King's protection, which produces documents favourable to the bishop's cause for the King's approval. In these circumstances the King was perhaps little more than a pawn in the monastic game.

The King's involvement in the English revival is underlined by the *see pp.132-3* royal nature of the monastery quarter in Winchester, and the proximity of the royal palace to the Old Minster. One wonders, indeed, whether excavation will one day reveal a physical connection between the palace and the minster of the sort which existed, for example, between Charlemagne's palace and the palatine chapel at Aachen. Not only the Winchester monks, but all who subscribed to *Regularis Concordia* acknowledged their indebtedness to the King; both Abbot Symons and *see pp.44,*
95-6 Professor Loyn place some emphasis on the *Concordia*'s collect for the King and the other invocations on behalf of the royal family. Prayers for royalty can be paralleled in at least one instance on the Continent; an example is quoted by Professor Bullough, who examines prevailing *Chap. 3* European attitudes of rulers to their monasteries and vice versa, as well as the effect on monastic life of political developments generally. One of the features of *Regularis Concordia* is the deliberate involvement of

Edgar's queen in the revival of regular life for nuns; the relations of the English queen with the nunneries under her protection, and those of her continental counterparts, are compared by Professor Bullough. This *see pp.35-6* involvement could be a mixed blessing, as Mr Farmer points out when he refers to the nuns at Barking securing the ejection of their abbess by *see p.17* appealing to the Queen; after the death of Edgar, the monasteries were a convenient whipping-boy in the squabble over the royal succession (see *Fisher I*).

Whether one regards it as the centre of a sophisticated educational system or as an oasis in a cultural desert, there is no doubt that there was something special about Winchester; Mr Biddle's choice of the words *Felix urbs Winthonia* for the title of his paper could hardly be more apposite. The thriving tenth-century town, with its monastic enclave secluded from the bustle of urban life, was a fitting setting for *see p.132* the Council. But was this equally true of the Old Minster, which is normally thought to have accommodated it? Taking Abbot Symons's conclusions about the date of the Council and the evidence of Mr Biddle's excavations together, there is at least a slight suggestion that it was not. Abbot Symons argues for 973 as the likely date for the *see pp.41-2* Council — right between the two translations of St Swithun in 971 and (?)974, a period when a start was made on the rebuilding of the Old *see pp.136-8* Minster; major building works at the west end of the church are not likely to have provided a conducive atmosphere for the Council's proceedings. Against this, one may argue for adherence to the traditional 970 date for the Council, for the completion of the rebuilding of the west end of Old Minster by 973, or for a later start to building work on the minster site. There remains the point made by Mr Biddle that the Old Minster was a small church cluttered with internal fittings and *see pp.131, 136* monuments: one wonders whether it could have coped with the number of people who attended the council. On this point Mr Biddle has drawn my attention to the church council which was held in Winchester Castle in 1072, and which was accommodated in a chapel one third of the size of the Old Minster; it is therefore possible that the Old Minster of 970/3 was perfectly adequate for the task. Unless further evidence on any of these points is forthcoming, nothing conclusive can be said. It would be premature to reject the Old Minster as the likeliest site for the Council of Winchester, but not perhaps unwise to bear in mind the possibility of an alternative venue: the obvious candidate is the New Minster. It too was a royal foundation *see pp.131, 134-6* and lay within the royal quarter of the city; kings had been buried there in the earlier part of the tenth century; it was larger than Old Minster, and moreover it was a 'public' church. It was certainly more up to date

see pp.136, 138
than the Old Minster, which does not seem to have been at all well suited to the use of a developed liturgy before the rededication in 980;
see pp.142-52 and Fig.13, p.151
it is almost inconceivable that the sort of processions which were a feature of the church of St Riquier could have been held there.

see p.141, 168
In this connection Dr Taylor emphasises the need to consider the liturgy of the tenth century in any attempt to understand church design of the period or to attribute a particular function to any given part of a church building: this approach has been employed for some time by our continental colleagues, but it has not so far received as much attention in this country as its importance deserves. Combining the
Chaps. 11, 5
evidence from Dr Taylor's and Mr Hohler's chapters, it looks as though the story of English architectural development in the tenth century is one of buildings being adapted to keep pace with liturgical needs; these needs developed in their turn as the English church service books, ultimately of Roman origin, were gradually rewritten to take account
see pp.81-2
of liturgical practices in Western Europe. A good example of this kind of liturgical elaboration is the dramatic element in the Easter services incorporated in *Regularis Concordia* itself. This element is discussed in
Chap. 9
relation to the development of medieval drama by Professor Wickham,
see p.116
who points out that the *platea* is a prerequisite for a dramatic presentation. In spite of the restricted action of the Easter drama in *Regularis Concordia,* the crowded Old Minster of the early 970s barely offered the space needed for this sort of dramatised service. The New Minster type of building, which apparently had a continuous transept or at least a reasonable amount of open space in front of the sanctuary, would have been better suited to this kind of use. It seems likely that this sort of ornamentation of the liturgy was one of the stimuli for the building and rebuilding of churches in the late tenth century; despite English architectural conservatism, churches like those illustrated in
see p. 143; Fig.17, p. 164
Fig. 7, or like Deerhurst with its raised sanctuary area and its open space between nave and altar, probably took shape about this time. It is a matter of some regret that there is an almost total lack of English
see p.60
liturgical manuscripts before about 900, so that it is impossible to tell how far such features as the *Regularis Concordia* Easter service were an innovation; could their novelty have been proved, the date of the Council of Winchester might have been taken as a convenient *terminus post quem* for the development of the relevant Anglo-Saxon church types, which are otherwise undatable.

*   *   *

One of the central themes of this book, which emerges in nearly every chapter, is the subject of Professor Bullough's 'great unwritten book': England and the Continent in the tenth century. It is rather a perplexing topic. There is no doubt that England was much involved with Europe during this period, whether directly and politically, as in the series of continental marriages of Edward the Elder's daughters, or more peripherally, by such matters as the reception of refugee clergy, the inscription of English names in continental confraternity books, the exchange of manuscripts and relics, or the possible importation of metalwork from as far afield as Austria (examples are given by Professor Bullough, Mr Hohler, Dr Alexander and Professor Wilson). But the extent and the nature of anything which could properly be termed 'continental influence' are difficult to define. Sometimes specific instances of influence can be quoted, such as the overt involvement of monks from continental houses in the compilation of *Regularis Concordia* and the clear parallels between parts of the *Concordia* text and the usage of the Cluniac and Lotharingian monasteries. Sometimes the connections seem more generalised, such as the wide-ranging sources for the *Concordia* text apart from those just mentioned, or the simple percolation of a climate of thought, as in the adoption in England of the Carolingian theocratic compromise in relations between Church and State. In the matter of the church service books, discussed above, Mr Hohler's final summary point is that no neat picture emerges of continental usage being taken over lock, stock and barrel, but that books of the traditional sort were adapted to bring them more into line with continental liturgical practice; as far as *Regularis Concordia* is concerned, Abbot Symons also emphasises the persistence of the traditional element in spite of general and particular instances of continental influence. Perhaps this is the key to tenth-century attitudes to Europe: a clinging to traditional English forms with a gradual, perhaps in some cases grudging, acceptance of continental ideas and practices, of which the English were clearly aware. The point is nicely made by Professor Clemoes when he notes that English scribes, while adopting the Caroline minuscule for Latin documents, retained, and indeed developed, the insular script for writing the vernacular that was such a distinctive feature of their inherited culture.

The architectural and art-historical evidence is similar. Dr Alexander (like Professor Wormald, in his paper in the *Whitelock Festschrift*) stresses the insular component of tenth-century English art, even though the strong Carolingian influence by the time of the Benedictional of St Aethelwold is indisputable. Professor Wilson shows the continuation of ninth-century traditions in metalwork, again in spite of interchange between England and the Continent (and here there is

see pp.33-4 and Fig.1, p.32

see p.45

see pp.48-59

see pp.46-8

see pp.95-6

see pp.44-5

see p.108

see pp.169-70

see p.207

Scandinavia to reckon with as well). Professor Cramp sees tenth-century sculpture as a natural development from what went before, but with an infusion of new ideas; here there may be a distinction between works of *see pp.185-6* an ecclesiastical or 'official' nature, where the new ideas were more in evidence, and vernacular products, in which traditional and local styles tended to predominate. There seems to me some similarity between this dual application of sculptural styles and the use, noted above, of Caroline minuscule for documents in Latin and of insular hands for those in the vernacular. Dr Taylor suggests that the church builders, *see pp.167-8* too, were conservative and venerated the past, although there is likely to be some connection between certain features in English churches and continental examples. The general picture is one of a fairly reluctant acceptance of some styles and fashions; except in a number of more or less isolated cases, there was no wholesale adoption of continental modes.

In view of this, it is perhaps not surprising that there is often a considerable time-lag between the production of those continental models which were in fact adopted and the appearance of fully-fledged English versions of them (where dates are ascertainable at all). A fairly long period of experimentation and acclimatisation seems to have been required before a motif became accepted as a part of the standard English repertoire: an example of this is the Carolingian version of the classical acanthus ornament, whose gradual adoption begins in the ninth century, about a hundred years before it finds a secure niche in the Winchester style. The Old Minster westwork and the rival New Minster *see pp.136-8, 134-5, 152-3* tower were built about a century after the parallel which Mr Biddle quotes for Old Minster, the westwork at Corvey. They are two hundred years later than the St Riquier equivalent, assuming that the evidence *see p.146* for western galleries in the original church implies a turriform westwork structure. There is, then, some justification for regarding the Old Minster westwork as somewhat old-fashioned by continental standards. The basic New Minster building, so far as it is revealed by excavation, appears to offer an earlier example of continental influence, but again the parallel which has been tentatively quoted is the Steinbach type, which belongs essentially to the early ninth century, although it enjoyed a revival later. If, however, developments in church building in tenth-century England depended upon the the gradual adaptation of the traditional liturgy to conform more closely with European practice, as has been suggested, then the matter is explained: we have to deal with indirect rather than direct influence.

The time-lag is less easily explained away in the case of manuscripts *see Chap. 12* in the Winchester style. The Benedictional of St Aethelwold is at least fifty years later than one of the accepted sources for the style, the Metz school, and about a hundred and fifty years later than its Reims models. Nor is it immediately apparent why these should have been selected as models rather than the contemporary Ottonian style; connections between England and Germany in the tenth century are well enough attested, and there is evidence of Ottonian manuscripts reaching this country. It may be that this, too, was influenced by that veneration for tradition which has been noted above: perhaps tenth-century Englishmen were still aware that King Alfred's connections had been with the Western Franks and the diocese of Reims; perhaps, too, they were not a little proud of the long tradition of the West Saxon royal family and felt themselves vastly superior to the upstart Ottonians. Maybe West Francia was slightly more respectable in their eyes — the Carling dynasty had been founded two hundred years before, and had survived into the tenth century. Nobody, though, in late tenth-century Europe could touch the English royal line for nobility and length of tradition, and it is almost a wonder that England bothered with the Continent at all.

If this indeed was the general climate of opinion in England at the time of the reform, it is small wonder that the ideals exemplified by *Regularis Concordia,* with its overt attempt to incorporate the current practice of contemporary reformed houses on the Continent, were unpalatable to many. To be generally acceptable, the reform would have needed to maintain a fine balance between conservatism and innovation. It is for the reader to judge from the ensuing papers how far it was successful in this.

Chapter 2

THE PROGRESS OF THE MONASTIC REVIVAL

by D. H. Farmer

The monastic revival of tenth-century England has been the subject of much research this century. Often it has been studied in purely internal terms, as a monastic movement inspired by monks, beginning with Dunstan's revival of Glastonbury, whose 'golden age' was the reign of Edgar and whose culmination was reached by the last decade of the tenth century, when its three principal leaders died. More recently the European context of the movement has been rightly stressed and studies in the fields of feudal, economic, artistic and literary history together with archaeology have resulted in further advance. This has coincided with a more critical examination of the traditional account, a realisation that Eadmer's account of the movement and, to some extent, those of Osbern and William of Malmesbury also, represent 'official history'. Unfortunately the relevant entries in the *Anglo-Saxon Chronicle* are sparse, the contemporary Lives of Dunstan, Oswald and Aethelwold unsatisfactory. Moreover the evidence for the development of the revival in the eleventh century is even more fragmentary. But in spite of these disadvantages, critical re-appraisal of the sources has enabled the solid achievements of the reform to be seen in clearer relief.[1]

These may be summarised as follows. First, the tenth-century revival led to the foundation of many of England's principal monasteries which were to be so important an influence in the national life until the Reformation: obvious examples are Glastonbury, Abingdon and Ramsey. Secondly, it formed the peculiarly English institution of monastic cathedrals, which included Canterbury, Winchester, Worcester and Sherborne before the Conquest; after it, these were the models for Norwich, Durham, Coventry, Rochester and later Ely. Thirdly, the movement provided most of the bishops for England from the reign of Edgar until that of Cnut: consequently it was then by far the most influential sector of the Church in England. This influence was felt not only in court, witan and cathedral but also, through vernacular writers like Wulfstan and Aelfric, at parochial level by both priest and people.

Fourthly, its influence was notable outside as well as inside England insofar as some of its members became evangelising or organising missionaries in Scandinavia.[2] Lastly, its best artistic products, whether in book-production, sculpture in metal and in ivory, polyphonic music or ecclesiastical architecture were of outstanding quality, some of them being exported to Normandy and elsewhere in the eleventh century. How did this revival begin, how did it progress, and how did it decline, if indeed it did decline?

* * *

The precursor of the revival was King Alfred. In his introduction to the translation of Gregory's *Pastoral Care* he both recalled England's former eminent monasticism and deplored its disappearance. His attempted foundation of monks at Athelney soon fizzled out, but his nunnery at Shaftesbury may have survived, with Edward the Elder's nunnery at Winchester, as recognisably monastic in the tenth century. The court of King Athelstan (924-39), which was famous for its visitors from Western Europe, especially for the marriage negotiations of *see pp.33-4* Athelstan's sisters, was most probably the place where the young noble courtier Dunstan (909-88) heard of the monastic revivals in Burgundy and Lotharingia. There too, no doubt, he was encouraged by Aelfheah, Bishop of Winchester and Oda, Bishop of Ramsbury (later Archbishop of Canterbury), both of whom were described as monks, probably because of confraternity with some continental house. It was one thing, however, to encourage and inspire, quite another to translate ideal into reality. This latter achievement belongs to Dunstan alone, who was the pioneer of the revival at Glastonbury, where he first became a hermit (soon after his priestly ordination by Aelfheah), and then in 940 was appointed Abbot by King Edmund.[3]

Little is known for certain about the details of monastic life at Glastonbury in those early days. The most ancient Christian centre in England, staffed at least in part by Irish exiles, may well have been tenacious of its traditions. It is certain however that Dunstan's reform was according to the Rule of St Benedict and likely that it resembled contemporary continental reformed monasticism. A purely antiquarian revival from, say, the pages of Bede, would have been scarcely viable owing to the selective nature of such information, the absence of any living tradition and the less well-defined status of the Rule in earlier Anglo-Saxon monasticism. The strong resemblance of the English revival to its continental counterparts became more and more clear as time went on. Here one may stress that this resemblance is especially notable in the main framework of the life: its essentially liturgical character, the abolition of private ownership, the strict practice of celibacy; all these, most significantly synthesised and symbolised by the Rule of St Benedict, are the features common to the three movements which far transcend any divergence of detail in their customaries.

But there were also differences. The most notable of these was the close English dependence on the West Saxon royal family. In Burgundy, where the local rulers were weak, Cluny forged strong links with the Papacy as its special protector: in England, papal influence on the reform seems to have been minimal in early days and indirect later on.

see pp.95-6 But links with the monarchy had always been strong. Some of these were mentioned above: the list could be increased by reference to Edmund keeping the royal treasure at Glastonbury, to Edred giving the defunct abbey of Abingdon to Aethelwold, to Edwig increasing its endowments and to Edgar's constant patronage of the reformers, his many gifts of lands, his role of 'protector' of individual abbeys and of the movement as a whole. This tradition was maintained by Cnut's foundation of Bury and patronage of Canterbury together with Edward the Confessor's lavish endowment of Westminster.

This special relationship with the King was seen most clearly in the *see pp.132-3; Fig.3, p.129* close physical proximity of the royal palace at Winchester with the cathedral. Here in 964 Edgar replaced the secular canons with monks from Aethelwold's monastery at Abingdon soon after Aethelwold had become Bishop of his native city of Winchester.[4]

This event is often and rightly regarded as a turning-point in the history of the movement. Monastic reforms have as their primary purpose the founding and good order of monasteries, which are centres of Christian life and learning, normally separated to a large extent from the world of both secular and ecclesiastical politics. Although a considerable number of early medieval bishops were monks, it is not a function of monastic life to be a nursery of bishops: the episcopal office lies well outside the monk's legitimate field of expectation. But in the England of Edgar the three most important monastic leaders held the two metropolitan sees, the see of the court 'capital' and that of an important border area. And whereas the appointment of Dunstan to Canterbury in 960 was a well-deserved and important personal promotion, destined to influence affairs of Church and State for the rest of the reign, it left the Canterbury chapter unaffected until after *but see Chap. 6* Dunstan's death. But at both Winchester and Worcester monks replaced the cathedral clerks. To accomplish this, royal intervention was necessary because it involved endowments being transferred from individual clerks (and their families) to the monasteries as communities. Once this was done, the monks not only had a strong base in these cathedral towns, but were in a strategic position to assure that the see was generally held by one of their number. In fact Worcester was held by monks until the death of St Wulfstan in 1095 and Winchester was held until 1006, while the extent of monastic influence in other sees is evident from the occupation by monks of Canterbury until the arrival of Stigand; of York until the death of Aldred; of Sherborne, Wells and Ramsbury for the greater part of the century 966-1066. It has been calculated that until 1042 nine-tenths of the bishops were monks, and over the century before the Conquest as a whole three-quarters of them were monks, including the occupants of several of the most important and influential sees.[5] The reform thus became a national instead of a sectional movement.

All this however could not be clearly foreseen in 963. Then the promotion of monks to the episcopate may have seemed to be on a purely personal basis. Aethelwold had been King Edgar's tutor at Abingdon (Edgar was only sixteen years old when he became King of England in 959), while Dunstan had been a courtier for much of his early adult life and had experienced in turn both favour and disgrace. This last, under Edwig, had seemed disastrous for the revival; in fact, it was transformed into an advantage, because Dunstan spent his exile in the reformed monastery of Mont Blandin, near Ghent. There he too, like Aethelwold's disciple Osgar and Archbishop Oda's nephew Oswald at Fleury, came for the first recorded time into direct personal contact with reformed monasticism on the Continent. These contacts contributed to the common observance worked out in the *Regularis Concordia* of *c.*970 at a great assembly at Winchester. Monks from both *see pp.40-42* Fleury and Ghent were present on that occasion and helped Dunstan and Aethelwold to draw up this most characteristic document of the revival. By then king and bishops had done much to extend it: the monks needed endowments, land and protection from the King, while he needed their advice on the government of church and state, their skill in the drafting of documents, their provision of centres of piety and learning, their intercessory prayers (which were unusually long) and their support for the mystique of royalty.

This close association had a political, as well as a religious significance. The monastic bishops and abbots, in practice nominated by the King, came to hold large estates in peripheral areas, and exercised much local government, including judicial and military elements. In fact they displaced, to some extent and in some areas, local thegns and ealdormen and became the heads of local hundreds. The geographical distribution of the monasteries, often sited in lands where the King's influence could be weak, especially in the Severn valley and Danelaw areas, strengthened royal power and control. Moreover the revival never got under way before the Conquest in Northumbria, largely because the King's estates there were almost negligible. The real extent of the revival corresponds closely with the main property and power base of Wessex and Mercia which the tenth-century English kings held.

The close co-operation of king and bishops, however, and the sincere respect for the monastic order usually attributed to Edgar must have seemed unlikely early in his reign. Even the official historians of the revival like Osbern, Eadmer and William of Malmesbury knew something of Edgar's less edifying traits, which one hinted at and another denied. Some light on this aspect of his character is thrown by Goscelin's Life of Wulfhilda, abbess of Barking. This heroine of his story was a novice or a young nun at Wilton when Edgar fell in love with her. She was invited by her aunt Wenfleda, abbess of Wherwell, who said she was ill, to come and see her about inheriting the abbey when she died. On her arrival Wulfhilda found her aunt in excellent health, 'royally dressed' and seated at table with the young King. She was told to change her clothes and join them for dinner, when Edgar vigorously pursued his quest, while Wulfhilda remained silent, pretending illness and planning her escape. This she achieved through the drains at night, eluding chaperones inside the abbey and guards outside, and returned to Wilton next day. After another unsuccessful assault there by Edgar when Wulfhilda took refuge among the relics in the sanctuary, he abandoned his purpose and bestowed on her instead the abbey of Barking, re-endowed with churches at Horton, Shaftesbury, Wareham, Wilton and Southampton. Edgar then married Wulftrudis (some authorities state she was his concubine), who was also a Wilton nun. She gave birth to a daughter Edith, who was brought up by her mother, now separated from Edgar and abbess of Wilton. Edgar married again in 964-5, which would seem to date his adventures at Wilton to the early 960s, perhaps a year or two before he replaced the canons at Winchester with monks.[6]

Whether or not his support for the revival had some character of reparation, whether or not the long delay until 973 of his coronation was due to Dunstan's mistrust of the young King who had shown himself even less trustworthy than his brother Edwig, reproved like a naughty boy on his coronation day by Dunstan, we shall probably never know. But the central fact of Edgar's reign cannot be denied: the close and constant co-operation between king and bishops who were members of the monastic Order, for the good of both kingdom and Church. The interests of both were believed to be best served by the multiplication of new foundations, by the promotion of monks to the episcopate, by the prominent part in local government taken by monastic bishops and abbots and by monastic influence at court, especially in formulating laws.

The turning point in the revival had been the appointment of monks to important sees, but the high point of the reform was reached during the last years of Edgar's reign (973-5). By then most of the larger houses had been founded: Milton and Chertsey, Peterborough, Ely and Thorney by Aethelwold, Ramsey, Worcester and Winchcombe by Oswald, the third prominent reformer. Oswald came of Danish stock, and was a nephew of Oda, archbishop of Canterbury; he had received his formation at Fleury and returned to England in 958. He was soon consecrated Bishop of Worcester in 961. Like some of his predecessors and successors he also held the see of York, but Ramsey, his most important house, was in neither of his dioceses. He did however found or revive the important group of Severn valley monasteries which included Evesham and Pershore as well as those already mentioned. Dunstan's own foundations seem to have been less important: Malmesbury, Bath, Athelney and Muchelney; but his Glastonbury was the first of them all and the substitution of monks for canons at Canterbury, accomplished after Dunstan's death, was prepared by his having a number of monks in his household.

Edgar died in 975, at the age of only thirty-one. The three great bishops outlived him for a decade or more. Aethelwold died in 984, Dunstan in 988, Oswald in 992. Although the monastic reform survived a political reaction in Mercia after Edgar's death,[7] the impression is often given that the high point of the movement was past by then and that a certain decline had set in. Is this impression correct? Did the revival reach its high-water mark at the turn of the century and decline thereafter until the Norman Conquest?

There is no simple answer to these questions. It is true that by the Conquest, when statistics are available, the numbers of monks in the monasteries were small by later standards. It is also clear from the pages of Eadmer and others that all was not well for the religious life in pre-Conquest Canterbury. Again, there are clear examples of property being held by individual monks in apparent defiance of one of the principal tenets of the reform.[8] In the intellectual sphere the monks seem to have been backward-looking: their libraries contained few of the standard patristic works, and the numerous bilingual books testify to a lack of familiarity with Latin, an impression strengthened by the poor latinity of many of their manuscripts including those of *Regularis Concordia.*[9] Again, the standard of the Lives of their notable *see pp. 72-4* members is not high. Both the biographies of Dunstan are poor efforts unworthy of one of the greatest men of his time, while the turgid rhetoric of Oswald's biographer obscured rather than clarified its subject. Perhaps the Lives of Aethelwold are the best, but even these, it may be thought, compare unfavourably with the best biographies of the age of Bede.[10] Yet against all this is the strong achievement of a *see Chaps. 8, 12-14* vernacular literature and art, described on other pages, and the statesmanlike activities of Archbishop Wulfstan, whose organising work in both Church and State has won growing recognition. In its later years also the movement produced the last saintly bishop of his kind in St Wulfstan of Worcester,[11] while soon after the Conquest the monasteries in the Severn valley were sufficiently lively to send off to the north pioneers who, inspired by the pages of Bede, would revive Northumbrian monasticism and eventually refound Durham, with all that that implied for the future.

Was there ever a real decline? The following considerations are advanced as a tentative answer. The revival has suffered from its own panegyrists in the past. Important though it was, it also had considerable limitations. The later achievements of several houses after the Norman Conquest are not a proof that the pre-Conquest monastery was of the same scale or importance. In 1066 there were thirty-five monasteries of monks and nine of nuns. Numbers of inmates are difficult to obtain, but where they exist they point to the existence of *see pp.136-9; Fig.6, p.137* many small and a few large houses. Winchester must have been large. Although it lacked the antiquity and fine library of Glastonbury, so admired by William of Malmesbury, its fine church, its impressive achievements in illumination and in music, its close proximity to the royal palace, its connection with the most energetic and intransigent of the reformers on the one hand and its formation of their principal vernacular writer Aelfric, on the other, gave it a distinction unmatched by the other houses. Such achievements would be almost impossible in a small community. Glastonbury, the richest of them all, was also likely to have been a large house, so also Christ Church, Canterbury, and Ely. But it is doubtful if more than six monasteries in England in 1066 numbered more than forty monks.[12] Evesham, for example, made famous by Aethelwig, numbered only twelve monks in 1058: *see Chap. 6* Worcester, as we know from a charter of Wulfstan himself, numbered only twelve when he became prior; as late as 1100 Abingdon numbered only twenty-eight, while the eleventh-century foundations of Bury St Edmunds and Coventry numbered respectively only twenty in 1020 and twenty-five in 1043. St Benet of Hulme in Norfolk numbered twenty-six monks in 1020, but it provided thirteen of these for the foundation of Bury. Westminster, greatly enlarged by the Confessor, was founded in 958 for only twelve monks. It is likely that other less notable houses such as Muchelney, Abbotsbury, Pershore and Gloucester were even smaller.[13] The very speed of the foundations in the 960s and 970s seems to point to *small* numbers of monks being sent to 'take over' existing foundations with, no doubt, a certain number of the existing inmates. The harsh words of the monastic writers about the 'unreformed' canons need to be qualified, not only by the consideration that their language was that of committed partisans, but also by the facts that St Oswald himself was a canon before he became a monk, that Thurketil, abbot and founder of Crowland, was previously 'abbot of Bedford',[14] presumably a semi-monastic foundation of some kind and that, by the standards of later reforms, the reform itself was not irreproachable.

In this connection it may be noted that its founders were virtually pluralists. Not only did Oswald hold both Worcester and York while living to a large extent at Ramsey, but Aethelwold was the real abbot of Peterborough, Ely and Thorney while still ruling the church and monastery of Winchester. Dunstan also, it seems, remained Abbot of Glastonbury while Archbishop of Canterbury, and Aldred of York more than once held two sees in plurality.[15]

Another weakness of the reform as well as its material strength, came from its dependence on royal support. It had begun, in part at least, as a protest against lay ownership of monasteries, seen as the principal cause of their decline. Yet the monks were ready to place their future in the hands of the monarch, whom they themselves exalted into a priest-like figure, neither fully lay nor fully clerical. Goscelin's Life of Wulfhilda, besides giving evidence for hereditary ownership of monasteries, also tells of the manoeuvres through which discontented nuns at Barking, by intriguing with Queen Aelfthryth their 'protector', could exile their abbess to distant Horton for twenty years. It would be rash to assume that this was the only time when royal control was a mixed blessing.

It may be that we have expected too much from the reform. Its continued provision of bishops must have considerably weakened communities which were rather small, as their most able members were repeatedly called on to fill vacant sees or further the Scandinavian mission. Again, the disorders of Aethelred's reign must have inhibited monastic development. By the time of Edward the Confessor the reform was already one hundred years old and must have lost some of its earlier vitality. Edward's appointments to bishoprics of both Lotharingians and Normans, and of royal clerks rather than monks, may well be a sign that the monasteries, never very large, were no longer producing so many able people: Edward's policy was no doubt good for the Church, but good also for the monastic Order. It is neither usual nor desirable for monks to have a virtual monopoly of episcopal appointments: perhaps we should ask, not so much why Edward changed the policy, but rather why the old state of affairs survived as long as it did.

Something has already been said of the limitations of the monks' intellectual life: they were out of touch with the new movements of thought on the Continent in the eleventh century. It is perhaps significant that Malmesbury, for instance, produced an unsuccessful amateur aeronaut while the community's education was so poor that they could only 'stammer at vernacular letters'.[16] Certainly there was need for the influence of Lanfranc and Anselm later to end their insularity and to introduce new currents of thought and new books in the libraries.

What should be thought of the more elusive spiritual quality of the movement, of the monks' fidelity or otherwise to their monastic ideals? It should be said at once that the evidence is lacking for a firm judgment on the movement as a whole. Allusion has already been made to some of the strengths and some of the weaknesses of the reform. One of its most enthusiastic partisans, Eadmer, could not but admit that pre-conquest monastic life at Canterbury left much room for improvement. His portrait of the monks who were more like earls, who gloried in gold, silver and fine clothes and who hunted and hawked has become famous, not only for its own sake but also because it inspired William of Malmesbury's more general treatment of the same *see pp. 71-2* theme.[17] What was true of one house may not have been true of all. Nor should it be assumed that there is a necessary 'decline of fervour' after the death of the first founders.

Nonetheless, it may be thought that the movement had considerable limitations, not only through the inevitable imperfections which are common to any community over a century or more of continued existence, but also through some internal weakness. The close connection with the King must have meant considerable loss of independence. The monks' involvement with society had consequences which were not uniformly advantageous. Their superiors, close in kin very often to the ruling families, identified themselves with local interests in a way which could be disastrous (as to some extent it was in 1066), and if they were bishops, they could not live a normal monastic life. Their geographical distribution emphasises their dependence on the King. Their intellectual interests and standards compare unfavourably with the best of contemporary and later European monasteries. One may well think that it was time for a change in 1066 and that the movement epitomised by *Regularis Concordia* had had its day. The cathedral monastery, which it created, proved in the end to be a source of weakness, especially in the separation of superior from convent which was a running sore in medieval monasticism. But the way of life, begun at the reform, was to survive the Norman Conquest for nearly five hundred years more, through varying changes of fortune, but in a form which was recognisably the same as that of 970. If it had concentrated on building up the internal life of a few monasteries, it might have contributed more to the achievements of the monastic Order. But by developing in the way it did, it made a unique contribution to the history of England.

Chapter 3

THE CONTINENTAL BACKGROUND OF THE REFORM

by D. A. Bullough

'England and the Continent in the Tenth Century' is one of the unwritten works of early medieval historiography. In the early decades of this century Mr Edmund Bishop and the Dean of Wells (Dr J. Armitage Robinson) indicated some of the paths that could be followed with advantage. More recently Mr Eric John has tried to open up several new ones and has provoked the now-familiar reaction from those who, regrettably, feel that there is only one legitimate approach to some of the central problems of early English history. In taking the continental background to *Regularis Concordia* as my theme I shall not try to emulate or improve on the contributions of these and other English scholars. Rather I shall be venturing on to terrain which has been elaborately — in some areas over-elaborately — developed by our continental colleagues in recent years and where we are all in danger of losing our way. In the absence of any obvious *via regia* or *strata publica* (the equation is Alcuin's) through it, I begin, therefore, with providing a few guide-posts — five short texts (or pairs of texts), taken from widely differing contexts and originating on both sides of the Channel.

The first of these is a blunt passage in the *Chronicle* of Regino of Prüm, written c.906 when the author was in fact at St Martin's in Trier: 'After the death of Charles the Fat (in 888) the kingdoms which had been under his rule, even as ones deprived of a lawful inheritor, broke apart and did not wait for a natural lord [to emerge] but each one settled on creating a king for itself out of its own guts'.[1]

The second guide-post is provided by two episodes in Regino's monastic career. In 899, having wittingly or unwittingly become involved in the struggles over the future succession to the kingdom of Lotharingia he was ousted from the abbacy of Prüm which he had occupied *aemulis agentibus* and a local lay magnate established in his stead; subsequently the Bishop of Trier gave him the monastery of St Martin's which had suffered severely from the attacks of the Northmen and which he duly 'restored to its pristine condition'.[2]

For my third guide-post I turn to the *Liber Confraternitatis* of St

Gallen and the entry which records the visit in October 929 of Bishop Cenwald of Worcester, in the course of a journey on behalf of King Athelstan 'to all the monasteries throughout Germany': after he had taken part in the patronal festival, the community granted to him 'the allotted portion [*annona*] of a brother' and accepted the obligation of praying for both Bishop and King and for other named Englishmen who henceforward figured in the Confraternity Book with the other *fratres conscripti*. I link this with a letter found and transcribed by William of Malmesbury in the early twelfth century, in which the prior of St Samson's at Dol tells Athelstan that his father has been regularly prayed for by the confraternity there and that it will now do the same for him, and that relics are being sent with the letter.[3]

My fourth is a part of Pope Leo VII's privilege of 938 for the monastery of Fleury (St Benoît-sur-Loire) which, the Pope has learnt, has recently been restored to a regular life through the efforts of Abbot Odo (of Cluny) and Hugh *dux Francorum*: henceforward 'neither the place nor any property belonging to it shall ever be put under any [outside] authority, except that of the king; neither the king nor any *princeps* shall ever give the place into the lordship of any bishop, canon, abbot, layman or any other person', but after Odo's death the community shall choose an abbot from among its own members or from another community as it wishes.[4]

My fifth and last is from the *Regularis Concordia* itself — the statement in the Prologue that King Edgar 'saw to it wisely that his Queen, Aelfthrith, should be the protectress and fearless guardian of the communities of nuns, so that he himself helping the men and his spouse helping the women there should be no cause for any breath of scandal'.[5] *see p.17*

* * *

The reunification under the Emperor Charles the Fat of all the territories which had once been under the *imperium* of Charlemagne and of Louis the Pious had in fact lasted a few brief months. The one enduring monument to the aspirations of his advisers and to his own undeniable if insubstantial achievements is the extraordinary *Deeds of Charles the Great* by Notker the Stammerer of St Gallen; the ninth-century equivalent of a cross between a modern tabloid newspaper and *Time* magazine, it was none the less intended to show what a real Emperor was like.[6] For the lands which made up the Middle Kingdom as established at Verdun in 843, Charles's rule formed a hardly-noticeable respite in decades of conflict, vicissitude and

uncertainty. The North Italian magnates' already-expressed impatience
for a decision over whom their country was to belong to[7] was not to
be appeased for a long time to come. In 888 the kingdom of Provence
or Lower Burgundy was re-established; and a new kingdom of Upper
Burgundy — in which a sovereign authority was probably less easy to
exercise than in the closely comparable Pyrenean territory of Wilfrid
the Hairy — had emerged by local demand.[8] Regino's Lotharingia,
the Middle Kingdom north of Luxeuil and Bâle and therefore embrac-
ing what was still thought of as the Carolingian heartland as well as
some of the best-endowed and best known 'Frankish' monasteries such
as Echternach, Prüm and Gorze, might have been expected to produce
its own monarch too. After all, it had once been a territorial kingdom
in its own right — under Lothar II who gave his name to it, and gave it a
lot of trouble also because he took too literally the injunction of the
Psalmist to take lifelong pleasure in the wife of one's youth; and it had
Aachen and its palace, although these were hardly what they had once
been, especially after the visitation of the Northmen at the end of
881.[9] In fact the magnates and bishops of Lotharingia threw in their
lot with those across the Rhine whose choice fell on Arnulf of
Carinthia, because he was a Carolingian, even though an illegitimate
one. In West Francia the nine-year-old Carolingian claimant Charles 'the
Simple' was passed over in 888 as he had been three years earlier and
the crown bestowed on Odo, count of Paris (and probably of other
counties round about): he owed his choice to the significant part he
had played in the successful defence of the city in 885/6, to the fact
that he had a substantial following among the middling landowners of
the Seine basin and because he was widely recognised as potentially the
most effective of the northern French magnates.[10] Not until 893 did
a discontented magnate element rally to Charles and in 'a legitimist
rebellion' proclaim him King in opposition to Odo.

Regino is, then, giving his readers a neat and graphic summary of
what happened to the Empire in 887/8.[11] His language, however,
belongs squarely to the late antique and early medieval rhetorical
tradition: and like all good rhetoric it is trying to convey something
more than could have been conveyed by a bare factual narrative. Like
much else in the Chronicle — which summarises the history of the
world from the Incarnation to 742 in a first short book and then begins
a very much longer *De gestis Francorum* — this passage proceeds from
the assumption that rule by a Carolingian is natural and necessary: an
assumption that would have been readily accepted by writers otherwise
very different from Regino, such as Notker.[12] At the same time it is
one of a number of passages which brings us into a thought-world

which is in sharp contrast with that prevailing a century earlier. A pessimistic view of the times is evident in Carolingian writing at least from the time of Einhard: one of the themes of the *Vita Karoli* is that the best days are already past unless (as seems unlikely) another ruler appears with the same *virtus,* the same *magnanimitas* as Charlemagne; and in this sense Asser's *Vita Alfredi* (whose author is usually supposed to have been inspired by Einhard's *Vita*), except perhaps for its extraordinary treatment of the king's illnesses, seems to breathe a very different spirit. Not surprisingly, however, the note of pessimism becomes very much stronger in the years either side of 900: the world was once again in travail and no instrument of the Divine will seemed at hand to bring about its end.[13]

Louis the Pious had been entrusted with authority over a *respublica Christiana* and had then allowed its unity to be threatened by his and his wife's love for their Benjamin and by savage quarrels of his older sons. The most conventional as well as the most thoughtful of churchmen had reason to deplore and resist the consequences. Unity was felt to be the natural condition not only of the Church but also of the secular polity that provided for its effective functioning: where it was lacking, there could be neither order nor peace, only *dissensio, fastus arrogantiae, iniustitia.* Exemplified in and secured by the un-divided authority of a divinely-ordained and morally unobjectionable monarch, it was at once a deeply-pondered abstraction and a pragmatic necessity.[14] Unity and what proceeded from it were therefore intimately linked with legitimacy — the legitimacy of a royal line or *generatio* (in more than one sense of that semantically complex word) which had been the recipient of God's favour, and which even when it splits into several branches is still seen to stem from a single root. (The Biblical analogies are obvious and are tentatively made from the mid-ninth century.)[15]

For Regino and most of his contemporaries 'legitimate' was still equated with 'Carolingian'. When King Odo died in 898 even his most ardent supporters almost inevitably rallied to Charles the Simple; and there were not many like Duke William, the founder of Cluny, who still cared for his soul more than a decade later. When the death of Lewis the Child in 911 left the East Franks without a 'native' Carolingian to be considered for the vacant throne, one party among the magnates and middle-rank landowners acted like their West Frankish counterparts in 888 and offered it to one of their own number. The leading laymen and clerics in Lorraine transferred their allegiance to the West Frankish king: for in no part of the former Empire was the sense of legitimacy stronger than in that region. Only after the ousting and imprisonment

of Charles the Simple in 922/3 and the succession of two non-
Carolingians on the throne did a significant element among the
Lotharingian magnates decide that their own future prestige or safety
lay rather with the East Frankish kingdom and its Saxon monarch; and
even then it needed an armed invasion and a massive change of
allegiance by the bishops finally to persuade them. The past associa-
tions of Aachen, Prüm and elsewhere may seem sufficient explanation
of this enduring attachment to the 'legitimate' monarch: and so in a
sense they are. They do not, however, satisfactorily explain why this
'Carolingian nostalgia' was very quickly transferred from the historic
royal and Imperial line to the Imperial idea, the title itself having lapsed
in 924. In this Aachen was no more than a symbol, although obviously
a powerfully evocative one. The circumstances of its rise to significance
and fame in Carolingian Europe worked against the subsequent
establishment there of a major church or a regular centre of learning:
the inheritance of its one-time resident scholars, artists and library — as
Professor Bischoff and others have taught us — must be sought
elsewhere.[16] There was obviously no one place in which memories of
the unitary Christian Imperial rule of the early part of the ninth
century were a living and fruitful study in its later decades and
probably no single centre in the time of the first Saxon monarchs:
Folz's and Beumann's explorations of the Saxon Carolingian tradition
and the preoccupations that underlie Widukind's *History* of the people
and dynasty who had inherited the *fortuna* of the Frankish rulers have
shown just how complex are the intellectual links between the two
centuries and the two royal lines.[17] There can be no doubt, however,
that the bishops and cathedral clergy of Trier, a city whose Imperial
memories were of the fourth century rather than the ninth and whose
exceptionally literate younger clerics in a period of general educational
decline had provided a major or distinctive element in the writing-
offices of the last Carolingian rulers of Lotharingia, now showed a
special interest in the concept of Christian Emperordom and apparently
envisaged a more glorious future for themselves in association with
it.[18] At the same time the metropolitan authority of its bishop or
archbishop over the dioceses of Verdun, Metz and Toul was no mere
formal one: clergy were exchanged between the four cathedral churches
and so even were the abbots of monasteries in different dioceses.

The notion of a *respublica Christiana* in which almost every facet of
the life of the Church reflected the political unity of the territorial
imperium had been prepared for in the time of Charlemagne when (in
the words of Professor Knowles) he 'aimed at securing conformity to a
general norm, and that the one consecrated by tradition' — the canons

of Gelasius or Gregory, the mass-book of Gregory, the Rule of Benedict
of Monte Cassino, an exact copy of the supposed autograph of which
was made available at Aachen.[19] What the first Frankish Emperor
did not attempt, however, was the imposition of a unity or uniformity
of practice on the monasteries of his dominions over and above that
which they could be expected to derive from a common dependence on
the one Rule and from the adoption of the liturgical reforms and
innovations which he inspired and to which those close to him gave a
wider currency. This, in so far as it was envisaged at all, was in Charles's
lifetime left to local or private initiative: it only became a feature of
Imperial policy when Louis succeeded his father and took his cue from
the ideas of Benedict of Aniane. The correction of the life of particular
communities prepared the way for the great reform councils of 816 and
817 at Aachen, which promulgated or inspired a whole series of
regulations for monks, canons and canonesses. The line between the
first two was, for the first time, firmly drawn: the result was not only
to make clear the distinction between the corporate life of, for
example, cathedral clergy on whom a rule had been imposed and the
conventual life of a monastery, but also to leave such well-known
abbeys as St Martin's at Tours on the 'canonical' side of the line, where
it remained in spite even of the reforming efforts of Odo of Cluny who
had once been a member of the community.[20] For the monasteries
uniformity was laid down as a principle; in the words of Benedict's
biographer: *Monasteria ita ad formam unitatis redacta sunt, acsi ab uno
magistro et in uno imbuerentur loco. Uniformis mensura in potu, in
cibo, in vigiliis, in modulationibus cunctis observanda est et tradita.* A
more elaborate pattern of liturgical observance, departing in several
important respects from both the letter and the spirit of the *Rule* and
distinct equally from the Roman observance, the *Laus perennis* and the
Cursus Scottorum, was envisaged. The involvement of monasteries in
the secular world and its affairs was reduced, most significantly by
providing that the school within the cloister was for monastic oblates
only.[21]

There was nothing unconsidered in all this: nor can it be said that
these reform decrees were the product of a mind that responded more
naturally to bureaucratic ideas than to the spiritual needs of the true
monk. Benedict had as a young man chosen the way of the desert: and
behind the regulations of 816 and 817 lie his personal collection of
older rules (including those of Greek monks) and an attempt to extract
the best from each of them, surviving as the *Codex regularum* and
Concordia.[22] The impact of Benedict's ideas and of the regulations
they inspired on later Carolingian monasticism is surprisingly difficult

to establish. It is certainly not proved by listing the liturgical and other innovations which subsequently became standard practice, since in many cases we have no decisive proof that they were generally adopted before they appear in the 'reform' monasteries of the tenth century. On the other hand it is not disproved by the lack of interest in the *Concordia*. It was, after all, the Aachen *Capitula* — those of the 817 council circulating widely at an early date in an expanded or interpolated version — that provided the foundations for the new order.[23] The impact of Benedict's modification and supplementation of the original Benedictine Rule is clearly evident in Abbot Smaragdus's *Expositio in regulam S. Benedicti,* written very shortly after 817 and perhaps in response to the problems created by the new regulations — just as our legal colleagues produce a new (and ever more expensive) edition of a standard work 'to take account', as they are careful to say, of a new statute. We will not be surprised to find that one of the earliest scribal products of the English tenth-century revival is a manuscript of the *Expositio,* written perhaps at Glastonbury in mid-century in the then new (to England) Caroline minuscule: or that Smaragdus's lesser work on the *Rule,* the *Diadema Monachorum,* was one of the first texts copied in that same script by members of the Christ Church, Canterbury community a quarter-century or so later.[24] Pater Hafner's convincing dissociation of any version of the so-called *Basil Commentary* on the *Rule* from Paul the Deacon, and his fairly firm dating of the basic text of this work to the mid-ninth century, not only leaves us without any pre-Benedict or pre-Smaragdus commentary: it requires us to look again at the possible textual links between the *Concordia* and *Capitula* on the one hand and the later *Commentary* on the other. Since the North Italian origin of this seems to have been made more rather than less likely by Pater Hafner's re-assessment, the clear if infrequent reflections of Benedict's innovations, mixed with what appears to be older Monte Cassino usage, are doubly interesting.[25] Nevertheless Professor Knowles's judgment that: 'The work of Benedict of Aniane was to all appearances undone within a few years of his death in the very decades during which Anglo-Saxon monasticism was disappearing before the Danes', that with the disintegration of the Empire 'went all hope of exact and controlled uniformity', seems to me very much nearer the truth than Professor Kempf's claim that on the eve of the tenth-century reforms most monasteries lived a way of life which made them the spiritual heirs of Benedict of Aniane, even if the details of their observances differed in small but significant ways.[26]

Just as the concept of Frankish Imperial unity went far beyond the achievable or at least the maintainable reality and after 843 was perpetually contradicted by the manifest development of separate kingdoms with recognisably distinct traditions of government and culture, formal adhesion to common norms for the monastic life was no guarantee that they would continue to be observed once the immediate stimulus or the limited means of enforcement were removed. It has been questioned, for example, whether they had any real significance for the great south German monasteries such as Reichenau and St Gallen, or even for Fulda[27] — the place in which teachers and scholars of the second and third generations after the foundation-laying Court circle gave a further dimension to the achievements of the 'Carolingian Renaissance'. It is, however, surely false to believe (as some have) that if Benedict's reforms had been properly enforced that great age of monastic culture would have been still-born. The biographer of Alcuin, writing in the late 820s, who thought it the highest of compliments to say of his hero that he was the pattern for canons as Benedict of Aniane was the pattern for monks, was clearly not suggesting that the life of the latter was a contemplative one without learning. Dom Leclercq, the most learned and sensitive living exponent of monastic culture, has drawn attention to Benedict's unduly-neglected *Munimenta Fidei*.[28] Although laying down an apparently limiting programme for 'monastic theology', the proper mental discipline for monks, this in fact presupposes a broad intellectual base; *grammatica* is to be transcended but obviously not passed over; and who could tackle Origen without a formidable preparation?: the comments of Jerome come immediately to mind. It is not apparent that Benedict would have taken serious exception to the presence in the Fleury library later in the century of, say, an (incompletely) illustrated manuscript of Terence's *Comedies* side by side with the now oldest-extant manuscript of his own *Concordia* — although he might well have found some of the texts brought there by Breton visitors very bizarre.[29] Enough books, orthodox or unusual, survived the sacking of the monastery by Northmen in 865 or were acquired in the next seventy years to give it an enviable reputation as a centre of learning at a time when a new generation of reformers had only recently re-established a proper monastic observance.

compare pp.65-6

The misfortunes experienced by Fleury or by St Martin's at Trier can easily be generalised to account for the decline of Western European religious life in the concluding decades of the ninth century, although one must be cautious in doing so. We must be even more cautious in associating ourselves uncritically with those reformers who thought that one of the main obstacles to a proper monastic life in the later

Carolingian period was the readiness of sinful laymen to misuse the resources of monasteries which their ancestors had founded or which were simply in the area in which they had territorial and judicial rights. It can be argued, I think, that what all Western European monasteries of the pre-reform period had in common — even more than their allegiance to the memory of St Benedict, since in this matter I can see no essential difference between the situation in Ireland and in Italy — was a comparable involvement in what for want of a better term must be referred to as 'the social structures' of the period. In raising this issue I am conscious that I am venturing not so much on to thorny ground as on to a minefield. Readers of recent numbers of *Past and Present* (or indeed of any number of *Past and Present*) will know that almost any sally into this field succeeds only in bringing out the worst in us: I suppose that this is because, much as in art-history, one creates for oneself a kind of mental construct against which particular problems are examined or judged and one feels exasperation that one can never produce arguments that will convince colleagues who favour a different construct. Perhaps none the less there will be broad agreement that the distinctions *we* make between the sacred and the profane are not necessarily those made in the eighth, ninth and tenth centuries: the history of innumerable monasteries, the succession of their abbots and the form in which they record the names of those for whom inter-cession is offered — the Confraternity Books, like those of St Gallen — even the familiar terminology of *pater, fratres, dominus,* are clear denials of the distinction which we (like later reformers) insist on making between the secular society of kinship and lordship and the monastic community.[30] The suffrages offered for dead founders and their descendants have as their necessary counterpart the suffrages being offered in Heaven by those who have already been admitted to the presence of God. The obliteration of the boundary between the natural and supernatural worlds is apparent in the communal monastic drinking and the *caritas*-songs (so impressively studied by Professor Bischoff) that accompanied it on certain festivals;[31] it is evident again in the well-documented, but still unstudied, practice of laymen's gifting vineyards to churches and monasteries with the specific require-ment that they shall be remembered at table with part of the proceeds and not merely in the prayers of the brethren, and the right accorded to certain privileged outsiders to participate in the communal eating and drinking whenever they are in the vicinity (which survives, I suppose, in the dining-rights enjoyed by some of us in our Oxford or Cambridge college).

What was recognisably an abuse of a 'family monastery' in the ninth and early tenth centuries was not the narrowing of the choice of abbot to members of the founding family, even when they lacked the spiritual qualifications for the position; nor even the behaviour of lay members of the family who regarded the monastery as they might any other piece of property that served their needs: it was, rather, when the monastery and its estates were treated in such a way that the intercessory activity which they were supposed to maintain effectively ceased. The appointment of a lay-abbot was doubtless always objectionable in ecclesiastical law: it was not so clearly objectionable socially, unless it deprived some *affinitas* or *cognatio* of its inherited rights. A formal division of the revenues between the abbot and the rest of the community had obvious attractions for all parties and was not uncommonly undertaken. It gave no safeguard against more serious abuses when central authority or responsibly-exercised local authority broke down, as it did in West Francia and Lotharingia in the late ninth and early tenth centuries: and in the process of trying to re-establish that authority even a king respectful both of tradition and the Church might feel impelled to treat monasteries and their possessions as a substitute for the domanial lands which he never longer owned or controlled. The fates of Regino's two monastic houses are typical of innumerable others, some of which suffered both in turn.[32]

Among the monasteries founded or revived within a period of twenty-five years in the early part of the tenth century which quickly became fountain heads of reform, Cluny (dioc. Mâcon) has traditionally attracted most attention. To many monastic historians of earlier generations, to many writers of text-books in our time it has seemed to offer the sharpest break with the past and the most obvious beginning of a new era. Recently, however, analyses of the phraseology of 'count and duke' William's foundation charter (909 or 910) and of comparable texts have demonstrated that the links established between the new monastery and the see of St Peter were limited in scope and not particularly novel.[33] It is still possible to maintain that the founder had been persuaded to turn his back on accepted current practice when — 'desiring', as he put it, 'to provide for myself while I am still able' — he sought to eliminate all future family or other lay interference: firstly, by transferring the proprietorship of the vill of Cluny and its appurtenances to the apostles Peter and Paul in whose honour a monastery was to be founded; secondly, by entrusting the new foundation to an abbot (Berno) who for more than a decade previously had been trying to follow the pattern of monastic life laid down by Benedict of Aniane in his own house at Baume (Jura).

Yet William's preoccupations were much the same as those of other founders. 'There', the charter declares, 'the monks shall congregate and live according to the rule of St Benedict . . . and prayers, beseechings and exhortations shall be sedulously directed to God as well for me as for . . . *the souls of my [late] lord and king Odo, and of my father and mother; for me salvation of myself and my wife [Ingelberga] and no less of Ava [my sister]*', of other relatives of the same or a younger generation and of 'our faithful ones (fideles) who are constant in our service'. (The passage in italics derives from the listing in an earlier part of the charter, to which the quotation in roman type refers back.) The practical problem remained of ensuring that the service of prayer in the interests of the founder, his family and dependents was safeguarded for the future. William is not known to have had other property in the vicinity (the vill and its appurtenances had come to him from his sister who had acquired it in unrecorded circumstances) and it is far from certain that he was ever count of Mâcon, in which territory and diocese it lay. It is often overlooked that the foundation charter was written at Bourges, of which William *was* count, and that it was subscribed by the Archbishop of Bourges (whose metropolitan area did not include Mâcon) and two other bishops but not by the Bishop of Mâcon.[34] In 926 Berno ensured that a man with the right attitudes and ambitions would succeed him as abbot when he bequeathed Cluny and two other monasteries — which implies a very different kind of proprietorship from that provided for in the foundation charter — to Odo; and this man was in all probability the son, otherwise a very close relative, of the most intimate of all the late Duke William's *fideles*, Ebbo, founder of the Cluny-inspired Bourg-Dieu at Déols.[35]

Protection by the West Frankish king of monasteries south and east of the Loire was not a realistic possibility in the early tenth century, even if it had been welcome to those who controlled — or sought to control — the region's destinies. The situation following the death of Duke William II in 927 and the emergence of a Poitou-based ducal dynasty may have made it easier for the Abbot of Cluny to seek the royal charters of confirmation which, with the parallel papal privileges, were the real foundation-stones of the monastery's distinctive *libertas*. That Odo himself felt no dogmatic opposition to royal supervision of see p. 21 reformed houses is clear from the previously-quoted papal privilege for Fleury which had been reformed by him in dramatic circumstances and of which he remained abbot until his death. This royally-protected house became the stepping-off point for Cluniac reform in northern France and, following Oswald's stay there in the time of Odo's successor, the main channel of Cluniac influence on the English reform movement.[36]

Brogne and Gorze are conveniently contrasted with Cluny in most accounts of tenth-century monasticism. In its origins Brogne has, however, much in common with Cluny, although with the difference that Gerard founded it on his own patrimony so that he might himself live the life of a monk. He took his lessons in the religious life at St Denis — a somewhat unexpected choice but possibly not unconnected with the lay abbacy exercised there by the ancestors of the Capetians who, as the history of Fleury in Odo's time shows, were responsive to the widespread demand for a stricter observance. The political changes in Lotharingia forced Gerard to seek secular protection in a different form and by 929 it is likely that it was provided by the German king. The monks of Brogne were thus enabled to maintain standards of observance which decayed houses in Lotharingia or just across the western border were soon eager to adopt.[37] One house that turned to Brogne for reform was St Peter at Ghent in the county of Flanders; and it did not seem incongruous or improper to contemporaries that the community should continue to have a close association with and serve some of the administrative as well as the spiritual needs of the count.[38]

Shortly after mid-century, but a year or two before Dunstan went briefly into exile there, St Peter's was reformed from Gorze. The latter had originated as a centre of reform in a very different way from Cluny or Brogne or even Fleury. Episcopal churches in Francia and Lotharingia seem for the most part to have escaped the worst consequences of external attack and the breakdown of political authority. A few, and not merely the expected ones, managed to maintain a significant educational and literary tradition which was subsequently taken up and enlarged by some of the reformed monasteries in the middle and later tenth century. But the spiritual life offered by their communities, whether dubbed 'canonical' or not, gave little satisfaction to those with higher aspirations, In southern Lotharingia it was discontented clerics from the cathedral churches of Metz and Toul, together with uneasy solitaries supported by the bishops of the two cities, who came together to establish a regular, fervent communal life: and after various abortive efforts they settled on Gorze. A one-time royal abbey thoroughly secularised in the late ninth century, it was recovered for the monastic way of life by the Bishop of Metz only by accepting the permanent loss to local laymen of most of its one-time estates. Bishop Adalbero's charter of 933 which consummated and sanctioned the revival of Gorze as a house of strict observance reveals an awareness that even bishops could treat monasteries and their lands in a destructively proprietorial way: after all they commonly came, like

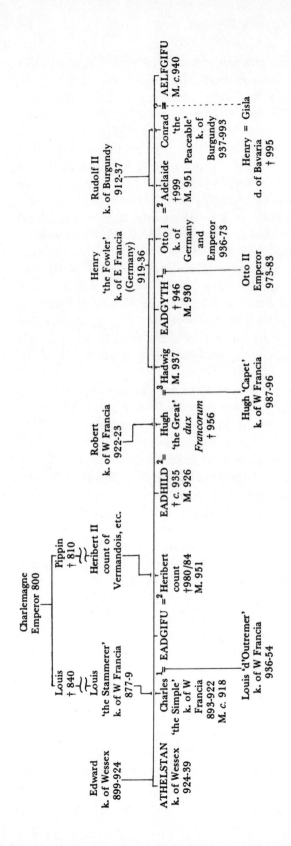

Fig. 1   The Continental Marriages of the Sisters of Athelstan

NOTES:

Only those names are included in the table which show the connections of Athelstan's family with continental royal and other families.

The children of Edward the Elder are in CAPITALS.

⊥ indicates that one or more generations in the descent
†   have been omitted.

- - - -   indicates uncertain descent

M indicates date of marriage.

Adalbero himself, from a local magnate family. Hence the *libertas monastice religionis* — a phrase which consciously or unconsciously looked back to Benedict of Aniane — of the houses founded (or re-founded) by men from the same circles as the first Gorze monks or which they helped to reform in the next three decades was felt to depend on the effective secular authority of someone transcending local rivalries and ambitions and interested in the prayers and personnel of the monasteries, not their properties: and, without it seems any conscious assertion of principle, their secure future was therefore identified with that of the Saxon royal dynasty to which by 955 the *fortuna* of the Carolingians could clearly be seen to have passed. [39]

Only a very bold or a very foolish man, as Dom Hallinger and Abbot Symons have taught us, would go to the judgment-seat asserting that characteristically Gorzean practices are or are not reflected in the *Concordia*. It would be an even bolder one who assumed that the *see pp. 48-9* attitudes to royal authority which I have associated with monasteries of the Gorze group were both familiar to and acted on by the leading figures in English reform circles: the transmission of general concepts and outlook rather than institutions and techniques — what I am sometimes tempted to think of as the ectoplasm of history — can rarely be demonstrated, even where the evidence of specific contact is considerable. Sir Frank Stenton assembled evidence for the presence of foreign and particularly German clerics in England during the second quarter of the tenth century: not all of it is convincing. [40] Brittany and southern Celtic Britain seem to have provided the most important textual and scribal influences in the opening phases of the English revival of learning and the religious life, which accords with the evidence of the Dol letter. [41] England's contribution to the European *see pp. 68-9* royal and princely marriage-market had hitherto been an intermittent and modest one. The success of the English kings against the Northmen and the situation in the Frankish 'disputed territories' in the second and third decades of the century were an obvious encouragement to the leading families in the continental kingdoms to seek a marriage with one of the many daughters of Edward the Elder. It is reasonable to think — although I would put it no more strongly — that as the network of marriage-relationships evolved the English court and its clerics absorbed something of the ideas then circulating in the East Frankish kingdom through the medium of its reformed monasteries.

After the death of his first (lawful) wife in 917, the ill-favoured Charles III 'the Simple' married Eadgifu: when he was deposed and imprisoned (922/3) she fled to England with their son, the future Louis *see pp. 67-9, espec. 68* IV; and significantly perhaps, contemporary French chronicles show an interest only in her later years as wife of the north-eastern French count Heribert. In 926 a ?younger sister married as his second wife Count Hugh 'the Elder', son of the briefly-reigning victor over Charles III, lay-abbot of St Martin's, Tours and from c.937 — when, however, his English wife was already dead and he was married to the late German king's daughter Hedwig — *dux Francorum,* in which capacity he supported Odo at Fleury.[42] To the French king Rudolf (923-36) Hugh's English connection may at times have seemed to constitute as great a threat as the Carolingians with *their* English backing. The preoccupations of the German king Henry (919-36) were at first sight similar: his rejection of consecration (for whatever reason) and reliance on personal prestige and military success left the future of the Saxon royal line at best insecure and at worst desperately weak.[43] If a 'dynastic' marriage were to be arranged for his teenage son and putative heir Otto it was hardly possible to look elsewhere than to the court of Edward's son and successor Athelstan; and a request was duly sent in 928 or 929. Aethelweard, writing at the very end of the tenth century, and two German writers a decade or two earlier, report the tradition that the English king responded by sending two of his sisters from whom, in the manner of a beauty-contest (for which there are in fact good ninth-century precedents) the choice was to be made: the leader of the English party, who was given enough additional resources to enable him to visit the major German monasteries and be welcome, was Bishop Cenwald. Otto or his advisers favoured Eadgyth as his bride. The second sister was disposed of to the Burgundian kingdom where, if it is true that she married Conrad, son and successor of King Rudolf, she found a husband whose biography is only slightly fuller than her own.[44]

Contacts thus established with the German court and monasteries were maintained in other ways. At an unknown date between 926 and 939 a Gospel manuscript of ultimately Metz origin with an English-written entry on the last leaf naming *Eadgifu regina* and *Athelstanus rex Angulsaxonum et Mercianorum,* and perhaps therefore commemorating entry into a prayer-community, was sent to Germany and subsequently found a home in the family and royal nunnery at Gandersheim. Another Gospel manuscript, written probably at Lobbes in the late ninth-century, was given to Athelstan by King Otto (after 936, therefore) and his mother Matilda and by him in turn to Christ Church, Canterbury.[45] Aethelweard, as is well known, dedicated his astonishing *Chronicle* to abbess Matilda of Essen, grand-daughter of Otto and Eadgyth.

It may well be the case that the responsibilities attributed to

Aelfthrith in the Prologue to *Regularis Concordia* mark a considerable enhancement of the traditional position of English queens and that this owed not a little to the Ottonian court and the circle of reformed monasteries associated with it. I readily admit that this is speculative: but it does not seem to me to be rebutted by the evidence for royal foundresses of monasteries or royal abbesses in the early post-conversion period or by the relatively favourable situation of women as landowners in their own right in early England; and although the position accorded to Cynethryth, wife of King Offa of Mercia, in contemporary texts is a remarkable anticipation of that of Edgar's queen it seems to be unique in the pre-reform period and I doubt if it has much bearing on the subsequent history of queenship in Wessex.[46] Individual queens had, of course, been figures of great influence in pre-Carolingian Francia. A formal recognition of the special position of the reigning monarch's wife and the attribution to her of some degree of constitutional authority is, however, a ninth-century development which is paralleled in the increased importance attached by some writers of the period to the maternal ancestry of public figures: the insistence of Agobard of Lyons in his famous, or perhaps notorious, critique of the Empress Judith that Louis needed a wife *quae ei posset adiutrix in regimine et gubernacione palacii et regni* would surely have been unthinkable in earlier reigns.[47] The new status of queens was reflected in the coronation-ceremonies devised in the later ninth century. It was, however, in the East Frankish kingdom and not among the Carolingians of West Francia that this tradition was most conspicuously maintained in the next century. Queen Eadgyth regularly figures as a petitioner on behalf of a third party or as 'intervener' in her husband's diplomas until the year of her death (946).[48] We will look in vain for similar clauses in contemporary English royal charters or in those of Louis IV, which reveal a striking indifference to both the king's wife and his mother. If Eadgyth had no particular relationship with the great German nunneries, this was because until long after her death responsibility for those linked with the royal family was in the hands of the queen-mother Mathilda, for whom Quedlinburg had been founded in her husband's last months.[49]

Entrusting a wider if looser responsibilty to the English queen-consort was one way of meeting in advance possible accusations of scandalous behaviour in the exercise of royal *dominatio* over religious houses. At the same time it enhanced the prestige of the queen both as consort and as mother of kings; and all the more so if — as we have some reason for believing — there were those who thought to bring the queen's position in her earthly kingdom into closer parallel with that of the Virgin Mary in her Heavenly one. Here again the precedents are to be sought in continental Europe in the ninth century: it is in the writings of the second generation of Carolingian scholars that the concept of Mary as *regina* first becomes commonplace in Latin texts, that she figures regularly as *adiutrix* or one of its synonyms and that her qualities as a petitioner are stressed.[50] Nunneries were almost without exception dedicated to the Virgin Mary. There is an obvious link here with the prominence given to feasts of the Virgin in the superb Benedictional of St Aethelwold — early but not the only

Plate X and   evidence for her special cult at Winchester — the miniatures of which
see pp.178-9   have a notable place in the development of the iconography of her Death and Assumption and in the pre-history of a representation of her Coronation.[51]

These, however, are speculations which others may pursue if they wish but in which many will not choose to follow me. They are at least a further reminder that the continental background of *Regularis Concordia* is not to be sought exclusively or even particularly in the

see Chap. 4   textual links with the recorded observance of foreign houses nor identified simply with the knowledge and understanding gained by individual English churchmen during their periods of residence on the Continent. The divergent political, ecclesiastical and cultural traditions of the various regions of Western Europe (including England) in the post-Carolingian decades evolved within a recognisably common framework — definable in terms of institutional and social structure, religious outlook, intellectual heritage. Such shared experiences determined the form of the challenge which faced English religious and political leaders who felt the Divine spark of discontent in the middle decades of the tenth century: they equally helped to determine the character and limits of their response.[52]

Chapter 4

REGULARIS CONCORDIA: HISTORY AND DERIVATION

by Dom Thomas Symons

The History of Regularis Concordia

The English monastic movement of the tenth century, which cul-
minated in the Council of Winchester and the issue of a code of
monastic law — the *Regularis Concordia* — can be traced back to the
reform of Glastonbury by St Dunstan. We might even go so far as to
consider that it was a natural consequence of the measures set on foot
by Alfred, nearly a century earlier, for the revival of education and
learning after their virtual extinction during the course of the Danish
invasions.

Alfred's work does not concern us here, neither is this the place in
which to review in detail Dunstan's early life and his reform of
Glastonbury. We shall therefore confine ourselves to the barest outline
of the first fifty-one years of Dunstan's career, that is, up to his
elevation to Canterbury. This will allow us to give a fuller account of
the Council of Winchester, of its immediate occasion — the spread of
the monastic revival in Edgar's reign — and of the *Regularis Concordia*
itself.

Born (c.909) near Glastonbury and connected with that monastery
from early childhood, Dunstan[1] took the tonsure there at the age of
about fourteen. After seven or eight years, spent partly at Glastonbury
and partly in attendance at Athelstan's court from which he was finally
expelled, there followed a long period of indecision which ended,
c.934, in his reception of the monastic habit at the hands of his
kinsman, Aelfheah the Bald, Bishop of Winchester. In the last year of
Athelstan's reign he was ordained to the priesthood and, in 940, he
became Abbot of Glastonbury.[2] During the following fifteen years, *see p. 209, n. 3*
while engaged mainly in the reform and reconstruction of his abbey, he
also acted as friend and counsellor to two kings, Edmund (who had
placed Glastonbury in his charge) and Edred. Then, in Edwig's reign, he
was forced to spend a year in exile at Ghent; but when Edgar was
chosen king by the Mercians and Northumbrians (957) Dunstan was
recalled, promoted to the bishoprics of Worcester and London and,

finally, after Edwig's death (959) and Edgar's accession to the re-united kingdom, to the archbishopric of Canterbury (960). Meanwhile the reform now flourishing at Glastonbury had been followed by the restoration of Abingdon in 954 by Dunstan's disciple and friend, Aethelwold.[3]

We may now enter into greater detail; for Edgar's appointments of Dunstan to Canterbury in 960, Oswald[4] to Worcester in 961 and Aethelwold to Winchester in 963 — three monastic bishops in the three most important sees — made possible a general extension of the monastic reform, a feature of which was the expulsion of secular clerks from some of the religious houses and the introduction of monks in their place.

It is from this period that we may date the beginnings of effective contacts with the reformed Benedictinism of the Continent. For Dunstan had seen this reform at work during his exile at St Peter's, Ghent; Oswald, for some years a monk at Fleury, had returned to England in 958 and was soon to recall his fellow-monk, Germanus; Osgar, sent by Aethelwold to Fleury, must have finished his training there early in Edgar's reign; and perhaps by then monks from Corbie had arrived to teach reading and chanting at Abingdon.[5]

All three leaders of the movement, Dunstan, Aethelwold and Oswald, are represented as founding or restoring monasteries; but when we look at their respective achievements, as described in their several Lives, we are struck at once by the amount of detailed information we possess concerning the remarkable founding activities of Aethelwold and Oswald compared with the scanty references to those of Dunstan. The *B Life,* for instance, tells us only that Dunstan 'went about visiting the monasteries', mentioning Bath in this connection.[6] Adelard is content to say that 'through Dunstan, a pillar of monastic religion spread throughout the land',[7] and also that the Archbishop allowed only monks to exercise episcopal authority — a slight but useful piece of information, borne out by the fact that some seventeen monks, as against five of the secular clergy, were promoted to bishoprics during Dunstan's lifetime.[8]

see pp. 12-13

Yet Edgar's choice of Dunstan as Archbishop of Canterbury is itself of considerable significance; so, too, are the striking references to Dunstan in *Regularis Concordia,* as 'archbishop of *our country*';[9] in Wulfstan, as that 'glorious and angelic archbishop of the *English nation*';[10] in the anonymous Life of Oswald, as the 'ornament of all *this land*' and as 'so great a senator of the *English nation*';[11] and in the *Old English Account of King Edgar's establishment of monasteries,* as '*his* [that is, *Edgar's*] archbishop'.[12] Moreover, the statement in the Life of Oswald that Edgar 'ordered Dunstan to see that Athelwold and Oswald should restore all the houses of both men and women'[13] could mean not only that the authority of the Archbishop was essential, but also that his was the guiding hand in the reform.

It is, however, Athelwold's biographers who are our chief witnesses to the Archbishop's active share in the reform. For both Aelfric and Wulfstan tell us that 'monasteries throughout the land were established partly by Dunstan's action', but while Aelfric adds 'and partly through that of Aethelwold', Wulfstan amends this to 'and partly by Aethelwold's sedulous co-operation'.[14]

Here the *Old English Account* seems to be decisive: '... [Edgar] began zealously to set monasteries in order widely throughout his kingdom ... he availed himself continually of the counsel of his archbishop, Dunstan; through his admonition he constantly enquired about ... all the religion and welfare of his dominion. He cleansed holy places ... drove out canons ... established monks ... and nuns'.[15]

* * *

The expansion of the monastic revival, referred to above and begun by Aethelwold, acting under Edgar's instructions in 964,[16] was pressed with such vigour that in less than ten years so many foundations and restorations had been made that the question of the consolidation of the reform movement as a whole had to be faced. This brings us to the Council of Winchester and the compilation of *Regularis Concordia*.

As our only definite authority for this Council and for the conditions that led up to it is to be found in *Regularis Concordia* itself, it is to that document that we must now turn.

There, after an introductory reference to the reform, we are told that King Edgar, delighted with the zeal of both monks and nuns, summoned a Synodal Council at Winchester. To this assembly of bishops, abbots and abbesses the King directed a letter of admonition and advice which was received with enthusiastic approval and acted upon forthwith. Monks were invited over from Fleury and Ghent and some of their customs were embodied in a code covering the whole range of the monastic life — the *Regularis Concordia* — to which all vowed obedience.[17]

This account suggests that, despite its dimensional advance, the reform was getting out of hand — 'drifting into incoherence', as the late Sir Frank Stenton wrote.[18] If we examine the *Concordia* more closely, we find that the monasteries are represented as united in one faith, but not in one manner of their observance [of the Rule of St Benedict]. In his letter to the Council, moreover, the King exhorts all to agree peaceably together, to follow the holy and approved Fathers in one and the same regular observance and to carry out the precepts of the Rule without discord, warning them lest the divergent use of one Rule and one country should bring their holy way of life into disrepute.[19]

When we call to mind that Aethelwold had not been wholly satisfied with the life at Glastonbury under Dunstan, that Oswald's work lacked the background of the early Glastonbury and Abingdon side of the movement and that effective relations had for some years been established with overseas monasticism, we begin to realise that detailed acquaintance with the elaborate observances of the great abbeys of the Continent had been gradually producing a state of unrest in the English monasteries — a state involving factions in individual houses and, possibly, a general want of harmonious collaboration prejudicial to the well-being of the entire monastic movement. Evidently the English houses needed some common bond of union if the reform was to have its place in the unifying process which was the great achievement of Edgar's reign.

The needed bond was provided by *Regularis Concordia,* the full title of which, found in the later of its two surviving manuscripts, aptly describes it as an agreement or settling of differences (*Concordia*), drawn up on lines in accordance with the Rule of St Benedict (*regularis*) for the guidance of the monks and nuns (*monachorum sanctimonialiumque*) of the English nation (*Anglicae nationis*).

A state of things that required a radical settlement in the interests of unity points to a date later than that commonly assigned to the Council of Winchester. For the want of agreement so expressly underlined in Edgar's letter to the Council could have reached serious proportions only if houses of each of the three centres of influence — Oswald's as well as Aethelwold's and Dunstan's — were in existence and on a firm footing.

Now by the year 970, besides Glastonbury and Abingdon, we can be sure of the two Winchester minsters together with Chertsey and Milton, all four of them monastic since c.964, Peterborough (c.966), Ely (c.970) and Westbury-on-Trym (962); besides these, St Augustine's (Canterbury) and Bath may very well have been reformed before 970 and, possibly, Malmesbury, Croyland, St Alban's and Deerhurst had also been taken in hand (Westminster and Thorney were not founded until c.971 and c.972 respectively).[20] To these we may be fairly safe in adding at least three houses of nuns: the Nunnaminster (Winchester),

Shaftesbury and Wilton.[21]

Our list includes none of Oswald's more important monasteries; yet these must surely have been in the picture since it is among them that we should expect to find the more notable elements of dissent. Westbury-on-Trym, for instance, though an early foundation and of importance as a seed-plot, was never intended to be a permanency; Deerhurst was in no way prominent; Ramsey itself (colonised from Westbury-on-Trym), Oswald's principal monastery, may not have been founded until as late as c.971, while Winchcombe and Pershore date from c.972.

Further, *Regularis Concordia* takes for granted that some cathedral churches were being served by monastic communities from which, normally, the bishops of such churches were, or were to be, chosen.[22] Winchester (the Old Minster) had indeed been monastic under Aethelwold since 964, but this was an isolated case; for Oswald's gradual introduction of monks into his cathedral church of Worcester *see Chap.6* can hardly have begun before 972 at the earliest.[23] Of Canterbury we know only that, in Dunstan's time, there is evidence for monks as well as clerks there. It could be that experiments on the lines indicated in *Regularis Concordia* were being made by monk-bishops (for instance, Aelfstan of Rochester from 964, Aelfstan of Ramsbury and Sidemann of Crediton from 970);[24] if so, they were not lasting, and this particular item of the reform programme had to wait for twenty years before a third cathedral became monastic (Sherborne, in 992). It looks as though the Council's legislation on what may be called monastic cathedrals, based as it was on historical precedent and consonant with Dunstan's unwillingness to appoint any but monks to bishoprics, owed not a little to Oswald's intention regarding his cathedral church at Worcester.

The foregoing considerations are not conclusive: too many uncertainties are involved and the dates of foundations are only approximate. Nevertheless, the general impression remains that Oswald's foundations, by comparison with Aethelwold's and even with those of Dunstan, were not sufficiently advanced to have helped to bring about the critical situation with which the Council had to deal.

A case can therefore be made out for moving the date of the Council from 970 to, say, 973 — giving a margin for an increase of personnel as well as for the development of the newer foundations. Thus whereas in 970 there would have been an attendance, besides the three leaders, of four other monk-bishops, Eadnoth (Dorchester 964-75), the two Aelfstans (Rochester 964-95; Ramsbury 970-81), Sidemann (Crediton 970-77), and of the abbots and abbesses of the houses listed above

under that year as certain or likely; in 973, on the other hand, there
would have been two more monk-bishops, Athulf (Hereford, from 973)
and Aelfheah (Lichfield, from 973), the abbots already mentioned
under 970 together with the Abbots of Ramsey, Winchcombe, Pershore
— a most important reinforcement from Oswald's group — Westminster
and Thorney (to say nothing of those houses for which it is difficult to
assign foundation dates) and, possibly the Abbess of Romsey. Moreover, by this late date, the transition from a secular to a monastic
condition may have been well on the way at Oswald's cathedral church
but see Chap.6   at Worcester.

The coronation of King Edgar at Bath on Whit Sunday, 973, would
not have been incompatible with the holding of the Council at
Winchester later in the same year; on the contrary, no more suitable
time could have been chosen for the carrying through of a project
designed to secure and to safeguard the unity and solidarity of the
monastic movement on which Edgar, now the 'anointed of the Lord',
had for long set his heart.

The whole-hearted acceptance of, and adherence to, the decisions of
the Council of Winchester, as embodied in *Regularis Concordia,* set the
seal on the revival initiated by Dunstan at Glastonbury more than thirty
years before. A fully organised system of monastic life for men, under
the guardianship of Edgar, and for women, under that of his consort,
Aelfthryth, had been called into being and was now firmly established
in the life of the country.

*   *   *

That Dunstan was present at the Council is a reasonable assumption:[25] otherwise we should have to believe that 'the noble archbishop of this country' who, according to the *Old English Account,* was
consulted by Edgar concerning 'all the religion and welfare of his
dominion',[26] was content to regard the Council with nothing more
than benign interest, and that his share in its proceedings was confined
to offering a couple of off-hand instructions dealing with the nuns of
the reform — instructions which, incidentally, were added by him in
order to confirm (*ad corroborandum*) the deliberations of the
assembly.[27]

If it was owing to the happy working together of King and
Archbishop that the danger of dissension was recognised and a common
norm of monastic observance decided on as a remedy,[28] the credit
for the working out of this common norm in detail must go to
Aethelwold. For though, strangely enough, neither of the early Lives of

Aethelwold has a word to say about the Council or *Regularis Concordia,* Aelfric tells us, in his Letter to the Monks of Eynsham, that 'in Edgar's reign, a book of customs had been put together from various sources and its use imposed on all the monasteries by Aethelwold with his fellow-bishops and abbots'.[29] The mention of 'fellow-bishops and abbots' is an obvious allusion to the Council of Winchester; but the work ascribed by Aelfric almost entirely to Aethelwold was, according to the *Regularis Concordia,* a joint production sanctioned by those present at the Council.[30] Thus, while Aelfric's statement cannot be accepted at its full face value, it may be interpreted as meaning that it was Aethelwold who arranged and codified the legislation agreed upon at the Council, thus producing the *Regularis Concordia* in the form in which it has come down to us.

Only two manuscripts of *Regularis Concordia* have survived,[31] one of the late tenth, the other of the late eleventh century, though we have evidence of two lost manuscripts. But its influence was far-reaching: Aelfric's Letter to the monks of Eynsham is almost entirely an abbreviation of the *Concordia;* passages from the *Concordia* are found in English service-books, charters (most of them, however, of doubtful authenticity) and other documents; while there is at least one trace of its introduction into Scandinavian lands.

see p. 223 n. 46

As St Anselm had heard that St Dunstan was the author of a rule of monastic life,[32] we may close this section with the suggestion that, in the course of a hundred years or so, *Regularis Concordia* had come to be regarded as the work of Dunstan himself.

The Derivation of Regularis Concordia [33]

The *Regularis Concordia* consists of a Proem dealing with the history of the monastic reform and the work of the Council of Winchester, followed by twelve chapters describing the monks' daily life through the year, the liturgy of the more important seasons and feasts, certain special features of claustral discipline, the reception of guests, the daily Maundy, the care of sick brethren and the rites accompanying the death and burial of a monk. A short Epilogue, found only in the later of our two surviving manuscripts, contains Edgar's exemption of religious houses from the payment of the 'heriot'[34] on the death of an abbot or abbess.

Like other customaries of its class, *Regularis Concordia* is based on the Rule of St Benedict; unlike them, it was drawn up in response to a specific need at a Synodal Council convened by royal authority. To meet this need the English, while preserving something of native tradition, went to considerable lengths in order to seek out what seemed best to them in the reformed monastic observance of the day. That, however, their work was not confined to the collection of monastic customs appears from the presence in the *Concordia* of passages witnessing to their investigations into historical, liturgical and devotional literature. In fine, with all the defects of style, structure and what we should call originality common to Latin documents of the period, the bulk of *Regularis Concordia* is a cento — a patchwork — made up of bits and pieces drawn from a wide field of enquiry.

If a large proportion of all this borrowed material still remains unaccounted for, it is hardly surprising; for, as we shall see later, many of the monastic customs of the tenth century were too widely observed to enable us to say exactly how or when any of them came to be introduced into this country; many, too, appear in the *Concordia* in forms suggesting that they have undergone a considerable amount of skilful editing.

*   *   *

From these preliminary observations we may turn at once to what may be called the native element in *Regularis Concordia*. A document which stresses the need for uniformity in the observance of 'one Rule and one country'[35] might be expected to contain some national or traditional customs. Here we are on sure ground, for a custom — the pealing of bells on the last three days of Christmas week — appears in the *Concordia* not only as 'the custom among the people of this country' but also in connection with the Winchester Council's decision that 'the goodly religious customs of this land ... be ... confirmed'.[36]

see pp.13, 30-5, 95-6 Specially prominent in their relationship with circumstances peculiar to the English revival are the prayers said daily for the King, Queen and benefactors: a total of eighteen psalms, twenty-three collects and, usually, the morrow (or early) Mass;[37] the ban on lay dominion over monasteries;[38] the directions that episcopal and abbatial elections are to be carried out according to the Rule and with the consent and advice of the King (here we have points of contact with the ruling on elections given by the legates George and Theophylact in 787, and with a passage from Bede's Letter to Egbert).[39]

In prescribing daily reception of the Eucharist[40] — an injunction found in no other customary — the *Concordia* quotes a short sentence from the *De Sacramentis* of St Ambrose; it is likely that the Council had also in mind the Letter to Egbert in which Bede deplores the neglect of daily Communion in Northumbria.

Another unique custom directs that a special room, with a fire, should be set apart for the carrying out of the normal claustral observance in the cold of winter.[41]

The following items may also be ascribed to traditional usage; the celebration of the principal Mass on Fridays and Saturdays in honour of the Holy Cross and of our Lady respectively;[42] the recitation of the entire psalter on the three last days of Holy Week;[43] the use of the chasuble by deacon and subdeacon in Lent and on Quarter Tense days only;[44] the prayer *Satisfaciat tibi Domine Deus,* said when news is received of the death of a monk of a nearby house[45] (in other customaries and in the service-books this prayer forms part of the burial service); the three prayers said at the Veneration of the Cross on Good Friday,[46] the first of which is in the *Book of Cerne,* the second in the Mozarabic rite, while the last is not found again anywhere until after the Conquest.

*   *   *

We may now consider the question of customs introduced from the Continent, the general evidence for which is given in the *Concordia* itself. There we find the members of the Winchester assembly recalling Pope Gregory the Great's direction to Augustine of Canterbury touching the introduction of good customs into the newly-founded English Church. We are then told how monks were invited over from 'St Benedict's monastery at Fleury' and from 'that eminent monastery known by the renowned name of Ghent' (St Peter's), and how some of their praiseworthy customs were selected for inclusion in *Regularis Concordia.*[47]

The mention of these two influential continental houses is most fortunate for our purpose; for Fleury had been reformed by Odo of Cluny c.930, and Ghent by Gerard of Brogne c.937. *see pp.21, 30 see p.31*

It might be thought that there would have been no difference between the customs of two monasteries both of which could claim descent ultimately from the reforms of Benedict of Aniane in the ninth century. But there would have been no reason to borrow customs from two different houses unless each had something of its own to offer. The reforms of Benedict had indeed influenced the whole course of western monasticism, but the elaborate customaries of the tenth and eleventh centuries have no real counterpart in the simpler writings of the ninth century: they form a new type of document. We must distinguish in the tenth century not so much between the main points of monastic practice, then more or less standardised, but between the various ways in which these were carried out. We may then consider Fleury and Ghent as representative, respectively, of the two major divisions of tenth-century reformed monasticism: the Cluniac and the Lotharingian.

This rough and ready distinction must not lead us to think of the movements which arose throughout the Lotharingian provinces as of so many isolated efforts cut off from one another. They would all have been in touch with one another in much the same way that the reforms emanating from Cluny were interconnected. Nor need we imagine that the main branches of reform, Lotharingian and Cluniac, stood entirely independent of each other.[48]

As, however, we possess no customary of Ghent and no early one of Fleury, we can hope to discern what the English reformers owed to these two monasteries only by comparing *Regularis Concordia* with such tenth- and eleventh-century continental customaries or documents as are available, referring parallels with those of Cluniac type to Fleury and parallels with those of Lotharingian provenance to Ghent.

Customs derived from continental sources may be considered under three heads: (1) those witnessed to by documents, mostly related with the monastery of Monte Cassino, belonging to a period before the ninth-century reforms of Benedict of Aniane; (2) those taken over from ninth-century Anianian documents; (3) those of the elaborated observance of the tenth-century reforms.

(1) Pre-Anianian practices include the drink allowed on Sundays and feasts after the Office of None (except from the 12th of November to the 1st of February), the recitation of the Divine Office when journeying, and the observances taken bodily from the eighth-century tract known as the *Ordo* (or *Memoriale*) *Qualiter*,[49] the only document of the period which has been extensively used in the *Concordia*. The first two customs are found everywhere in the tenth century, and may have been derived through the Cluniac or Lotharingian reforms; but passages taken from the *Ordo Qualiter* may well have been survivals of much older English usage.

(2) Here, attention must be called to general parallels between the tenth-century English reform and that of Benedict of Aniane in the ninth.

We have, in the literature of both movements, the usual story of the extinction of monastic life followed, first, by a revival of observance, then, by a recognition of this as a work of national moment and, lastly, by conciliar legislation. In England King Edgar, abroad the Emperor Louis the Pious, appear as the leading figures; to the Council of Winchester correspond the two Councils of Aix-la-Chapelle in 816 and

817; from Winchester we have the *Regularis Concordia,* from Aix we have, *inter alia,* the *Rule for Canons*[50] in 816 and the *Capitula*[51] for monks in 817.

It seems that the English reformers had the Anianian movement in mind, for one short passage of the Proem to the *Concordia* describes the reception of Edgar's letter to the Council of Winchester in terms modelled on the corresponding account (given in the Preface to the *Rule for Canons*) of the reception of Louis's speech by the first assembly at Aix.[52] Here, the *Concordia* weaves into its paraphrase of the account in question brief verbal quotations from the *Exultet* of Holy Saturday and from Aldhelm's *De Virginitate.*

In a second passage, the *Concordia* borrows directly from the *Rule for Canons,* adding the words 'I will sing with the spirit, I will sing also with the understanding' to the injunction of the *Rule* of St Benedict that, at the Divine Office, 'mind and voice should be in accord'.

Since the English knew of the Aix meeting of 816 it is surprising that their acquaintance with that of 817 should be directly evidenced by only three points of the Anianian observance: one, dealing with visits to the 'villas' (or possessions) of the monastery, another, forbidding abbot or monks to eat outside the common refectory, and a third, dealing with the admission of faults at the daily Chapter — all three taken from the *Capitula* of Aix.

It is still more surprising that there are divergences from the injunctions of the *Capitula*: thus in the *Concordia,* 'pinguedo' (lard or fat) is forbidden during the whole of Advent instead of only during the eight days before Christmas; the Lenten abstinence from 'pinguedo' begins at Septuagesima instead of at Quinquagesima; the 'rasura fratrum' (shaving and hair-cutting) takes place during the middle of Lent as well as on Holy Saturday instead of on Holy Saturday only.

The recitation before Nocturns of the *Trina Oratio* (a threefold form of prayer)[53] and the Gradual psalms,[54] which had its origin in the discipline in force at Benedict of Aniane's model monastery of Inda (Kornelimünster) and was widespread in the tenth century, forms, as it stands in the *Concordia,* a custom for which no exact parallel is to be found.

(3) In what we have called the 'elaborate observance' of the tenth-century reforms, we find liturgical as well as monastic customs. Purely liturgical usage, however, will be touched on very briefly here since, by and large, the liturgy of the customaries of the period, like that of the *Concordia,* was celebrated according to the Roman Rite as more or less stabilised in the tenth century. Thus the ceremonies of Christmas, Candlemas, Ash Wednesday, Lent, Holy Week, Easter and

Pentecost, incomplete as they are in the customaries, can nearly all be found in the various types of Service Books of the day. We may however mention that the *Concordia*'s descriptions of the Liturgy of Holy Week and Easter are partly based on, and contain three rubrics quoted verbatim from, some form of the *Ordo Romanus Primus*; and that the substitution of the Roman Office for that of the Rule on the last three days of Holy Week, during Easter week and at Nocturns on Whit Sunday comes nearer to Lotharingian than to Cluniac practice.

*   *   *

Turning to monastic customs, we must begin by noting the more important documents on which we rely for our knowledge of the 'sources' of the *Concordia*. [55]

Many of the customaries of Cluniac type are of a date too late for inclusion here. We have, however, the *Life of St Odo of Cluny*;[56] the oldest known customs of Cluny, of the late tenth century and existing in three recensions:[57] these will be referred to as *Cluny*; the customs of Cluny, drawn up shortly before the middle of the eleventh century, and hitherto known as the customs of *Farfa*,[58] under which name they will be cited here; the customs of *Fleury*,[59] of the thirteenth century, but included because they preserve some valuable primitive practices.

Documents of Lotharingian type are the closely related customs of *Einsiedeln* and *Trèves* together with those of *Verdun,* all cited under these names. [60]

Cluny, Farfa and *Fleury* are very different in character from *Einsiedeln, Trèves* and *Verdun*: the Cluniac customaries forming compact guides to the monks' choir duties, while the Lotharingian, to some extent rambling and discursive, frequently offer useful sidelights on monastic observance.

It is obvious that agreements established between any of these customaries and the *Concordia* will indicate only indirectly the 'source' of the latter. It is equally obvious that as the observances of these customaries rarely afford us a certain clue to somewhat similar observances found in the *Concordia,* a number of *Concordia* customs must, for the present, be referred to what is known as 'common observance'. This is the case with the two extra Offices (Of all Saints and Of the Dead) the seven psalms and Litany after Prime, the five psalms said after the Chapter, the Penitential and Gradual psalms said in Lent after each of the day hours and the Penitential psalms begun at the grave of a deceased monk. The appearance of all these in the earliest

Cluniac as well as in the Lotharingian customaries affords us no satisfactory explanation of the presence of these very practices in the *Concordia.*

Even a clear agreement between the *Concordia* and another document may not always help in our search for 'sources'. The Advent fast prescribed in the *Concordia* is an example of this: the eleventh-century Cluniac customary of *Farfa* seems to be the only one to afford an adequate parallel with the *Concordia,* and it might be argued that the *Concordia* derives its custom from primitive practice at Cluny as represented by *Farfa* were it not that on this point the earliest Cluniac customaries (*Cluny*) differ from *Farfa.*

We can now give a list of *Concordia* customs that may, with reasonable assurance, be assigned to one or other of the two main branches of continental reformed monasticism.

Each *Concordia* custom will be given in abstract form and will be followed by a parallel abstract from, or a general observation concerning, the document claimed as a 'source', the Latin originals being quoted in the right-hand column.

It is taken for granted that readers are conversant with such features of monastic life as the Chapter, or meeting of the brethren at which the day's duties were distributed; the Divine Office consisting of the night hours, Nocturns and Matins (now known as Matins and Lauds), the day hours Prime, Terce, Sext and None (said at daylight, 9 o'clock, noon and 3 p.m.), Vespers and Compline; the two daily public Masses, the Morrow (or early) Mass and the Principal Mass.

1. Relations between Master and Schola (the children of the cloister as a body).

Concordia

Not even the master himself may be in company with any boy without a third person being present as witness. Master and Schola are to be together and to go about together according to the requirements of reason or necessity.	Nec ad obsequium privatum quempiam illorum *nec saltem* sub spiritualis rei obtentu solum deducere *praesumant, sed* uti regula praecipit sub sui custodis vigilantia iugiter maneat; *nec* ipse custos cum singulo aliquo puerulo sine tertio qui *testis* assistat migrandi licentiam habeat, *sed* solito cum tota schola, si res rationabilis exigerit, quo necesse est . . . cum benedictine eat.[61]

This is in complete agreement with the discipline observed at Cluny, as known to us from the *Life of Odo of Cluny*:

> . . . mos enim eiusdem loci fuerat ut magister scholae solus cum solo puero *nec* quoquam iret *saltem nec* ad naturae digestionem, *sed nec* solus puer secretius illi loqui *praesumeret*; *sed* et propter bonum *testimonium* alium e pueris aut unum ex fratribus in comitatu vel locutione semper assumeret.[62]

2. *The change from night to day shoes.*

Concordia

No one except the ministers (that is, the various officials) may put on his day shoes until the signal is given after *Prime*.	Tunc facto signo eant et se diurnalibus induant calceamentis; nullus enim hoc debet praesumere antequam illud audiatur signum, exceptis ministris, neque tunc ab aliquo intermittatur sine licentia.[63]

With this *Cluny* agrees, though it places the signal before *Terce*. But 'after *Prime*' and 'before *Terce*' come to much the same thing; since the lengthy devotions and other additions to *Prime* were always followed by *Terce*:

> Post Primam namque nullus fratrum debet se calciare diurnalibus, nisi illi fratres quibus iniuncta est cura obedientiae. . . . Cum autem tempus fuerit *horae Tertiae sonet custos signum* pusillum modice et tunc pergant in dormitorium et calcient se diurnalibus.[64]

3. *Chapter custom on Christmas Eve and Holy Saturday*

Concordia

On Christmas Eve, when the feast is announced in Chapter by the reader, the brethren rise and then genuflect, giving thanks for	*Vigilia Natalis Domini,* dum eiusdem natalis mentio a lectore recitetur *in capitulo,* omnes pariter surgentes genua flectent,

the loving-kindness of Our Lord who came to redeem the world from the snares of the devil. They shall do in like manner on Holy Saturday when one of the boys announces the Resurrection ... in honour of the victory by which Our Lord overthrew the gates of Hell, drew with Him into the heavens some of his faithful ones and gave to us ... the hope of ascending thither.

gratias agentes propter eius ineffabilem pietatem qua mundum a laqueis diaboli redempturus descendit. Sabbato quoque Sancto Paschae, dum *a puero Resurrectio Domini Nostri Ihesu Christi* legitur, quamquam in martyrologio id non habetur, propter eius gloriosissimi victoriam triumphi qua, destructis Herebi claustris, secum fideles quosque in coelos advexit, nobis etiam redivivis spem ascendendi c o n c e s s i t, u n i f o r m i t e r agatur.[65]

The *Fleury* parallel runs:

On Christmas Eve, when the feast is announced in Chapter by one of the boys, all shall prostrate themselves saying thrice: Glory be to Thee, O Lord, who wast born of a Virgin ... On Holy Saturday, when the Resurrection is announced in Chapter, all shall beg pardon, that is, genuflect or prostrate themselves, saying silently: Glory be to Thee, O Lord, who didst rise again.

In Vigilia Nativitatis Domini quando *in capitulo* Nativitas Domini *a puero* pronunciatur, omnes in faciem cadant et tunc in silentio dicant ter Gloria Tibi Domine qui natus es de Virgine ... Ad initium Capituli debent omnes congregari, ut dum pronuntietur *Resurrectio Domini Nostri Iesu Christi* omnes petant veniam et dicant sub silentio Gloria tibi Domine qui surrexisti.[66]

Here, the *Concordia*'s devotional comments, suitable to the two feasts, may well be paraphrases of the two doxologies prescribed by *Fleury*.

4. Blessing of the New Fire on Maundy Thursday

Concordia

The brethren proceed to the Church doors bearing with them a staff on which is a candlestick shaped like a serpent; fire is

... pergant [fratres] ad ostium ecclesiae ferentes hastam cum imagine serpentis, ibique *ignis de silice excutiatur*; illo benedicto

struck from flint and is blessed
by the abbot; then the candle
which is in the mouth of the
serpent is lit from that fire.

ab abbate, candela, quae *in ore
serpentis* infixa est, ab illo
accendatur.[67]

Fleury

For the consecration of the new
fire at the door of almsgiving,
fire is struck from a beryl or
from flint . . . In the procession a
staff is borne on which is a
dragon. One of the boys shall
hold a lighted candle, ready to
re-light, if necessary, the fire in
the mouth of the dragon.

. . . *ignis* industria praecentoris
. . . *e silice excutiatur* . . . ad
processionem portatur . . . draco
in pertica. Unus vero de infanti-
bus in sconsa a magistro suo
praeparata affert candelam ut
praesto sit ignis si extinguatur
[? cereus] qui *in ore draconis*
portatur.[68]

The Blessing of the New Fire was general in the tenth century and
was carried out also on Good Friday and Holy Saturday. In *Fleury*, the
'door of almsgiving' may be a misreading for 'door of the Church'. The
difference between 'serpent' and 'dragon' is probably a question of
nomenclature. The *Concordia*'s 'lighted candle *in the mouth of the
serpent*' is a remarkable equivalent to *Fleury*'s 'fire (that is, a lighted
candle) *in the mouth of the dragon*'.

5. *The four extra psalms after Prime*

Concordia

After Prime, two psalms are
recited, one against fleshly temptation, the other for deceased
brethren; there follow the psalm
Inclina Domine, the Penitential
psalms, the Litany, said prostrate, the psalm *In Te Domine
speravi,* prayers.

Deinde finita Prima duos psalmos
Domine ne in furore tuo (ii) et
Miserere mei Deus (i), canant:
primum   pro   carnis *ten-
tatione* . . . sequentem vero *pro
defunctis* fratribus . . . Et   sic,
more solito, paenitentiae psalmos
percurrant   devote   interposito
psalmo *Inclina Domine.* His vero
finitis subsequatur *letania* quam
universi, more solito *prostrati*
humiliter nullo excepto, signo
pulsato compleant. Qua expleta,
post orationem dominicam inter-
canitur psalmus *In te Domine
speravi* (ii) consequentibus
precibus et orationibus.[69]

The corresponding arrangement in *Trèves* is as follows: three psalms for deceased abbots and against temptations, the Penitential psalms, the Litany prostrate, the psalm *In Te Domine speravi,* Prayers:

> Post Primam *pro defunctis* abbatibus et *tentatione* tres psalmi quarum non estis ignari; hos itaque sequuntur septem psalmi cum *litania quae cantatur terraneus, congregatione prostrata,* praeter *In Te Domine speravi* adiungentes ceteras quoque *orationes* multiplices.[70]

It is not certain that the third *Concordia* psalm, *Inclina Domine* comes exactly where I have placed it: it is described in the *Concordia* as 'interposed'. Yet only *Trèves* agrees with the *Concordia* in giving a total of four extra psalms in connection with the customary Penitential psalms and Litany after Prime.

6. *The offering at the Morrow and Principal Masses.*

Concordia

At the Morrow Mass on Mondays, the offering is made by the brethren of the right-hand choir, while those of the left-hand choir offer at the Principal Mass; on Tuesdays, the brethren of the left-hand choir offer at the Matin Mass while those of the right-hand choir offer at the Principal Mass; this is done alternately throughout the week.

Inde Missam matutinalem celebrent ad quam *secunda feria dexter offerat chorus, sinister* ad principalem *Missam*: *tertia* rursum *feria sinister offerat* ad matutinalem, *dexter* ad principalem, sicque alternatim in eo hebdomadam percurrant.[71]

So also *Einsiedeln* and *Trèves*:

Einsiedeln

At the Principal Mass on Mondays, the left-hand chorus makes the offering, and on Tuesdays the right-hand chorus, and so by turns to the end of the week.

Ad generalem vero *Missam secunda feria sinister [offerat] chorus, tertia dexter,* et suis vicibus sibi succedant usque ad sabbatum.[72]

Trèves

> *sinister chorus secunda feria,*
> quarta et sexta; *dexter tertia,*
> quinta et septima *feria ad* publi-
> cam Missam *offerat* et pacifi-
> cet. [73]

At first sight this may seem confusing. But a little thought shows us that in the *Concordia, Einsiedeln* and *Trèves,* at the Morrow Mass on Mondays, Wednesdays and Fridays, the offering is made by the right-hand choir; on Tuesdays, Thursdays and Saturdays by the left-hand choir: at the Principal Mass this order was reversed.

7. *Reading of the Rule and Gospel in Chapter.*

Concordia

At the Chapter, the brethren being seated in their stalls, the Rule or, on feasts, the Gospel of the day is read and the prior (that is, the Superior) discourses on what has been read.

> Iterum autem *residentibus lega-*
> *tur regula vel,* si dies festus
> fuerit, evangelium ipsius diei, *de*
> qua lectione a *priore* prout
> Dominus dederit dicatur. [74]

All three points are found in *Einsiedeln* where the 'homily' evidently equals the 'gospel' of the *Concordia.*

> ...itemque *residentibus legitur*
> *Regula vel* in festis diebus
> omelia... et *prior*... faciat ser-
> monem   *de*   praesenti
> *lectione.* [75]

8. *The Morrow Mass of the Trinity.*
Concordia

The Morrow Mass on Sundays is always of the Holy Trinity except on feast days.

> ... [Missa   matutinalis]   die
> dominica *de Trinitate* celebranda
> est . nisi   alia   festiva   dies
> fuerit. [76]

With this both *Einsiedeln* and *Trèves* agree.

> *Dominicis agitur [Missa prior] de*
> *Trinitate,*   diebus   exceptis
> Sanctorum. [77]

9. Psalmody during the manual labour.

Concordia

During the manual labour the brethren recite the Canonical Cursus (that is, the Roman Office or Cursus) and the Psalter.

Tunc cum decantatione canonici *cursus et psalterii* operentur...[78]

Einsiedeln prescribes the recitation of the Roman Cursus (that is, the Canonical Cursus or Office) and the Psalter, in the same connection.

Post hos vero [psalmos] incipiant Romanum *cursum* per ordinem, quo completo *psalterium* per totum.[79]

10. Chapter custom special to Christmas Day and Maundy Thursday. (here the word 'Vigilia' refers to 'Nocturns' on Christmas Day).

Concordia

At the Chapter meeting on Christmas Day the abbot gives a conference after which the brethren ask pardon on their knees for all their negligences. The abbot then begs pardon in like manner for his faults.

[In cuius noctis Vigilia] ... finita Prima venientes ad *Capitulum,* post cetera spiritualis aedificationis colloquia, petant humili devotione omnes fratres veniam ab abbate, qui vices Christi agit, postulantes multiplicium indulgentiam excessuum dicentes Confiteor; et abbas respondeat Misereatur. Demum ipse abbas solotenus ac se prosternens eadem a fratribus petat. *Idem* modus confessionis prima Paschalis sollemnitatis die ita agatur.[80]

This custom is to be repeated on 'the first day of the Paschal solemnities'. The *Trèves* parallel to this is unique, though *Trèves* describes the custom as carried out on Maundy Thursday, enjoining its repetition on Christmas Day.

In die sancto Cenae Domini abbas *ad Capitulum* sermonem faciat, et ut iterum confessionem de neglegentiis suis faciant admoneat. Deinde ipse surgat et

ad pedes se omnium fratrum pro-
volvat ut veniam neglegenciarum
suarum a deo sibi postulent, et
idem in Vigiliis Natalis Domini
faciat.[81]

The apparent discrepancy between the 'Maundy Thursday' of *Trèves*
and 'the first day of the Paschal solemnities' of the *Concordia* is easily
reconciled; for the Maundy Thursday ceremonies are referred to in the
Gothic, Bobbio, Gelasian and Mozarabic Sacramentaries as 'the
beginning of the Paschal solemnities'.

11. *The Weekly Maundy carried out by the boys.*

Concordia

The Saturday Maundy is carried
out by the boys of the right-hand
choir, accompanied by one
master: on Sundays it is carried
out by the boys of the left-hand
choir, led by the other master.

... *sabbato pueri dexterioris
chori* cum uno custode illud
peragant: sequenti *die dominica*
residui pueri *sinisterioris* chori
cum altero custode ...[82]

This same custom is found only in *Trèves*.

... nam *Sabbato pueri de dextro
debent* hoc facere *choro,* die
dominico de *sinistro,* sequenti
eos   uno   magistro;[83]
... *sabbato* unus magister [cum
pueris] de *dextro* choro,
dominica alter cum pueris *de
sinistro choro mandatum*
faciant.[84]

12. *Masses for a deceased brother.*

Concordia

For thirty days after the death of
a monk, each of the priests of
the monastery shall celebrate
thirty Masses for the repose of
his soul.

His tamen *triginta* diebus cotidie
sacerdotum unusquisque ... pro
eo *Missas* celebret.[85]

This is the same as in *Verdun.*

...unusquisque sacerdos triginta Missas cantabit pro defuncto fratre.[86]

13. In memory of the death of a monk of another monastery.

Concordia

The name of a dead monk of a nearby house shall be written down in the (book of) anniversaries.

...et nomen eius notetur in anniversariis...[87]

This is as in *Einsiedeln* where, however, 'the (book of) Anniversaries' is specified as 'the Breviarium and Martyrology'.

...nomenque eius notetur in breviario et martirologio, ne tradatur oblivioni eius anniversarium.[88]

14. The Triple 'Kyrie eleison' custom after Tenebrae in Holy Week.

This custom needs some preliminary explanation. On the last three days of Holy Week the Offices of Nocturns and Matins, celebrated according to the Roman or Canonical Rite, went by the name of *Tenebrae*. Candles were lit at the beginning of *Tenebrae*: in the course of that office, these candles were extinguished one by one until, at the end of the antiphon of the canticle, *Benedictus,* with which Tenebrae closed, the church was in darkness. It was then that the triple 'Kyrie' custom began. According to the *Concordia,* this custom, which had come to the knowledge of the English from 'certain churches of religious men', though recommended, is not to be imposed as of obligation.

The scheme given by the *Concordia* is as follows:

When the antiphon of the Gospel (that is, the *Benedictus*) is finished and the candles are extinguished, two boys of the right-hand choir sing *Kyrie eleison* sonorously; two boys of the left-hand choir answer *Christe eleison*; two more, to the westward, sing *Domine, miserere*

... peracto quicquid ad cantilenam illius noctis pertinet, evangeliique antiphona finita nihilque iam cereorum luminis remanente, sint duo ad hoc idem destinati *pueri* in dextera parte chori qui sonora psallant voce *Kyrie eleison,* duoque similiter in sinistra parte qui respondeant

nobis; the entire chorus then sing *The Lord was made obedient unto death*; then, beginning with the boys of the right-hand choir, the scheme is repeated a second and a third time. This order is uniformly kept for three nights by them [that is, by 'certain churches of religious men'].

Christe eleison, necnon et in occidentali parte duo qui dicant *Domine miserere nobis*; quibus peractis respondeat simul omnis chorus Christus *Dominus factus est oboediens* usque ad mortem. Demum pueri dexterioris chori repetant quae supra, eodem modo quo supra, usquequo chorus finiat quae supra; idemque tertio repetant eodem ordine. Quibus tertio finitis agant tacitas genuflexo more solito preces; *qui ordo trium noctium uniformiter teneatur* ab illis.[89]

Forms of this rite were widespread; but the *Concordia* version is almost certainly connected with or derived from that found in *Verdun,* the last sentence of which closely resembles the last sentence given in the *Concordia,* as will be seen by comparison of the Latin texts.

... ubi ultima antiphona insonuerit, necabitur simul et novissima candela. Tunc demum cantico de evangelio finito in tenebris, stabunt *duo pueri* contra dexteram partem altaris alte inclamantes *Kirie eleison* et nihilominus alii duo ad levam respondentes *Christe*. Rursumque primi Kyrie eleison, sed et duo levitae paulo minus in inferiori gradu cancelli stent, altius quid a vocibus puerorum, intonantes versus Qui passus quibus respondeant e contra duo sacerdotes *Domine miserere*. Deinde chorus *Dominus factus est oboediens*. Hoc ergo tertio repetito et finito, unus puerorum coram altare clamabit gemendo Mortem autem crucis. Post cuius vocem fratres canonice dicent preces

> silenter et ubi prior signum ded-
> erit surgent . . . *Qui ordo uni-*
> *formiter servabitur tribus noct-*
> *ibus.* [90]

It is true that *Verdun* differs from the *Concordia* in details, the most noteworthy of which is the insertion of a special verse: *Qui pass[?ur]us es.* The terms of this verse suggest that there must have been two more verses, one special to Good Friday, the other to Holy Saturday. It is likely that neither *Verdun* nor the *Concordia* gives full details of their respective practices, for an eleventh-century manuscript, CCCC 190 (one of the books given by Bishop Leofric to Exeter, which frequently agrees verbatim with, or possibly copies from, the *Concordia*) follows the *Concordia* closely here, but with the addition of three special verses, one for each day: *Qui passurus advenisti* (compare *Verdun*), *Qui prophetice* and *Vita in ligno.*

*   *   *

The general derivative nature of the customs of the *Concordia* show not only how comprehensive that document is, but also how independently and how skilfully its borrowed material has been adapted, blended and even altered.

As for the list of particular customs which has been given, it is perhaps not an impressive one; for few of the parallels adduced suggest more than remotely a literary connection with any given document. Nevertheless, as it stands, our list shows a higher proportion of agreement with the Lotharingian customaries of *Einsiedeln, Trèves and Verdun* than with those of *Cluny, Farfa* and *Fleury*. It may be that the customs of Ghent, indirectly discernible in the *Regularis Concordia* through Lotharingian parallels, had specially commended themselves to the English.[91]

We may sum up with the following quotation: ' . . . the *Concordia*, for all its spirit of national independence, reflects the ideas of an age when monasticism, pursuing the course into which it had been directed by Benedict of Aniane, was finally settling down to a type of observance that remained generally typical of Benedictine life until the days of St Bernard'.[92]

Chapter 5

SOME SERVICE-BOOKS OF THE LATER SAXON CHURCH

by C. E. Hohler

The surviving service books of the Old English church are commonly overlooked by historians of the Roman Latin rite. The principal reason is that nothing beyond fragments survives from England earlier than c.900.[1] The genesis of the books approved by the Council of Trent can be adequately illuminated from c.800 from extant 'Frankish' manuscripts, this being roughly the date when the Frankish authorities made serious efforts to bring all their books into line with those used in Rome in general, and by the Pope in particular. There is every reason to suppose they were more or less successful. The process by which what was done by the Pope c.800 was arrived at, and to what extent (and, if at all, since when) it was distinctive to the Pope himself, to the City of Rome, to Lazio, or to Central Italy as a whole is however a great deal more obscure; and the total disappearance of early Italian manuscripts likely to be relevant, apart from the manuscript called the Leonine Sacramentary and some fragments, means that scholars are thrown back on a variety of indirect sources. The authority behind the few complete earlier manuscripts, which are French, is arguable, and the fragments are usually puzzling; but, by way of limiting the field, it is tacitly agreed that manuscripts later than c.850 need not be brought into the debate. This, owing to accidents of survival, excludes pretty well all material from both England and Italy which are, in fact, the two areas most likely to be relevant: and it is marvellously unsatisfactory.[2]

It is not merely that it is a bore to an Englishman, attempting to understand the early books of his own church, to be endlessly told they are Carolingian, when they are nothing so simple. It is more than that. Down to and including the Sarum missal (when one gets it, in the thirteenth century) English books are liable to exhibit 'Italian features' which are distinguishable precisely because they do not reappear on the southern shores of the Channel; and to exhibit other features which do appear across the Channel but only in some, apparently non-standard, books. The peculiarities of these last are, historically speaking, more likely to have been initially transmitted from Italy via England to the

Frankish realm than via the last to England. There is no evidence whatever that the churches of the Frankish Empire applied direct to Rome for service books before c.790. Until c.750 the principal churches of Gaul used versions of their own, Gallican, rite. The change took place under the influence of Englishmen, the tediously familiar names being those of Willibrord, Boniface and Alcuin; and, as some form of the Roman rite had necessarily been used at Canterbury since 600, it is an inescapable conclusion that the books used to effect the change of rite in the Frankish Empire must often have been copied from English models, or at the least have been influenced by English models. All this will, of course, be difficult to detect, since the English books can hardly have been 'wrong': though they may well have been differently arranged, and, in terms of what the Pope did, out of date. But since it is often nowadays suggested that the Roman use in Italy in 600 had no properly codified books (because the use had simply grown up and the clergy knew what to do), it cannot be too firmly emphasised that, in so far as this may have been so, St Augustine will have had to codify it himself. His mission was the first occasion when there was any question of Roman liturgical usages in a developed form being transported bodily to a remote pagan area: and St Augustine was faced with the task of training scores of Anglophone priests to conduct services decently in Latin. If he was under any illusions about the Englishman's natural aptitude for foreign languages, he will soon have lost them. His priests must have been provided with books which made clear exactly what they had to say and sing, never mind whether they understood it. In the light of these considerations the Vatican (or 'Old') Gelasian[3] must, it seems to me, represent an assemblage of Roman materials put together with a view to use in England in the seventh century. The book may, and no doubt does, contain features subsequently introduced in France, since it is a French manuscript of c.750, but its obvious distinctive aspects — apart from its 'Roman-ness' — are its archaism, its separate sanctoral, and its inclusion in that sanctoral of prayers for several central Italian saints. Special pleading has not made it look a whit more likely that these last can ever have been part of any sort of official liturgy in Rome: and my impression is that the study of (necessarily later) Italian books will confirm that these saints did not belong to the Gelasian tradition as it was known in Italy.[4]

So far as the separate sanctoral is concerned, the next oldest surviving European mass book with one is the Leofric Missal,[5] and all the other Anglo-Saxon missals conform. In particular the Winchcomb Sacramentary appears to be in this respect an English rearrangement of a type of book from Saint Denis which in Ratoldus's copy has the two propria combined.[6] For the saints of Capua etc. one of the few things that is quite certain about English service books of the eighth century is that they made generous provision for central Italian saints.[7] There was, of course, no reason why St Augustine should impose on England a lot of lesser feasts from the local calendar of Rome. or exclude saints venerated elsewhere. Subsequent developments on those lines seem to be an accidental consequence of books, which happened to embody a particular Roman calendar, being taken as standard in the Frankish empire. But St Augustine had companions and we do not know where they were born. If they were not native Romans, and I should say the English liturgical evidence proves they were not, then, as lonely Italians contending with pagan barbarians in a land of fogs, they are likely to have wished to remember the patronal festivals of their homes. No one can have thought it, as such, important that the feast of St Magnus of Fabrateria should be kept by every church in England, Gaul and Germany: but some individual may easily have wished it should be kept at Canterbury in 597. The purpose of the separate sanctoral would then have been, not to predetermine the liturgical calendar of any church, but to make it easy to check whether an Italian prayer was available for a saint who happened to figure in such a calendar. The process of forming a separate sanctoral, other than one logically assembling all immoveable feasts including Christmas, implies a feeling that saints' days are secondary; and that this feeling is still alive is shown when Candlemas and Lady day, as feasts of our Lord, join Christmas in the temporal. This is rare: but the Leofric Missal and the Durham Ritual put them there.[8] In England the separate sanctoral is clearly at home. There seems no obvious objection to this view which clearly gets rid of some difficulties, and the model for the Gelasian could then have been brought to the region of Paris in the 660s by its Bishop Agilbert. He must have got to know the Roman rite while he was Bishop of Dorchester, and his date removes the possible difficulty (which I do not actually find a difficulty) that if the Vatican Gelasian were an English text it would contain propers for English saints. When Agilbert left the country the first Englishman at all likely to have received a proper, St Cuthbert, was still alive.[9]

* * *

I do not, however, wish to devote more space to Gelasian books since the surviving English books, of the tenth and early eleventh centuries, are not of this kind. They are Gregorians together with several pontificals and some rather scrappy material for the office.[10] They have features which suggest that, whatever the answer about the Gelasian, there was other Italian material, not contained in it, in use in the earlier English church: and the limited Gelasian element in them is the aspect which at the present moment is least inviting to investigate. Any discussion of Gregorians is, however, to some extent a function of the view one takes, or considers the evidence compels one to take, of the history of this type of text in the North. Since this paper in its original form was delivered, Dom Deshusses's marvellous edition of the ninth-century manuscripts of the Gregorian has appeared.[11]

This absolves me from combatting the unreasonable view that all European missals descend from two sub-archetypes exported from Rome to France in the course of the eighth century. From whatever, highly discutable, date the Gregorian in any recognisable form came into regular use in any important church in Rome, it must have been possible to order a copy from a scribe, if copies were not actually offered for sale. The number of sub-archetypes exported is undiscoverable, but must, especially in Italy, have been substantial. One can, however, detect the influence of particularly authoritative copies; and (provided one is not determined to use only early manuscripts) one can discover the geographical distribution of peculiarities and try to discern the implications of the pattern. An existing liturgical manuscript is often, I should say usually, not the clean lineal descendant of the approved typicum of some edition, but copied from a 'practical' book, based on some much older form of the text than the one it purports to represent. This will have been brought more or less efficiently up to date at successive recopyings by collating what was supposed to be a 'good' text. Most ninth-century Gregorians appear to survive because they were 'good' texts, and it does not at all follow that peculiar readings etc. which surface in books of the late ninth or tenth centuries are of recent origin. In theory they can always be survivals which ought to have been corrected out and were not. The possibility of demonstrating this sort of thing formally too often depends on the survival of single early manuscripts as it is. One cannot usually know: one can only make a case.

The basic problems of the Gregorian have been endlessly discussed but remain as puzzling as ever. Essentially they are that for some 200 years after the saint's death we have no copy of the text or clear allusion to it. There are statements about his alterations to the Canon, and he is mentioned in connection with the chant, and prayers occur in eighth-century manuscripts which appear to be from his pen or to embody modifications for which he is responsible. But at the end of these two centuries Gelasians, though incorporating what is taken to be his work, are still being copied. Conceivably his book, though widespread, was considered unsuitable for monks, or was only used by the Pope himself, or perhaps it was not used for a long time, or the individual masses in it not even assembled to form a sacramentary.[12] It is very difficult to believe that, once it had been published as a work of St Gregory, copies would not speedily have found their way to England; or, as Dom H. Ashworth has emphasised, that Bede regularly and knowingly said mass from a book composed by St Gregory without alluding anywhere to the fact. All options for the present must, however, be left open. The only contribution I can offer to Gregorian prehistory is that some of the textual peculiarities of the Sundays after Whitsun in the notorious Padua copy can be found in the thirteenth-century missal of Uzès in the Cévennes.[13]

*   *   *

I turn now to more concrete matters relating to the circulation of texts specifically associable with tenth-century England, and begin with the Sacramentary of Ratoldus.[14] This manuscript was, of course, copied in France, for a Frenchman. A note in the calendar says that it was copied for Ratoldus, who was Abbot of Corbie (near Amiens) and died in 986. The book is not according to the use of Corbie. Indeed the text of the Canon it originally contained has had to be removed and replaced by the text approved at Corbie to make it usable there. The statement in the calendar is nevertheless compatible with the facts, provided Ratoldus's book was not primarily meant to be used at the altar. There is, however, no special reason to think it was. It is a typical standard text, very complete, legible, accurate, with numbered sections and a table of contents, such as anyone wishing to 'improve' the services in his church might find valuable. But those who have supposed, reasonably enough, that a tenth-century sacramentary can only be according to the use of a specific church, and that it must have been copied at and for the church whose use it gives, seeing that it was clearly not of the use of Corbie, have said it was copied at and for the monastery of Saint-Vaast at Arras.

Alas! It is not according to the use of Saint-Vaast at Arras, even though its calendar is a calendar of Saint-Vaast, and it has proper masses for St Vedast on both 6 February and 1 October. The Saint-Vaast calendar must have been a physical insertion in the model, in the same way that the Corbie Canon is a physical insertion in the copy we possess. The masses for St Vedast must have been on a fly-leaf or the margin. For we know, from one earlier and several later manuscripts, which masses for St Vedast were said on which days.[15] The mass here assigned to 1 October belongs to 6 February: that actually assigned to 6 February belongs to 13 February: and in any case no mass for the Translation on 1 October is included in the Table of Contents. The muddle must be the result of Ratoldus's scribe attempting to make sense of some Saint-Vaast modification. Conceivably the mass for the Octave had been added on the margin against the mass for 6 February and he took it to be intended as a replacement: and then decided the displaced mass must belong to the second feast noticed in the calendar. In any case he cannot himself have been a monk of Saint-Vaast: and the book he was copying was not initially intended for Saint-Vaast. As for the copy he made, it is not entirely according to the use of anywhere.

There is, however, one more mass which is not listed in the table of contents, and which points, more instructively, to a third church. This is a mass for St Samson of Dol and St Pair of Avranches jointly, copied as if it were a second mass for St Samson's day.[16] Together, these two saints can only mean the church of Saint-Symphorien at Orleans, which was given in the 930s to the refugee clergy of the Breton and Norman cathedrals concerned, who had joined forces in their flight before the Normans.[17] St Symphorian duly has a (very peculiar and I think unique) mass in which he is described as especial patron.[18]

But the original 'edition' lies further back than the arrival of the refugees at Orleans. There is no mass for St Pair alone or for any Orleans saint: while the episcopal blessings are, exceptionally, included in the orders for the services at which they were to be said.[19] The compilation must initially have been prepared for the Bishop of Dol while he was still at Dol. The table of contents gives no further assistance: the book contains (with the exceptions noted) the items the table lists. Of these items the mass for St Symphorian, at least, must have been modified after arrival at Orleans; but so must the mass for St Samson.[20] To get further one has, however, to follow a different tack. The book contains masses for St Denis and companions, with propers for Vigil and Octave, and a mass for St Cucufas of Barcelona whose relics, since the mid-ninth century, had been at Saint-Denis.[21] There are three other tenth- to eleventh-century books which make the same provision. Two are Breton.[22] The third is the sacramentary once at Fleury and written in an English hand, referred to earlier as the Winchcombe Sacramentary and as having a separate sanctoral.[23] It *see pp.61-2* has a mass for St Kenelm and his name is in capitals in the Litany. But otherwise, apart from the hand and the separate sanctoral, there is nothing obviously English about it; on the face of things it should give the text of a sacramentary of Saint-Denis. All four books need collating (a forbidding task as they are all lengthy), since their relationship is probably complex. Their sanctoralia are not identical: in particular the Winchcombe book has no mass for St Samson, Ratoldus has the 'new' mass for St Samson, and the two Breton books have, one his 'old' mass, the other the 'old' one on the day, and the 'new' one on the vigil.

The 'old' mass is a selection from the prayers prepared for the saint before the date, whenever that may have been, that Dol abandoned the Gallican rite. It is a fantastic illustration of that *multiplex sermo* of the Celts which so infuriated William of Malmesbury. The normal English version of the secret was reached simply by striking out twenty-four words: the sense is not thereby altered. The text of the first collect is corrupt in all known copies: in two books it survives, still not making sense, as sole collect, a purpose for which it is quite unsuitable. But the 'old' mass continued to enjoy favour in Brittany where the clergy, who cannot have understood it since they failed to correct it so that it would make sense, must have thought it sounded well.[24] The 'new' mass, therefore, which (though still preposterously verbose) does make sense and fits into the Roman framework, must have been composed during the exile when the Dol clergy found that the old mass was regarded outside Brittany as a joke. Its distribution would agree with composition at Orleans, and it no doubt took the place of the 'old' mass as part of the Orleans contribution to the final shape of Ratoldus's text.[25] It would seem in any case that the vehicle for the intro- duction of the Roman rite into the Breton monasteries was a sacra- mentary or number of sacramentaries prepared at Saint-Denis. The same type of text clearly reached England, presumably in the baggage of Breton refugees. The mass for St Samson may well have been dropped from the Winchcombe text when the sanctoral was extracted in England; but actually Ratoldus's book has closer connections with England than any of the other three. In the first place it contains a mass for St Cuthbert,[26] duly noted in the table of contents. In the second place, the original Saint-Denis sacramentary has been combined in it with an English pontifical. Not only does it contain the English coronation service, imperfectly adapted for a king of the Franks: it also contains the episcopal blessing in which St Andrew is called especial patron.[27] This is otherwise peculiar to English books and was presumably written at and for Wells; and, if so, has a limiting date, since Wells did not become a see till 908.[28]

The mass for St Cuthbert is excessively rare and excessively odd. St Cuthbert is persistently called a martyr in it, and the collect is actually adapted from a prayer for martyrs in the Bangor Antiphoner.[29] One would assign the whole mass to Brittany, were it not that at least the preface of the same mass is included in that added in a blank space in the Anglo-Saxon pontifical now at Sidney Sussex College, Cambridge.[30] A possible explanation is that the Cambridge pontifical is West-country, and that the Celtic element in the mass means that it originated at Glastonbury.

* * *

Before pursuing this line it will be as well to try to dispose of the problems set by the Coronation order.[31] This is, by some two centuries or so, the oldest surviving copy of the French version of the English Coronation service: French because it has the French coronation oath which never appears in a purely English book: English because in this form the man, though called in one place King of the Franks, is called in another King of the whole of Albion. In later, standard, French copies he no longer appears under this style but is elsewhere in the same prayer called King of the Saxons, Mercians and Northumbrians. The English titles cannot have been deliberately introduced for a French king, they must survive from an English text which had been carelessly adapted for one: and, what is more, the French copies must descend from two distinct English manuscripts adapted by two different, though equally careless, men. The revision, incidentally, was never properly done: Charles X in the nineteenth century was still crowned ruler of the three Heptarchic peoples. From the English point of view Ratoldus's text is an adaptation of the Second Coronation Order, a combination of the First Coronation Order (found in the Leofric Missal) with the order found in pontificals of Sens (and variously called the Sens, Delalande's and Erdmann's *ordo*) which seems to be genuinely French. There is, however, a paragraph included in the text of the French prayer *Omnipotens sempiterne deus creator et gubernator caeli et terrae* which is not present in the earliest known versions used at the Coronation of Louis the Stammerer in 877, though it appears in the Sens text and in German copies. It is in this, in forms varying with the individual French or English copies, that references to the realm of England occur; and owing to the uncritical approach of Ratoldus's scribe traces of successive corrections can be detected. The most important is the one where Ratoldus's and all other French copies (except those of the pure Sens *ordo*) have the words *utrorumque horum populorum* while all English and German copies omit *utrorumque*. In Ratoldus's text 'both peoples' is left referring nonsensically back to *solium viz Francorum,* i.e. one people; and in the later French copies, equally nonsensically, to the throne of the three peoples named above. The English copies usually, and the German copies always, name no peoples at all; but in three English manuscripts the text reads *solium Anglorum vel Saxonum.* It is clear that *utrorumque* must have come from England and be original; and the successive modifications made in England must have been (1) the naming of two peoples (2) the naming of three peoples (3) the cancellation of *utrorumque* (4) the substitution of two names again for three (5) the cancellation of all names. The French copies are at stage (2) except that Ratoldus's scribe has got further than the others in adapting the text for France and has put the Franks in place of the three peoples. He, on the other hand, has managed to preserve earlier in the prayer the expressions *regnum N. Albionis totius viz. Francorum* (i.e. he has copied two successive interlinings) and *totius Albionis ecclesiam* where other French and most English copies do not specify whose realm or church; and the three English ones that do, have the Angles and Saxons. The French texts in general, and therefore Ratoldus's text in particular, must be using copies of the English service, as it was adapted for some English coronation where, in order to emphasise the king's dominion over the whole of his territory, the number of peoples named had been raised from two to three, and the unity of the realm emphasised by the expression *Albion totum.* As the English copies, none of which is earlier than the later tenth century, reflect a further change, it is not in theory possible to be sure whether the two peoples originally named were the Angles and Saxons rather than the Saxons and Northumbrians, both pairs being used in the English royal style in charters. But for the Mercians to be named as one of three separate peoples in the precise way found in the other French manuscripts is not, I think, paralleled in the charters at all; and the coronation in England which immediately preceded the export of this order for use at the coronation of some French king must have been one where flattering the Mercians seemed exceptionally desirable. The Second English Order was certainly used at the coronation of King Edgar in 973 and is commonly, though on slight grounds, held to have been composed for the occasion. But the putting together of Ratoldus's text was certainly not done in the 970s, it was done in the 920s; and the coronations for which it was successively modified are manifestly those of Athelstan in 925 and Louis d'Outremer in 936. The important period for contacts between England and Brittany is just this period. Alain Barbetorte (as well as Louis d'Outremer) was a refugee at Athelstan's court, and we have the text of a letter from the provost of the Dol clergy in Orleans to Athelstan which tells us that his father King Edward the Elder had his name on the confraternity books of Dol. Edward and Athelstan are the only tenth-century English kings who are known to have had links of this kind with Brittany: and Athelstan had quite as much need as Edgar to please the Mercians at his coronation. Moreover, there is no king of France between Louis and Hugh Capet who is in the least likely to have imported a new coronation service, and by 987 Ratoldus was dead.

That this analysis of Ratoldus's Sacramentary is broadly correct I am confident: and it means that its text was transmitted in successive recopyings from Saint-Denis to Dol and from Dol to Wells (with a journey to Orleans before or in the course of its stay in Wells) and then to Arras and thence to Corbie, gathering fresh material and sundry modifications at every move. The details are arguable, but the general picture is not. The only reason all this is traceable is that the items collected en route are so rare and extraordinary: but there is no reason to suppose that plenty of more commonplace looking texts do not have similar pedigrees. If a text circulates between churches dedicated to our Lady, St Peter and St Michael, does not belong to a bishop interested in coronations, or passes through the hands of a careful reviser who cancels irrelevant items before letting a copy be taken, unmistakeable indications will be lacking. But that is all.

* * *

Reverting, then, to Glastonbury, it is time to take a preliminary look at the Leofric Missal, and first at 'Leofric B', the Glastonbury calendar of about 980 prefixed to the main book. This introduces us to Glastonbury before the legends. St Benignus and St Indract do not appear in it: St David is an eleventh-century addition. St Patrick of Ireland on 17 March and St Brigid on 1 February appear, but without grading. The Patrick who does appear, as *Patricius senior* with a graded feast (of the second rank) is the man who, I feel sure, was the actual founder of Glastonbury, assigned to 24 August.[32] The other native feasts include Sts Aidan and Ceolfrid *in Glastonia,* in the second rank: St Cuthbert and St Guthlac and St Augustine of Canterbury are the only ones graded in the first rank.

In 'Leofric A', the original core of the volume written around 900 in a continental hand, there are no proper masses for English saints: but the Litany which is in the same original continental hand includes successive invocations of St Patrick (pretty clearly of Glastonbury) St Cuthbert and St Guthlac.[33] This choice of invocations should be earlier than the acquisition by Glastonbury of the supposed relics of the Northumbrian saints Aidan and Ceolfrid. Rival traditions about when their relics arrived were current in the twelfth century, but this litany, in conjunction with the calendar, suggests that the correct date for the translation is in the tenth century not the ninth.[34] The popularity of St Cuthbert in Wessex is sufficiently attested. He has a little group of dedications in the West Country, the most important being that (of unknown date) of the principal parish church of Wells. The credit for King Alfred's victory at *Ethandune* was attributed to his intervention (though there were rival claims on behalf of St Neot). And, most important, the proper office or history for St Cuthbert, *Cuthbertus puer bonae indolis* appears to originate in Wessex. The main early manuscript of this is the copy of Bede's Two Lives of St Cuthbert given to St Cuthbert's clergy by King Athelstan during the *Brunanburh* campaign of 934: later Durham copies seem to derive from this particular book. The Durham text is distinguishable from the Wessex one and it is the Wessex one which is represented in both the other Anglo-Saxon manuscripts which contain it. In one, and probably once in both, it is associated with the usual history of St Benedict, *Fuit vir vitae venerabilis*, and also with that of St Guthlac, *Celebri fama*, of which only the one copy is known.[35]

The history *Cuthbertus puer* is mainly in verse, a thing most advanced for a text of this character written as early as the mid-930s: and I am inclined to suppose that its author must have been a Belgian. Its obvious prototypes are the offices composed by Stephen, Bishop of Tongres/Liège,[36] and it seems not impossible that the Office Book prepared by Bishop Stephen and represented, in an eleventh-century redaction, by the Leofric Collectar,[37] was introduced to England at this stage. Stephen's collectar and *Cuthbertus puer* are both designed for the secular as opposed to the Benedictine office: and although this consideration is far from decisive in terms of usage in monasteries around 900 (it is actually quite probable that Glastonbury adhered to the secular cursus until St Dunstan's time) these things seem to combine with the blessing for St Andrew's day to suggest a 'Wells' (rather than a 'Glastonbury') phase in the history of English liturgical development, preceding the 'Winchester' phase which was the occasion of this paper.

The only Anglo-Saxon book which seems to have an indisputable direct connection with Wells is the mid eleventh-century sacramentary Vitellius A.xviii in the Cotton collection,[38] the connection being established by the appearance in its calendar (only) of the feast of St Congar of Congresbury who had no cultus outside Somerset.[39] Later

Wells tradition pretended that this man was actually an early bishop of the see, and it seems likely enough that there was a Celtic monastery at Congresbury between whose endowments and those of Wells there was some continuity. But Somerset from the time of its conquest to 908 was part of the diocese of Sherborne: and it is therefore with considerable interest that one notices the close connection Wickham Legg was able to shew existed between Vitellius A.xviii and the only surviving missal (which happens to be fifteenth-century) of the abbey of Sherborne. This could mean that the two books are witnesses to the missal of the undivided diocese: the type of text must have been fairly widespread, for there exists a 'rogue' Sarum missal[40] of c.1300 in which the rubric and collects are as specified in the Sarum Ordinal but the secrets and postcommunions not specified in the Ordinal, are not Sarum but those of the Wells-Sherborne books. Such a missal could in theory descend, revision after revision, from whatever book was favoured by St Aldhelm. But in fact, as will be seen, the explanation of this text is probably rather different.

* * *

Coming now to the period of monastic reform, I fear I must simply admit that my views on the late old English clergy tend to agree with those of Abbot Paul of St Albans and Lanfranc. They were no doubt doing their best, but their best was so often absurd. It will be recalled how the Abingdon chronicler in the twelfth century, writing for private circulation only, explains with gratitude how St Aethelwold, by moderating the rigours of St Benedict's stern Rule, made it possible for gentlemen to live in monasteries. The fur bed-covers were all very well, but it seems to me that more of the effects of the three gallons of beer a day are to be detected in manuscripts of the 'reform' period.[41] Even the austere Abbot Aelfric felt obliged, when inserting a version of the Miracle of Cana into his Life of St Aethelwold, to have everyone concerned intoxicated by the inexhaustible profusion of Abingdon mead.[42] Wulfstan the Cantor's account of the bibulous celebration of the completion of Winchester Cathedral is well known.[43] And among the few apparently indisputable contributions of England to the Latin liturgy is the formula, to be read over the cask by the priest, to improve the quality of beer in which mice or weasels have got drowned.[44] It was not that the English were alone in wishing, for gastronomic or economical reasons, to drink such beer; the penitential embedded in the Romano-German pontifical expects the priest specifically to ask at confession whether his German penitent has drunk beer flavoured in this way. Admission of the offence involved forty days penance. But in England the view was different; and, by calling in the priest first, it was possible to indulge in this recondite vice with impunity.[45]

In any case, whether for this reason or another, the critical faculties even in the higher ranks of the Old English clergy seem to have been numb. In the *Concordia* one finds that the assembled abbots of England, attempting to line up the lessons and tracts on Whitsun Eve, have managed to put a chant from Isaiah into the mouth of Moses.[46] Then, by what must be an accident of manuscript transmission, some Frankish canons got copied between the preface and the text of the Penitential of St Egbert of York. A conviction that the canons were an important document of early English church discipline and that the preface belonged to them, not the Penitential, followed. It took such a hold that the canons were copied with the preface, and the title naming St Egbert as author, into three of the surviving Anglo-Saxon pontificals: though, at the level at which this must have happened, the order to pray, not for the King of Northumbria, but the Emperor should have roused some suspicion.[47] And this slipshod state of mind runs right through and it goes with, and stands in some close relation to, a low level of competence at Latin and the grimmest superstition. In the Red Book of Darley[48] the text that is in capitals is not the Canon of the Mass but the Ordeal by Hot Iron; most of the rubric has been prudently put into English, and the arrangement is so disorderly that one has to know the book well to find the place. The most valuable record surviving of office chants from the period is not a liturgical book at all, but a series of entries on the margins of an English translation of Bede's *Ecclesiastical History*. [49] The form for blessing milk and honey added by some member of St Cuthbert's Clergy to the Durham Ritual is clearly nonsensical: what has happened is that the man has interpolated into the middle of it the greater part of the form for blessing an altar-cross.[50] It is not really obvious why Archbishop Wulfstan, supposedly a learned Canonist with previous experience as a bishop, and with the resources of the churches of both Worcester and York at his disposal, should have been impelled to ask Abbot Aelfric to provide the not very recondite matter included in his Pastoral Letters. It is definitely shocking that, when they arrived in Latin, he should have had to send them back to get them translated.[51]

Faced with this, it can hardly be an accident that the life of St Edmund was written by Abbo of Fleury, the Miracles of St Swithun by Lantfred, and most of the rest of the Lives of Old English saints by Goscelin of St Bertin. Abbo's passage through Ramsey does seem to have produced one pupil capable of writing the Life of St Oswald, and I suppose Byrhtferth; but it seems to have been without much further echo; and I have the strong impression that, for a long time, the only place there was a chance of anyone seriously learning Latin was Winchester, at a guess because Lantfred was qualified to teach it. The propers for Old English saints (which, as has been truly said, have a very strong family resemblance) seem more likely to come from Winchester than anywhere else,[52] certainly all surviving Worcester service books stem from there. Thus the Portiforium of St Wulfstan[53] gives two prayers for St Hedda, three for St Grimbald, three for St Byrnstan and three for St Judoc, though none of these holy men can have been of much interest at Worcester; while St Swithun gets six collects for one feast and four for the other. The English saints for whom blessings are provided in Bishop Samson's pontifical[54] include Swithun (both feasts), Aethelwold (both feasts) and Birinus: there is nothing for Kenelm or even Oswald. The only fragment of an Anglo-Saxon missal still at Worcester[55] gives full details for the route of a funeral procession, assuming that the deceased is a monk of Winchester Cathedral. One Benedictional,[56] apparently from Exeter, in which the texts have been largely recomposed, shews remarkable self-confidence in Latin; but it is clearly a Winchester text. Canterbury shews some independence but not, I think, before the eleventh century, when the light from Winchester was beginning to spread. The most ambitious product of this period in Latin, and not on the face of things from Winchester, in the versified history *Sacrosanctum* for St Alban[57] which the *Gesta Abbatum Sancti Albani* say was composed, words and music, by the local Abbot Aelfric II.[58] But the opinion of most commentators is that there never was a second Abbot Aelfric of St Albans, and the question is how the intricate confusions at this point in the *Gesta Abbatum* can ever have arisen. There must have been some dated document which compelled the local historian to put an Abbot Aelfric into the eleventh century, and I am tempted to suggest that the author of *Sacrosanctum* was the Homilist. I do not know where the Homilist was abbot: the tone of his letter to the monks of Eynsham seems to exclude the possibility that he was their head; but as he never says where he was abbot in his covering letters, and as, if he had written *Sacrosanctum,* he would certainly, on form, have sent a letter with it, and as any St Albans monk would have supposed an unnamed house of which the author of *Sacrosanctum* was abbot was his own, if that letter was in any way dated the confusions would certainly have followed.

This picture makes no claim to be balanced; to achieve that would involve considering the charters and Aethelweard's chronicle and considering also what level of competence at what sort of Latin one would be prepared to call competence. But everything conspires to suggest that the knowledge of Latin among the clergy was almost universally low, and that, except in so far as an insignificant minority of scholars was prepared, as well as able, to provide translations, the Church was cut off from the general cultural heritage of the West. That the Worcester service books should come from Winchester is, of course, unexpected. The survival of so much of the early Worcester library has created a presupposition that it was intellectually active. But probably the high proportion among its early books of things written in English is to be taken rather as evidence that this was not really so. Moreover the impression made on me by the various miscellanies from Worcester is that they are neither the compilations of independent scholars nor intelligently prepared manuals of instruction. They look more like fair copies of notes taken by pupils following a course, during which useful items were dictated or circulated for copying, and my instinct is to suggest that that course was held at Winchester.[59] The principal force upholding competence at Latin seems to have been relentless pressure from kings. King Alfred had called everybody's bluff: and King Edgar, by telling St Aethelwold to produce him a translation of the Rule of St Benedict, no doubt had a most stimulating effect on higher education. There is, however, one major monument of scholarship from the period, the collection of Alcuin's letters in BM Cott. Tib. A.xv. To assemble this will have involved serious research in continental and English libraries. There are excerpts from it in the Worcester books, but the important question from the point of view of scholarship is where the main manuscript was kept. The inclusion of St Dunstan's correspondence along with Alcuin's suggests Canterbury.[60]

The only early service books which show indisputable signs of the influence of the *Concordia* are the missal fragments in Oslo with the Good Friday devotions, and the Missal of Robert of Jumièges with the *Concordia* muddle on Whitsun Eve.[61] So far as later books go, we managed, as Mrs Gjerløw has pointed out, to pass on, to our shame, the Whitsun Eve muddle to our daughter church of Norway, where it was accepted into the thirteenth-century ordinal of Nidaros and duly appears in print in the sixteenth century missal of the Province.[62] The Missal of Robert of Jumièges has an unusual super populum in the mass for the Saturday after Ash Wednesday,[63] and I can find it at this place again only on the margins of the Corpus Christi College English Bede. The day has no mass in the Hadrianic Gregorian, though it has one in all Gelasians and 'practical' books. If this means that

Robert's mass was put together in England, it should follow that the whole editorial process of expanding a Hadrianic or some analagous Gregorian to the form found in Robert's book was done in England. The immediate model of the existing manuscript should have come from Peterborough,[64] while the Bede is one of Leofric's books from Exeter. One of the many difficulties about the surviving Anglo-Saxon missals is that they differ substantially from one another, and there is no rapid way of telling whether any one of them represents a widely circulated text or is, on the contrary, a unicum due to the scribe happening to have a foreign book to copy or collate. But the link between Robert and the Bede suggests that this text was widespread, and this in conjunction with the *Concordia* muddle makes it probable that Robert (and still more the Bede which, when it differs, seems more 'primitive'[65]) should be taken as a type of text generally current in English monasteries, and this view extended to cover the office texts also in the Bede. Of other missals, that now represented by fragments divided between the Bodleian and Westminster Abbey Library[66] has a mass for St Samson who has none in any other pre-Conquest book. It is the same revision of his 'old' mass (except that it includes a Preface) which later appears in the Sarum Missal, and is presumably the mass used at Athelstan's foundation of Milton Abbey in Sherborne diocese. The Missal from Winchester New Minster[67] depends on some sacramentary of the Saint-Amand type, a class of text not demonstrably reflected in other pre-Conquest books; the fragments at Uppsala may come from a related text, but it was not identical.[68] No surviving book has a sanctoral corresponding to that implied for Glastonbury by the calendars of the Leofric Missal and the Bosworth Psalter.[69] A further element of confusion is introduced by the Drummond, Corpus and Rosslyn Missals,[70] shortened missals from Ireland or the Hebrides, of which the two latter, so far as prayers go, are certainly shortened from something very like the Sarum Missal. The Drummond Missal had an analogous source since its gigantic common (it has no propers) used, for example, the prayers found in the Sarum Missal as collects for St Alban and St Leger, secrets for St Etheldreda and St Batildis and postcommunions for St Dunstan, St Leo, St Augustine of Hippo, St Lucy, St Praxedis, and St Germanus of Auxerre. Some of these reappear with different affectations in other members of the 'Sarum group'; but apart from the prayers for St Etheldreda and St Germanus which are Leonine[71] (St Etheldreda's also Ambrosian), I know no continental sources for them, though I am confident all are ultimately Italian. Drummond and Corpus at least seem now agreed to be eleventh-century. So unless it can be established that the sacramentary found later used at Salisbury is that of, say, Pavia (an exempt diocese) or Aosta (in the province of Tarentaise), introduced into England and Ireland by Lanfranc or Anselm (and in that case passed to Ireland very speedily), it must in some form be a pre-Conquest book.[72] There is a yawning gap it could quite easily fill since, with the dubious exception of the Missal of Giso of Wells, all pre-Conquest missals appear to be in some sense monastic; and there is nothing to indicate what sort of book would normally have been in the hands of a body of secular clergy. Allowing for the inevitable collations and revisions, the book used at Salisbury could be substantially eighth-century, and its success could be due to the fact (if it is a fact) that it was broadly the book to which Old English seculars were accustomed. I am the more persuaded this may be so because the rubric for Candlemas in the Corpus Missal differs in phraseology from all English and accessible continental rubrics for the day, except that in the ordinal of Besançon.[73] Why this church should have been influential in the British Isles is not easy to guess: but it was. The (unpublished) *ordines* in the Missal of Giso of Wells briefly discussed earlier, also come from the ordinal of Besançon.[74] This ordinal is thought to have been prepared under the early eleventh-century Archbishop Hugues de Salins, but Fr Aubrey Gwynn has produced quite different reasons for thinking the text represented by the Corpus Missal reached Ireland in the second quarter of the eleventh century and the Besançon constituent makes it fairly certain, in conjunction with the evidence of Giso's book, that it was fetched from England. The Sarum-type sacramentary should, therefore, already have been available here to accompany the Besançon rubric.

*   *   *

In the light of this it becomes desirable to take another look at the text of Giso's missal. It is not a Sarum type of book. It is, on the other hand, the only pre-Conquest missal with a mass for St Patrick. This, however, is not the mass used in Ireland (and found in the Corpus Missal), I know it otherwise only from Fécamp;[75] and I take it to be the mass for the founder of Glastonbury moved to 17 March after the two Patricks, in the early eleventh century, had been identified with one another.[76] It duly contains masses for St Aidan and St Guthlac and both feasts of St Cuthbert, and Glastonbury influence seems sure. It has, however, a very rich sanctoral with many foreign saints: and these have been attributed to the personal requirements of Bishop Giso who, by his own account came from Saint-Trond, which is in the archdeaconry of Hesbaye, the diocese of Liège and the province of Cologne.[77] The sanctoral is conformable to what one might then expect, except that it includes all the feasts of Winchester New Minster as well, and omits Trond himself. The calendar, besides including many feasts which do not have prayers in the sanctoral, omits Guthlac (AD), Leo IX, the Invention of St Denis (WN), Florian, Basil the Great, German of Auxerre (AD, WN), Aethelwold (WN), Arnulf (16 Aug. AD), Timothy and Apollinaris (AD), Antoninus (AD), Trs. Birini (WN), Trs. Ethelwoldi (WN), Januarius (19 Sep), Cyprian and Justina (AD), Willibrord and Chrysanthus and Daria, who do have prayers in the sanctoral. AD means the feast is an early addition to the calendar, which is practically equivalent to inclusion: WN means the feast is in the Sanctoral of the New Minster Missal with the same prayers. The rejection from the calendar of both feasts of St Aethelwold and the second feasts of St Denis and St Birinus prompts the question why these Winchester celebrations were included in the sanctoral at all. It looks as if they were simply in the model, with the implication that that model was a New Minster book and that, between its copying and the copying of the quite different later Missal from the New Minster, that establishment had changed or completely revised the sacramentary it used. The New Minster feasts are essentially unlike the other feasts omitted from the calendar, which are foreign and can be regarded as private devotions of the Bishop which did not find their way into the formal calendar of his see. St Florian (the martyr of Linz with the correct prayers as found in the books of Salzburg), St Januarius (the Bishop of Naples, on his Italian, and Cologne, day, but with prayers I have not elsewhere met for him) and Pope Leo IX (from Toul, d.1049, who receives unusual attention in English books but whose cultus never established itself) are clearly in this category; and St Willibrord (since he has prayers not, I think, otherwise found for him) appears to be so. If, then, it is right that this is basically a New Minster book, then this type of text, whether at Wells or Sherborne, should be a relatively recent intrusion into western Wessex. It is thus permissible to hold that something like the later Sarum missal was already earlier in general use in the region, could equally unite with provisions from the Besançon ordinal there, and could be exported to Ireland in the earlier eleventh century.

Now every one of these books, with the possible exception of the Drummond Missal, derives in some sense from a standard Frankish edition of the Gregorian. Somewhere along the line, possibly several times, an editor has had two books before him, one of them a standard Frankish edition of the Gregorian and one not, and he has modified one of them to accord more or less with the other. I am hesitant about using the word Frankish because the ninth-century Frankish liturgists were trying fairly hard to bring their books into accord with those of Rome. It is normally, therefore, impossible to assert with much justification that a particular feature or reading was introduced by a Frank and not by some Italian of whose book an indeterminable number of barbarians of varied origin can have procured independent copies. But the English books reflect the influence of the 'Supplement' (Grimold's, Benedict of Aniane's or Alcuin's according to one's theories), and it is certainly neither Italian nor English. But whereas this kind of collation or fusion of a 'Frankish' Gregorian with something else is absolutely normal throughout Europe, provided the something else is (or cannot be proved not to be) an eighth-century or Frankish Gelasian of a well-documented type and no more, in the case of the Sarum Missal and the Leofric Missal this is not so. The Sarum Missal is not in this context any further my concern, but the Leofric Missal is.

* * *

see p.69   The original core of this book, Leofric A, which Mr Ker dates ninth to tenth century,[78] is, as I have already said, written in a foreign hand, and has more than once been irresponsibly claimed as a purely Lotharingian text. Anyone wishing to establish that should produce another Lotharingian book with a separate sanctoral, St Mark on 18 May,[79] the English coronation oath and an invocation of St Guthlac in the Litany. When he does, I shall say it is derived from an English book. The Leofric Missal is patently English. There were plenty of foreign clerics in England in the reigns of Alfred and his immediate successors who could have copied it; but one is faced with the question of the extent to which its contents and text have been subjected to Frankish (as opposed to Italian) influences or indeed based on purely Frankish models. It is an extremely complicated book, analogous to Ratoldus's. It too, since the blessings are included in the formularies for mass, must at some stage in the transmission of its text have been adjusted for a bishop: and one is again faced with the task of trying to unravel its complexities. A 'Lotharingian' constituent is demonstrated by the presence high up in the Litany, among the Fathers, of invocations of three archbishops of Trèves; and an Artesian constituent is proved by St Vedast's name being in capitals in the Litany and by the invocations of the singularly obscure saints Ragnulf (of Arras) and Eusebia (of Hamage). But there are no proper masses for any of these; the non-Roman saints who have propers are St Denis (of Paris), St

Maurice (probably as of Tours) and St Benedict (both feasts). Of these, St Denis was not of much interest to whoever inserted his mass, only his collect is the standard one, the secret and postcommunion are from the common, and a hunt through the missals of some two hundred churches has so far failed to reveal another that used them for him. They may yet turn up, but I have abandoned hope. I suspect he was merely given an *ad hoc* set of prayers because there were chants for him in the gradual used. The cues for the gradual are on the margins against the various mass-prayers in the original hand; and comparison with Dom Hesbert's six graduals suggests that this one was French (i.e. not Lotharingian). There is a rare extra prayer for St Michael (not apparently used on the Mont-Saint-Michel); [80] and there is an exceedingly rare choice of prayers for the third Thursday in Lent which I can parallel only from Tours.[81] But I consider all these features save the last to belong to the latest stratum, and links with Tours are particularly ambiguous because of Alcuin's presence there and Tours being the metropolitan see of Brittany. What appears to me significant is the relatively large number of rare and early forms. Thus the *propria* have been fairly efficiently normalised: and now that Dom Deshusses has given us the variants of the ninth-century Gregorian from St Vedast at Arras, it appears, most obviously in the secret for St Stephen, that a book closely related to it must (as one might have supposed) have been among those used in normalising. But the reviser must have got weary towards the end of his task; for he has left St Thomas, the last mass in the sanctoral, with a proper preface adapted from one used for St Peter in the (seventh-century) Leonine Sacramentary[82] and not, I think, otherwise preserved in any book at all. Another curious feature with possibly similar implications is the text of the collect for the Monday following the Third Sunday in Lent. This is as in the Tridentine Missal, with *gratiam tuam* and *carnalibus*; and, thanks to Dom Deshusses, we now know that Leofric must be the earliest witness to *carnalibus* surviving. Provisionally I take it to be an Italian variant of some antiquity.[83] The most remarkable survivals are, however, in the pontifical. Here the prayers of the mass during which the bishop is consecrated are also found for this occasion in the early eighth-century *Missale Francorum*[84] but in no other book. The prayers of the mass at the ordination of a priest include two otherwise unknown and two known only from the Leonine Sacramentary. The prayers used at the ordering of a deacon include one used for the same purpose in the Leonine Sacramentary but otherwise not to be found.[85] It is hardly disputable, in the face of all this, and even if scattered parallels are eventually found in France, that the basis of, at least, the Pontifical, however much revision it may have undergone, is a sixth- or seventh-century book of a kind which cannot have come into use at any time or place where Gelasians, let alone Gregorians, of the familiar kind were actually normative. That book was pretty certainly the pontifical of Canterbury (if this somewhat anachronistic expression may be allowed) since there is an alternative main consecratory prayer for the bishop which is not, I think, found in genuinely French books and whose origin is unknown:[86] but which is retained in the pontificals usually called Robert, Dunstan and Lanalet, and also (of course) in Ratoldus, and survives the Norman Conquest.

It would be inappropriate to continue with the discussion of minutiae of this kind, though it is perhaps worth pointing out that the coronation service has to be reconsidered in the light of the rest of the evidence. It is not merely that too many scholars who have discussed this have dated the manuscript too late and supposed it to be straightforwardly Frankish; it is that so many of the other texts which distinguish the book as a whole from its Frankish contemporaries prove not to be of recent origin but to go back to a source represented otherwise only by one seventh-century Italian manuscript. The presumption is not merely that the *ordo* is English, this was accepted by Bouman: it is, as for the other English features, that by 900 it was old. The evidence for coronations in England begins early, and it is evident from the continental circulation of Ratoldus's *ordo* and from the Milanese *ordo* (which combines the general form of the English service with the variants in the text of individual prayers characteristic of German books) that the English coronation, for whatever reason, was admired and imitated.

*　　*　　*

There are three points which I should like to emphasise in conclusion. The first is that the fact that a liturgical book is 'late' does not mean that it can be disregarded for early liturgical history, and particularly not if it comes from an important centre from which the evidence of earlier books is inadequate. Even Dom Deshusses seems to have fallen into this trap, since he and Dr Gamber, in their controversy over the Trento Gregorian, agree that its Thursday masses for Lent can be found in no other manuscript and gravely discuss their possible authorship on this assumption.[87] In fact, however, these masses were widespread, though normalisers were liable to retain only the mass for the Third Thursday (for which the Hadrianic text was unsatisfactory), and my notes are anyhow really extensive only for that day. In the present connection the distinctive feature on the Third Thursday is the super populum, the other three prayers being much commoner. My list of churches, then, where at some date or other precisely the same prayers were used on the Third Thursday as in the Trento book is: Burgo de Osma and Leon; Saint-Malo and Angers; Vienne; Arles; Bazas (as an alternative); Toulouse; Reims; Cambrai and Saint-Denis; not to mention the 'Winchcomb Sacramentary' which has the same mass as an alternative. The only German book I know which used this mass with the super populum *Purifica* is from Augsburg diocese, but I do not doubt that the Trento book will prove to have full support from other south-east German missals. This distribution, historical considerations and such notes as I have on the distribution of books using the Trento masses on the other Thursdays, suggests that the main northern focus of all this is Reims;[88] it is in any case obviously not Salzburg.[89] It is not my fault there are no suitable Reims books earlier than the thirteenth century: nor does this mean that services were conducted at Reims for a thousand years by dumb-show. What it means is that it is a mistake to leave so manifestly influential a church as Reims out of account, and that, if the evidence one would like to have from Reims does not survive, one must not throw in one's hand but use, with due precaution, what evidence there is. It remains perfectly possible that Reims and Salzburg got these masses, independently, from somewhere in Italy; and the same is true of various sees in the south of France and Spain. But the matter cannot be settled inductively; someone has got to look at a great many Italian books, never mind about the date provided they are not standard Franciscan Roman, to find out.

The second point is that all these early books are complicated, indeed Dom Deshusses's admirable dictum that each successive copy of a liturgical manuscript was 'une petite édition critique' is liable, though I should hesitate slightly about the word *critique,* to be true down to the thirteenth century. This means that, if one is to understand them historically one has got to compare them with a fair number of related books; and not least of the problems, since the body of surviving medieval liturgical texts is so gigantic, is finding the books with which comparisons are most likely to be instructive and fruitful.

My last point, which I hope emerges in any case from what I have said, is that the tenth- and eleventh-century English books do not present a neat picture of continental usages being adopted, but rather stages in the adjustment, by fairly stupid men most of the time, of some pre-existing body of texts and usages of Italian origin current in England to what, by the tenth century, was fashionable in Northern Europe. The differences between the books used wherever the Roman rite was followed were certainly at no period formidable in terms of regions; they depend, if anything, more on the purpose of the book. Thus the two papal collections of prayers, the Leonine and the Hadrianic Gregorian, both imply the presence of clergy who know what to do, supplied with other books for practically everything except the text of prayers. Even for these there were plenty of days when services must have been held, for which specific provision is not made, but on which an assisting minister must have been able to produce some suitable set of prayers for a busy pope to read. At the other end of the scale the Drummond Missal may or may not be shortened and selected from the properly organised books of a large church. But it is the sort of book that must have been used by priests before all the usual round of variable chants and prayers were composed or written and accepted as standard. Pending detailed examination, it may well be that it originated as such a book; and has been modified in transmission by endless rewritings and additions, rather than because someone sat down in the ninth or some later century with the complete services of a large church before him and made a selection. Such shorter books made by selection do, however, exist: in addition to the Rosslyn and Corpus missals, the Red Book of Darley is a pre-Conquest English example. It is this difficulty about types of books that makes it impossible to evaluate on English evidence alone peculiar survivals such as the Leofric preface for St Thomas or of course, assuming they survived continuously in England, the more numerous features of the same kind in the Sarum books. We do not know whether we have to postulate a really early English edition of the services for the year in which these prayers were included from the start but which has been normalised, or whether they circulated in collections resembling the Drummond Missal and were rescued from these and inserted at suitable places in the course of some eighth-century reception of a standard Gregorian. The only thing that is fairly sure is that the greater English churches must have used books which, since they were Roman, could have been 'corrected' without appalling difficulty over the years till they were nearly indistinguishable from Carolingian ones. The possibility of getting much further light on this from English evidence seems (in view of the trifling amount of evidence provided by the few English liturgical fragments earlier than 900) to be negligible. One can only extract and list variants and, as I said, make a case. But this cannot yet be said of the Italian evidence. The English survivals must go back to the period before the abolition of the Gallican rite: that must be why they are found in England and not on the far side of the Channel. But there clearly ought to be similar survivals in books from Italy where the spread of Roman texts and usages must have begun long before it did in France; and in fact, in the only accessible body of 'non-standard' material from Italy, the Ambrosian books, there are. Only the Ambrosian books differ too fundamentally from the Roman to be directly helpful.

It will thus probably be possible, by pin-pointing distinctive features and referring to the French evidence, to determine with some precision the source of books used for revision in the tenth century. A little more editing of English material is still essential, the most important being the texts on the margins of the Bede. What is going to be much more difficult is to determine what difference this adjustment to continental fashion made, to determine just what was displaced, if indeed that was not already so similar that modification would be a more appropriate word than displacement. But it seems clear that anomalous things did come through to the tenth century from the first century and a half of English Christianity, when this country was an isolated outpost of the Roman rite; and the implication is that the 'standard' Frankish books are an inadequate basis for reconstructing the liturgical scene in Rome during that century and a half. Whether anything substantial can ever be made out of such scrappy materials will, however, depend entirely on whether a common pattern emerges when the central Italian books can be subjected to proper study.

Chapter 6

CHARTERS OF THE REFORM MOVEMENT:
THE WORCESTER ARCHIVE

by P. H. Sawyer

The value of Anglo-Saxon charters for the study of the reform movement has long been recognised. The five hundred and fifty diplomas, leases, wills and memoranda that survive for the period 940-1000 provide important evidence of the activity of benefactors, showing how the monasteries acquired, and sometimes lost, land and privileges, and the leases make it possible to see how some houses used their endowments and rewarded their friends.[1] The charters of the tenth century are, however, more intimately connected with the reform movement than has commonly been supposed, for they were themselves prepared by leading churchmen and were written in monastic scriptoria. It has long been recognised that in the eleventh century royal diplomas were drawn up by beneficiaries or interested ecclesiastics[2] and, as Dr Chaplais has pointed out, some eleventh-century charters reveal their local provenance in their script.[3] A good example is Stowe Charter 38, a grant of Cnut to Bishop Aelfstan dated 1018 and written in the same 'Canterbury' hand as the purported original of Wihtred's grant of privileges to the churches of Kent. The same scribe also wrote Cnut's writ about the liberties of Christ Church, Canterbury into an early eleventh-century gospel book belonging to that church. In the eighth and ninth centuries beneficiaries were similarly responsible for drawing up their charters.[4] It has, however, been generally accepted that there was an interval in the tenth century when this function was assumed by a royal chancery. The case for this, argued by Stevenson and elaborated by Drögereit[5] was based on the similarity of form of royal charters from 931 to 963 and the recognition that the original charters from that period were all written by a small number of scribes. Miss Harmer expressed some reservation about this and recently Dr Chaplais has demonstrated that there is 'not a shred of evidence to indicate that at any time between the seventh and the eleventh centuries Anglo-Saxon diplomas were drafted or written in what might be called, even loosely, a central royal secretariat, that is to say in a single organized department staffed with scribes who specialized in royal business.'[6] He has shown that the diplomas were produced 'not in a self-staffed royal secretariat, but at all times in monastic or episcopal scriptoria' and that 'among these charters the largest group, including the earliest, were written in the scriptorium of Winchester'. He remarks that it is not surprising that most charters in the Winchester group were 'issued during the episcopate of Aelfheah, the prime mover of the monastic renaissance, the teacher of St Dunstan and St Aethelwold' and he shows how the writing of royal charters 'which had been concentrated at Winchester in the 940s, came to be done also at Glastonbury under Dunstan in the 950s and at Abingdon under Aethelwold in the 960s.'[7] As the number of houses capable of drawing up royal charters grew, so too did the variety of their productions, but that variety was due to the progress of the reform, not to the collapse of the royal chancery. Despite the growing variety of forms and scripts, the surviving originals from the second half of the tenth century demonstrate in a very remarkable way the great and continuing influence of Winchester in this, as in other aspects of the reform.

*   *   *

The archive of Worcester is one of the most interesting of all those closely connected with the reform movement. It is not the largest, (there are more charters from both Winchester and Abingdon) and very few originals have survived, but it does contain perhaps the most famous and controversial charter of the whole movement, Edgar's general grant of privileges to Worcester in 964. In addition, the unusually early cartularies of Worcester [8] contain a remarkable series of leases, mostly from the time of Oswald. Fortunately some scholars took a keen interest in the charters of Worcester before they were dispersed and lost, and although their notes and copies show how great the loss has been, they do, at the same time, compensate for it. Dugdale visited the cathedral in 1643 and made a list of ninety-two original charters there and about twenty years earlier Patrick Young made some detailed notes from them.[9] At the end of the century the Dean, George Hickes, copied, and later printed, fifteen Worcester charters that have since disappeared[10] and a further twenty-four charters that were destroyed by fire at Lincoln's Inn in 1752 had fortunately been printed thirty years before.[11]

Edgar's great charter to Worcester of 964, sometimes referred to by its opening word, *Altitonantis,* was described by Maitland as the most celebrated of all the land books.[12] It is apparently a grant by Edgar to St Mary's, Worcester, of extensive privileges for the estates of the church of Worcester and it creates the triple hundred of Oswaldslow. There are many copies of this charter, mostly made in the seventeenth and eighteenth centuries when it attracted a lot of attention, but the earliest is the purported original, BM Harley 7513. This is written in an early twelfth-century hand, but that need not damn it, for several authentic documents have only survived in later copies that pretend to be originals.[13] There are, however, good reasons for doubting whether *Altitonantis* can be trusted, and no critic has ever suggested that it can be accepted as it stands. At best it has been claimed, by Maitland, that 'there has been some improvement in favour of the monks'. Recently Mr John has argued that a genuine *Altitonantis*, drawn up in Edgar's time, underlies this charter and he has been bold enough to print a text in which he indicates what, in his view, are the original, authentic passages.[14] Mr John supports his case with detailed arguments based on the formulae of the document and the circumstances at Worcester, all of which merit, and should receive, detailed attention, but perhaps the strongest argument against his theory is that the Worcester cartularies contain no trace of an uninterpolated *Altitonantis* charter. Had such a notable privilege existed it would certainly have found a place in one of the eleventh-century collections. It may be urged in support of Mr John's case that other charters are similarly omitted from the cartularies and that arguments from silence are therefore unsound, but an examination of these documents shows that there were good reasons for their omission. One of them, Edgar's grant of privileges dated 972, formerly in the Somers Collection, is a manifest forgery and was based on Edgar's charter for Pershore.[15] The three apparently genuine texts that were not included in the cartularies were all grants to laymen and there is no indication that the estates in question were transferred to Worcester before the Norman Conquest.[16] These documents did not, therefore, belong in the cartularies of that house. For the period 900 to 1015 there are only thirteen royal diplomas known to have been in the Worcester archive. Of the eight that are found in one or more of the early cartularies, five were grants to Worcester,[17] two were grants to laymen accompanied by evidence that the estates in question had been transferred to Worcester,[18] and the eighth is a grant to another religious community, *Deowiesstow*.[19] It appears that the tenth-century diplomas that were included in the early cartularies of Worcester were either grants to the church or to laymen with evidence of transfer to Worcester. Grants to laymen without such evidence were omitted. A similar policy was followed at Rochester in the twelfth century by the compiler of the *Textus Roffensis* who also omitted grants to laymen that are only known because the originals have survived or because they were included in the fourteenth-century *Liber Temporalium.* [20] Both *Altitonantis,* even in its uninterpolated form, and Edgar's charter of 972 would have been well within the terms of reference of the compilers of the Worcester cartularies and their omission shows that neither was in existence when the cartularies were being compiled. They belong not to the tenth-century reformation but to the later, post-Conquest, history of Worcester.

*   *   *

The relative poverty of Worcester in royal diplomas is balanced by the remarkable series of leases that have been preserved in the cartularies. Seventy-nine were granted by Oswald as Bishop of Worcester and seventy-one of these have lists of witnesses who were probably members of the community. Many of the grants were made with the consent of the community and the implication is that the witnesses were its consenting members.[21] They are normally described as clerk, deacon, priest, or — rarely — monk. All but six of witnessed leases are dated and a chronological sequence can therefore be established. The general run of subscriptions in these leases is remarkably consistent and it is possible to observe the progress of individuals in the community. For example, Aethelstan, who is described in 962-3 as a clerk, or as the sacrist, was by 966 a priest and eventually he became the leader of the community. Sometimes the neat pattern is broken by an unusual or irregular subscription but there are very few of these and some are certainly due to copying mistakes. That such mistakes could occur is shown by two eleventh-century copies of a lease dated 990 (*ASCh.* no. 1363) in one of which Leofwine is called a monk while in the other he is a clerk.[22] The order in which the witnesses were listed was certainly significant and the leader of the community was generally named first, but copyists have sometimes muddled the order and it is therefore unsafe, at present, to base detailed arguments on the arrangement of the lists.[23]

The information that can be gained about the witnesses of Oswald's leases is summarised in the table based on the seventy-one leases with witness lists from Oswald's episcopate with the addition of *ASCh.* nos.1290 and 1381, dated 957 and 996 respectively, for comparison. The dates assigned to the undated leases are as follows: no.1367: 985, no.1369: 987, no.1370: 969, nos.1372-74: 977. The chronological distribution of these leases is as follows:

Fig. 2, pp. 90-91

Date	No. of leases	*ASCh*. no.
957	1	1290
962	4	1299-1302
963	6	1297, 1303-7
966	3	1309-11
967	5	1312-16
969	11	1317-20, 1322-27, 1370
977	10	1330-36, 1372-74
978	3	1337-39
979	1	1340
980	2	1341-42
981	1	1343
982	1	1344
983	1	1345
984	4	1346-49
985	4	1350-52, 1367
987	3	1353-54, 1369
988	4	1356-58
989	3	1359-61
990	2	1362-63
991	3	1364-66
996	1	1381

The monastic reformation of Worcester is not well documented. Oswald is said to have accomplished it at various dates. According to *Altitonantis* the change occurred abruptly in 964 and this date has been accepted by Mr John;[24] Florence of Worcester put the reform in 969, a date that was accepted by Miss Robertson[25] but rejected by Armitage Robinson who himself suggested that it happened with 'no violent breach of continuity' some years after 969, but before 977.[26] Armitage Robinson believed that Oswald did not violently eject the clerks in the manner of Aethelwold at Winchester because the witness lists of 977 show no sign of such a dramatic change since 969. Mr John has recently accepted Armitage Robinson's conclusion on this point but has himself claimed that the earlier leases reveal a disruptive change between 963 and 966.[27]

Fig. 2, pp. 90-91   A detailed study of the witness lists shows that the change in the community was, in some respects, greater in both these periods, 963-966 and 969-977, than at any other time covered by these leases. Between 977 and 991 there are twenty nine leases with witness lists in which only nine new recruits appear, only two of whom appeared with any regularity, Aethelstan 'secundus' and Oswig. Five of the nine recruits only occur once. The change in the community after 977 was

brought about by the gradual disappearance of witnesses rather than by
any great and sudden loss, as may be seen by the following list of last
appearances of witnesses in those years:

977 Byrhstan
978 Wynstan
980 Eadwine
981 Aelfgar, Wulfheah
983 Aelfstan, Cynestan, Wulfric
984 Wulfhun
985 Aethelwold, Eadward, Wynsige
988 Ufic
989 Aelfnoth
990 Wulfweard

Of the twenty nine regular witnesses in 977, only fourteen survived
until 991. To judge by these leases the last fifteen years of Oswald's
episcopate saw a gradual decline in the size of the community at
Worcester.

The fact that between 963 and 966 seven witnesses disappeared, four
of them regular, and that seven new witnesses appeared, all fairly
regular, shows that in those years there was some change at Worcester,
even though it may have been inadequate to justify Mr John's
conclusion that 'the community must have undergone a thorough purge
between 963 and 966'.[28] The loss of seven witnesses in that interval,
three of whom were infrequent, is no more dramatic than the loss that
occurred in the years 983-985, and both could easily have been the
result of what is nowadays called natural wastage. But if there was no
purge, there was certainly some recruitment. More new members were
added in the interval 963-966 than in the following three years or in the
last fifteen years of Oswald's episcopate.

The changes between 969 and 977 cannot, however, be dismissed as
slight. In 969 itself there were apparently five new recruits, three of
whom had disappeared by 977, and by then there were no fewer than
eight new witnesses, all of whom appear regularly in later lists. In the
ten years after 967 there were, therefore, at least thirteen new recruits,
and all but three were regular witnesses in and after 977. In the same
period there were few losses. Apart from Iohan, Cynesige and Wulfheah
who all appeared for the first, and last, time in 969, the only witness to
disappear in those years was Aelfred. The decade after 967 was
therefore also a time of significant change, but it was by way of
recruitment rather than loss. The development of the community
during Oswald's episcopate as revealed by the witness lists is best
described as a process of gradual change with much continuity through

Name	Dates of Appearance	No. of sub-scriptions	No. of possible sub-scriptions[i]	Descriptions[ii]	Regular changes of description[iii]
Aelfgar	966-81	34	36	c(17), d(14), p(2), m(1)	d from 977 (2 irregular)
Aelfnoth	977-88	21	37	c(21)	
Aelfred	957-69	27	30	c(21), p(5)	
Aelfric	957-63	11	11	d(3), p(7)	p from 962 (1 irregular)
Aelfsige	969-96	45	54	d(3), p(41), m(1)	p from 977 (1 irregular)
Aelfstan	957-83	36	49	c(35)	
—	977	2	8	c(2)	
Aelfward	988	1	4	c(1)	
Aethelnoth	962-63	3	10	p(3)	
Aethelric	981	1	1	d(1)	
Aetheric[iv]	977-96	41	43	c(12), d(28)	d from 979 (2 irregular)
Aethelsige	977-96	41	43	d(15), p(25), m(1)	p from 983
—	991	1	3	p(1)	
Aethelstan	957-91	71	72	c(8), *cirward* (2), p(46), *primus* (12), m(2)	p from 966 (3 irregular) *Primus* from 987 (2 irregular)
—	977	1	10	m(1)	
—	984-96	20	24	p(19), *secundus* (1)	
—	985	1	4	p(1)	
—	991	1	3	d(1)	
Aethelwold	963	2	6	c(2)	
—	977-85	20	26	c(20)	
Byrhstan	962-77	38	39	c(37), p(1)	
Cynesige	957-63	10	11	c(10)	
—	969	5	10	c(5)	
Cynestan	962-63	9	10	c(9)	
Cynestan	977-83	17	18	c(17)	
Cynethegn	957-63	11	11	c(11)	
—	969-96	46	54	c(45)	
Eadgar	962-91	69	71	c(2), d(6), p(61)	d from 962, p from 963
Eadward	966-85	35	46	c(11), p(24)	p from 977 (2 irregular)
Eadwine	962-80	39	45	c(39)	
Goding	977-96	42	43	c(1), d(41)	
Godwine	982, 991	3	—	c(3)	
Iohan	969	3	10	p(3)	
Leofric	981	1	1	c(1)	
Leofstan	977-96	43	43	d(43)	
Leofwine[v]	966-96	59	62	c(45), m(14)	m from 984 (10 irregular)
Oswig	985-89	10	14	c(3), m(6)	
Tuna	966-82	15	37	c(15)	
Ufic	966-88	33	49	c(33)	
Wistan[vi]	966-91	51	61	p(51)	

Fig 2. The Com⟩

Name	Dates of Appearance	No. of subscriptions	No. of possible subscriptions[i]	Descriptions[ii]	Regular changes of description[iii]
Wulfgar	962-96	69	72	c(69)	
Wulfheah	962-81	43	46	c(27), p(15), m(1)	p from 977 (1 irregular)
—	969	3	10	c(3)	
Wulfhun	957-84	49	52	c(47), p(1)	
Wulfnoth	957	1	—	c(1)	
—	966-96	47	62	c(47)	
Wulfric	957-83	46	49	c(1), p(44)	
—	957-63	4	11	c(2), p(1)	
Wulfweard	977-90	39	39	c(2), d(36), m(1)	
Wulfwine	966	1	3	c(1)	
—	977	1	10	c(1)	
—	982-96	25	26	c(25)	
Wynsige	977-85	26	27	p(24), *primus* (1), m(1)	
Wynstan	962-78	36	42	c(36)	

Notes

i Including all documents for the first and last years of the witness.

ii The following abbreviations are used: c for clerk; d for deacon; p for priest; m for monk. The number of appearances under each description is noted in brackets.

iii The number of irregular designations within the relevant period is given in brackets.

iv Aetheric deacon witnesses ASCh., nos. 1384, 1385, the first dated 1017.

v Leofwine monk witnesses ASCh., no. 1384, dated 1017.

vi There may have been some confusion with Wynstan in 962-63.

the whole period, with no very dramatic losses at any time, but with two main periods of recruitment, 964-65, and 969-977.

Whatever disagreements there have been about the date and method of Oswald's reformation of his cathedral church at Worcester, there has apparently never been any doubt that he did reform the church and that it became one of the leading reformed monasteries in England. It is, however, strange that the description 'monk' should occur so infrequently in these leases. As the summary table shows, witnesses are normally described as clerks, deacons or priests, and apart from one very unusual document in which ten witnesses are called monks,[29] only three witnesses are ever given that description: Aethelstan once, Leofwine fourteen times and Oswig six times. The fact that Leofwine and Oswig were called monk quite often, in contrast to other witnesses, suggests that the term had some significance at Worcester; this only serves to underline the apparent reluctance to use it for others, a reluctance that casts a rather curious light on Oswald's monastic reformation. Even Wynsige who returned after his conversion to lead the community is normally called priest in the witness lists. There are some references to him as a monk, but most of these are suspect.[30] There is however one clearly authentic reference to him as a monk in a lease of 977 when he was himself the beneficiary and was given a lease of an estate at Little Washbourne in Gloucestershire, formerly held by his father.[31] This perhaps suggests that many, if not all, these clerks, deacons and priests may, like their leader Wynsige, have been monks, and that the witness lists give a misleading impression of the true monastic character of Worcester. It would not be surprising if deacons and priests were so described in preference to the more general term monk, but the use of the term clerk rather than monk would be hard to understand if the clerks really were monks.

The suspicion aroused by these witness lists that Oswald's community was less monastic than has commonly been supposed, is strengthened by the substance of some of the leases. The grant to Wynsige himself was an extraordinary arrangement for a true monk. Mr John has defended it by speculating that it may have been to support a wife and children who had to be abandoned when he entered the new way of life and he adds the comment that 'had it been a flagrant breach of the Rule one feels it would have been a larger grant'.[32] Despite this pleading, it is hard to escape the conclusion that the leader of Oswald's reformed community was setting a rather strange example. Several other grants were made to clerks and priests who could have been the same men who appear as witnesses,[33] but there is one where we can be fairly confident that the grantee was a member of the community. In an undated lease, which was probably granted in about 987, 'a certain clerk (*preost*) called Goding' was given a lease, for three lives, of three hides of land at Bredicot, about three miles east of Worcester, a yardland at *Genenofer* which Grundy identified as near Battenhall in St Peter's-without-Worcester, seven acres of meadow belonging to Tibberton, which also lies about three miles from Worcester, and a messuage 'which he has before the gate', meaning the gate of the city or the church.[34] A note in Hemming's Chartulary explains that this grant was made on the condition that Goding acted as scribe and that he wrote many books for the monastery.[35]

Both the witness lists and these grants to members of the community suggest that Oswald was indeed a gentle reformer. At no point was there any change that can reasonably be called a purge and it is hard to see what difference Oswald actually made at Worcester. Several of the leading members of the 'reformed' community were witnessing leases in 962 and 963, and some were there in 957. Wulfric, who had been the head of the unreformed community continued to head the witness lists for at least the first seven years of Oswald's episcopate and when Wynsige returned to become the new leader, Wulfric was merely pushed into second place. Aethelstan, who had been sacrist in 963, remained a member of the community and eventually became its head, and at least four others, Eadwine, Wulfgar, Wulfheah and Wulfhun survived from the early days until the 980s. The members of the community were much more frequently called clerks than monks in the leases that they granted, despite the reformers' hostility to clerks, and at least two members of the community, its leader and its scribe, accepted grants of estates for three lives. The community of Worcester certainly grew in size under Oswald, at least for a time, but how far its character was changed is open to some doubt.

Chapter 7

CHURCH AND STATE IN ENGLAND IN THE TENTH AND ELEVENTH CENTURIES

by H. R. Loyn

The concept of Church and State in early medieval England is trite and yet to some extent misleading. Is it sensible to talk of an institutional Church in England in the tenth century? Should the word 'state' be used of corresponding secular institutions? Is not 'monarchy' more precise and less sullied by Romanic overtones? What is a State but the channel by grace for transmission of God's authority? Convenience alone justifies the use of the terms with their suggestion of inexactness. And yet the framework of political ideas in which discussion of the problems takes place is clear enough, especially on the ecclesiastical side. We recognise the basic division of organised Christianity into the institutional church and gathered groups. In the great crisis of the sixteenth century the institutional church remained dominant, Catholic, Anglican, Lutheran, or Calvinist. Only slowly do gathered groups, Brownist, Baptist, Congregationalist, become significant though their historic roots can be traced far back through Anabaptists, Hussites, and Waldensians to the primitive church. Most professing Christians therefore discover, in tracing their own origins, that the division between Catholic and Protestant is by no means fundamental, and the story of the institutional church, above all its relationship with the state, becomes a matter of direct personal interest to most of the principal Christian churches.

Gradually, although not uniformly throughout Western Europe nor without dissent, an agreed picture has emerged of the development of the institutional church. The basis is the Church of Gregory the Great, Pope Gregory I, 590-604, the heir of Rome. In the successor states of the West the heritage was preserved and the consequences of the heritage experienced, notably in matters of land-ownership, alms-giving, education, and teaching relative to social discipline. There persisted an element of reluctance in this transmission of Rome through the Church. The dominant ideal remained otherworldly, monastic, withdrawn, celibate. An occasional active governor-bishop, such as Wilfrid of York, was thrown up by temperament and circumstance, but penitence and not governance was the general first concern. A change came about in the eighth century, probably associated with large-scale movements in the Mediterranean, perhaps with the emergence of Islam as another and rival universal faith. Under Charles the Great, 768-814, Emperor in 800, the beginnings of a new phase in the life of the institutional church in the West was reached. The propriety and essential rightness of the involvement of the Church in the workings of secular society was now recognised, fully on the part of the secular rulers, partially on the part of the Church. It was right that the bishop should be a ruler, provided that he was a true servant of God, and some would add, of the king.

To describe this Carolingian situation at the top level of society the term theocracy becomes helpful. A crime against the State had almost the force of a sin against God. Charles the Great himself legislated boldly for the Church. At Frankfurt in 794 the *filioque* clause was accepted and rulings on image-worship acknowledged in line with the views of Frankish theologians. The capitularies of Charles, govermental orders, were full of ecclesiastical matter. The influential early imperial capitulary of Aix, one of the products of the intellectual and ecclesiastical ferment of the new Empire, 802—3, was typical in heading its ordinances with prayers for the Emperor and for the Emperor's family.[1] Quite reasonably the term Carolingian is applied to this whole phase in the life of the institutional church. The secular power was dominant. Under the Saxon and Salian emperors in tenth- and eleventh-century Germany the process was exaggerated. Bishops were appointed and bishops were rejected by the king in the so-called Ottonian church. Monastic revival came about in consequence of royal and imperial concern for the health of the church, in part too as a reaction against excessive ecclesiastical involvement in government. Nowhere in Europe is this development more marked than in England. *see pp. 12-14* King Alfred performed Charles the Great's work on a smaller scale. St Dunstan and King Edgar in mid-tenth century provided a fruitful partnership during the very decade when Ottonian authority reached fresh heights. The monastic revival, directed actively by Dunstan himself, Aethelwold of Winchester, and Oswald of Worcester appeared almost in its purest form. And the consequences in England were altogether salutary. Most typical of manifestations of this activity was the growth of the monastic cathedral, the great church served by monks at the centre of a diocese. Bishops were elected, if possible from the community, under the guidance of the king. The Collect in the *Regularis Concordia,* drawn up about 970 A.D., is appropriate and revealing: *for the date see pp.40-42*

We beseech Thee, Almighty God, that Thy servant, our king, who has received of Thy mercy the government of this realm, may obtain also an increase of all virtues, wherewith being fittingly adorned he may be able to avoid the evils of wickedness, to overcome his enemies, and to attain to Thee who art the Way, the Truth, and the Life.[2]

see pp. 34-6

The Collect, which was followed by a similar Collect for the Queen, accurately conveys the tone of the movement's attitude to the monarchy. For a full generation and more the Carolingian compromise was exercised in the interests of both Church and King. Not, of course, that it was completely satisfying. The great European crisis of the eleventh century, the Investiture Contest, was concerned with the inadequacies of this very Carolingian compromise, with the freedom of the institutional church to regulate its own affairs. But to Canossa in this paper we must not go. Our concern is with the central phase in medieval church history, with the Carolingian phase, and it is not always easy to catch the subtle variations in meaning within the central themes. Indeed, a whole set of terminology has been constructed to cope with ideas connected with the relationship between Church and Society, between Church and State: 'Augustinian' or monastic where the dominant ideal is that of withdrawal from society; 'monarchic' where the royal Carolingian theme predominates; and 'sacerdotal' or 'Hildebrandine' when the papacy asserts its leadership. It is commonplace that whereas monastic and monarchic can flourish together — our monk-bishops of Worcester and Sherborne, and for long of Canterbury and Winchester — monarchic and sacerdotal cannot. It is recognised too that the balance of withdrawal and monarchic was often uneasy in the Carolingian world, and that the bishops themselves at times adopted strong ecclesiastical attitudes independent of papal direction and influence.

As means of testing this balance and of assessing signs of tension and of possible conflict to come, the Old English situation can be helpful in a variety of ways. This paper will be concerned with two aspects which offer help, with some of the substance of royal enactments concerning the church and with the attitude of the one key figure to emerge as articulate on these problems during the period, Wulfstan, Bishop of Worcester and Archbishop of York 1002–23.

Old English royal enactments are exceedingly complicated in nature and in detail. They may well be taken as a working-out in practice of the sentiments expressed obliquely in a famous passage in Alfred's preface to the translation of the *Cura Pastoralis,* an attempt to reconstruct a Golden Age when kings 'upheld peace (*sibbe*) and morals (*siodo*) and authority (*onweald*) at home, and also extended their territory abroad'.[3] Good kingship was Christian kingship. Successful kingship was Christian kingship. For all the occasional lack of sophistication and crudity in drafting and presentation, the Anglo-Saxon laws of the tenth and eleventh centuries represent a remarkable body of work in the vernacular. They offer evidence especially relevant to the problem of assessing the relationship between Church and State in the fields of law, of finance, of general social sanction and of concern with and for the integrity of the institutional church.

The care that is often taken to separate regulations relating to the Church as an institution from regulations relating to the laity is an important legal feature of the enactments. Such separation was not always possible. The demands of a general theme sometimes compelled unity, such as regulations relating to *mundbyrd,* to special peace, to protection of a hand-given peace.[4] But many of the key statements of law remained separate. Athelstan I on tithes, Edgar II as opposed to Edgar III which was the secular half of the composite code, Cnut I as opposed to Cnut II on the Edgar model. The reason for this was partly procedural. The ecclesiastical wing of the witan acted independently, almost as a national synod. There was more to separation, however, than mere procedure. Matters of substance and not merely of form were hived off. The Church and the bishops were heavily involved in law, national and ecclesiastical, and there has been a tendency rightly to emphasise the activities of the bishop in the public courts, notably in the shire-courts where he could preside jointly with the *ealdorman.* We should not neglect other aspects of his jurisdictionary rights. He had rights over his household and rights over his priests, as well as a general right to supervise ordeal and compurgation. It is hard to see how business could have been transacted without the existence of a formal bishop's court, a genuine *forum externum.*[5] Unless we dismiss extensive concern with canonical rulings and collections as mere antiquarianism we must recognise elements of a genuine ecclesiastical jursidiction, elusive in record though it might be. There are hints of a hierarchy of courts, a bishop's synod, even provincial synods with it is true the king active in the background. The church was deeply involved in the workings of secular government. It continued to enjoy a legal life of its own.

A similar pattern can be observed in the financial field. No institution can survive long without finance. The closeness of the tie between church and state is sometimes exaggerated in financial matters. Compulsory payment needs support to compel, and the secular power alone possessed such physical support. So in the tenth century the payment of tithes became compulsory, and also the method of payment. Tithes were to be paid to the old minster to which the church belonged, from the thegn's demesne, and from the land of his tenants (*geneatland*). The nature of the apportionment was also defined. Some was to go for the maintenance of churches. If on a thegn's bookland one third of the tithes if the church had a graveyard, and one ninth if not, was to be used for this purpose. Church-scot was to be paid to the old minster, plough-alms and the tithe of young stock by Pentecost, the fruits of the earth by the Equinox, and all by Martinmas. Physical royal sanction was surely needed to enforce such payment.[6] The king also played a prominent part in the collection and transmission of Peter's Pence to Rome. Failure to pay by St Peter's Day involved severe penalties, culminating at the third offence in total forfeiture of property.[7] Tensions undoubtedly existed and developed but attempts were made to safeguard the integrity of the institutional church in financial matters. Was it right that property that was owned by God who could commit no fault should be forfeit by the action of his unworthy servant? Yet the main theme was one of co-operation and support for God's acres and their renders.

In relation to general social sanctions and to the inner working of society the Old English royal enactments show clearly that church festivals, church fasts, as well as payments to the church, gave rhythm and continuity to the routine of the year. For the individual, christening, confirmation, possibly marriage, and burial provided such rhythm: for the community protection from plague and all affliction, and recovery from plague and all affliction. The bishops were great political figures who should not be disobeyed in any of the things they prescribed for the good of the Christian people. They were also immensely important social figures in their dioceses, conspicuously different in dress and way of life from all lay folk around them and so permanent conspicuous symbols of the separate life of the church.

General concern for the maintenance of the integrity of the Church as an institution is indeed the last of the big themes to discuss here in connection with royal legal activity. This concern is strong in the reigns of Aethelred and Cnut. The involved, complex, and interrelated statements of law that we know as Aethelred V and VI, and Cnut I, give full expression to it.[8] There was to be no heresy, but one Christian faith under one king. Vagrant monks were dealt with curtly. They were to return to their monasteries or else to observe what were clearly regarded as the three necessities, chastity, the monastic rule, and the Lord's service, by means of a pledge to the bishop. Celibacy was to be observed. Canons with refectory and dormitory were to live chastely. All priests were to preserve chastity on pain of forfeiture of a thegn's wergeld. All Christian folk were to avoid illegal intercourse. Moral teaching on sex was to be enforced. Simony in some of its wider attributes was to be suppressed. Each church was to be under the protection of God and of the king. No church was to be brought under subjection. There was to be no illegal traffic with a church. Just as moralists 'fulminated against men who dealt with churches as if they were mills, so did the lawyers insist on the enforcement of moral teaching against the sins of Simon Magus. No minister was to be expelled without the bishop's consent.[9] This theoretical English reservation of the rights of the hierarchy approaches the heart of the mysteries of the territorial church. There was genuine concern in England over the integrity of the Church. The king, the witan, and responsible opinion were anxious that the Church should not be treated merely as property. Rejection of simony and insistence on celibacy and chastity pointed the way to moral reform under royal direction for the good of the Church.

Such at least was the theory, but law-codes provide in their way no more than the refined top layer of evidence. It is not easy to probe behind them. Fortunately enough material has survived associated directly and personally with Archbishop Wulfstan to give us some insight into the true workings of society.[10] Wulfstan was a most active ecclesiastical statesman and scholar, deeply involved in the framing of the law-codes of Aethelred and Cnut, a homilist and stylist of distinction. Apart from his polished completed material he has left *but see p.225, n.59* us in manuscript not one but a series of commonplace books, collections of canons, selections from capitularies, homiletic material, and drafts of laws. Sir Frank Stenton long ago, in warning us against judging the Old English Church by ideal standards not achieved elsewhere pointed out that much still remained to be done on these Old English collections of canon law.[11] A conspicuous example occurs in the manuscript Nero A.i of the Cottonian library, now in the British Museum. This contains a massive series of extracts long known as the *Excerptiones Ecgberti,* or the Pseudo-Egbert. This was a working collection, annotated, corrected, and added to by the Archbishop *see p.72 and p.223, n.47* himself. The sources of the *Excerptiones* were diverse, including laws, scriptural statements, canons and Carolingian capitularies, sometimes word for word, sometimes rearranged. The very capitulary of Aix 802–3, that was mentioned above, reappears but with prayers for the *see p.95* emperor relegated to an inferior place — in the same order indeed as in the collection made by Ansegisus in 827. The impression of a hotchpotch is at first sight overpowering. But the material itself is grouped sensibly not only into obvious short topical divisions on baptism, communion, excommunication, sanctuary, or tithes, but into larger, basic divisions. There are thirty-four continuous chapters on bishops, nine on the monastic order, sixteen on the priestly order in relation to society, and no fewer than twenty-five on marriage and sexual problems. The last twenty folios of the manuscript constitute a penitential woven around Abbo of St Germain's powerful *Sermo de reconciliatione post penitentiam*. [12] Public penance with consequent visible signs of episcopal pre-eminence was a thing to be desired. Not that all was quite as orderly as may appear from this description. There were isolated chapters on the treatment of pagans and of Jews. There was a powerful isolated exhortation against selling believers to unbelievers. Contradictions appear within the various sections. But the fact remains that this collection and others like it provided a practical document, useful to those anxious for the smooth running of the institutional church, a reminder of the ways things were developing within the Carolingian framework.

Archbishop Wulfstan was indeed in the full Carolingian tradition in his attempts to put system into legal dictates on matters affecting proper order, baptism, excommunication, penance, and the duties, privileges and safeguards of the institutional church. It is still assumed that the unity of Christian society will be preserved. Only in the very nature of the systematic approach is there an indirect hint to later difficulty. In time the institutional growth of the Church and the relative efficiency of its legal definitions led to conflict. The special and permanent dignity of the episcopal office gave a reserve of non-royal authority to its chief officers. To a Europe anxious for judgment the bishop's court offered much advantage. But this was in the future. There is no obvious sign of conflict between Church and State in Wulfstan's collections.

An examination of the most important Old English document dealing directly with Church and State will lead to very much the same conclusion. There has survived, again from the pen of Wulfstan, a remarkable tract, or series of drafts of a tract, that we know as the *Institutes of Polity*. [13] In his rhythmic prose, not quite poetry and not quite prose, Wulfstan aimed to give condensed statements of the ideal of an ordered society in which each would play his proper part in his proper station. 'It is right that' or 'It is seemly that' are the link-phrases used to introduce the separate orders of men. It is right that a king, or an earl, or a bishop, or a monk, or a canon, should follow such and such a pattern of life. The hierarchy moves from the heavenly king, 'the true king, and glory of kings that ever were or shall be', to the earthly king, the comfort of the *folc*, the righteous herd over all the Christian flock, with his prime duty of protecting and comforting God's Church on earth. The eight virtues that uphold a kingdom are said to be truth, patience, generosity, good counsel, correction of evil-doers, the lifting-up of the righteous, modest taxes, and equitable judgments. The king should possess seven attributes: fear of God, love of truth, humility, resolution against evil, the will to succour the poor, to help the church, and to be equitable in judgment to friend and to foe. The throne was to be upheld by three supports, *oratores, laboratores,* and *bellatores.* Each rank of society was then treated in similar fashion — councillors, bishops, earls, reeves, abbots, monks, canons, priests, nuns, widows, God's servants, the laity, the clerisy, and so on through the clerical grades to sections on the rule of canons and on all Christian folk. Great prominence is naturally given to the bishop and finally, in order to illustrate the absence of theoretical strain between Church and State, Wulfstan's own view of the ideal bishop should be considered. We can sense from the writings of Wulfstan and of his contemporaries some of the paradox in the position of the bishop, who was to do right and to look after weights and measures, to be patient and wise and yet to preside over the shire court, to be humble, and yet to be set apart by clothing and dignity. A Bishop's day-work was:

First to his prayers and then to his book-work,
Reading or writing, teaching or learning,
And to see to the canonical hours in their due time
And all things that pertain to them,
To wash the feet of the needy, and to distribute alms,
And to give instruction where it is needed.

Also good craftsman's work is proper to him
And that men in his household should know such skills
So that no one shall remain too idle
And also it is seemly that he teach God's law,
Portion it to the *folc,*
Often and frequently at the courts. [14]

Moral exhortation was not lacking. A bishop should not waste his time over useless things, follies and stupidities. He should not drink too much, nor be infantile in speech with empty jests in any wise, whether at home or on his journeyings. But wisdom and discretion were proper to his order, and seemly behaviour to those who served him. The emphasis was on moral strength, not physical power, on instruction not government, on wisdom above all. Such a bishop could fit well into the Carolingian setting, the institution that he served snug and secure in a monarchial world.

Wulfstan's picture is indeed an idealised picture of an English bishop in the tenth and eleventh centuries. Z.N. Brooke in a fine piece of historical analysis showed that Lanfranc, the great Norman archbishop, was something of a pre-Investiture man.[15] In this as in so much else Lanfranc proved himself effective, strong, and full in the tradition of the English church he had come to serve — monarchic, Carolingian, but sound and stable in the pre-Investiture mould.

When Sir Frank Stenton in a memorable ending to a memorable chapter in *Anglo-Saxon England* stated that the English Church in 1066 had created a religious literature in the native tongue, had not yet lost the impact of the revival of religion and learning, and was faithful to the memory of its great men,[16] he was reminding us of the success of the tenth-century reformation and also incidentally of the fruitful co-operation of some of its great men — Dunstan, Edgar, Aethelwold, Oswald, Aelfric, Wulfstan, and Cnut. Their careers and achievements vital to the healthy development of the institutional Church in England, show us the Carolingian compromise operating at its best, in the fullness of active and vigorous reforming effort on the part both of Church and of State.

Chapter 8

LATE OLD ENGLISH LITERATURE

by Peter Clemoes

We should not conclude too easily that the period between the reign of
Edgar and the Norman Conquest was a poor one in the history of
English poetry. In the first place, of course, there is *The Battle of
Maldon* to give us a glimpse of the poetic power with which that age
could invoke heroic tradition when courage and loyalty were displayed
in contemporary events, as in these ringing words of young Aelfwine,
exhorting his comrades to remember the vows they had made and
declaring the pride in his noble ancestry that impelled him to avenge his
dead kinsman and lord:

> 'Gemunað þara mæla   þe we oft æt meodo spræcon,
> þonne we on bence   beot ahofon,
> hæleð on healle,   ymbe heard gewinn:
> nu mæg cunnian   hwa cene sy.
> Ic wylle mine æþelo   eallum gecyþan,
> þæt ic wæs on Myrcon   miccles cynnes;
> wæs min ealda fæder   Ealhelm haten,
> wis ealdorman,   woruldgesælig.
> Ne sceolon me on þære þeode   þegenas ætwitan,
> þæt ic of ðisse fyrde   feran wille,
> eard gesecan,   nu min ealdor ligeð
> forheawen æt hilde.   Me is þæt hearma mæst:
> he wæs ægðer min mæg   and min hlaford.'
> þa he forð eode,   fæhðe gemunde,
> þæt he mid orde   anne geræhte
> flotan on þam folce,   þæt se on foldan læg
> forwegen mid his wæpne. [1]

This is pregnant language, in which, for instance, the mere particle *þa* in
þa he forð eode, by connecting what is said with what is done, can
express the essence of heroic integrity. This is not the poetry of
decadence or decline. And there is too the warning we receive against
the dangers of drawing conclusions from negative evidence when we
remember that this great poem has survived only because the solitary,

imperfect, manuscript to outlive the Middle Ages had been copied early in the eighteenth century before it was destroyed by fire in 1731: circumstances such as these should remind us vividly on what slender chances our knowledge depends. For all we know, Ulfcytel of East Anglia, who, the Danes said, put up a harder fight than anyone else they encountered, and others like him were celebrated in verse as Byrhtnoth was.

When we turn to religious poetry where, if anywhere, we should expect to find the finest achievement of an age as ecclesiastical as this we are beset with the doubts and difficulties of an attempted chronology that is hardly ever linked to datable historical events as secular poems sometimes are. It is true that we have good reason to believe that much fine poetry was composed in earlier days — *The Dream of the Rood* (in some form), *The Wanderer*, *The Seafarer* and Cynewulf's poems for example; but we ought to acknowledge honestly that there is other fine poetry about which we cannot be sure. When, for instance, was an imaginative poem such as *Exodus* composed? A poet of that kind of individual genius might be born at any time. Because there is good early poetry it would be wrong to argue that a poem must be early because it is good. Rather, I think, we should reserve judgment and admit that we do not certainly know whether by the late tenth century the inspiration of conceiving Christian experience afresh in terms of Germanic heroic poetry had become a largely spent force. At any rate we can be sure that this period preserved and valued poetry of the past, for almost our entire knowledge of Old English poetry of any time of composition depends on anthologies of the second half or the end of the tenth century. What we experience today is a share — a small share, no doubt — in late tenth-century taste.

For prose, on the other hand, the evidence is copious and clear-cut: there can be no doubt that in this age it was a vitally important medium of expression. That it was vernacular prose was largely due to the lead King Alfred had given nearly a hundred years before. He himself had written English prose versions of some major Latin works. He had encouraged others to do the same. The large-scale, original undertaking of *The Anglo-Saxon Chronicle* had been initiated in his reign. He had believed that it was necessary for all men to know the basic works which he or others had translated. He had devoted royal resources to their dissemination. He had enunciated an educational policy of training all available young men of free stock to read English. That the tradition he had established was still alive in the monastic reform period and beyond is clear from a number of signs — from the recopying of Alfredian works; from the renewed continuation of *The Anglo-Saxon*

Chronicle; from the rewriting of Wærferth's translation of Gregory the Great's *Dialogues*, extant in fragmentary form in Bodleian Hatton 76 of the first half of the eleventh century;[2] from Aelfric's reference to the 'books which King Alfred wisely translated from Latin into English' or Aethelweard's tribute to the influence that Alfred's translation of the *De Consolatione* had had in enabling more than scholars to share the moving experience of Boethius;[3] or, again, from the careful revision which Wulfstan gave to the preface of Alfred's translation of Gregory the Great's *Cura Pastoralis* and which the Bishop entered in his own hand in Bodleian Hatton 20, the copy which the King had sent to Worcester.[4] With the reform period a new phase in the fulfilment of this tradition opens up. Whereas Alfred had initiated a programme of making known single great works such as Boethius's *De Consolatione Philosophiae* or Orosius's *History of the World,* the reform period aimed at the diffusion of the elements of Christian education among the population at large, through media such as the homily, for the salvation of souls. English prose became the means of communication for the pastoral evangelism of a confident religious orthodoxy. How far this process continued the educational practice which Alfred had advocated is hard to say. Had the priests to whom pastoral letters in English were directed, the ealdormen and thanes who asked Aelfric for writings in the vernacular, been trained in any systematic way to read English? I know of just one scrap of evidence that prompts me to speculate that training of this kind may have existed in some form for some people. In his homily for St Gregory's day Aelfric draws on Paul the Deacon's *Life of Gregory* as his main source, with secondary use of Bede's *Historia Ecclesiastica* for a fuller account of Augustine's mission to England.[5] But when he comes to the story of Gregory's meeting with the Anglian slave-boys in Rome, then, and then only, he uses the Old English Bede, a work of which he nowhere else shows any first-hand knowledge. It looks as though he knew the Old English version of this famous story as an extract. Perhaps he knew it by heart. Perhaps — and here is my speculation — he knew it like this because he knew it as a 'set text'. The training to read English envisaged by Alfred could profitably have been based on just such set texts as this.

The front across which English prose supplied the educational movement that was in action in the reform period was a broad one. Besides Christian doctrine, the Bible and its exposition and lives of saints, it comprehended history, ancient, national and contemporary; geography; natural science; medicine; grammar; philosophy; government, both secular and ecclesiastical; and fictional narrative, valued perhaps for its wholesome moral tone. English prose was not to be used

again with a range like this before the fourteenth and fifteenth
centuries. For instance, the version of the first six books of the Old
Testament extant in the Bodleian manuscript Laud Miscellaneous 509
and in BM Cotton Claudius B.iv[6] and the West Saxon Gospels[7] are
the only English prose translations of the Bible before the Wycliffite
ones.[8] English prose, it is fair to claim, was part of the fabric of
national life in the latter part of the tenth century, throughout the
eleventh, and even to a significant extent still in the twelfth. Its
distribution interpenetrated that of Latin writings: one has only to
think of the way in which Wulfstan wrote in both Latin and English, or
of the way in which English items and Latin ones stand side by side in
the early eleventh-century part of BM Cotton Nero A.i, a collection of
material which, as shown by many entries in his own hand, was
planned, supervised, corrected and augmented by Wulfstan for his own
use as adviser to the King.[9] Sometimes English prose was combined
with illustrations. The original parts of the first volume of BM Cotton
Tiberius B.v, those in handwriting of the first half of the eleventh
century, exemplify this association as well as the intermingling of Latin
and English. In this miscellany of computistical, astronomical and
geographical material Aelfric's English prose piece *De Temporibus Anni*
keeps company with such Latin texts as a metrical calendar; the *Aratea*,
Cicero's versified translation of a Greek astronomical text; and
Priscian's *Periegesis*, another verse translation, this time of a description
of the world in Greek verse. And there is both a Latin text and an
English one of an account of 'Wonders of the East'. Illustration is
lavish. As well as a Mappa Mundi there are three major sets of coloured
drawings, one accompanying the calendar, one Cicero's text and one
the Latin and English *Wonders*.[10] Or again, in one of its two extant
copies, Claudius B.iv of the first half of the eleventh century, the
English prose version of the first six books of the Old Testament which
I have already mentioned accompanies, section by section, a set of
some four hundred coloured drawings.[11] A study of the educational
materials in use at particular ecclesiastical centres during the first half
of the eleventh century would be interesting. The treatment given to
Aelfric's homilies in this, their period of maximum circulation, is an
example. At Canterbury, typically, they were modified in verbal details,
reorganised in ordered sets in combination with items not by Aelfric
and given massive circulation. We can see reflected in this treatment the
'official' status accorded to them. In the reorganisation that they
received at Worcester, a sense of the identity of Aelfric as an individual
author was retained. At Exeter, by about the time of the Conquest,
they were one source among others which had been drawn on to form

pastiche preaching material emphasising direct exhortation more than abstract exposition. We have here an impression of provision for preaching needs of an elementary kind.[12] The intimate, two-way relationship that existed between vernacular materials and contemporary thinking is revealed in a number of ways: for instance, when Aelfric supplies a note to inform interested readers that a rather striking point in one of his homilies comes from a certain, rather rare source;[13] or when in a mid-twelfth-century manuscript, BM Cotton Vespasian D.xiv, we find excerpted from the first Old English pastoral letter which Aelfric wrote for Wulfstan a passage in which Aelfric relates specifically to priests a point concerning purity of body and mind which is given only general application in the source from which he took it, Alcuin's *Commentary on the Apocalypse*;[14] or, again, when from the text of Aelfric's pastoral letter for Bishop Wulfsige that was copied into CCCC 190 at Exeter during the second half of the eleventh century we find omitted, perhaps because it embarrassed someone, the section in which the priest is enjoined not to leave the church to which he has been ordained and move to another *for ænigre gitsunge* ('out of greed');[15] or, again, indeed, when in a Worcester manuscript, Bodleian Hatton 114, against Aelfric's note to the effect that church custom forbids any preaching on Thursday, Friday and Saturday in Holy Week,[16] we find written in a hand of the second half of the eleventh century *Ðis nis no well gesæd*.

In fulfilling its diverse educational role the English prose of the reform period and onwards drew much intellectual strength from Englishmen of former times. Bede, pre-eminently, and then Alcuin were the great English teachers of the past in Aelfric's eyes: Bede he calls *se snotere Engla ðeode lareow*, 'the wise teacher of the English people', and Alcuin he alludes to as *sum geþungen lareow*, 'a distinguished teacher', who taught many, first in this country and then on the Continent. Aelfric was thoroughly familiar with Bede's *Historia* and used it with independent ease, notably for information about English saints. He also knew well and made good use of Bede's homilies, books of biblical exegesis, scientific treatises and prose and verse lives of St Cuthbert. For instance, as Professor Cross has demonstrated, he knew books of scriptural commentary and homilies by Bede well enough to recall them by memory when his line of thought prompted him to do so.[17] As for the writings of Alcuin, besides the *In Apocalypsin* which I have already mentioned, Aelfric knew and used at least his *Interrogationes et Responsiones in Genesin*[18] and *De Virtutibus et Vitiis*,[19] and Wulfstan drew on his letters — for a passage in the *Sermo Lupi* for instance.[20] In chronicling and legislating English prose writers stood directly on the shoulders of their forebears, so to speak. The mid-eleventh-century part of BM Cotton Nero A.i neatly illustrates this point, for, all in Old English, it contains the laws of Cnut accompanied by the earlier codes that were their background. Nothing reveals the sense of Englishness in the vernacular literature of the late tenth century more clearly than the continued use of the traditional insular script for writing it down side by side with the continental, Caroline script used for the writing of Latin. And that this was no mere dead hand of tradition is evident from the new character this insular script took on in the tenth century. Anyone looking at the handsome square minuscule of such manuscripts as the Exeter Book of poetry, of the second half of the tenth century, or the two-volume homiliary Bodley 340 and 342, of the beginning of the eleventh, knows that these books were the products of an age of intellectual breadth and clarity.

The main source of intellectual enlightenment was the works of the Fathers. Aelfric thought of Augustine, Gregory and Jerome as the great fountainheads of orthodox teaching, and his vernacular prose writings, especially his homilies, transmitted their thought — above all, that of Augustine and Gregory — intelligently and intelligibly. Ambrose and Basil were other Fathers drawn on. Carolingian writers provided much source material for English prose too, notably concerning ecclesiastical organisation and practice; as examples one thinks of the Rule of Chrodegang of Metz, Halitgar of Cambrai's Penitential, the *capitula* of Theodulf of Orleans, and Amalarius of Metz's *De Ecclesiasticis Officiis* and *De Regula Canónicorum*. Aelfric used Ratramnus's treatise on the Eucharist, *De Corpore et Sanguine Domini*, as a source,[21] and Wulfstan likewise a *Sermo in Cena Domini ad Penitentes* by Abbo of St Germain[22] and Adso's *Libellus Anticristi*;[23] Byrhtferth of Ramsey, author of a manual of cosmic philosophy, partly in English and partly in Latin, studied under Abbo of Fleury while Abbo was in charge of the monastic school at Ramsey. The historical sources drawn on by writers of English prose to supplement their full range of ecclesiastical histories, like Rufinus's Latin version of Eusebius, include Gregory of Tours's *Historia Francorum*. Their sources for saints' lives include Sulpicius Severus, Hilduin of St Denis and Abbo of Fleury. The works of Isidore of Seville furnished them with a store-house of material; the *De Correctione Rusticorum* of Martin of Braga and Julian of Toledo's *Prognosticon Futuri Saeculi* are other examples of Iberian contributions. Celtic influence is apparent when English prose writers treat of the cardinal sins, and it was an ultimately Irish source of the seventh century that gave them the topic of the 'Twelve Abuses of the Age'; they drew denunciatory strength from Gildas's *De Excidio*

Britanniae. Other kinds of source material are exemplified by Priscian's *Grammar* and the *Vitae Patrum.* The medical material which had been in circulation in English prose since King Alfred's reign or soon after and the late Old English prose treatises on remedies derived from plants and on remedies derived from animals embody, as Dr C. H. Talbot has shown,[24] some of the best medical knowledge of the time. Carolingian compilations such as Paul the Deacon's homiliary and that of Haymo of Auxerre were important channels for the transmission of patristic thought and, we may be sure, many a saint's life was rendered into English prose because a Latin text of it had come from the Continent. For example, the Old English version of the legend of the Seven Sleepers of Ephesus, included by Skeat in his edition of Aelfric's *Lives of Saints* though not by Aelfric, was based on a Latin text which almost certainly had arrived from the Continent during the second half of the tenth century.[25] Paul the Deacon's homiliary, as Father Smetana demonstrated,[26] was Aelfric's basic source for his *Catholic Homilies.* Clearly its importance to him was not just as a source of material but also as an example, a model. What Paul's collection of homilies, compiled at the request of Charlemagne, had been intended to do for the Empire, Aelfric's homilies, dedicated to the Archbishop of Canterbury, were intended to do for England. Each man provided his church with the essential body of orthodox preaching material for standard use. The difference was that, whereas Paul's was a collection of patristic Latin homilies, Aelfric's was a vernacular adaptation. Paul's task had been to compile; Aelfric's was to think through, simplify and re-express in the English language. I wonder whether similarly Aelfric had a continental model in view when he composed his set of vernacular saints' lives? Others would be better able to answer that question than I.

Aelfric's English prose works constitute, in effect, an epitome of the religious knowledge of his day. Such an aim and the ability to carry it out argue a highly educated background. And indeed late Old English prose has the marks of educational training stamped upon it. For one thing it distinguishes between what is correct doctrine and what is not: 'Precor modo obnixe almitatem tuam, mitissime Pater Sigerice', Aelfric writes to the Archbishop about his *Catholic Homilies,* 'ut digneris corrigere per tuam industriam, si aliquos nevos malignae haeresis, aut nebulosae fallaciae in nostra interpretatione repperies'.[27] It also distinguishes between true religion and superstition: 'Ne sceal nan cristenman nan ðing be ðam monan wiglian; gif he hit deð, his geleafa ne bið naht', Aelfric writes.[28] And it distinguishes too between correct and mistaken knowledge. Aelfric again, after explaining how the shape of the moon depends on the direction from which the sun's light falls on it: 'Nu cweðað sume men . . . þæt se mona hine wende be ðan ðe hit wedrian sceall on ðam monðe, ac hine ne went naðor ne weder ne unweder of ðam ðe his gecynd is.'[29] Then there is a critical attitude towards the status of sources: *qui aestimatur Sancti Hilarii fuisse* Aelfric says of one of the tracts that he uses.[30] And a critical attitude towards their text: (Aelfric again, of the Bible) 'Quidam dicunt non dixisse Salvatorem "Satane, uade retro", sed tantum "Uade"; sed tamen in rectioribus et uetustioribus exemplaribus habetur "Uade retro Satanas".'[31] And there is the concern that Aelfric shows for the uncorrupted transmission of his writings.[32] Basic, of course, are a complete mastery of the Latin language on the one hand and the use of a standard form of English on the other. Professor Gneuss has recently shown how directly the education in Aethelwold's school at Winchester was focussed on this relationship. In his book on hymnals and hymns in England in the Middle Ages, Professor Gneuss presented evidence that a systematic equivalence between certain Latin words and certain English ones is shared by Aelfric's writings and some other specimens of English (including glosses) which are likely to have had a Winchester connection. Subsequently, in a lecture published in the first issue of the new periodical *Anglo-Saxon England,* he has developed a convincing argument that these are all products of the educational system of Aethelwold's school.[33] Certainly this regularity of lexical choice that they show is but the twin of the desire for grammatical regularity that Aelfric displays in hundreds of small alterations that we know he made to the text of his *Catholic Homilies.*[34] Evidently regularity was accepted as an ideal aim in language, and Aethelwold's school directed this aim towards English.

Education gave Old English prose writers a conscious sense of the difference between one language and another, of the process involved in transferring thought from one language to another, of the process involved in using language to communicate understanding, and of the aptness, the fitness of style. More particularly it taught them to apply a number of expository and rhetorical techniques. They understood and used, for example, the exegetical form of the 'continuous gloss' and various types of the 'question and answer' device. They had a range of rhetorical figures at their command. For instance, alliteration, rhyme and parallel structure are used with great skill in this characteristic sentence of Wulfstan's, prompted by some verses in Paul's second epistle to Timothy:

He sæde hwilum þam biscope Tymothee þæt on ðam endenyhstan dagum þissere worulde beoð frecenlice tida for manna synnum, and men þonne lufiað, he cwæð, ealles to swyðe þas swicolan woruld and beoð ofergrædige woruldgestreona, and to manege weorðaþ to wlance and ealles to rance and to gylpgeorne, and sume weorþað egeslice godcundnessa hyrwende and boclare leande and unriht lufiende, and sume weorðað swicole and swæslice ficole and butan getrywðum forscyldgode on synnan.[35]

There is, of course, a great deal of efficient plain, informational prose. Here, for example, is a short medical piece included in BM Cotton Tiberius A.iii, a manuscript written in the middle of the eleventh century, almost certainly at Christ Church, Canterbury. It concerns the development of the human foetus during the nine months before birth:

Her onginð secgan ymbe mannes gecynde, hu he on his modor innoþe to men gewyrðeð. Ærest þæs mannes brægen bið geworden on his moder innoþe. Þonne bið þ brægen utan mid reaman bewefen on þære syxtan wucan. On oðrum monþe þa ædron beoð geworden. On lxv and þreo hundræd scytran and lengran hi beoð todælede and þ blod þonne floweð on þa fet and uppan þa handa, and he þonne byþ on limum todæled and tosomme gearwað. On þam þriddum monþe he biþ man butan sawle. On þam feorþan monþe he bið on limum staþolfæst. On þam fiftan monþe he biþ cwica and weaxeð, and seo modur lið witleas, and þonne þa ribb beoð geworden. Þonne gelimpð þæræ manigfeald sar þonne þæs byrþres lic on hire innoþe scypigende bið. On þam syxtan monþe he byþ gehyd and ban beoð weaxende. On þam seofoþan monþe þa tan and þa fingras beoð weaxende. On þam eahtoþan monþe him beoð þa breost þing wexende, and heorte and blod, and he bið eall staþolfæstlice geseted. On þam nigoþan monþe witodlice wifum bið cuð hwæþer hi cennan magon. On þam teoþan monþe þ wif ne gedigð hyre feore gif þ bearn accenned ne biþ, for þam þe hit in þam magan wyrð hit to feorhadle oftost on tiwes niht.[36]

The high quality of English prose between the reform of the monasteries and the Conquest — unique in the European vernaculars of the time — can be simply demonstrated by two or three examples of narrative. Within the traditional *Chronicle* mode of simple sentence structure and simple connectives there is now a power — as in, for instance, the E version of the episode of Eustace at Dover in 1051[37] — to present a situation as it develops step by step so that the reader grasps what is involved at each stage and realises the connection with national politics. The late Old English prose version of the romantic adventure story of *Apollonius of Tyre* — the one that was later to supply the plot for the play *Pericles* — shows a civilised sensitivity to refined feeling in personal relationships. Take, for instance, this first meeting between the shipwrecked Apollonius and the daughter of the king who has befriended him:

Mid-þi-ðe se cyning þas word gecwæð, ða færinga þar eode in ðæs cynges iunge dohtor and cyste hyre fæder and ða ymbsittendan. Þa heo becom to Apollonio, þa gewænde heo ongean to hire fæder and cwæð: 'Ðu goda cyningc and min se leofesta fæder, hwæt is þes iunga man þe ongean ðe on swa wurðlicum setle sit mid sarlicum andwlitan? Nat ic hwæt he besorgað.' Ða cwæð se cyningc: 'Leofe dohtor, þes iunga man is forliden, and he gecwemde me manna betst on ðam plegan, for-ðam ic hine gelaðode to ðysum urum gebeorscipe. Nat ic hwæt he is ne hwanon he is; ac gif ðu wille witan hwæt he sy, axsa hine, for-ðam þe gedafenað þæt þu wite.' Ða eode þæt mæden to Apollonio and mid forwandigendre spræce cwæð: 'Ðeah ðu stille sy and unrot, þeah ic þine æðelborennesse on ðe geseo. Nu þonne, gif ðe to hefig ne þince, sege me þinne naman, and þin gelymp arece me.' Ða cwæð Apollonius: 'Gif ðu for neode axsast æfter minum namon, ic secge þe ic hine forleas on sæ. Gif ðu wilt mine æðelborennesse witan, wite ðu þæt ic hig forlet on Tharsum.' Ðæt mæden cwæð: 'Sege me gewislicor, þæt ic hit mæge understandan.'[38]

In his *Lives of Saints* Aelfric gives to their central episodes a stylisation that is expressive of their spiritual perspective. Take, for instance, the little scene of King Oswald's almsgiving.[39] Oswald and Bishop Aidan are eating together on Easter Sunday. A thane tells the King that there are many beggars outside. Oswald sends out a silver dish to be divided among them. Aidan grasps the King's right hand, crying out 'May this blessed hand never rot!' And so it has turned out, Aelfric says: that hand is still preserved undecayed. Aelfric presents the elements of this episode in a sequence of rhythmical phrases paired by alliteration. For instance, he uses four phrases — two pairs — to set the scene:

Hit gelamp on sumne sæl   þæt hi sæton ætgædere
Oswold and Aidan   on þam halgan Easterdæge.

In the first phrase an occurrence and a point of time are singled out but not specified; in the second phrase, the second of its pair, an action is identified — sitting together. In the third phrase, the first of its pair, two people are named — Oswald and Aidan; in the fourth phrase, closing its pair, the occasion is identified as Easter Sunday. The narrative situation is thus used only to bring together two illustrious people on the supreme occasion of the church year. Only what is essential to that universal meaning is allowed to be present. Or again, when Aidan speaks:

'Ne forrotige on brosnunge   þeos gebletsode hand.'

Brosnung, 'decay', and *gebletsode*, 'blessed', are set off against one another by the rhythm. The essence of the thought is that the one concept is overcome by the other: that is what the hand symbolises and that is what the pair of rhythmical phrases gives shape to. The linguistic means are at once simple and stylised. And so throughout the story. The reader's imagination is presented with a collocation of narrative symbols just as it would be if he were looking at a narrative panel in an illuminated manuscript or in a stained glass window.

Late Old English prose was not an instrument of original, speculative thinking. But that is not to say that it only transmitted inert information. At least at its best, it conveyed an attitude on the writer's part towards his subject matter, a view of it to which he intended his reader to respond. Think, for instance, of the scorn for bungling, cowardice, treachery and soft-centredness felt by the author of the annals of the wars of Aethelred's reign in the C, D and E versions of the *Chronicle,* and of the rhetorical skill with which he communicates his contempt and anger to the reader: 'Ond naðelæs, for eallum þisum griðe ond friðe ond gafole, hi ferdon æghwider flocmælum ond hergodon ure earme folc, ond hi rypton ond slogon.'[40] Or think again of the impact of Wulfstan's impassioned view of the demoralisation of English society:

Her syndan þurh synleawa, swa hit þincan mæg, sare gelewede to manege on earde. Her syndan mannslagan and mægslagan and mæsserbanan and mynsterhatan, and her syndan mansworan and morþorwyrhtan, and her syndan myltestran and bearnmyrðran and fule forlegene horingas manege, and her syndan wiccan and wælcyrian, and her syndan ryperas and reaferas and worolstruderas, and, hrædest is to cweþenne, mana and misdæda ungerim ealra. And þæs us ne scamað na, ac us scamað swyþe þæt we bote aginnan swa swa bec tæcan, and þæt is gesyne on þysse earman forsyngodan þeode.[41]

First a comprehensive, general statement: *Her syndan þurh synleawa, swa hit þincan mæg, sare gelewede to manege on earde.* Then a series of fourteen exemplifications joined to one another without a break by thirteen *and*s and forming five groups linked to the general statement and to each other by repetition of *her syndan.* Then a recapitulating generalisation *and, hrædest is to cweþenne, mana and misdæda ungerim ealra,* leading to a reference to our lack of shame and to the mark of this on this wretched, sinful people, each component in this threefold sequence of thought — sins, lack of shame, consequent

wickedness — being connected by *and* to what precedes it. The language
with its various figures of repetition is relentlessly linear; but pace and
tone vary and the continuous rhythmical phrasing, comprising parts
that are all the same as one another, comprehends both the sequence
and the wholeness of the thought.

Aelfric's method, as we have seen in the short scrap of narrative we
have looked at, was to use language so as to set up a formal
correspondence between parts, whatever the particular subject he was
writing about. This, to him, was of the essence of the relationship
between thought and expression. This is what reflected the thematic in
his thought, what came to the fore when he was treating such subjects
as the Trinity, Creation, Redemption, Judgment, or was making
transitions from the material to the spiritual, from the symbol to the
symbolised. For instance, in these two sentences in his homily on the
Parable of the Vineyard, written before he used his rhythmical style:
'Se hiredes ealdor is ure Scyppend, se ðe gewylt ða ðe he gesceop, and
his gecorenan on þisum middanearde geagnað, swa swa hlaford his hired
on his healle.'[42] And: 'Þes wingeard sprytte Godes gecorenan, fram
ðam rihtwisan Abel oð ðam endenextan halgan ðe on ende þyssere
worulde acenned bið, swilce he swa fela winboga getyddrode.'[43]
Each of these sentences has four main members of approximately the
same length. The first member in each case establishes the equivalence
between the symbol and its signification; in the middle two members
the signification is amplified; and in the fourth there is an amplificatory
return to the symbol. The effect is to enclose the spiritual sense within
the symbol. Applied to intellectual subject matter language thus
formalised partook of the regularly patterned character of the divinely
created universe. It was, I believe, this ideal view of language that
caused both Aelfric and Wulfstan to adopt in their English prose an
abstractly conceived structure of continuous rhythm.[44] Let me close
with an example. In his letter to the thane Sigeweard, on the Old
Testament and the New, Aelfric describes in turn the six ages of this
world. Concurrent with these six is a seventh — that of the faithful
departed awaiting final judgment. Beyond these seven is an eighth:

> Seo eahteoðe yld   ys se an eca dæg
> æfter urum æriste,   þonne we rixiað mid Gode
> on sawle and on lichaman   on ecere sælþe,
> and ne bið nan ende   þæs anes dæges,
> þonne þa halgan scinað   swa swa seo sunne deð nu.[45]

The balance and proportion of the rhythmed prose common to the
account of all the ages alike signify that this world in its entirety, with
its sun shining like the saints and its schematic sequence of time, is the
prelude to the ordered harmony of the eternity ahead.

PLATES

a: Winchester, the Old Minster: the northern apse of the *martyrium* built *c.* 971–4 around the site of St. Swithun's grave. Photo: R. C. Anderson.

b: Winchester, the Old Minster: the central area of the *martyrium* showing the sunken chamber surrounding the site of St. Swithun's grave. The foundation in the foreground marks the south side of the medieval chapel of St. Swithun. Photo: R. C. Anderson.

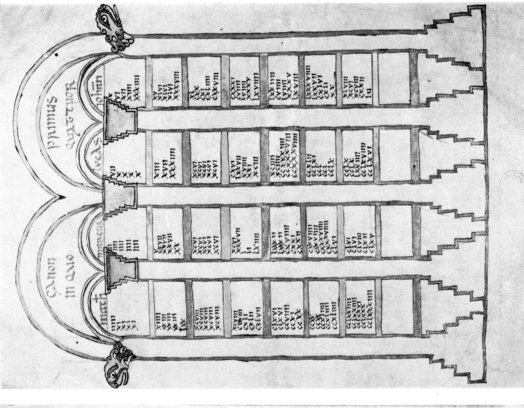

a: Gospels, Boulogne-sur-Mer, Bibliothèque municipale, MS 10, Vol. II, folio 2. Initial P. By courtesy of Bibliothèque municipale, Boulogne-sur-Mer. Photo: J. J. G. Alexander.

b: Gospels, Boulogne-sur-Mer, Bibliothèque municipale, MS 10, Vol. I, folio 5. Canon 1. By courtesy of Bibliothèque municipale, Boulogne-sur-Mer. Photo: J. J. G. Alexander.

a (top left): Athelstan Psalter, BM Cotton Galba A.xviii, folio 120ᵛ. The Ascension. By courtesy of the Trustees of the British Museum. Photo: BM.

b (left): Athelstan Psalter, Bodleian MS Rawl. B. 484, folio 85. The Nativity. By courtesy of the Bodleian Library, Oxford. Photo: Bodleian Library.

c (above): Athelstan Psalter, BM Cotton Galba A.xviii, folio 2ᵛ. Christ in Majesty with choirs of Saints. By courtesy of the Trustees of the British Museum. Photo: BM.

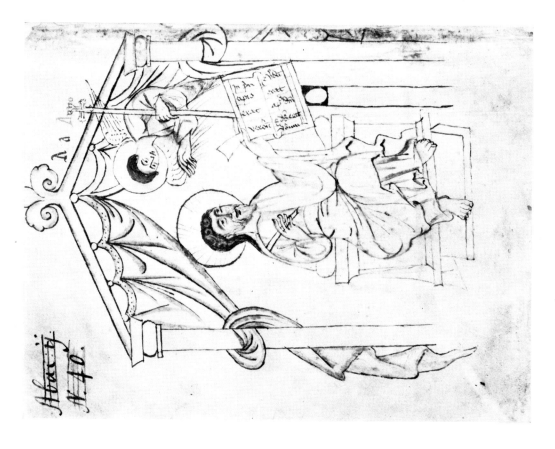

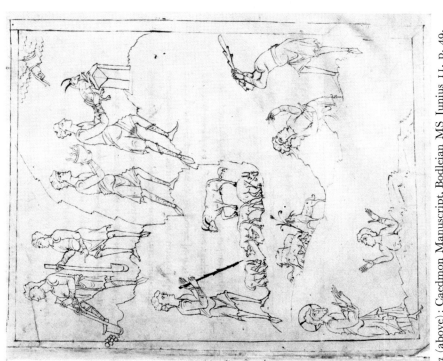

a (above): Caedmon Manuscript, Bodleian MS Junius 11, p. 49. Cain and Abel. By courtesy of the Bodleian Library, Oxford. Photo: Bodleian Library.

b (right): Gospels, St. John's College, Oxford, MS 194, folio 1v. St. Matthew. By courtesy of St. John's College, Oxford. Photo: St. John's College, Oxford.

b: Ivory cover of the Lorsch Gospels. Detail showing Christ...

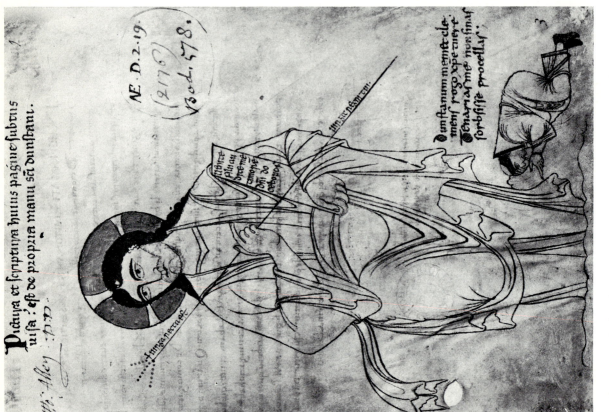

a: St. Dunstan's Classbook, Bodleian MS Auct. F.4.32, folio 1. St. Dunstan at the feet of Christ. By courtesy of the Bodleian Library, Oxford Photo:

b: Leofric Missal, Bodleian MS Bodley 579, folio 49. Paschal Hand. By courtesy of the Bodleian Library, Oxford. Photo: Bodleian Library.

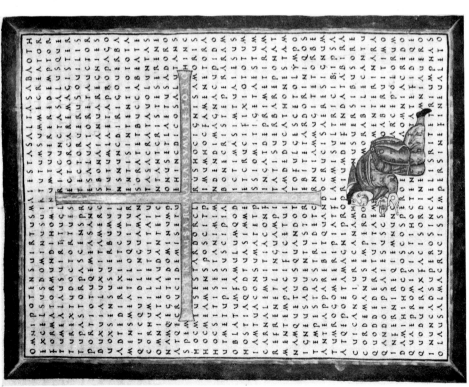

a: *In laude sanctae crucis*, Trinity College, Cambridge, B.16.3, folio 30v. Hrabanus Maurus adoring the Cross. By courtesy of the Master and Fellows of Trinity College, Cambridge. Photo: Trinity College, Cambridge.

Benedictional of St. Aethelwold, BM Add. 49598, folio 25. The Baptism. By courtesy of the Trustees of the British
Museum. Photo: Warburg Institute.

Ivory casket showing the Baptism. By courtesy of the Herzog Anton Ulrich-Museum, Brunswick. Photo: Herzog Anton Ulrich-Museum.

Benedictional of St. Aethelwold, BM Add. 49598, folio 102ᵛ. Death of the Virgin. By courtesy of the Trustees of the British Museum. Photo: Warburg Institute.

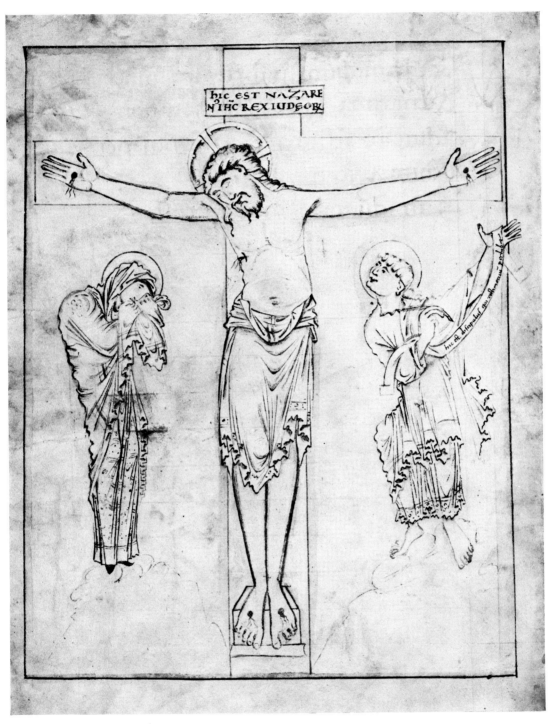

Harley Psalter, BM Harley 2904, folio 3ᵛ. The Crucifixion. By courtesy of the Trustees of the British Museum. Photo: BM.

Benedictional of St. Aethelwold, BM Add. 49598, folio 45ᵛ. The Entry into Jerusalem. By courtesy of the Trustees of the British Museum. Photo: Warburg Institute.

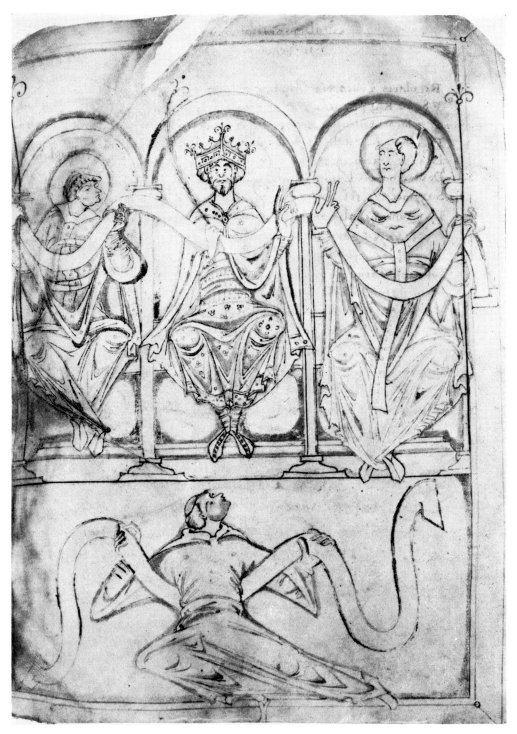

Regularis Concordia, BM Cotton Tiberius A.iii, folio 2ᵛ. Frontispiece: King Edgar, St. Dunstan and St. Aethelwold. By courtesy of the Trustees of the British Museum. Photo: BM.

Benedictional of St. Aethelwold, BM Add. 49598, folio 22ᵛ. Feast of the Circumcision. By courtesy of the Trustees of the British Museum. Photo: Warburg Institute.

replen . ut cum eıſ caeleſtaſ ſpon
ſı thalamum ualeatıſ ıngre
dı . quod ıpſe .

Benedictional of St. Aethelwold, BM Add. 49598, folio 118ᵛ. A bishop blessing (St. Aethelwold?). By courtesy of the Trustees of the British Museum. Photo: Warburg Institute.

a: The Wolverhampton Column. By courtesy of the Trustees of the   *b*: The Wolverhampton Column. Photo: A. F. Kersting.
British Museum. Photo: W. F. Taylor.

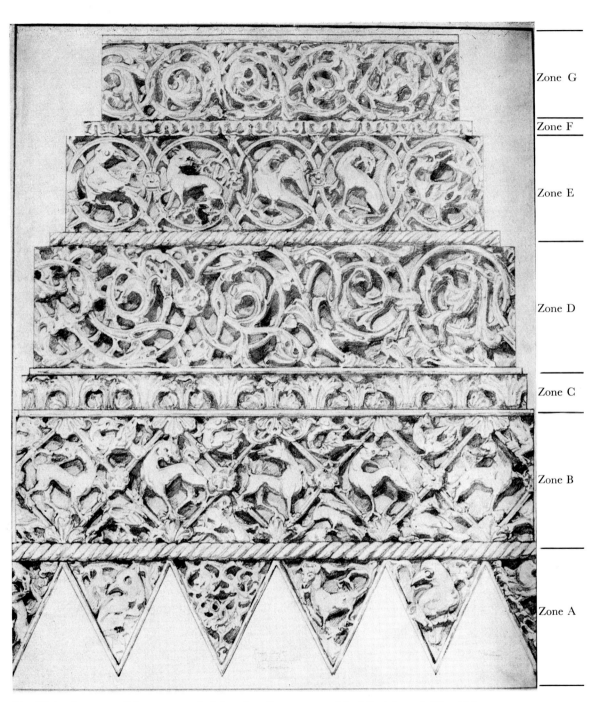

Zone G

Zone F

Zone E

Zone D

Zone C

Zone B

Zone A

The Wolverhampton Column: extended drawing. By courtesy of the Victoria and Albert Museum.

Cross-shaft from East Stour, Dorset. By courtesy of the Trustees of the British Museum. Photos: BM. *left*: East face; *right*: West face.

...e-stone from Hanley Castle, Worcs. By courtesy of the Lechmere Collection. Photos: D. Wright.

a: Trial piece or mould from St. Augustine's Abbey, Canterbury. By courtesy of the Trustees of the British Museum and the Department of the Environment. Photos: BM.

b: Stinsford, Dorset: St. Michael's Church, angel. By courtesy of the Royal Commission on Historical Monuments (England). Photo: RCHM (Eng).

c: Ivory plaque from North Elmham, Norfolk. By courtesy of the Museum of Archaeology and Ethnology, Cambridge. Photo: The Museum of Archaeology and Ethnology, Cambridge.

Melbury Bubb, Dorset: font, formerly cross-shaft. Photos: R. J. Cramp.

a (above left): Melbury Osmond, Dorset: St. Osmond's Church, stone fragment. By courtesy of the Royal Commission on Historical Monuments (England). Photo: RCHM (Eng).

b (top right): Bronze mount from Southampton. By courtesy of Southampton Museum. Photo: BM. (Actual size.)

c (right): Bronze strapend from Winchester. By courtesy of Winchester Excavations Committee. Photo: University College, London. (Actual size.)

a: Gilt-bronze jug. No provenance. By courtesy of the Trustees of the British Museum. Photo: BM. (Actual size.)

b: Bronze censer-cover with inlaid nielloed silver plates, from Canterbury. By courtesy of the Trustees of the British Museum. Photo: BM. (Actual size.)

a (top left): Bronze enamelled brooches: *left* from Bedlington, Northumberland (British Museum); *right* from Hyde Abbey, Winchester (Winchester Cathedral). Photo: BM. (Actual size.)

b (bottom left): Enamelled brooch. No provenance. By courtesy of the Trustees of the British Museum. Photo: BM. (Actual size.)

c (right): Plate from binding of Henry II Gospels. By courtesy of Bayrische Staatsbibliothek, Munich. Photo: Bayrische Staatsbibliothek. (Actual size.)

Chapter 9

THE ROMANESQUE STYLE IN MEDIEVAL DRAMA

by G. W. G. Wickham [1]

Historians of English drama have traced often enough the supposed development of medieval drama from 'sequences' within the liturgy of the Roman Catholic Church in the tenth century into the lengthy Mystery Cycles, Moralities and Saints Plays of city streets and market places in the fifteenth century. Prejudice, however, the product in part of three centuries of Protestantism and in part of a century of scientific humanism, has led many of these historians to view this development (mistakenly as I believe) as a single evolutionary process. Small beginnings have been seen to lead naturally to bigger (and thus better) things. It has been left to scholars during the past two decades to challenge this view and to suggest that the early history of English drama may have to be re-written to encompass at least two traditions of religious drama which were as separate in origin as they were different in their respective purposes and growth.[2]

This suggestion has been carried into practice first by efforts to get behind the smoke-screens of prejudice and look again at the factual evidence, and secondly by attempts to view the surviving facts as manifestations of religious beliefs expressed in artistic forms. An immediate result of this new approach has been the discovery of factors which clearly and sharply differentiate the chanted Latin drama of the liturgy from the spoken vernacular drama of a later epoch: these factors include differences of subject matter and of presentation so large as to warrant division of both into two distinct dramatic genres — liturgical music-drama and vernacular didactic drama. The former, broadly speaking, represents an elucidation and an ornamentation of the existing liturgy by means of art: the latter, equally generalised, represents a deliberate deployment of dramatic art as an aid to the preaching of repentance. The former is a product of monasticism and the latter a product of the friars-preachers. Thus where one may be labelled, for convenience, Romanesque, the other may be labelled Gothic. As in architecture, from which these descriptive terms are borrowed, there is in drama also a recognisable if imprecisely defined transitional style.[3]

In the context of this publication devoted to the celebration of the millennium of *Regularis Concordia* it is my purpose to discuss only the first of these dramatic styles, that which I have labelled the Romanesque; but in doing this I cannot avoid, if only by way of comparison, dropping some hints at least about the ways in which the other two styles differ recognisably from it.

* * *

When we talk about the performance of a play we are automatically, if uncritically, speaking about five things at once. We cannot think of a performance without assuming the existence of a theatre, that is, a stage and auditorium to contain it. We assume imitation of actions in sequence, that is, a story-line. We take for granted some means of identifying person and place, costumes and settings: and we assume the existence of both actors and audience. Let us now apply these concepts to drama contemporary with the *Regularis Concordia* and in the period of some one to two hundred years following its promulgation in the diocese of Winchester; and let us start with the word 'theatre'.

Only one word is used in the original stage-directions of this earliest form of English drama, the Latin *platea*, a word that is surprisingly accurate in its very vagueness. It means the *place*, no more, no less. The only qualifications, assumed but not specified, are that this place should be flat and open enough for actors to move about and be seen. Our own word 'acting-area' is a near equivalent. This concept is of course as appropriate as it is admissable in the context of Byzantine and Romanesque church architecture.

The fact, however, that the *platea* is contained within a church at once endows it with a special quality: it is an integral part of a place of worship. What is done on or in the *platea* will reflect some of this quality; if it does not, it will appear discordant, even offensive. It will absorb this quality of worship not only from the architectural environment, the Church, but also from the people assembled in the church, priests and congregation.

Turning next to the action of the drama we notice that worship itself is a response to instinct, something that we both feel and perceive to be desirable: it is neither an exclusively emotional response nor an exclusively intellectual one. The double-barrelled quality of this response is apparent in the Latin words chosen to describe the function of the *platea* in respect of the stage action. These are *officium, ordo* and, somewhat later, *representatio*.

Officium, or office, simply means a ceremony or rite. The strong ritual quality of any ceremony accords with what we take to be emotionally fitting to the occasion: at the same time we recognise with our intellect the appropriateness of marking the occasion in this way. In Christian terms of reference, Good Friday is a time for sorrow, penance, contrition; Easter is a time for joy and thanksgiving. The Church therefore commemorates the occasion *per se* by reliving the event in a ritual that is calculated to awake as vivid an emotional response to the significance of the event as possible. To this end, dramatic imitation becomes the servant of worship.

What the use of the words *officium* and *ordo* tells us therefore is that this drama was never thought of as some sort of visual aid to Bible reading for illiterate peasants — why, in heavens name, should it be conducted in plain-chant and in Latin if it were? — but as a new dimension to the depth of the emotional response to the event commemorated and thus as an enhancement to its abiding significance.

Nevertheless, hand in hand with the concepts embraced by the words *officium* and *ordo* went consciousness of the fact that re-enactment of the event by means of dramatic imitation involved the use of artifice for a specific purpose. This came to be expressed in the word *representatio*, or representation. Use of this word implies consciousness of both the symbolic purpose and the emblematic, or figurative, means of commemoration through drama.

So much for the *platea* and the environmental atmosphere of worship in which this acting area was centred.

I want to consider next the nature of the actions imitated and the responses which mimicry provides in both actors and spectators. A moment's reflection will show that the sort of dramatic imitation implicit in *representatio* not only looks back to its genesis in *officium* and *ordo* but looks forward to independent existence in its own right: for it soon becomes possible to assess the quality of the imitation as good, bad or indifferent by reference to previous standards. In other words a new element of assessment asserts itself, the ability of the actors to give pleasure through what they are doing: and once this has occurred, drama is no longer simply an artistic extension of a ritual but an entertainment. In short, once we recognise that we have been moved to tears by the skill of the performers or that we have been reduced to laughter by their wit, or by the absurdity of the behaviour imitated, we realise we are being entertained. This transition is faithfully reflected in the early Middle Ages by the shift from the use of the words *officium, ordo* and *representatio* to use of the Latin word *ludus.*

Ludus, in this context, shared the same ambiguity of meaning as it had possessed in Roman times and that is preserved in the German

Spiel, the Anglo-Saxon *pleg* and the English 'play' or 'game'. All these words can be translated to mean 'recreation' or 'entertainment' in a general sense; but each of them can be applied equally appropriately to recreation of either an athletic or a mimetic kind.

Given this ambiguity in the meaning of the words 'game' and 'play', there are at least some common factors in the sense of them in whichever of these two directions they are stretched. Chief among these is the idea of activity, of doing, of a release of energy in which both body and feelings are engaged. Scarcely less important to the sense of the words are the ideas of order and pretence; for the order or structure of the game controls its nature and provides the boundary between the make-believe action and the reality for which it is in some sense a substitute or preparation. For example, tournaments were often violent affairs and could result in the death of a combatant; but they were organised invariably as battle-schools for training in the arts of war, and were never regarded as a form of war itself. Similarly, where the death of the hero at the hands of the villain and his subsequent revival by the doctor is an obligatory scene in the Mummers' Play, both the death and the resurrection of the champion are feigned, not real. Use of the words *ludus, pleg,* 'play' or 'game' therefore to describe any such activities implies frank recognition of a recreational element. Time is needed, however, for the activity to develop sufficiently for these recreational elements to be recognised.

In the tenth century liturgical music-drama had not developed that far: the actions imitated by the clerical performers were not described as a *ludus,* but under the titles of *ordo* or *officium.*

Commemoration of an historical event, the first Easter, the first Christmas, by means of mimetic imitation covers two aspects of the original occasion: the facts and the emotions associated with or arising from the facts. It also involves the provision of suitable techniques to meet these two objectives. In other words the imitation must both narrate the facts and demonstrate their emotional quality. The facts of the Easter story could scarcely be simpler. Three women are looking for a tomb intending to dress the corpse of a friend: they meet an angel who tells them that the corpse has risen from the tomb. The accompanying emotions are equally simple. The women are overcome with grief as they approach the tomb. The angel's news translates this grief into joy. The events of Christmas, Epiphany, Whitsun and so on are equally straightforward.

The means adopted to meet these needs only involved the application of existing rituals to the new forms. Processions, song, symbolic gesture and vestments appropriately geared to the emotion of the occasion had long since been used and codified by the Church; and in dramatic representation of these events nothing more was needed than to apply these audible and visible emblems to each new sequence of actions. It is here that the *Regularis Concordia* becomes so important to the historian of the drama as a document: for the strictly liturgical nature of this early drama is made explicit in its regulations for the proper conduct of the Easter Introit and accompanying tropes:

While the third lesson is being chanted, let four brethren vest themselves. Let one of these, vested in an alb, enter as though to take part in the service, and let him approach the sepulchre without attracting attention and sit there quietly with a palm in his hand. While the third respond is chanted, let the remaining three follow, and let them all, vested in copes, bearing in their hands thuribles with incense, and stepping delicately as those who seek something, approach the sepulchre. These things are done in imitation of the angel sitting in the monument, and the women with spices coming to anoint the body of Jesus. When therefore he who sits there beholds the three approach him like folk lost and seeking something, let him begin in a dulcet voice of medium pitch to sing *'Quem quaeritis . . . ?'* And when he has sung it to the end, let the three reply in unison *'Ihesum Nazarenum'*. So he, *'Non est hic, surrexit sicut praedixerat. Ite, nuntiate quia surrexit a mortuis.'* At the word of bidding let those three turn to the choir and say *'Alleluia! resurrexit Dominus!'* This said, let the one, still sitting there and as if recalling them, recite the anthem *'Venite et videte locum'*. And saying this, let him rise, and lift the veil, and show them the place bare of the cross [*i.e.* the altar cross placed in the sepulchre below the altar on Good Friday] but only the clothes laid there in which the cross was wrapped. And when they have seen this, let them set down the thuribles which they bare in that same sepulchre, and take the cloth and hold it up in the face of the clergy, and as if to demonstrate that the Lord has risen and is no longer wrapped therein, let them sing the anthem *'Surrexit Dominus de sepulchro'*, and lay the cloth upon the altar. When the anthem is done, let the prior, sharing in their gladness at the triumph of our King, in that having vanquished death, He rose again, begin the hymn *'Te Deum laudamus'*. And this begun all the bells shall chime out together.[4]

The importance of these instructions can scarcely be exaggerated: not only do they inform us that the Easter Introit was conceived of as an office and not as a play, but they give us a vivid picture of the style of acting, and the means adopted to identify character and locality in this 'imitation of the angel sitting in the monument, and the women with spices coming to anoint the body of Jesus'. It was clearly intended that the congregation should be confronted with a double image. The Maries are men, not women. They wear copes, not fashionable female attire or historical 'period' dress. The dialogue is in Latin, not English, and is punctuated with anthems and hymns. The climax is the *Te Deum,* the most famous and familiar of Christian hymns of praise and thanksgiving, in which actors and audience participate together. Thus the event of Christ's resurrection is commemorated by re-enactment in the most artificial and formal manner imaginable; yet what is patently a highly ornate ritual from one standpoint is just as patently a dramatic representation of a turning point in Christian history when viewed from another. The dichotomy of this double image within the Easter office and others modelled upon it is carried over into more self-consciously dramatic representations, religious and secular, in the Middle Ages, but with a difference: the latter are not and cannot be described as an *ordo* or 'office' for they have become *ludus,* or 'play' in its sense of mimetic illustration. What then were the implications for the actors, the priest and deacons conducting these liturgical ceremonies in dramatic form?

The primary emotions to be covered did not extend beyond 'sorrow', 'joy', 'fear', 'serenity' and 'rage'. Nevertheless a distinction had to be observed and made between the behaviour of Christian and non-Christian characters. Yet this too was simple. Christians were, *a priori,* serious and therefore good: non-Christians were bad and therefore ridiculous. Impersonators of Christian characters therefore, if true to their cloth, had only to handle emotions ranging between joy and grief. Non-Christians however, or Christians behaving in a non-Christian way, had a wider range of emotions, being normally regarded as angry, fearful, envious, greedy or likely to rejoice in a vicious way. That they were lecherous could be taken for granted. With the possible exception of joy, which could be expressed in a manner thought to be unseemly, the imitation of Christian emotions within the forms of dramatic ritual, *ordo,* did not present a serious problem; but if the solemnity implicit within the ritual of an *officium* or *ordo* had to be sacrificed then only non-Christians could be a party to it. The problem, however, could not end there, for it is within this bad or ridiculous behaviour that the germ of entertainment through laughter reposes. The devil has all the best lines!

The special relationship between the frame of *officium,* therefore, and the imitation of emotion in liturgical music-drama ensured that motivation played no part in the actors' thinking: the characters they represented were stereotyped in advance by the faith and works of the characters. The emotions were pre-set, as it were, even in the matter of degree, together with the appropriate actions indicative of them. Thus respect or reverence could be represented by a bowing of the head, genuflexion, kneeling accompanied by a bowing of the head, or total prostration. For one Christian greeting another, simple inclination of the head would suffice; but a Christian greeting an angel or God himself would just as naturally prostrate himself. This code of conduct did not have to be invented by these early actors. It was taken over wholesale from the existing rituals of the Imperial Court in Byzantium: and as the earlier Roman Emperors had been styled Gods, so the deference and respect accorded in Court protocol to the Christian Emperor seemed appropriate as a code of conduct towards the Pancreator brooding over Christian basilicas.

Conduct unbecoming for Christians in such an environment sufficed, by simple contrast, to indicate the character, actions and emotions of non-Christians. Unlike the serene joy of Christians, their joy would be overstated in fiendish convulsions. No less important, the modesty and humility of the Christian Emperor's behaviour before his own master, God, was contrasted in non-Christian rulers by the adjuncts of tyranny — uncontrolled anger, vain boasting and general ostentation expressed in the Latin stage-direction *pompabit*.

However, just as it is a relatively small step to equate bad conduct with ridiculous or absurd conduct, so only a small further step is needed for absurd or ridiculous conduct to become comic. In other words the impersonation of non-Christian characters carried with it a risk that the means adopted to represent them would come to possess an entertainment value: and any actor knows that if an audience responds warmly to the manner in which he executes an action this carries with it an automatic temptation to repeat or enlarge this same device.

In this way the entertainment value of non-Christian characters and non-Christian emotions became an embarrassment to the begetters of liturgical music-drama, and doubly so when the impersonators are themselves clerics. Thus it is this lack of seemliness, or appropriateness, and not drama *per se* which gives rise to ecclesiastical doubts and protests in the early Middle Ages, since this indecorum is clearly at odds with the solemnity of the ritual form and with the occasion which the ritual exists to illuminate. Similar discordant notes may be seen both in the elaboration of polyphonic music and in the number and quality of the visual aids required to identify character and place. The expression of non-Christian emotions encourages the use of music drawn from secular sources, while the need to distinguish one disciple from another or to identify Old Testament characters, as in the *Play of Daniel,* encourages some degree of visual realism.

The awareness within the Church of the incursions made by these discordant elements upon the gravity of the original *ordo* or *officium* is apparent in the adoption of the word *ludus* as an alternative. The word is used to distinguish these more developed, commemorative impersonations where entertainment, however appropriate to the occasion, came near to destroying the original emotional purpose of the ritual: *Ordo Prophetarum* is one thing, *Ludus Danielis* quite another.

These changes obliged the Church to rethink its attitude to the representation of biblical history in drama. It is thus the major concern of what we may term 'the transitional style' to deal with two problems: first, where non-Christian characters and emotions were concerned, to try to distinguish between the malignant and the absurd, and secondly to try to endow Christian characters with a dramatic vitality to match that of their enemies by injecting a greater degree of realism and motivation into actions that were serious and good. The solutions to these problems inform the Gothic style. They were effected gradually and were the product of direct borrowing from secular traditions of dramatic entertainment via clerical minstrelsy as much as of changes within the thinking and personnel of the ecclesiastical hierarchy itself, and of attitudes to Christ as God and Man.

The primary feature of the Gothic style is the frank recognition of a recreational element — diverting, pleasurable and instructive — in dramatic representation, implicit in the words *ludus,* 'game' and 'play'.

Ordo and *officium,* in the sense of ritual, survive as a frame on which the new *ludi* are structured; but the rituals used were no longer strictly liturgical. They could be derived from the occasion, the subject, or both, and there was inevitably some degree of cross-fertilisation between them all.

Chapter 10

FELIX URBS WINTHONIA: WINCHESTER IN THE AGE OF MONASTIC REFORM

by Martin Biddle

By the year 1000 Winchester was the principal seat of the English kings and contained the greatest complex of ecclesiastical buildings in the country. To discover how this had come about, and why, and what it implies, we must look back to the reign of Alfred, and behind that to the period when Anglo-Saxon *Uintancaestir* was emerging from Roman *Venta Belgarum*.

Roman and Saxon Winchester

In the later fourth century, when *Venta Belgarum* was still a function-ing, and perhaps even a flourishing, Roman town, its defences were strengthened by the addition of bastions to the city wall, possibly as part of the general reconstruction of Britain undertaken by Count Theodosius in 369.[1] Such bastions were apparently designed to mount *ballistae,* a complex form of artillery which would have required a specialist force for its maintenance and use.[2] The presence of such a force is suggested by the discovery at several points within the walls of distinctive kinds of late Roman belt-fittings which are now recog-nised both in this country and on the Continent as military equipment.[3] This evidence is greatly strenghened by a series of graves found at Lankhills in the northern cemetery of the Roman town in which the dead were buried with belts, knives, and brooches which can be closely paralleled in military graves of the second half of the fourth and early fifth century on the Continent.[4] The rite of burial is paralleled most closely in southern Germany,[5] and in the current state of research it is to this region that we must look for the origin of the defence force of Winchester in the second half of the fourth century. These troops were accompanied by their women, as the female graves of this kind show quite clearly, and they must have been brought in by the official Roman administration while the provinces of Britain were still part of the empire.

This first appearance of alien elements in the late Roman *civitas* was soon followed by a further implantation of barbarian people from another area of Germany, and under quite different auspices. Pottery of continental Saxon character and dating from the early fifth century has been found in Winchester at Lower Brook Street and at Southgate.[6] This kind of pottery is normally found in pagan Anglo-Saxon cemeteries and has recently been the subject of an extensive study by Dr J. N. L. Myres.[7] Although its discovery in towns is still unusual, it has been found in Canterbury,[8] at Dorcehster on Thames,[9] at Portchester (a fort),[10] and now at Winchester, to name only places on or south of the Thames. The date of this pottery is so early in the fifth century that it seems that it must belong to a phase when Germanic peoples were being settled in or close to towns to act as defence forces in return for grants of land and direct payment.[11] The pottery from Winchester can be closely paralleled in the latest settlement of the Feddersen Wierde, on the right bank of the Weser estuary, north of Bremerhaven,[12] and is evidence that Germanic people from the Saxon homelands were already present in the city in the early decades of the fifth century.[13]

By the early fifth century Winchester thus contained a mixed population, with at least two phases of Germanic settlement imposed on the Romano-British community: an earlier phase in which people from south Germany were brought over under imperial control, and a later phase when people from north Germany were employed by the British rulers of the independent post-Roman province, or were perhaps engaged directly by the surviving administration of *Venta Belgarum*. Before we can say that the origins of Wessex lie in this period rather than a hundred years later, as the *Anglo-Saxon Chronicle* would seem to suggest, there must be reasonable evidence for continuity between the Germanic mercenaries of the early fifth century, and the settlers of the early sixth. This problem can be approached in two ways: by assembling physical evidence for the presence of Germanic people in the area throughout the fifth century, or at least by a date substantially earlier than the traditional dates for the settlement of Wessex given by the Chronicle; and by arguing back from the situation in Winchester in the seventh century in an attempt to explain the presence there of a royal church founded about 650 and shortly after to become a cathedral.

Although the pagan Saxon cemeteries so far known in Hampshire are few in number compared with areas to the north and east, there are several immediately outside the walls of Winchester.[14] Two of these were certainly in use in the sixth century, while a third at King's Worthy, about three miles north of the city, began before 500.[15]

The gap between the fifth-century Anglo-Saxon finds from the city and the beginning of the King's Worthy cemetery may not be more than about sixty years. Furthermore the concentration of pagan Saxon cemeteries around Winchester suggests that the site of the former Roman city was still a focus of some significance in the sixth century, at least a hundred years before the establishment of the first church within the walls.

The Old Minster was built by Cenwalh of Wessex in 648 and dedicated to SS Peter and Paul.[16] Although a royal foundation, it was not at first the seat of a bishop, and did not become a cathedral until the transference of the see from Dorchester on Thames in the 660s.[17] This fact seems of particular importance, for it is necessary to seek some explanation of the presence of the church within the walls of the Roman town at this early date. From Cenwalh onwards the kings of Wessex were usually buried in the Old Minster and some at least were crowned there.[18] Furthermore the site of the royal palace, for which there is direct evidence from the later tenth century, lay immediately west of the church. If the evidence of the sixth-century cemeteries around the city can be taken as indicating a focus of interest in the former urban area, it may not be unreasonable to suggest that this interest was centered upon a royal estate within the walls, and that the Old Minster was founded to serve as a palace church. The origins of an Anglo-Saxon royal presence in the city would on this argument date from at least the sixth century. It may not be too fanciful to wonder if they do not in fact go back even further, to a period when the Germanic mercenaries employed for the defence of the late Roman town took over control and lordship of the land from the failing administration of the Roman *civitas*. [19] This is not a matter of mere speculation: the site of the royal palace is immediately adjacent to the Roman forum, and may partly overlie the south end of the basilica, the administrative centre and chief public building of the Roman town. The excavation of this site could be expected to provide clear evidence of the correctness or otherwise of these suggestions.

By the second half of the seventh century, it may thus be argued, Winchester was the residence of both king and bishop; in two centuries the antique town had yielded to the medieval order. The new community was in no sense urban, and the greater part of the old walled area appears to have been quite unoccupied, for the extensive excavations of 1961-71, and over twenty years of smaller excavation and constant recording, have failed to produce evidence of occupation in the period between the middle of the fifth and the latter part of the seventh century. For something approaching quarter of a millenium

Fig. 6, p.137

see pp. 132-3

much of the town lay deserted. This is not indeed evidence that the town was entirely unoccupied, for the areas where observation has been possible are not large compared with the whole town, and are moreover unevenly distributed, so that there are many places where no observation has been possible at all. The relative lack of finds of the fifth, sixth, and seventh centuries is however evidence that there was little activity within the walls away from the suggested site of the early palace, where there has been no excavation or opportunity for observation in modern times.

Settlement may thus have been continuous only in this very limited part of the walled area, and with the special character of a royal estate. In the mid-seventh century the occupied area was increased by the creation of a second enclosure for the church and the community which served it, and towards the end of that century there is evidence for a third component in the form of an unknown number of private estates, lesser reflections of the two great enclosures for king and church.

A small estate including at least one stone building among its otherwise timber structures, and with evidence of the assaying and working of gold, was found at Lower Brook Street in 1971.[20] The earliest element, dating to the second half of the seventh century, was a small cemetery of probably Christian character in which one of the burials included an elaborate necklace of gold-and-garnet pendants and silver rings. Occupation continued through the eighth and ninth centuries until the area was completely altered by the laying out of the new street pattern late in Alfred's reign. There is so far no archaeological evidence for other estates of this kind within the walls, but the second element of the name *Coitburi,* attached to an area just within east gate, may indicate the existence of at least one other enclosure of this type.[21] It seems likely, however, that there were never many of these estates, since had this been the case many more objects of the eighth and ninth centuries would have been found in excavations or as chance finds throughout the city.

This then was the nature of Winchester for another two hundred years: from the middle of the seventh century until late in the reign of Alfred, it was a settlement of dual character, a royal and ecclesiastical centre with a limited number of private estates, but with no trace of the intensive occupation, market economy, or industrial production, which are necessary for urban status. In this it stood in stark contrast to Hamwih, Saxon Southampton.[22] The two settlements seem to have been complementary, the one the old ceremonial centre, seat of the bishop and perhaps the principal residence of an itinerant king; the other the focus of trade and industry for early Wessex. This contrast is reflected in the contemporary terminology, Winchester was *urbs* or *civitas*, Southampton, *mercimonium* or *wic*. [23]

The renewal of urban Winchester

Late in the reign of Alfred the defences of Winchester were refurbished as part of a general reorganisation and fortification of the burhs of Wessex. The work is unlikely to have begun before 880 and was probably completed by 892, or possibly in some cases, including Winchester, before 886 when Alfred was involved in the restoration of London, on the borders of his kingdom. [24] As an integral part of their new defences, most of larger and some of the smaller burhs were provided with rectilinear street systems which seem to reflect the organisation and apportionment of the enclosed land for permanent settlement. If this view is correct, these regular street plans must reflect a deliberate policy of urban formation in response to the Danish attacks: military effectiveness was to be based on economic viability and a permanent population. [25]

It was precisely because Winchester was not densely built up at this time, that the laying out of a comprehensive new street system was possible. If the situation had been otherwise, the difficulties of cutting across a complex of existing rights and boundaries would probably have made so thorough-going a reorganisation impracticable. As it was, the only important route within the walls seems to have been High Street, and it was around this axis that the new system was fashioned. South of High Street there were existing complexes which had to be considered, notably the Old Minster and the palace, but both were still small enough to be incorporated into the *insulae* of the new system without apparent difficulty. The original boundaries of the New Minster site show quite clearly that the new street pattern did originally cover even the south-eastern quarter of the city, where its course was to be completely obscured during the tenth century by the growth of monastic precincts and palace enclosures. [26]

Fig.3, p.129

The expansion of the royal and ecclesiastical complexes in this area of the city began soon after the establishment of the street pattern. By the early years of Edward the Elder's reign two new monasteries had been founded in this area, the New Minster and the Nunnaminster. Although both houses were formally founded by Edward, steps towards their foundation seem in each case to have been undertaken before Alfred's death in 899. Very little is known of the origins of Nunnaminster, later St Mary's Abbey. It appears to have been established on an urban estate belonging to Ealhswith, Alfred's queen,[27] and it seems likely that the royal couple were jointly involved in the moves leading to its foundation.[28] As an important nunnery it seems unnecessary to seek beyond an act of royal piety for the reason for its foundation.

Much greater uncertainty surrounds the foundation of New Minster, for the obvious course would have been to rebuild and extend the already existing church of the Old Minster, which was by this time two hundred and fifty years old, a cathedral, and the hallowed resting place of many kings and bishops. Instead a new and entirely separate monastery was created on the north side of Old Minster, the new

Fig.4, p.130 church lying only four metres away from the older building which continued in uninterrupted use. Excavations between 1962 and 1969 showed that the Old Minster church was not enlarged at this time, but remained as originally built, a small aisleless structure, which was by now filled, not to say cluttered, with internal fittings.[29] The New Minster church was over twice as large and of a quite different type, with a nave and aisles capable of accommodating a considerable congregation.

It is impossible to separate the origins of New Minster from some consideration of St Grimbald, but this is not the place to offer more than a summary account of a most complex matter.[30] Grimbald seems to have arrived in England c.886-7 and, pending his appointment to a bishopric, to have been established temporarily by Alfred in a *monasteriolum* in Winchester.[31] This *monasteriolum* can probably be identified with the wooden church and stone dormitory belonging to Old Minster which formed part of the land obtained by Edward the Elder for the foundation of New Minster. If correct, this would mean that Grimbald had been accommodated by Alfred in a temporary residence set up on land belonging to Old Minster. There is no indication that there was any initial intention of turning this residence into a permanent monastery, although this idea seems to have arisen before Alfred's death in 899, perhaps after Grimbald's supposed refusal of the archbishopric of Canterbury in 889.[32]

In the two years between 899 and his death in 901 Grimbald encouraged Edward to proceed with the foundation of a new monastery in accordance with Alfred's wishes. The actual foundation took place after Grimbald's death on 8 July 901, for he did not witness any of the three surviving grants of land made to New Minster in that year, something which would have been inconceivable had he still been alive.[33]

The foundation of the monastery must of course be carefully distinguished from the construction and dedication of the church itself.

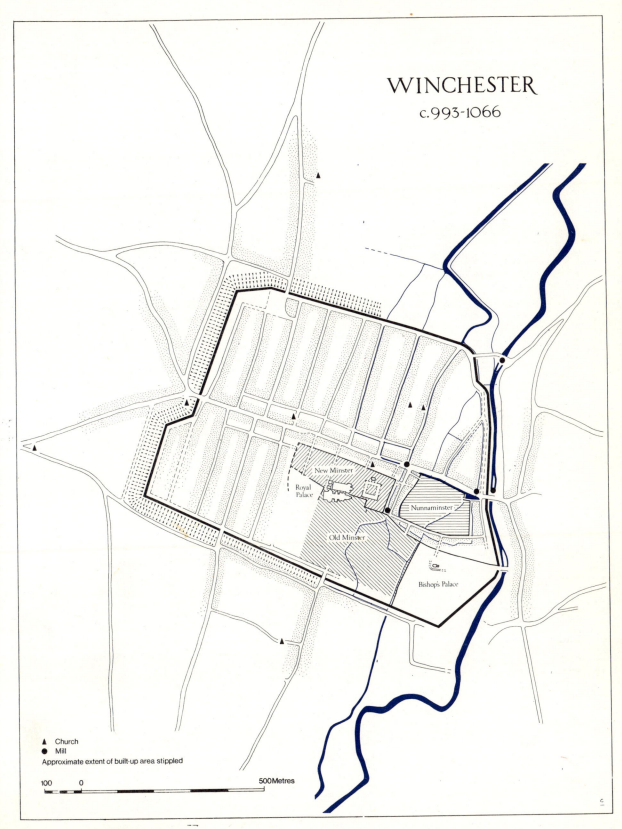

WINCHESTER
c.993-1066

New Minster

Royal
Palace

Nunnaminster

Old Minster

Bishop's Palace

▲ Church
● Mill
Approximate extent of built-up area stippled

100   0   500 Metres

Fig. 3.   Late Saxon Winchester

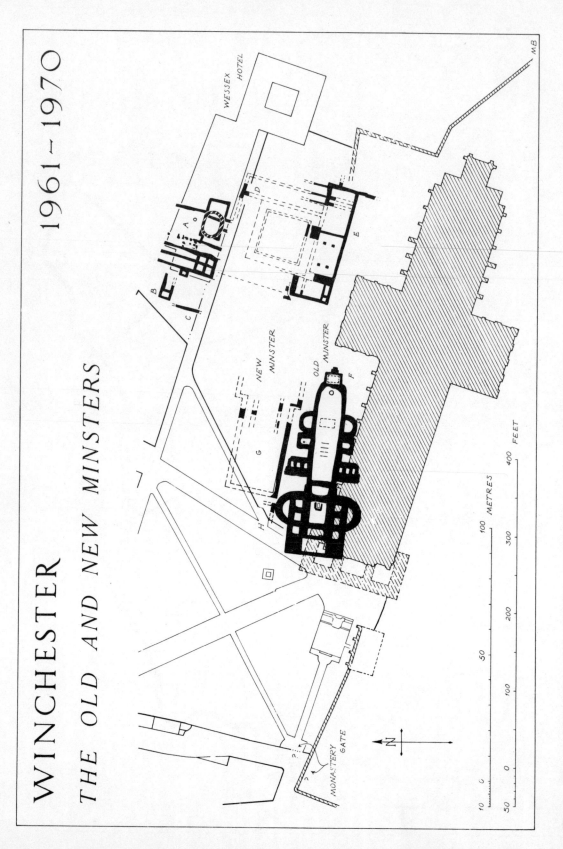

Fig. 4. The sites of the Old and New Minsters as revealed by the excavations of 1961-70

This dedication seems to have taken place in 903, the work of building having lasted two years,[34] and was the occasion for the granting of a formal foundation charter, and for the public acknowledgment by the *witan* of the steps taken to acquire the site.[35] It was probably at this time or very shortly afterwards that Alfred's body was translated into the New Minster from his original grave in the Old Minster.[36]

Although this outline reconciles the confused and frequently distorted accounts of the foundation of New Minster, and clarifies the part played by Grimbald, it does not explain why the new foundation was thought necessary. The explanations that have so far been put forward are either fanciful or inconsistent with the known facts; that it was to be primarily a seat of learning, or a royal burial church, or that it was founded by Alfred for Grimbald. The physical contrast between the actual structures of the Old and New Minster churches at this time may however suggest a more reasonable possibility. The New Minster was a large church, suitable for considerable congregations; Old Minster was small, and crowded with internal fittings. The New Minster was used from the first for burials inside the church; inside Old Minster there were very few burials, and these of the highest rank. The citizens of Winchester enjoyed the right of burial in New Minster and its cemetery, free of the control which the Old Minster appears to have exercised elsewhere in the city.[37] These facts suggest a close relationship between the New Minster and the people of Winchester, and it is possible that the real reason for the new foundation was that it should serve as the burh church of the replanned city. Old Minster was perhaps too ancient and too venerated for the complete rebuilding and change of character and function that would have been necessary.

The original boundaries of the New Minster site were defined by the streets of the rectilinear system that had been laid out about twenty years before. Already by c.901-3, when Edward the Elder was acquiring the site, land-prices were high and much of it had to be obtained from those who were *circummanentibus iure hereditatis*.[38] Further evidence for the economic success of the refounded city comes only in the 960s, when it is clear that the central area was densely populated,[39] or in the 990s with the first occurrence of street-names which indicate that distinctive industrial processes had already left their mark on various parts of the town.[40] There is one other source of evidence: the first coins bearing the Winchester mint-signature appear only at the very end of Alfred's reign.[41] It now seems likely that these were the first pennies struck in the city, and that the unsigned coins of Beorhtric, Ecgbeorht and Aethelwulf previously attributed to Winchester were in fact minted at Southampton.[42]

After an interval of over four hundred years, Winchester was once again an urban community. Refurbished defences, new streets, a mint, a market, and the foundations of economic viability and even prosperity can all be traced to this period late in the reign of Alfred, beginning in the years between 880 and 892.[43] The success of this policy was already apparent early in the following reign, when Edward the Elder completed his father's wishes by the creation of New Minster and Nunnaminster. It was in this setting of a diverse and burgeoning urban community, that the path of monastic reform was to be found and followed.

Winchester in the age of reform

Fig.3, p.129

The period with which we are now concerned is that of the episcopates of Aethelwold (963-84) and Aelfheah (984-1005). We must once again concentrate on the south-eastern quarter of the city, and on the three great monasteries, which were the immediate setting for the events of reform movement in Winchester, but this must be prefaced by some account of the city itself, and of the royal and episcopal palaces, as they were in the second half of the tenth century.

Documentary evidence for the development of urban life in Winchester does not become relatively plentiful before the twelfth century, but all the indications that survive point to a steady intensification of urban conditions and activities from the early tenth century onwards. The action taken by Edgar in the 960s and 970s to secure the privacy of the three minsters shows that they were already lapped by a rising tide of urban life, and although phrases such as *a civium tumultu remoti* may reflect a monastic bias heightened by the fervour of reform, it is clear that secular dwellings had to be removed, boundaries extended, and walls and fences erected, to ensure a reasonable degree of peace and solitude.[44] It is against this background of a developing city that the growth of the royal and ecclesiastical quarter must be set.[45]

see p.125

The early history of the Winchester palace is very obscure, although its existence from a very early date, as argued above, seems required to explain the apparent focal character of Winchester from at least the sixth century onwards. A hint of the royal house's interest in the city is provided in the mid-ninth century by a grant of land made to Bishop Swithun in 854 for the expenses of distinguished foreign visitors,[46] but it is not until the later tenth century that the palace (*de palatio regis, in obsequio regis*) is specifically referred to for the first time.[47]

The site of the palace lay immediately west of the Old Minster, in the area east of Little Minster Street, and south of the New Minster cemetery. This is made clear by the extension of the site northwards for the construction of William the Conqueror's hall about 1070.[48] The Anglo-Saxon palace thus lay within forty metres of the seventh-century church and in the immediate vicinity of the west-work added to the Old Minster in 971-80.[49] Nothing at all is known of the plan of the palace, or of the buildings which composed it, although it seems likely that these will have included a chapel and perhaps a treasury, possibly combined in one and the same building.[50]

The bishop's palace lay in the south-east corner of the walled area and from at least the early thirteenth century was known as Wolvesey.[51] Until the excavations of 1963-71 there was no indication that the palace was of pre-Conquest origin, but there is now ample evidence that it was in existence by the latter part of the tenth century.[52] The greater part of the early palace seems to have lain north of the Norman complex, where its remains must have been extensively destroyed by the digging of a later moat. An east-west arrangement of timber and stone buildings forming the southernmost range of the pre-Conquest palace was however preserved below the north range of the Norman palace, and was excavated in 1963-8. The early range was bounded to the south by a drainage ditch, and consisted of a double-apsed chapel with a rectangular eastern addition, extended *Fig.5, p.135* further east by a line of timber structures.[53]

Documentary evidence throws very little light on the origin of the bishop's palace, even now that the reality of a pre-Conquest phase has been established by other means. The archaeological evidence points to the episcopate of Aethelwold as the time when the palace was first built. In some part of the 970s Aethelwold was living in the royal palace.[54] Between 975 and 979 he enclosed the south-eastern part of the Old Minster precinct with a wall which probably ran on the line which still today forms the boundary between Wolvesey and the cathedral close.[55] The formation of the palace precinct should date from this moment, which agrees with the date derived from archaeological evidence for the first phase of the buildings. The earliest specific reference to the bishop's house (*in domo episcopi*) occurs in the Winchester Annal for 1042, but it is impossible to be sure that this statement is not influenced by the conditions of the twelfth or thirteenth century when the Annals as we have them were composed.[56] The first unequivocal reference to the palace does not occur until 1138.[57]

The evidence suggests that the physical separation of the bishop's household from the community of the Old Minster belongs precisely to

the period of the reform movement in Winchester, and that it should be
seen as part of the series of actions by which Aethelwold secured
privacy and seclusion for the great monasteries of the city.[58] The
bishop himself seems to have moved first to the royal palace, perhaps as
early as 963-4 and to have remained there until the 970s, when he built
his own residence at Wolvesey, in an area deliberately set off from the
cathedral monastery by the construction of a new boundary wall.

It is now time to consider the three great monasteries of Winchester,
the Old Minster, the New Minster and the Nunnaminster, and to
examine the changes brought about in their structures and grounds by
the attitudes and requirements of reform.

The Nunnaminster was refounded by Aethelwold early in 964, at
Fig.3, p.129   about the same time as the reformation of New Minster.[59] Nothing
else is known of how this house fared under reform, except that it
shared in the general adjustment, enlargement, and enclosure of the
lands of all three monasteries by which Aethelwold sought to reduce
disputes and to provide a more secluded setting for their reformed
monastic life.[60]

During the first part of the tenth century New Minster was the
principal burying place of the English royal house, including Alfred,
Ealhswith, Edward the Elder, and other members of their family.[61]
This practice ceased with the death of Athelstan who was buried at
Malmesbury in 939. In addition to these royal tombs, New Minster was
also notable for its relics, at this date principally those of St Judoc and
Grimbald.[62] The monastery was reformed by Aethelwold early in
964, and placed under Aethelgar, who was brought from Abingdon as
the new abbot. The original site provided by Edward the Elder was
enlarged to the west, north and east,[63] boundary disputes with the
Old Minster and Nunnaminster were settled,[64] and the conventual
buildings (*omnia monastici ordinis domicilia*) were restored.[65] Two
years later in 966 Edgar issued to New Minster the famous 'Golden
Frontispiece   Charter', virtually a charter of refoundation, which clearly reflects (cap.
xii) not only the efforts of Aethelwold to secure the privacy of the
monasteries, but also the reconstruction of the monastic buildings on
more regular lines.[66] Among these buildings, most of which lay
north of the New Minster church, there is mentioned the infirmary
Fig.4, p.130   (*domo infirmorum*) which may perhaps be identified with the first
stage of the claustral building found east of the church in 1970.[67]

More striking, but perhaps less the result of reform than of monastic
emulation, was the great tower added to New Minster at the expense of
King Aethelred between 979-80 and 988. The tower seems to have been
built at the west end of the church, perhaps before the west front.[68]

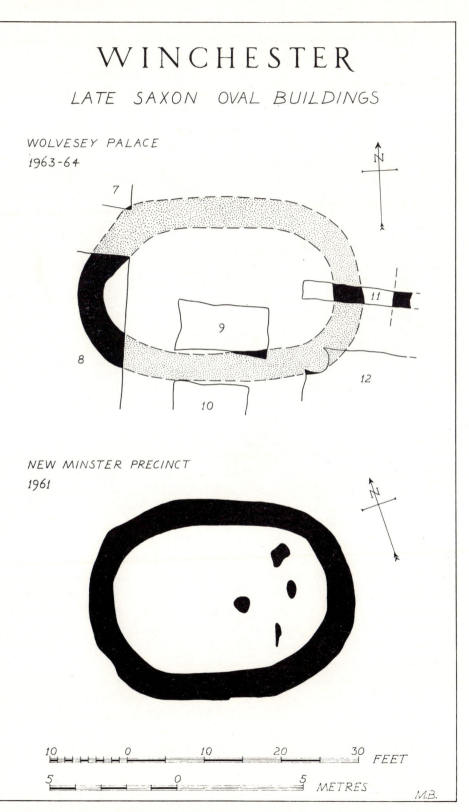

WINCHESTER

LATE SAXON OVAL BUILDINGS

WOLVESEY PALACE
1963-64

N

7

9

11

8

12

10

NEW MINSTER PRECINCT
1961

N

10   0   10   20   30   FEET

5   0   5   METRES

M.B.

Fig. 5.   Late Saxon chapels in Winchester: the Wolvesey building represents the earliest form of the chapel in the bishop's palace, *c.* 980; the New Minster building is a cemetery chapel, possibly that dedicated to St. Michael the Archangel (see Turner, *op. cit.* in note 50, p. 68)

It is described at length in a notoriously obscure passage of the *Liber Vitae,* analysed in detail by the late Roger Quirk.[69] His conclusions suggest a tower of six storeys embellished with external carving and sculpture throughout its height, the decorations at each level apparently corresponding to the dedication of each storey. The west-work of the Old Minster was dedicated in 980, and it seems hard to avoid the conclusion that the construction of the New Minster tower, standing only twenty metres from the west-work, was undertaken in a spirit of ostentatious competition with the new buildings of the older community.

see pp.39-42

The church in which about ten years earlier *Regularis Concordia* had been agreed would not have aroused such a reaction among the monks of New Minster, for at that time Old Minster was by far the smaller church, and had remained virtually unaltered since its foundation more than three centuries before. Its interior was further constricted by a series of altars and monuments, and an unknown number of tombs.[70] Externally it was surrounded on all sides by a cemetery, the most important graves lying before the west door.[71] It was here that Bishop Swithun had been buried in 862, his grave marked by a tomb structure (*sacellum, tugurium*) that still existed in 971.[72]

Fig.6, opposite

The Old Minster was reformed by Aethelwold on 21 February 964, the first Saturday in Lent, in a memorable confrontation between the clerks and the monks who had been brought from Abingdon to replace them.[73] During the following years it took part in Aethelwold's general reorganisation of the monastic precincts, gaining some land from New Minster, and a considerable extension eastwards from private lands, the whole being surrounded by a new boundary wall.[74] The monastery was rebuilt, and provided with a water system;[75] as with the New Minster this rebuilding was probably made necessary by the introduction of regular monks in the place of secular canons.

Fig.6, opposite

Plate IIa

On 15 July 971 Swithun was translated from his original grave into the church, and on 2 October, possibly three years later in 974, he was translated a second time and his remains placed in two shrines, one attached to the high altar and another kept in the sacristy.[76] It was probably during this period that the reconstruction of the Old Minster church began. The first plan was to build over the cemetery west of the old church, linking the west end to the detached tower of St Martin to the west. The new building was centred upon the site of St Swithun's original burial, the importance of which was emphasised by flanking apses of immense size to north and south.[77] It seems clear that this structure was intended to be a shrine-church or *martyrium,* but it is doubtful if it was ever finished, for the building dedicated at the west

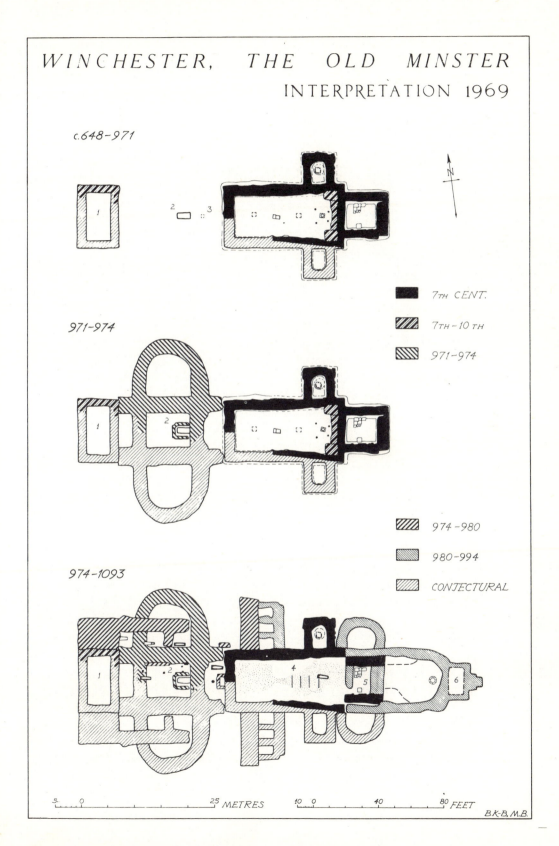

Fig. 6.   The development of the Old Minster, *c.* 648-1093

end of the church in 980 was of a quite different character. Mr Roger Quirk suggested that the written descriptions of this building by Lantfred and Wulfstan implied a west-work comparable perhaps to the
see pp.146-52
west-works at Corvey on the Weser or Werden on the Ruhr.[78] This is precisely what the excavation of the west end of the Old Minster in
Fig.6, p.137
1966-69 revealed.[79] By a skilful adaptation of the two apses, and by massive additions to the north and south of St Martin's tower, the rectangular plan of a large west-work very much of the Werden pattern was produced. The scale was immense: the new west-work was about twenty-three metres square and seems likely to have risen to a height of more than thirty-five metres.

Such was the structure dedicated in 980.[80] It would have provided an axial entrance to the church and a raised western choir, a suitable
see pp.118-120
setting for choirs taking part in the Easter liturgy.[81] It was moreover centred upon the site of St Swithun's original grave, over which a
Plate IIb
monument had now been raised on the axis of the church.[82] The connection between west-works, the tombs of saints, and the cult of relics, well known on the Continent,[83] seems clearly reflected here, not least in the circumstance that this west-work had emerged from an adaptation of an earlier and apparently unfinished *martyrium*. There is, lastly, the question of the relationship between west-works and the ruling house, for it is a striking feature of Corvey that there is provision for the seat of a ruler at second-floor level, commanding a comprehensive view of the church.[84] At Winchester such a connection with the ruler is particularly appropriate, for the west-work stood immedi-
Fig.3, p.129
ately opposite the royal palace, and was part of a church which for three hundred years had been closely associated with the house of Wessex. Royal burials had apparently taken place in the cemetery underlying the west-work, while after its construction some of the most important burials of the late Saxon period seem to have taken place within it, rather than elsewhere in the building.[85] Construction cannot have begun before July 971, for St Swithun's grave was in the open at the time of his translation. The design may have been changed about the time of the saint's second translation in (?) 974, and must have been altered early enough for the completion of this very large project by the time of the dedication of the rebuilt west end in 980. It seems possible that the inception of so grand a scheme, closely connected with the royal house, may have been the work of Edgar (d. 975), who 'showed by his impressive coronation ceremony at Bath in 973 that he grasped the political value of external magnificence'.[86]

The reconstruction of the Old Minster continued after 980 with the rebuilding and extension of the east end, which was dedicated in

993-4.[87] A long eastern arm terminating in an apse was constructed beyond the original east end, which was itself converted into a crypt below the new high altar, and flanked to north and south by apses reminiscent on a smaller scale of the great apses originally intended to flank St Swithun's tomb in the unfinished first stage of the west-work. A second crypt was built outside the new eastern apse, and a five-storey tower was erected, possibly over the high altar, but conceivably as the final adornment of the west-work.[88]

Fig. 6, p.137

The most distinctive part of this arrangement was the length of the eastern arm, which ended in an external crypt, probably reached from within the apse near an altar dedicated to St Mary. It is clear that this eastern arm could now have provided a proper setting for the bishop's throne and the monastic community, but it is by no means certain that it did serve this function. It could also have been occupied by important tombs in stone coffins which would have left no trace if laid on or into the stone paving, all but one slab of which was removed in the demolition.[89] It is too early to attempt a definitive answer to these questions, while the results of the excavations of 1962-69 are still being evaluated, but it must be clear that the Old Minster was rebuilt in the years between 971 and 994 in a manner which suited the needs of the reformed monastery, and provided a suitable setting both for the liturgy as set out in *Regularis Concordia* and for the accommodation of the large numbers of pilgrims now congregating at St Swithun's tomb and relics.[90]

The Old Minster was by this time a large church, some eighty metres in length, and entered through a west-work that must have been one of the greatest architectural achievements of the Old English kingdom, yet it was still only one element in the great complex of monasteries and palaces which filled the south-eastern quarter of Winchester. Between 963 and 975 Edgar ordered that fences or walls should be erected to separate the three monasteries from the rush and disorder of the town.[91] Within this framework the three communities followed a way of life that had been profoundly altered both inwardly and externally by the reform of their houses in 964. Even the setting of their daily lives had been changed, their churches rebuilt or enlarged, and their convent buildings regularised to conform with the requirements of a rule that had itself been promulgated in the most ancient of their churches.

Fig. 4, p.130

Fig. 3, p.129

L'an mil

In the year 1000 Winchester was an astonishingly diverse and complex community, filling a walled area of fifty-eight and one fifth hectares and already beginning to extend into suburbs beyond the gates. Urban conditions had long been dominant, and by the end of the tenth century covered a wide range of industrial and trading activities. As the principal seat of the kings first of Wessex and later of England it enjoyed a tradition reaching back into, and perhaps even beyond, the faintly discerned days of settlement in the fifth and sixth centuries; for was it not believed by the monks of Old Minster that Cerdic lay buried in their church, which was itself founded on the temples of Dagon and Apollo?[92]

The three great monasteries of the city had grown from a single stock, the Old Minster founded by Cenwalh in the middle of the seventh century. Onto this at a time of national revival another king had grafted two new foundations, and now the three houses together, pruned and blossoming afresh, secure in their new life, and under the tutelage of saints, were the principal adornment of the city of Swithun:

> *Gratuletur et exultet felix urbs Winthonia*
> *Que virtute tanti patris meritisque rutilat*
> *Cuius sacra fovet ossa sentit et miracula*
> *Incessanter illi plaudat odas cum letitia.* [93]

Chapter 11

TENTH-CENTURY CHURCH BUILDING IN
ENGLAND AND ON THE CONTINENT

by H. M. Taylor

Introduction

The purpose of this study is not to give a comprehensive list of
buildings of the tenth century but rather to consider only a few, with
special reference to the uses to which the different parts of the
buildings were put. The lack of comprehensive contemporary records
about the nature of the services makes for difficulty in this task; and
there is always the danger of falling into error by interpreting buildings
of this early date in terms of the uses to which corresponding features
are put in the services of the present day. But for some continental
churches there are detailed records of early liturgical use, and therefore
the first part of this essay has been devoted to a study of three
continental buildings which seem to give help in interpreting the
English examples.

In selecting a small number of English churches for study it seemed
natural to include two with which St Dunstan was closely associated,
namely Glastonbury abbey and the cathedral church at Canterbury.
The Old Minster at Winchester is excluded because it is fully treated by
Mr Biddle elsewhere in this volume. St Augustine's abbey in Canterbury *see Chap. 10*
is included as being possibly the only foundation in which the regular
monastic life survived unbroken through the general decline during the
Danish invasions. The choice of St Mary's church at Deerhurst may
seem less obvious; but it was included in order to have one English
example of a building which still stands above ground, to a height of
several storeys, in sufficient detail to justify reliable assertions about its
state and use during the monastic revival.

Shortage of space precludes any comprehensive discussion of the
typology of transepts, but the classification and brief notes in Fig.7 *p.143*
may serve to fill this gap, and to excuse the omission from this
essay of the great transeptal churches of Stow and Norton which belong
to the first type shown in the figure.

The continental evidence
Gernrode
The abbey church of St Cyriac at Gernrode near Magdeburg in the Harz Mountains is particularly appropriate for study because its date of foundation is known with certainty, in the period of the monastic revival in England; and also because it has survived with remarkably little change from its original form. The church was founded by Count Gero, a friend of Otto the Great, and although it was not completed at the time of Gero's death in 965 it was far enough advanced to allow of his burial before one of its altars.[1] Its first abbess was Gero's daughter-in-law.

The original west entrance of the church and a west gallery above it were destroyed in the twelfth century to make way for the present western apse, and about the same time low galleries were built above the arms of the transepts. The north wall of the north aisle was largely rebuilt when the church was restored in 1858-9, and the western stair towers were completely rebuilt between 1907 and 1910.

p.144
p.145
The original state of the church is shown in Fig.8 and the present state in Fig.9. The features which call for special mention are the west gallery A which disappeared in the reconstructions of the twelfth century, the lateral galleries D which have survived unchanged, and the lower transeptal galleries G which were inserted in the twelfth century. These later transeptal galleries have stone floors carried on ribbed vaults whereas the original galleries have wooden floors.

There is good historical evidence to show that in the many early German abbeys for canonesses it was common practice to provide lateral galleries for the ladies while the abbess had a separate place, probably here represented by the western gallery.[2] The later provision of galleries over the arms of the transepts seems to have been undertaken to bring the canonesses nearer to the service which was conducted by their priest in the sanctuary. Unlike most churches of monks and nuns the churches of the canonesses made special provision for parish services.[3]

Centula: St Riquier
In 799 Angilbert, friend of Charlemagne, completed at Centula, near Abbeville, an abbey on a scale that was not to be surpassed in France until the great foundations of the twelfth century. The golden age of this splendid establishment was brought to an end by the Norman onslaughts in 881, but Angilbert's great church seems to have survived with little material change until reconstructed in the developed Romanesque style under Abbot Gervin II (1075-96). Successive later rebuildings have left a stately Gothic church which seems out of place

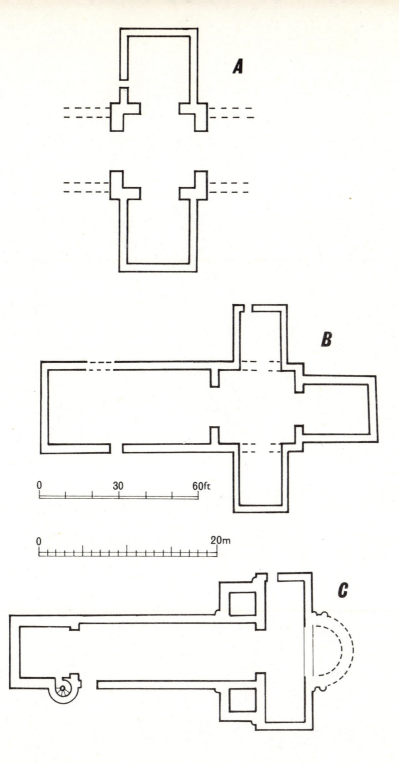

Typology of transepts in pre-Conquest England

he noblest example of Type A is at Stow in Lincolnshire, here illustrated. The characteristic feature is that the central
is wider than any of the four arms, and the type seems to be peculiar to England. At Stow all four arches are preserved,
the same height and width, thus indicating that all four arms were approximately of the same height. The transepts
ve complete but the nave and chancel were replaced in the Norman period.

he plan here shown to illustrate Type B is that of Dover, Kent. This type, with transepts appreciably lower than the
occurs widely both on the continent and in England. The central space is the same width as the nave. Sometimes the
al space carries a tower but this is not always the case in England and even less frequently on the continent.

he continuous transept of Type C is early Christian in origin, but it had revivals in Carolingian and Ottonian Europe.
only examples so far known in England are at Peterborough and North Elmham, probably both dating from the latter
d. The latter, here illustrated, is almost complete in plan, whereas the remains of the former are fragmentary.

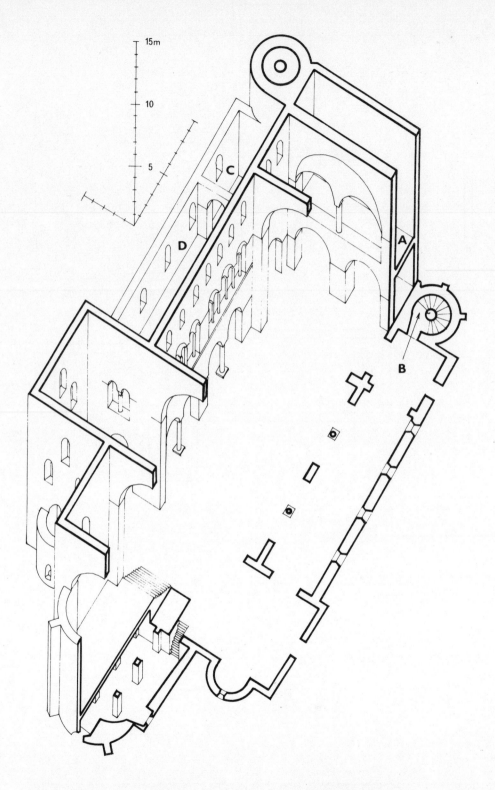

Fig. 8. *Gernrode: Isometric reconstruction of the church as built*
The west gallery A as shown here has entirely disappeared but is reconstructed
from evidence provided by the side walls and stair turrets. The northern half of
the building has been cut away in the diagram to show more clearly the spiral
stairs B, the south gallery D and the connecting chamber C. Note also the
continuous transept, and the stone-vaulted crypt beneath the apsidal sanctuary.

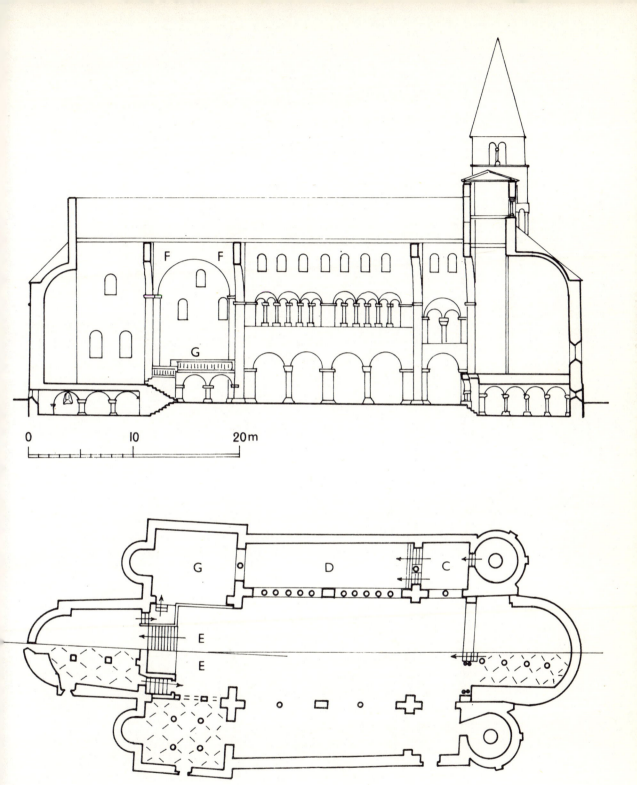

Gernrode: Section and plan of the church as it now is

both plan and section the west is to the right for easier comparison with the reconstruction in Fig. 8. It will be ted how the west gallery has been replaced by a western apse and crypt, how galleries G have been built in the ansepts, and how transverse arches F now divide the arms of the transepts from the central space E. In the plan the uthern half shows the details at the level of gallery and apses, while the northern half shows the details at the level the main floor and crypts.

in the present small township of St Riquier. But, although the Carolingian church and abbey have vanished, their general form can be reconstructed from early records; and a study of the church is of particular importance because the records specify the nature of the services and the position of altars and other fittings.

Three separate sources give us this information: the first is the *Chronicon Centulensae* written at the abbey by a monk named Hariulf, who left Centula in 1105 to become abbot of Oudenberg where he died in 1143;[4] the second is a *Life of Angilbert* by another monk named Anscher, who in 1096 became abbot of Centula;[5] and the third, now in the Vatican Library, is a copy by an unknown scribe of a record of Angilbert's works at Centula and of the order of services which he instituted there.[6] The only known early manuscript of Hariulf's *Chronicon* perished by fire at the abbey in 1719, but not before substantial parts had been copied and published,[7] including a drawing of the abbey.[8] Anscher's life of Angilbert seems largely to have been taken from Hariulf's chronicle, but it gives one further interesting detail to which reference is made below. The Vatican manuscript is in close agreement with related passages in the copies that were published from Hariulf's chronicle before it was destroyed by fire.[9]

Fig. 10, opposite

Much work has been done on the problem of reconstructing the layout of the Carolingian church from the text and picture in Hariulf's chronicle, and in recent years our knowledge has been further advanced by excavations on the site of one of the smaller churches shown in the picture. For our purpose it must suffice to describe the results in outline, and to refer the reader to the published works for confirmatory evidence and fuller detail.[10]

Fig. 10, opposite

It is clear from Hariulf's chronicle that the church had very much the appearance indicated in his drawing and also that the transeptal western area was covered by a great gallery which was itself overlooked by upper galleries on the north, west, and south, all of which were reached by spiral stairs. This great western gallery was virtually a separate church with its own altar and its own name *ecclesia Sancti Salvatoris*. It could accommodate three hundred monks and a hundred boys and there was still space for men and women of the village at certain special services. It has generally been assumed that this western gallery-church was carried on stone vaulting such as has survived on a smaller scale in the later church at Corvey and such as is indicated for the large Carolingian cathedral of Reims by foundations discovered there by excavation in 1927.[11] On entering the west doors one passed under this gallery and so into the main church known as *ecclesia Sancti*

Fig. 10. *St Riquier: The churches about the close of the 11th century*
This drawing, copied from the frontispiece of P. Petau's *De Nithardo* (1613), is here reproduced by kind permission of the Trustees of the British Museum. It was copied by Petau, or at his order, from the miniature in Hariulf's manuscript. The dress of the figures seems to belong to Petau's date rather than Hariulf's; but the churches correspond to the buildings described by Hariulf.

Richarii. Hariulf's text also described two other churches, dedicated to St Mary and St Benedict, both of which are shown in the drawing, connected to the main church by covered ways like those of a medieval cloister. But modern study has shown that the drawing is only schematic in this respect and that the three churches lay much further apart than the drawing indicates, while the covered ways were like town *opposite* walls enclosing a substantial built-up area.[12] As is indicated in Fig.11 excavations begun in 1960 have located the church of St Mary about three hundred yards from the main church; and, although the church of St Benedict has vanished, Hariulf's drawing shows it beside the stream where surviving place names give added confirmation. It is therefore possible to say with certainty that the cloister-like enclosure shown in the drawing was indeed the very large walled area shown in Fig.11. Moreover the chronicle describes passages of two storeys along these walls, for use by the monks in bad weather when going in procession from one church to another, whereas in good weather they walked along the intervening streets.

Angilbert's orders of services provided for such processions twice daily, and for regular services in all three churches. Moreover they allow us to settle with considerable certainty the placing of the eleven altars in the main church, while Anscher's *Life of Angilbert* specifies the nature of four liturgical stations which are referred to in the services. These stations, known respectively as the Nativity, Passion, Resurrection, and Ascension, are described by Anscher as:

> of wonderful workmanship, made of plaster and gold,
> beautifully set with mosaics and other precious colours.[13]

p.150 Fig.12 shows the placing of the four liturgical stations and the eleven altars in accordance with the latest study.

The chronicle also makes clear the great size of the church and the elaboration of ritual. There were three choirs each of a hundred monks, and a choir of a hundred boys sometimes singing as a unit and sometimes divided between the three choirs of monks. The three monks' choirs each had its special place in the church: the Choir of the Saviour in the western gallery, the Choir before the Passion in the eastern part of the nave like the choir stalls in many later medieval cathedrals, and the Choir of St Richar with its place in the sanctuary.[14]

In providing in this lavish way for monastic services, Angilbert did not overlook provision for the people living nearby and attached to the abbey. There were five special chapels for their use elsewhere in the monastic city,[15] and in addition they had access to the ground floor of the great western church, indeed it was in a special way marked out

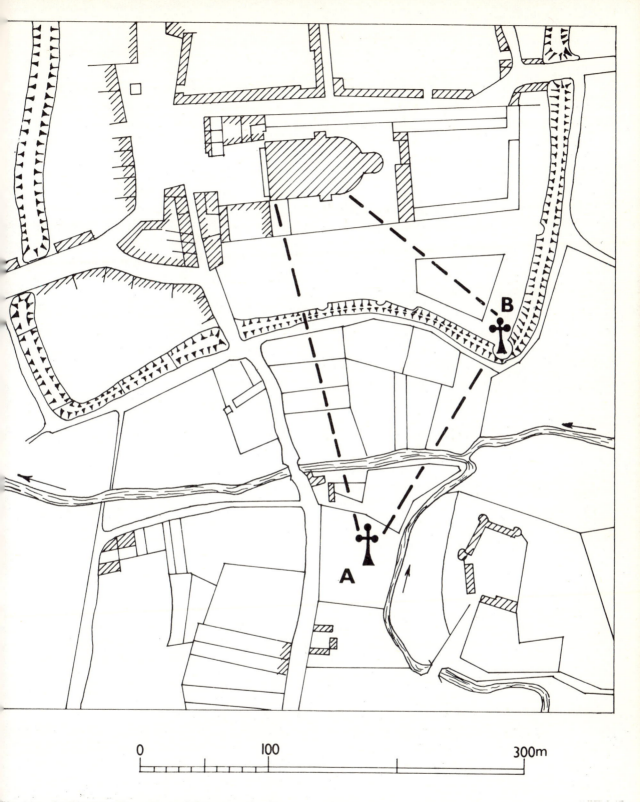

Fig. 11. *St Riquier: The extent of the monastic city*

This drawing is based upon an early 19th-century plan published by Durand in 1911. In the original, the field here marked A carries the caption *Emplacement de l'église Notre Dame en 1790*. According to Hubert (see n.10), the bastion B in the town walls and a fountain nearby both still carry the name St Benedict. Excavations begun in 1960 have disclosed in the field A foundations which seem certainly to belong to the circular sanctuary of St Mary's church as illustrated and described by Hariulf; and thus the 9th-century monastic city walls are reliably indicated as having enclosed the very extensive area shown in this plan by the heavy broken lines.

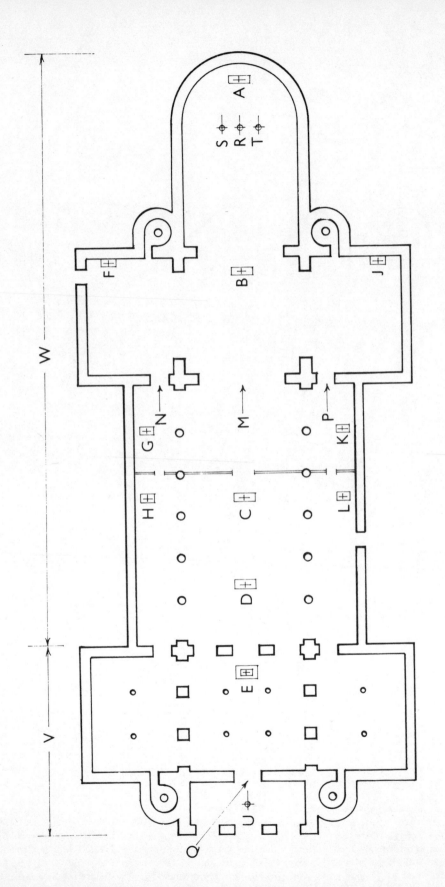

Fig. 12. *St Riquier: Altars, stations, and burial of saints*
The plan shows the division of the church into two components: the western gallery-church, V, known as *ecclesia Sancti Salvatoris*; and the nave, transepts, and sanctuary, W, known as *ecclesia Sancti Richarii*. The layout of altars and stations is that derived by Lehmann, and is in substantial agreement with that given by Hubert (see n.10).
Altars: A, St Richar; B, St Peter; C, Holy Cross; D, St Denis; E, Holy Saviour (*in the gallery*); F, St John; G, St Stephen; H, St Quintin; J, St Martin; K, St Laurence; L, St Maurice.
Stations: M, Passion; N, Resurrection; P, Ascension; Q, Nativity.
Burial of Saints: R, Richar; S, Frigor; T, Caidoc; U, Angilbert.

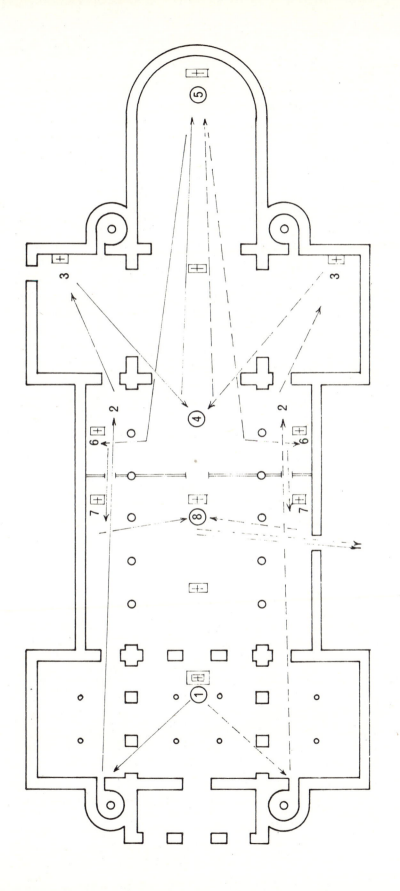

Fig. 13. *St. Riquier: One of the daily circuits of prayer and praise*

Even in the incomplete form in which they have survived, Angilbert's statutes provide for two different circuits. The one here illustrated starts with all the monks assembled at the altar of the Saviour in the western gallery. After the completion of prayer and praise there, the monks divided into two separate groups whose progress is shown separately by full lines and broken lines. It will be noticed how the groups progressed separately to the altars and stations in the aisles (shown by simple numbers), and how from time to time they re-assembled as a unit at altars and stations along the axis of the church (shown by numbers enclosed in circles). The route here shown was worked out in detail by Lehmann.

as their parish church since it contained the baptismal font.[16]
Moreover at the special Easter services the public, both men and
women, were admitted to the great western gallery-church for the mass
which was celebrated at the altar of the Saviour, and the statutes made
provision at the end of the service for the elements to be taken down
the turret stairs to be served on the ground floor to those members of
the public who had not been able to come up into the gallery.[17]

Angilbert's statutes not only made provision for special services on
the great feast days but also specified a daily circuit of prayers which
involved movement of the whole body of monks from altar to altar,
sometimes as a single body, and sometimes divided into two groups of
which one visited altars on the south side of the church while the other
visited those on the north. In addition to prayers at the several altars,
the circuit made provision for visits to three of the special sculptured
stations to which reference has been made above, namely the Passion,
Resurrection, and Ascension.[18] Diagrammatical representations of
p.151   these processional routes are shown in Fig.13. The station of the
Nativity at the main west doors of the church did not enter into the
daily circuit of prayers but was used for prayer at the beginning and
end of the special Easter processions which went from the main church
to neighbouring villages on several days from Easter to Ascension.[19]

These matters have been described here in some detail to put beyond
doubt the remarkable size of the great gallery-church of the Holy
Saviour, and also to indicate the rich provision of altars and stations
which gave the setting for prayer and praise in services which moved
round the whole of the interior of the church in accordance with a well
ordered plan.

Corvey on the Weser

Our final continental example, at Corvey, lies roughly midway in time
and space between the two previous churches. This abbey was founded
in 822 under patronage from Louis the Pious and was dedicated to St
Stephen. At first its church seems to have had essentially the form of a
great mission hall, with most of the space available for the laity, and
only a small sanctuary reserved for the monks. This church was
damaged by lightning in 870 and was thereafter given a much more
ambitious form. The small sanctuary which had not been damaged was
retained without change, but much more space was provided for a
greatly increased number of monks by enlarging the transepts and
crossing. Moreover a great new western church was provided on an
upper floor, on the general pattern of Centula but on a smaller scale.
This gallery-church was dedicated to St Vitus, and it still survives

almost intact although the earlier basilical church to the east was swept away at the close of the sixteenth century.[20]

The 'westwork', or western church of St Vitus, is referred to in contemporary writings as *tres turres*; and, although only the two western towers have survived, it is easy to visualise the larger eastern tower which formerly stood above the surviving gallery-church. All three towers are shown in the reconstruction, where it will be noted that the floor of the gallery-church is a stone vault carried on massive piers and lighter columns. Of the upper galleries to the west, north, and south, only the western has survived, but there is clear evidence for the others. As at Centula, these were used for choirs; and it is of special interest to note that a series of marks found in the original plaster of the western range during recent works of restoration have been interpreted as a musical score for the boys' choir.[21] Fig.14 shows the church as it must have been about 885 and indicates the division into the eastern church of St Stephen and the western gallery-church of St Vitus. It also shows how in the western church there were three special places for the choirs, known as *chorus angelicus, chorus supremus* and *chorus infimus*.[22] There were two more positions in the eastern church, known as *chorus superior* and *chorus inferior*; and, although no contemporary record of services has survived like that at Centula, the historian Letzner, writing about 1604, gave examples of the movement of three choirs between the five stations mentioned above, and of the antiphonal singing during these services of movement.[23]

Fig.14, p.155

The English evidence

By contrast with the continental evidence which is so richly supported both by standing buildings and by contemporary records, the English evidence may appear somewhat disappointing in completeness; but when the two groups are taken together each serves to improve our understanding of the other.

St Augustine's Abbey at Canterbury

It is tantalising that for the period of the monastic revival there appears to be an almost complete gap in historical records of the buildings of St Augustine's abbey. For the foundation period in the seventh century the principal church of St Peter and St Paul is perhaps the best documented Anglo-Saxon building for which we have substantial remains; and there are also fairly full and almost contemporary records of the alterations which were made by Abbot Wulfric (1047-59). But there is no contemporary account for the additions which on stylistic grounds are commonly dated to the tenth century and have accordingly been associated with a late record of a rededication of the church by Archbishop Dunstan in the year 978.[24] These alterations comprised the adding of a narthex to the west of the original church, with a vestibule still further west.

It is, however, of importance to note that throughout the active period of the monastic revival in the latter part of the tenth century the layout of the buildings at St Augustine's continued in the primitive form of a number of comparatively small churches on a single alignment, and that it was not until the middle of the eleventh century that Abbot Wulfric began his ambitious project of joining two of these together with his circular crypt and ambulatory.[25]

It is also interesting to note that in the general loss of the regular monastic life during the Danish invasions there seems to be a real possibility that at St Augustine's rather than anywhere else the regular life persisted unbroken.[26] During excavations in the 1930s in the area of the Norman cloister, remains of a domestic building were found that seemed to date from a period before the layout of a rectangular claustral plan, as well as substantial parts of a rectangular claustral building of pre-Norman date.[27] Unfortunately the interpretation of these excavations has recently been called into question and there is an urgent need for further work on the site to confirm the plan and dating.[28]

The Cathedral Church of Christ at Canterbury

In default of excavation beneath the present cathedral church at Canterbury we have no structural evidence for the pre-Conquest church which was destroyed by fire in 1067 and entirely rebuilt by Archbishop Lanfranc. But it is possible to form some sort of picture of the building from the description given of it in words by Archbishop Anselm's secretary and biographer, the monk Eadmer, who was a child at the time of its destruction and was shortly thereafter a pupil at the cathedral school. Any attempt to turn Eadmer's description into a detailed plan and elevation is fraught with risk because of the differences in the use of words over a period of nine centuries and also because medieval writers often drew comparisons where we should see little resemblance.[29] The difficulties inherent in this problem are shown by the divergent views recently expressed in four essays about the Anglo-Saxon church at Canterbury, and it seems best at this stage to record here only some very general observations and to leave readers to consult the original works.[30] The following brief summary of

Fig.15, p.156   Eadmer's words in translation, and the schematic layout, may serve to illustrate the cathedral church in the form specified by Eadmer without introducing subjective interpretation of his words in a way that can lead to controversy:

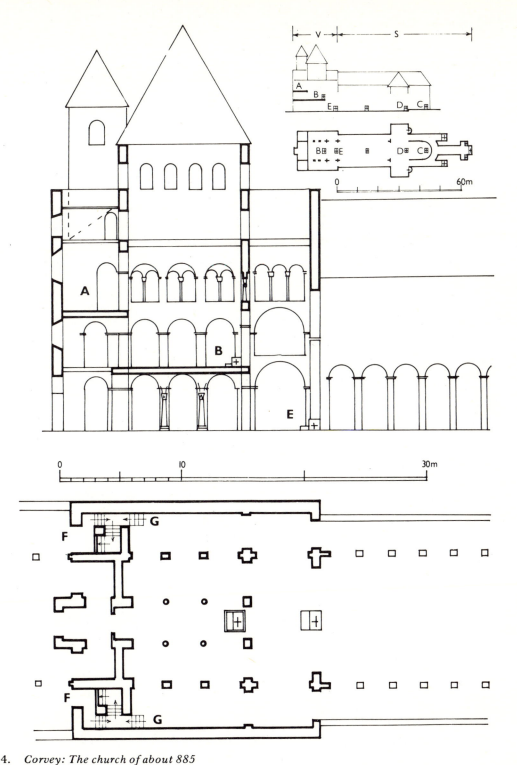

Fig. 14. *Corvey: The church of about 885*

The main drawing shows the western gallery-church of St Vitus as it must have been about 885. The great central tower has disappeared but the main gallery B survives intact as does the west gallery A, as well as the two stair turrets, much of the outer walling, and the west transept E. The inset shows the whole church of about 885, as established by recent excavation. As at St Riquier it was divided into two components, here known as the church of St Vitus, V; and the church of St Stephen, S. The five positions of choirs described by Letzner are indicated: A, *chorus angelicus*; B, *chorus supremus*; C, *chorus superior*; D, *chorus inferior*; E, *chorus infimus*. The stairs up to the gallery-church and its upper galleries can be entered from the atrium by the doors F or from the church by the doors G.

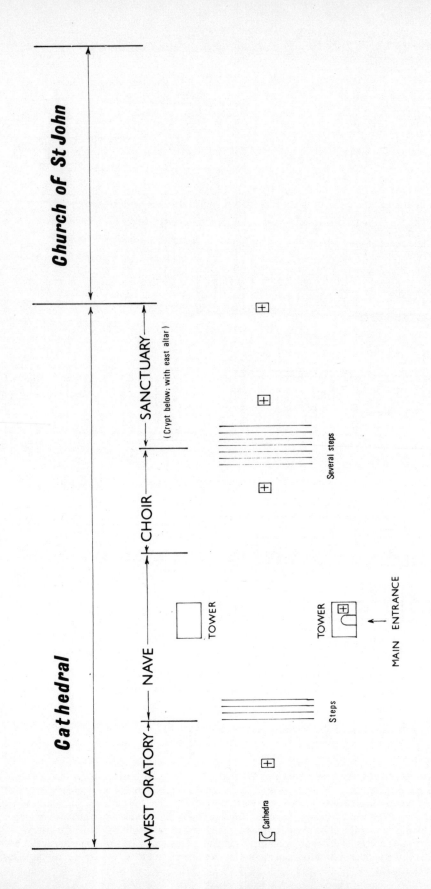

Fig. 15. *Canterbury Cathedral: Schematic layout about 1066*
This diagram is an attempt to represent objectively Eadmer's description of the pre-Conquest church.

At the extreme west in an oratory dedicated to the Virgin Mary and reached by steps from the nave, the archbishop's stone chair stood against the west wall. This oratory had an altar at the east, where the priest celebrating mass stood facing east toward the people standing below. About the centre of the church were two towers, in one of which on the south was the main entrance to the church and also an altar in honour of St Gregory, while the one on the north was built in honour of St Martin. Eastward was the enclosed choir of singers and in it was the matutinal altar close to the steps that led up to the sanctuary. St Dunstan's burial place was before these steps and deep underground. In the sanctuary were two altars, one of which was close to the east wall while the other, dedicated to our Saviour, stood some distance in front. Below the sanctuary was a crypt which had an altar at the east. Almost touching the great church, and to its east, was another church built by Archbishop Cuthbert in honour of St John the Baptist, for baptisms, for certain trials, and for the burial of the archbishops.

It will be seen that while the reconstruction in Fig.15 has eliminated most of the grounds of disagreement between recent writers it has also produced a picture which gives little precision. It may be best to admit that precision cannot yet be attained, but it seems worth while to spend a moment on two features which are the subject of disagreement.

opposite

(a) *The western oratory.* There is nothing in the texts to imply that the western oratory was apsidal, and the many instances of western galleries now known in Anglo-Saxon churches naturally make it attractive to think that this was the form of the oratory. But two of Eadmer's observations seem to give a strong indication in a different sense. In the first place Eadmer says that the main entry to the church was through the south tower, whereas all other examples of west galleries are associated with a principal entry from the west.[31] Secondly, Eadmer says that the priest celebrating mass faced east toward the people standing below, and this seems strongly to suggest that they were taking part in the service in a way that would hardly be possible if the priest stood in a gallery above their heads. It should be noted that at Centula the order of service made provision for lay people, both men and women, to receive the sacrament in the gallery-church when mass was celebrated there. If it be assumed that at Canterbury the priest celebrating mass would have similar direct access to people attending the service then Eadmer's words would not suit a western gallery. The western porch which survives at Barnack with a stone seat in its western wall and aumbries in the north and south may give a clue to the arrangement at Canterbury if we assume such a porch with a few steps leading down into the nave.[32]

(b) *The separate church of St John the Baptist.* Criticism has been raised against my suggestion that this baptistery-mortuary church stood directly east of the sanctuary of the cathedral church, connected to it by covered ways laid out like an atrium.[33] Dr Gilbert says that 'baptisteries were rarely or never placed immediately east of the sanctuary of the church' and that 'it would be difficult to give one example'.[34] In putting forward this suggestion in 1969 I had particularly in mind not only that this church was a baptistery but also that it was designed from the outset as the burial place of the archbishops, and that therefore there would be good reason to place it close to the sanctuary so that the archbishops would lie buried near the place where they had celebrated mass. But the position is by no means as unusual as Gilbert suggests. To this day the Lateran baptistery stands close to the sanctuary of St John in the Lateran, connected to the ends of the aisles of the church by just such atrium-like passages as were shown in my figure; and in the churches of Tripolitania ranging in date from the fourth to the sixth century, out of eleven baptisteries recovered, four were found directly behind the sanctuary, connected to the ends of the aisles by similar passages.[35]

Glastonbury

Shortage of space precludes discussion of the historical evidence for the early buildings at Glastonbury, and only a brief account can be given of the results of many years of excavation.[36] In Fig.16 the Anglo-Saxon *opposite* walls which have been recovered are shown by continuous lines, while broken lines are used to indicate the nave and cloister of the much larger and later medieval abbey. The following details are particularly worthy of mention here:

(a) There is no possibility of recovering any trace of the early wattled church which is known to have stood within the area S now occupied by the ruined Norman Lady Chapel. The large late medieval crypt beneath this chapel has removed all evidence of earlier structures.

(b) To the east, and partly overlaid by the medieval nave are the foundations of an extensive church whose walls are indicated as of three different dates by the use of differently coloured mortars. The western part A, B, X consists of a nave with narrow flanking *porticus,* and this part is interpreted as the church known to have been built by King Ine in 688. To the east of this a chancel C is of later work which cannot be associated with any historical record. Still further east, the thick walls of the central part of D suggest the foundations of the tower built by St Dunstan; while the wide lateral chambers E, F on either side

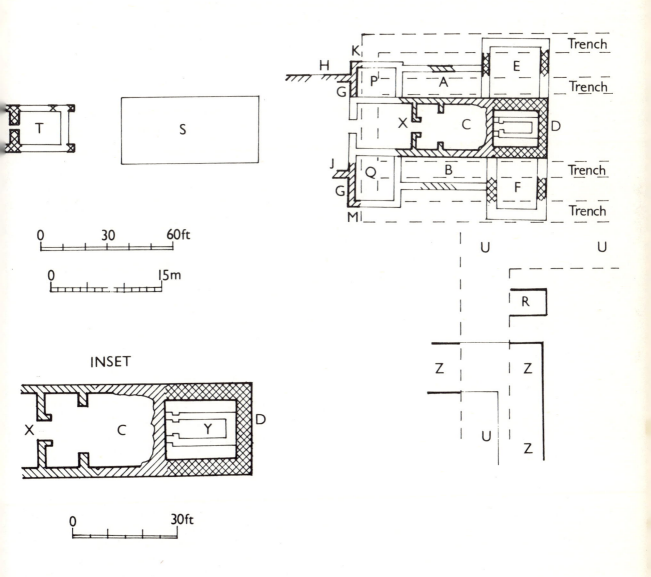

Fig. 16. *Glastonbury: Excavations in the abbey ruins*
The grids of broken lines marked *Trench* show the foundations of the main walls and arcades of the medieval church, thus indicating where the later builders have destroyed all evidence of Anglo-Saxon fabric.

A, B, Lateral porticus flanking King Ine's nave; C, later chancel; D, St Dunstan's tower; E, F, lateral porticus of St Dunstan's church; G, west wall of shortly after King Ine's time; H, J, westward extension; K, M, eastward turn of west walls, serving to define width of church shortly after King Ine's time; P, Q, lateral porticus shortly after King Ine; R, wattled chapel in cemetery of Dunstan's time; S, Lady Chapel of about 1186 enclosing site of Old Church; T, Dunstan's western church of St John; U, medieval cloister; X, King Ine's nave; Y, early burial chamber enclosed within and destroyed by Dunstan's tower (shown in inset at larger scale); Z, pre-Norman cloister.

would represent the *porticus* which he added to make a square plan.

(c) Beneath Dunstan's tower Peers, Clapham and Horne found in 1928 an interesting, much earlier, chamber Y which they compared to the hypogeum at Poitiers.[37] It seemed to have been a burial chamber, originally outside the earlier east end of the church, and later incorporated within it by St Dunstan in a way for which there are parallels elsewhere in Britain and on the Continent.[38]

(d) To the west of the late Norman Lady Chapel traces were found of a square church T with pilaster-buttresses at its corners. Peers and Clapham identified this as the church which Dunstan built and dedicated to St John.

(e) In the excavations of the seasons 1951-55 to the south of the church, the Anglo-Saxon burial ground was found, and within it a series of post-holes defining a wattled building R which was interpreted as a chapel for which there is no historical evidence.

(f) These seasons also yielded fragmentary remains of the walls and walks of a pre-Norman cloister Z whose east wall was aligned with the east wall of the church of Dunstan's period. It will be noticed that this cloister was separated from the church by the extent of the burial ground.

In summary it can be said that the buildings at Glastonbury during and after the monastic revival seem to have consisted, like those of St Augustine's abbey at Canterbury, of a family of smallish churches rather than a large abbey church like that at Centula or Corvey. Moreover, again like St Augustine's, the family of churches was laid out along a single axis; and there was also evidence of a rectangular complex of domestic buildings round an open cloister.

St Mary's Priory Church, Deerhurst

St Mary's church at Deerhurst differs from all the English sites which have so far been under consideration in this essay in that, instead of a ruin, the fabric there preserved is almost the complete main body of an Anglo-Saxon church which remained in monastic use down to the Dissolution, and has thereafter served as the parish church until the present day.

Unfortunately there is still disagreement about the detailed association of recorded history with the surviving fabric; but I believe there would be little dissent from the view that the fabric as it stands today contains the greater part of the church which was in use during the monastic revival. Some would claim that it was built during that revival; while others, including myself, believe that much of it is older and was adapted during the revival so as to serve more efficiently the new needs of that time.

The historical evidence for Deerhurst so far as it is relevant for our purpose may be summarised as follows:

(a) A religious body was in being there in 804 when a nobleman of the Hwicce, Aethelric, son of Aethelmund, gave lands to this *congregatio* on condition that his body be buried there and that the community 'carry out their vows as they have promised'.[39]

(b) Edward the Confessor granted the church of Deerhurst to the abbey of St Denis, and this grant (made about 1060) was confirmed by William I in 1069.[40]

(c) St Alfheah was a monk at Deerhurst before moving to Bath about 970.[41]

None of this historical evidence serves to establish the date of any part of the surviving buildings, but on stylistic evidence the main fabric of the church can confidently be claimed as Anglo-Saxon. Further study of the fabric may before long settle the question whether substantial parts go back to the date of Aethelric's charter or even earlier; but even in our present state of knowledge we can assert that there are few, if any, other buildings in England which survive so completely in the state in which they formed an integral part of the monastic revival. Moreover we know from Aethelric's charter that a monastery existed on the site in 804 even if we cannot yet say what parts of the building belong to that period.[42]

The buildings at Deerhurst have often been described in detail,[43] and we may therefore confine attention to the features that are of particular relevance to our study of liturgical use. Figs.17 and 18 show the principal features and record most of the problems; these may be summarised thus:

pp.164-5

(a) The ruined polygonal sanctuary stood on a foundation of stilted semicircular plan. One panel of the south wall stands almost complete, along with enough of the adjoining panel to settle the polygonal (not curved) form of the upper walls. It is not at present agreed whether this sanctuary is the first which stood on the foundation; and the sharp drop of ground-level from that of the nave raises a question whether there was some form of crypt beneath the sanctuary.[44]

(b) Eastern side-chambers to north and south of the apse are now in ruins. Of the southern chamber only the foundation of the eastern wall remains; but for the northern chamber there is a similar foundation as well as much of the body of the north wall.

(c) A great round-headed arch (now blocked) formerly connected the choir and the sanctuary. There is disagreement whether this arch is a primary feature of the choir or a later insertion in this wall.

(d) The choir is now an integral part of the nave, but was formerly separated by a cross wall whose foundations were seen by Butterworth during repairs in 1861.[45] He also recorded traces of the junction of the cross wall with the side walls of the nave and said that the opening between the nave and the choir was about the same width as the blocked chancel-arch. These observations need to be checked by removal of modern plaster on the walls and by careful study of the foundations.

(e) The principal side-chambers were clearly of two storeys because of doorways at two levels. But there is disagreement about dates, particularly whether the wide upper doorways are later than the lower ones of narrower and more primitive form.

(f) Subsidiary side-chambers lie further west, and are indicated as being later by the straight joints between their outer walls and those of the main chambers to the east. On the north of the church this straight joint runs from the ground to the eaves, but on the south it seems to extend from the eaves only about half way to the ground. Thus on the south there is some reason to think that the original two-storeyed main chamber may from the first have had a one-storeyed western annexe.

(g) The western porch of entry is divided into two chambers by a wall which seems to be original in the ground-floor chamber. In this wall, facing west, over the doorway is a carved slab with a representation of the Virgin and Child, a representation which seems appropriate at the entry to a church dedicated in honour of St Mary.[46]

(h) The first-floor chamber above the entry porch has an original square-headed window in each of its north and south walls, and an original doorway towards the nave. This doorway is round-headed on the east and square-headed on the west, and it is placed in the extreme north angle of the chamber. South of this doorway and roughly in the centre of the wall is a small triangular window. At a later time a cross wall was built above the wall of the lower chamber and partially blocking the north and south windows.[47] Still later the floor of this chamber was removed, so that the original ground and first floor chambers are now united.[48] A west window of dubious date now lights the entry porch and has been omitted from Fig.17.

(i) On the west wall of the nave two long corbels are placed at a height appropriate to support the western end of a gallery to which access would be gained from the first-floor room of the tower through the doorway J. No positive evidence is now available to suggest how far east this gallery extended unless it be thought that the small triangular windows in the side walls of the nave may have served to light the gallery; if so, it would have extended over about a half of the nave, much as seems to have been the case at Tredington.[49]

(j) The second-floor chamber above the entry porch has a western doorway, an elaborate eastern window with double triangular heads, and square-headed windows to the north and south. These are all framed in well dressed stone, and the framing of the north and south windows forms an integral part of the framing of adjacent round-headed aumbries. The western doorway, with its sill about twenty five feet above the ground, is a puzzling feature which has analogies elsewhere, as at Barnack and Earl's Barton. A possible use seems to be the occasional display of relics either from the door itself or from a balcony outside it; there are early precedents for such a custom on the Continent, and at some places it continues to the present day.[50]

(k) High up in the original west wall of the nave (now the east wall of the tower) is a doorway of which the upper part now appears as a window above the lowered ridge of the roof of the nave. Like other Anglo-Saxon doorways in the church, this doorway is rebated and its head is semicircular on one side (west) but flat on the other. Now in all the other examples the rebated side with the flat head faces into the interior (no doubt for the convenient seating of a rectangular door). It therefore seems safe to deduce that this was the entry to a large upper chamber over the flat ceiling of the nave,[51] and that access to it was by stairs in the western porch.

(l) On the east wall of the choir, two long corbels are placed at a height of about twenty five feet above the floor as if to carry the east edge of a gallery which would stand clear of the arch to the sanctuary and of the upper openings to the lateral *porticus*.[52]

Before passing on to consider other details at Deerhurst, it seems appropriate to compare the western gallery and tower with the much larger and more elaborate western gallery-churches at Centula (c.800) and Corvey (c.880). At all three there was a western entry to the principal church beneath a porch and a gallery; at all three the gallery covered the western part of the nave; and at all three a still higher area opened towards the church at the west of the gallery. Of course there are great differences of scale: the arrangements on the upper floors at Deerhurst are for a handful of people, while those at Corvey were for scores, and those at Centula for hundreds; also there are differences of elaboration: for at Corvey and Centula the gallery-church had upper galleries not only on the west but also on the north and south; moreover the surviving galleries at Corvey are of stone whereas all the upper floors at Deerhurst must have been of wood. But although the continental examples differ from Deerhurst in scale and elaboration

Fig.10, p.147;
Fig.12, p.150;
Fig.14, p.155

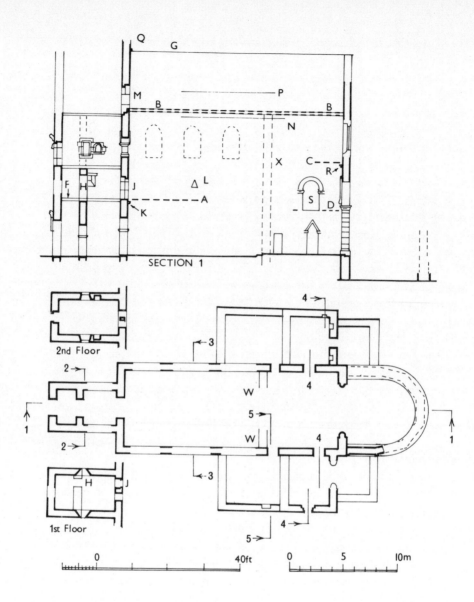

Fig. 17. *Deerhurst: Longitudinal section, and plan*

Figs. 17 and 18 are based on the details given by W. H. Knowles in *Archaeologia*, 77 (1927), but with certain additions, particularly in connection with the nature and position of early floors and galleries. Features which appear in more than one of the diagrams are marked with the same distinguishing letter in each diagram, for ease of identification. The following key relates to both figures.

Lost early features reconstructed from other evidence in the building: A, Position and possible extent of western gallery; B, Floor of upper chamber above nave; C, Eastern gallery in choir; D, Floor of upper chamber in north porticus; E, Floor of upper chamber in south porticus; F, Lost first floor in west porch; G, Original ridge of roof of nave, as defined by stones Q on tower.

Surviving features: H, J, Doorways which define level of gallery A and floor F; K, Corbels which proclaim former existence of gallery A and confirm its level; L, Window suggesting eastern extent of gallery A; M, Doorway defining level of upper chamber B; N, Present ceiling of nave; P, Present ridge of roof of nave; Q, Stones on east wall of tower defining original gable of roof; R, Corbels suggesting former existence of gallery C; S, Upper doorway to north porticus, related to floor D; T, Upper doorway to south porticus, with sill now lower than floor E; U, West doorway to upper floor of south porticus, confirming level of floor E; V, West window.

Features recorded but no longer visible: W, foundations of wall between nave and choir; X, Marks of this wall on the side walls of the nave.

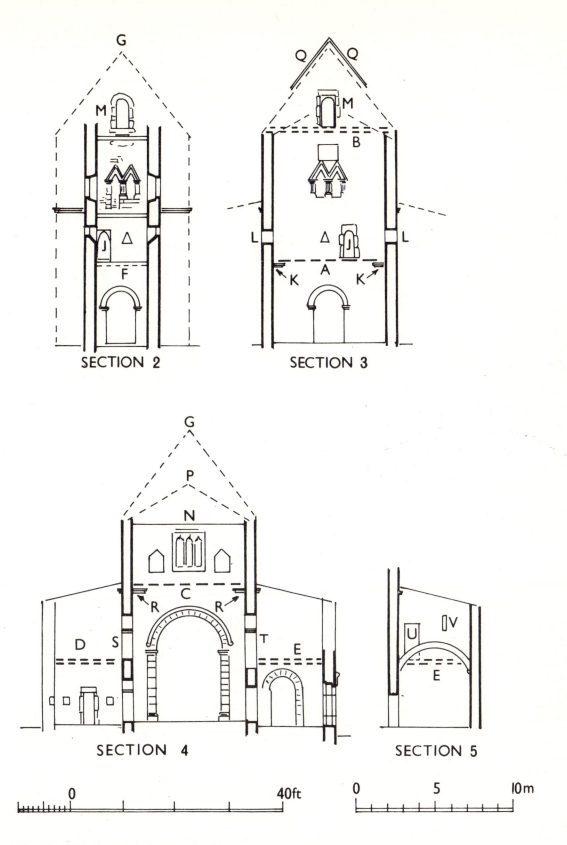

SECTION 2

SECTION 3

SECTION 4

SECTION 5

0   40ft

0   5   10m

Fig. 18. *Deerhurst: Transverse sections*
The position of each section is shown by the corresponding numbers on the plan in Fig. 17.

there is a similarity in principle, suggesting some similarity in use.

It is also worth giving some attention to the question of stairways at Deerhurst. There is no evidence of stone stairs and it therefore seems clear that access to upper floors was by wooden stairs or ladders. The degree of elaboration of upper chambers would suggest that stairs should be assumed in preference to ladders; and the modern wooden stair which leads from the second to the third floor of the tower shows that a stair can be provided within the tower while still leaving about two-thirds of each floor unencumbered. Moreover access to the first-floor gallery could have been by a wooden stair leading up from the nave along the north or south wall just as stone stairs still lead up from the nave into the west gallery at the ninth-century church of Sta Cristina de Lena near Oviedo in Spain.[53] Free movement between the upper space of the nave and the upper spaces of the tower was clearly something upon which the occupants of the church at Deerhurst set considerable store, for there are not only the two surviving complete doorways, on the first and third floors respectively, but also at some later time it was thought desirable to make a doorway at the level of the second floor by cutting away the lower part of the wall beneath the northern light of the elaborate double triangular-headed window. The

p.165 evidence is clearly to be seen in Fig.18 for this rather heartless mutilation of a very elaborately built window.

If we turn next to the main body of the church, with its nave formerly divided from the square choir by a cross wall, we may note that there are analogues for the square choir flanked by *porticus* at places such as Breamore, Brixworth, and Repton, but that no other is so far known with its *porticus* of two storeys. The large openings at Deerhurst on the upper floor contrast sharply with the very small doorways on the ground floor, thus giving a strong impression that they were intended to allow a clear view from the upper floor towards the choir and the apsidal sanctuary. In this respect they show a close resemblance to the galleries at Gernrode, particularly the eastern double windows of those galleries. But even more striking is the resemblance which they show to the arrangement of the church which is drawn on

Plate XV fol. 118b of the Benedictional of St Aethelwold, beside the blessing for the dedication of a church. Even after making all due allowance for the schematic liberties taken in drawings of this type, the picture seems clearly to indicate the space immediately in front of the altar, with clergy facing the bishop who pronounces the blessing, while a group of lay persons including at least one lady are looking down from a gallery.

It would be wrong to leave Deerhurst without a reference to the second piece of sculpture which is also almost certainly *in situ,* namely the figure of an angel seen in full frontal view in the sole surviving panel of the apsidal chancel. Reasons for believing that it is *in situ* were given by Baldwin Brown in 1925, and inspection on several occasions has given me no reason to doubt this opinion. It seems to me reasonable to assume that the apse contained at least three such carvings and perhaps even seven.

Conclusion

The general impression which is given by this brief survey of English and continental buildings of the tenth century may be summarised under five heads.

First, the majority of English buildings give a clear impression of simplicity and veneration for the past; there seems to have been an unwillingness to sweep away old buildings to make way for modern innovations. At Glastonbury the wattled church from before the time of King Ine in the seventh century was still standing to be seen by William of Malmesbury in the twelfth; and at Canterbury the original buildings of St Augustine's abbey remained substantially unchanged for over four centuries until Abbot Wulfric's adaptations in the middle of the eleventh century.[54]

Secondly, a parallel can be seen (even if on a different scale) between the galleries and west porches of the English churches and the continental western gallery-churches such as those at Centula and Corvey. Even without precise knowledge of the distance to which the gallery at Deerhurst extended eastward over the nave it provides a clear analogue to the gallery-church of St Vitus at Corvey, especially if we bear in mind the second floor *chorus angelicus* at Corvey and the second-floor chamber of the porch at Deerhurst, with its elaborate double window looking toward the nave. Moreover, although we have considered only one English gallery, at Deerhurst, there is evidence for western galleries and upper chambers in west porches at a considerable number of English churches, of which the most clearly defined examples are Brixworth, Dover, Jarrow, Ledsham, Monkwearmouth, Tredington and Wing. At Jarrow the western gallery must have been of narrow rectangular shape like that at Gernrode; while at Tredington (and probably at Deerhurst) it was wide enough to cover almost half the nave, and was therefore roughly square in plan like that of Corvey (and probably Centula).

Thirdly, it is possible to compare the arrangements for processional stations in the abbey of Centula with some of the otherwise un-explained sculptural fragments in the English churches. For example in the large late Anglo-Saxon church at Bitton, between Bath and Bristol, there is still *in situ,* over the chancel-arch, the lower part of a great stone Crucifixion which corresponds in position with the similar image at Centula where the *Chorus ante Passionem* had its place. There is no known historical evidence for a monastery at Bitton, but the large scale of the church, and its lateral *porticus,* suggest strongly that it was no mere parish church. There is no surviving evidence in England for the Resurrection or Ascension as sculptured stations in a church, but the Madonna and Child over the west doorway at Deerhurst seem to provide a close parallel to the station of the Nativity in the western entry porch at Centula.

Fourth, the upper chambers in the lateral *porticus* at Deerhurst closely resemble on a smaller scale the galleries over the aisles at Gernrode; and, as has already been noted, the presence of upper chambers of this sort in more important English churches is indicated by the picture, in the Benedictional of St Aethelwold, of a bishop consecrating a church.

Finally, an important matter that should not be passed over in silence is the need for much more study of important surviving buildings such as Deerhurst (and others not mentioned in the text such as Brixworth and Repton) if we are to gain a clearer picture of the history of Anglo-Saxon church building and of its connection with the liturgy. At Deerhurst important historical evidence is hidden beneath Victorian plaster; and, until evidence recorded in sketchy outline last century can be re-investigated in detail, the present areas of disagreement in the architectural history of this important building are unlikely to be greatly reduced. The type of investigation needed to lead to a clear understanding of this (and other equally important buildings) involves excavation within and outside the building and comprehensive clearing of plaster from the walls. That such investigation is possible without damage to the structure, or desecration, or indeed undue interruption of services is admirably shown by the detailed investigation which has led to clear understanding of important continental churches, both ones which have suffered damage during the war and others.[55] Excavation of churches which exist only as foundations, such as St Augustine's abbey at Canterbury or the Anglo-Saxon Cathedral at Winchester can, of course, be carried out in more completeness, and can yield results of first-class importance; but it is only by detailed investigation of standing buildings like Deerhurst, particularly ones which seem to show evidence of modification at a series of dates, that we can hope to build up a reliable framework of historical evidence about doorways, windows, arches, galleries, stairways and similar features all of which occur above ground and which constitute so important a part of the background for understanding the use to which the churches were put.

Chapter 12

THE BENEDICTIONAL OF ST AETHELWOLD AND
ANGLO-SAXON ILLUMINATION OF THE REFORM PERIOD

by J. J. G. Alexander

'A bishop, the great Ethelwold, whom the Lord had made patron of
Winchester, ordered a certain monk subject to him to write the present
book . . . He commanded also to be made in this book many frames
well adorned and filled with various figures decorated with numerous
beautiful colours and with gold . . . Let all who look upon this book
pray always that after the term of the flesh I may abide in heaven —
Godeman the scribe, as a suppliant, earnestly asks this.' This is an
abbreviated version of the long Latin poem written in gold capitals at
the beginning of the text of the Benedictional of St Aethelwold,
formerly at Chatsworth in the Library of the Dukes of Devonshire, now
in the British Museum.[1]

This Benedictional is certainly the greatest surviving artistic monument of the Anglo-Saxon monastic reform movement. The object of
this paper is to try to set its illumination in its context, in particular by
contrasting it with what precedes it. The evidence we have on which to
base our conclusions is only a small fraction of what must once have
existed and on that score alone the conclusions reached cannot be
anything other than tentative. Very much more study of even such
evidence as we have will be necessary before we can hope to understand
fully the genesis of the Benedictional.[2]

The Anglo-Saxon illuminated manuscripts surviving from the period
before the production of the Benedictional are not numerous. We may
start with a group which belongs to the first half of the tenth century.
There are seven manuscripts in all, of which some are associated with
King Athelstan (925-39). If we study their decoration we can observe
three main sources, insular art of the eighth century, late antique art
from the Mediterranean in the period probably of the fifth to seventh
century, and Carolingian art of the ninth century.

Taking these three sources in order, we may demonstrate the
continuance of the insular tradition into the tenth century by examin-
ing a Gospel book now at Boulogne-sur-mer, which does not appear to

Plate III have been reproduced and which has been very little discussed.[3] Its initials are close in style to those in the Junius Psalter to be discussed below, and in the Tollemache Orosius,[4] both probably from Winchester and both accepted as belonging to the second quarter of the tenth century. The illumination consists of Canon Tables and initials only, though a faint drawing of the Evangelist St John with symbol perched on his halo has been added, perhaps in the first half of the eleventh century. The Canon Tables have stepped imposts as in the Lindisfarne Gospels. There are also bird and animal heads as capitals and on folio 14 a human head as in another eighth-century insular Gospel book, BM Royal MS. 1 B.vii, in which a manumission made by Athelstan early in his reign was entered. Other features are found in the Canons of the eighth-century Gospels now at Trier, in which the illumination is insular in style.[5] The infilling of the capitals in the Boulogne Gospels with orange and yellow also recalls insular practice.

The initials with figures in the Junius Psalter[6] can also be shown to derive from insular sources. They can be compared with the initial in the Leningrad Bede of the second quarter of the eighth century showing St Augustine, apostle of the English, in which similar tubular folds over his shoulder and schematic features, round head and large oval eyes, occur.[7] The historiated initial of David and the lion in the Psalter, though it differs in certain respects, is still close enough to the Vespasian Psalter of the second quarter of the eighth century, to suggest that some such insular manuscript was the source.[8]

The motif of David kneeling on the lion's back is taken over, as is well known, from the classical composition used to represent Mithras slaying the bull. This is a good example of our difficulties in differentiating the artist's sources if we use iconographical comparisons alone. For late antique motifs could be transmitted to the tenth-century artist by insular as well as by Carolingian copies.

Turning to this second source, late antique art, another of this group of seven manuscripts, the so-called Athelstan Psalter, may suggest that we have to do with direct as well as indirect debts to the art of that period. This little Psalter, made in a continental scriptorium in the late ninth century, received additions in England in the tenth century.[9] Edmund Bishop showed that there were good reasons to believe that this Psalter was at Winchester in the Middle Ages and that the inscription in it by its sixteenth-century owner, Thomas Dackombe, recording a connection with Athelstan is trustworthy. The evidence of the added illumination is quite consistent with this view.[10]

The additional matter includes a calendar and tables and a series of Psalter Collects with a Litany and prayers in Greek transliterated. This

matter is on five added gatherings, two at the beginning and three at the
end of the manuscript. In addition there were at least four miniatures,
two in the first two gatherings, fols.2^v and 21, and two as single leaves,
one preceding Psalm 1 and another Psalm 101. There was no doubt
another before Psalm 51.

The miniature on fol.120^v, preceding Psalm 101, shows the Ascen-   *Plate IVa*
sion. Below in the centre is the Virgin with her arms outstretched in the
'orans' position common in early Christian art. The Apostles flank her
on either side and above Christ is enthroned in majesty in a mandorla
accompanied by four angels. This is the common Eastern iconography
of the sixth century, seen, for example, in the Syrian Rabbula Gospels
of the year 586 (where, however, the Christ stands) and in the oil flasks
brought back by pilgrims from Jerusalem, now preserved at Monza and
Bobbio.[11] In the West a more literal representation of Christ
ascending the mount of Olives is used as in the fifth-century ivory in
Munich.[12] This second type, normal in Carolingian art, is later used
in the Benedictional of St Aethelwold.

A second miniature shows the Nativity of Christ.[13] It is now a   *Plate IVb*
detached leaf in the Bodleian Library, but originally prefaced Psalm 1,
as is clear from the offprint of the interlace at the top of the initial 'B',
'Beatus vir', on fol.35 of the Psalter. Again the normal Carolingian
iconography is different and one may suspect earlier models. The
earliest example of the midwives preparing the bath for the child, as
they do here, is Eastern. The scene then appears in Rome in the seventh
to eighth centuries, and later becomes common in Middle Byzantine
art.[14]

For the style of these miniatures the closest parallels are with Italian
rather than Eastern works, for example the ivory, apparently showing
the Apotheosis of an Emperor, of the late fourth or the fifth
century[15] and the late sixth-century Gospels of St Augustine,[16]
traditionally thought to have been brought from Italy to England by
Augustine himself. In the latter we find a division of the ground line
into two, which may be reflected in the line dividing the upper and the
lower parts of the Nativity scene. A similar stratification occurs in the
Junius Caedmon to be discussed later. The small figures with their sharp   *see p.172*
profile faces should also be compared with the ivory and the Gospels.

These are just the sorts of models that were available to insular
artists, but the remnants of classical space construction and landscape
conventions and the absence of insular stylisation seem to me to make
it unlikely that the models were transmitted via insular art. The
originals may still have been accessible to the tenth-century artists.

The other two miniatures in the Athelstan Psalter both represent

Christ in Majesty surrounded by choirs of saints. One precedes the
calendar of fol.2ᵛ, and the other follows it on fol. 21. In the latter we
see a Christ of the Last Judgment showing his wounds and holding the
Plate IVc   cross. In the former behind the throne are the symbols of the Passion.
These features are so unusual and so emphasised in this miniature that
it seems very likely that there is a reference intended to a famous relic,
the lance which pierced Christ's side and which had belonged to
Charlemagne. This had been given to Athelstan with other relics in 926
by Hugh the Great on the occasion of his marrying a sister of
see p.34   Athelstan.[17] If so, this gives a *terminus post quem* for the illumination. There do not seem to be any parallels for the combination of this
Last Judgment picture with the saints in bands in this way, though it is
not altogether dissimilar from miniatures in illustrated Apocalypses
showing the Elders adoring the Christ.[18] Perhaps these two miniatures, and the standing saints painted in small frames in the added
calendar, and the choirs at the beginning of the Benedictional of St
Aethelwold all reflect some monumental source available to artists at
Winchester. Carolingian miniatures of this subject exist but are rather
different.

It should also be mentioned at this point that Professor Wormald has
suggested that the famous so-called Caedmon manuscript in the
Bodleian Library, Oxford, copies an earlier manuscript related in style
to the Athelstan group.[19] The style and particularly the colouring of
the figure of the Creator on page 11 are strong evidence for this. A
small iconographical detail also supports this suggestion. In the first All
Plate IVc   Saints miniature of the Athelstan Psalter on fol.2ᵛ we see Abel offering
a ram and a figure opposite him with a vase with three prongs sticking
Plate Va   out of it. In the drawing of the offering of Cain and Abel on p.21 Cain
holds a bowl with similar prongs. Perhaps they represent steam rising
from Cain's offering (the Bible text speaks only of the fruit of the
earth). The two miniatures must be connected and the probability is
that they both stylise an earlier prototype in a more illusionistic style.
Late antique sources undoubtedly lie behind some at least of the
miniatures in the Caedmon.[20]

For two of the three remaining manuscripts of our group Carolingian
sources are absolutely certain. The text of the first, Hrabanus Maurus's
Plate VIIa   *In laude sanctae crucis,* was composed and its illustrations made at
Fulda in the first third of the ninth century.[21] This enormously
popular text exists in a great many copies. In his *stemma* of the
manuscripts Prochno derives our manuscript and a ninth century
manuscript, now in Amiens, from a lost manuscript 'W'.[22] The
Amiens manuscript, like Cambridge, shows the presentation scene

under an arcade, which is not found in the earlier copies which are closest to the original dedication copy now lost. From the photographs available the Amiens manuscript seems to belong to the so-called Franco-Saxon school. One cannot for the moment be more precise about the date or the place of the model of the Cambridge manuscript, but certainly a provenance in north France would fit in with other hypotheses about the kind of Carolingian manuscript imported into England. A reference exists to a gift of a manuscript of this text to Glastonbury by Archbishop Aethelnoth of Canterbury (1020-38), who was a former monk of Glastonbury.[23]

The second manuscript is a ninth-century Gospel book now in St John's College, Oxford.[24] It was written probably in Brittany like a number of other manuscripts which reached England in the first half of the tenth century. A colour wash drawing of St Matthew was added to *Plate Vb* it, which belongs stylistically with this early group of manuscripts. It is, in fact, a close copy of the St Matthew in a Gospel book which was given by Athelstan to Christ Church, Canterbury, now in the British Museum. This Gospel book, of the late ninth or early tenth century, was assigned to Lobbes in Belgium by Edmund Bishop on the strength of its *capitula* and may have been a present to Athelstan from Otto the Great (912-73), whose name it contains.[25]

The last of the seven manuscripts of this early group is the well-known Bede Life of St Cuthbert, now at Corpus Christi College, Cambridge, in which King Athelstan is shown presenting his book to a standing St Cuthbert.[26] This has been identified from a list of books given to Durham by the king and can be dated before 934. The presentation scene to a seated figure, such as is represented in the Hrabanus manuscript, is much commoner. Nevertheless, there are some examples of illustrations where a book is presented to a standing recipient, though the only earlier example in a manuscript seems to be the St Gallen Folchard Psalter of c.870.[27] A Carolingian model seems quite possible, therefore, for this miniature too.

It should also be mentioned that Althelstan gave to Durham at the same time a Gospel book which was in the Cotton collection, but which was destroyed in the fire of 1731. The descriptions of Smith and of Wanley tell us, however, that besides the Canon Tables and Evangelists there was a miniature of Athelstan on bent knee, crowned and with a sceptre, offering the book to an enthroned St Cuthbert.[28]

*　　*　　*

If we now turn to manuscripts which can be connected with the reform, I think we can reach some conclusions. It would be wrong to speak as if there were a complete stylistic break after the mid-century, and to imply that the artists turned to a totally different set of models. The lack of evidence would not justify us in doing this in any case, and it is possible to point to some positive evidence of continuity as well. But the important point is that the sort of insular influence we detected in our first group of manuscripts is now absent. There is some evidence of late antique cycles being copied, but in many cases these can be shown to be received via Carolingian intermediaries. At any rate Carolingian sources now predominate and this implies a conscious choice by the reformers. Earlier it seems to be a matter of almost haphazard and uncritical copying and adaptation. Now the impression is of an intentional programme.

The earliest work in a new style for which we have any evidence of date is the prefatory drawing to St Dunstan's Classbook from Glastonbury.[29] This is a collection of texts of different origins but all of grammatical interest, put together no doubt at Glastonbury where it remained until the dissolution. The famous drawing on fol.1 shows St Dunstan at the feet of Christ who is portrayed as Divine Wisdom.

Plate VIa

There are a number of problems about this drawing. The first is whether the figure of Dunstan was drawn at the same time and by the same artist as the Christ. It seems to have been Saxl who first made the suggestion that it is a later addition.[30] The position of Christ who looks away from rather than at the kneeling figure is unexpected. On the other hand it is hard to see why the Christ should be represented in this unusual three-quarter length view unless the kneeling abbot was intended from the first. This is a device to increase the contrast between the monk's humility and the Lord's majesty. Professor Wormald has called attention to the presence of three-quarter length figures emerging from the clouds in the Utrecht Psalter and they are found also in the Junius 'Caedmon'. On the other hand, very similar but full-length figures are found in the Sherborne Pontifical and in a manuscript at St John's College, Oxford,[31] so that it seems likely that here too the model was full length.

Stylistic comparisons for this and other early Anglo-Saxon drawings have been made with the group of early Carolingian ivories of the so-called 'Ada school'. The figure of Christ on the ivory binding of the Lorsch Gospels, deriving probably from a sixth-century model, provides a good parallel for the soft yet complicated drapery folds.[32] No drawings in this style are known and this presupposes that the artist was transposing his image from one medium to another.

Plate VIb

The stylistic discrepancy between the classical rhythmical figure of

Christ and the contained angular kneeling abbot below, which Saxl very acutely noticed, can be explained, however, not by the latter being an addition but by its being copied from a different model. A very similar contained figure is found at the end of Hrabanus Maurus's *In laude sanctae crucis* representing Hrabanus, Abbot of Fulda, adoring the cross. The Anglo-Saxon copy of this text at Trinity College, Cambridge, which was discussed above, is earlier than the Classbook, and it seems likely that this — or its exemplar — provided the model for the Dunstan figure. The kneeling abbot is not, therefore, an addition, but an integral part of the original composition.[33]

Plate VIIa

see pp.172-3

The second question concerns the inscription written above Dunstan in the first person, *Dunstanum memet clemens rogo Christe tuere,* 'I ask thee, Christ, in thy clemency to protect me, Dunstan'. Dr Hunt has discussed the script of this, his Hand 'D', which is found in other parts of the book. He is willing to believe that it is Dunstan's own writing and Mr T. A. M. Bishop concurs in this view.[34]

If the kneeling figure is integral to the composition and if Hand 'D' is Dunstan's own, there is some reason to accept the theory of the much later inscription at the top of the page, added perhaps in the sixteenth century, that Dunstan himself was the artist. For we know from the life of St Dunstan by the author 'B' that he 'cultivated diligently both the art of writing and also skill in playing the harp and painting'.[35]

Dunstan himself may, therefore, have introduced to England the practice of illustrating manuscripts with self-sufficient outline drawings. This becomes of the greatest importance in Anglo-Saxon art, reflecting the English artists' predilection for expressing themselves in linear terms. The added miniature in the St John's College, Oxford, Gospels already discussed, preceding the Dunstan drawing in date is already moving in this direction, for, though there are colour washes there, it is still a linear reduction of a painted model.

Plate Vb

The next manuscript to be considered is the Leofric Missal, a Carolingian manuscript, to which a calendar and other material was added at Glastonbury before the death of Edward the Martyr in 979.[36] Here also the illumination consists of drawings which, unfortunately, are faded and rubbed. They are in coloured inks and two of them represent *Vita* and *Mors*, Life and Death, illustrating a text giving instructions for prognosticating the chances of survival in illness. The iconography has been brilliantly elucidated by Dr A. Heimann who suggests the sources of the illustrations lie ultimately in the same milieu as the texts to which they belong, that is Egypt. Another drawing shows a Paschal Hand. If we contrast the monumental style of the Christ with its fluid but comparatively restrained drapery folds with the

*see pp.69-70,
78-80*

Plate VIIb
Plate VIa

shivering punctured line of the Leofric drawings, it is clear that a great change has taken place. Though it is possible to ascribe this in part to an internal development in a direction to which Anglo-Saxon art was already prone, it seems likely that the Leofric artist owes something of his style as well as of his iconography to his model. In that case the obvious source is the Reims style of drawing of the second quarter of the ninth century. One famous manuscript in this style still surviving, the Psalter now at Utrecht, was brought to England and had a tremendous effect, being copied at Canterbury about the year 1000 and also later.[37]

Carolingian art then is the stimulus here too, but again the important point is that of the various possible Carolingian or other models it is the more linear that were sought out and copied by Anglo-Saxon artists. Though, of course, there is no evidence whatsoever for such a guess, who is more likely than St Dunstan himself to have imported various manuscripts of the Reims school, manuscripts which were copied at Glastonbury in the Leofric Missal, and at Canterbury in the Harley Psalter and, perhaps, in a series of calendar illustrations?

The earliest monument of the new Anglo-Saxon outline drawing style is connected with St Dunstan. The most important early monument of the new Anglo-Saxon painted style is connected with St Aethelwold, and at least the majority of its sources also lie in Carolingian art. The Benedictional, as we know from its colophon already quoted, was written for Aethelwold whilst he was Bishop of Winchester, that is between 963 and 984. The dates can probably be narrowed down to 971-984, since there is a reference to miracles performed recently at the shrine of St Swithun, who was translated in 971.[38]

The Benedictional contains twenty-eight full-page miniatures, two historiated initials and nineteen pages with elaborate frames but no figures. In addition there were probably miniatures of the Massacre of the Innocents, of the Nativity of the Virgin and of St Michael on pages now missing.

There are also pages missing from the beginning of the manuscript. The illumination starts with seven miniatures of the Choirs of Confessors, Virgins and the twelve Apostles. Using the miniatures of the Athelstan Psalter as guide, Professor Wormald has suggested that the book originally began with twelve miniatures on six leaves now missing, showing Christ in Majesty, and Choirs of Angels, Prophets, Patriarchs, Apostles and Martyrs.[39]

If the Athelstan Psalter provided the idea for this unusual sequence it would be evidence of some continuity between the Athelstan period and the period of the reform. Choirs are found in a Carolingian sacramentary but their arrangement is different.[40]

The other miniatures in the Benedictional, including the three now lost, divide into seven scenes of the early life of Christ, five scenes of the events preceding and following the Passion, eleven miniatures of saints and finally the famous drawing, only partly coloured, of the Dedication of the Church, possibly showing St Aethelwold himself. *Plate XV*

With regard to the iconography of these scenes Homburger in 1912 first called attention to a number of striking similarities with ivory carvings of the so-called Metz school, that is of the second half of the ninth and the early part of the tenth centuries. He compared for example the miniature of the Baptism (fol.25) with the same scene *Plate VIII* represented on an ivory casket now in Brunswick.[41] The same five *Plate IX* figures, Christ, St John the Baptist, the two angels and the personification of the river Jordan as a classical river god, occur in both scenes. Christ has a mandorla in both and in both there is the exceptional detail of a double ampulla for the annointing of Christ carried in the beak of the Dove.[42] The way in which the figures in the Benedictional are squeezed together suggests a model with a broader format such as the ivory panel.

In spite of this extremely close similarity it soes not seem possible that this actual casket was used as model, since St John the Baptist is wearing a cloak of skins, a detail which appears in two other Metz ivories, one being the cover of the Drogo Sacramentary and the other an ivory now in Antwerp.[43]

We see a similar effect of crowding in the miniature of the Presentation in the Temple (fol.34v). This can be compared to a Metz group ivory of c.900 in the Victoria and Albert Museum.[44] In the Benedictional, Anna the Prophetess is on the right but otherwise the two scenes are remarkably similar, with Joseph carrying the Doves. Homburger drew attention to the fact that the artist of the miniature confused the cloth on the altar and that covering Simeon's hands, which may confirm that his source was an ivory not a painted illumination.

The Eastern type of Ascension picture in which Christ is enthroned in majesty, and of which we saw an example in the Athelstan Psalter, is *Plate IVa* rejected in the Benedictional (fol.64v) in favour of the Western type of Christ walking up the side of the mountain. This is used in various Carolingian ivories and in the Sacramentary made for Drogo, a natural son of Charlemagne, who was Bishop of Metz from 826-855.[45] Here there is no mandorla. It occurs on a ninth-century Carolingian ivory from Narbonne, however.[46] In the Benedictional there are four not two angels and they fly in the air rather than, as Acts narrates, walk on the ground. It seems likely that the artist of the Benedictional went back to the Athelstan Psalter or its model, for the angels, especially as the gesture of pointing up to the Christ occurs in the Psalter as it does in the Benedictional, and the angels are half-length there too.

In the scene of the three Maries at the Grave (fol.51) Homburger drew attention to the form of the tomb as a long narrow building with two towers. This is not like the usual round building with cupola found in the early Christian examples and still in the Utrecht Psalter and in the Drogo Sacramentary. It does occur in two ivories of the later Metz school, however. These ivories of the later Metz school omit the soldiers, and the gesture of the angel is different, but these particular details are shown similarly in the Drogo Sacramentary.[47]

Homburger was able to find parallels in Carolingian art, particularly the Metz group ivories, for almost all the scenes in the Benedictional. There were three, however, for which he was unable to cite comparisons. The first is the Christ of the Second Coming preceding the Benediction for the Third Sunday in Advent (fol.9^v). This magnificent page shows the Christ in a mandorla with the same feature of the broad band to the left behind Christ as in the Ascension. It is possible that the artist based his picture on the Ascension miniature. However, it has an obvious sense of incompleteness, which suggests that it is an extract from some large composition. One possible source would be an illustrated Apocalypse since the grouping of Christ and the attendant angels recalls St Michael and the Angels attacking the Dragon.[48] Homburger, however, spoke of the possibility of a Byzantine source for this composition, having in mind the iconography of Anastasis. Professor Wormald has noted that the Angels carry the Spear, the Sponge and the Cross of the Passion as in the Athelstan Psalter, and this detail may confirm Homburger's interpretation.

Another scene apparently without a Carolingian parallel is the Pentecost miniature (fol.67^v). Here the Apostles are seated round in a half circle with the Dove descending above as in Middle Byzantine examples and in Ottonian examples deriving from Byzantine sources.[49] An exceptional detail which is found also in the Pontifical of Archbishop Robert in Rouen,[50] is the way the tongues of flame enter the mouths of the Apostles.

The third scene without Carolingian parallel is the Death of the *Plate X* Virgin (fol.102^v). This appears to be altogether unique, for the figure of Christ standing behind the bed to receive the Virgin's soul as seen in Byzantine examples, is absent.[51] The composition is clearly based on the Nativity scene found earlier in the book (fol.15^v). It should be noted that the mourning women in the centre are very close to the figure, if reversed, of the mourning Virgin in the Crucifixion in the Harley Psalter. Niver believed that this Psalter was made for Ramsey and it may, therefore, be connected with the third leader of the reform, St Oswald.[52] Script and text, however, suggest it was written at Winchester. The group of Apostles, below, resemble the standing figures at the beginning of the Benedictional, and, even more closely, the Apostles in the Ascension miniature of the Athelstan Psalter. It looks as if on this page we have an invention of the Winchester artist put together from other scenes known to him. Professor Zarnecki has drawn attention to the importance of the motif of the Crown, since it is in England on a capital at Reading Abbey of c.1130 that we have the first example of the Coronation of the Virgin.[53]

    Plate XI

    Plate IVa

Homburger was inclined to suggest that there may have been Byzantine or early Christian sources available to the Winchester artists, presumably having in mind these three scenes, though he was not specific about this. This possibility still requires further investigation, but the fact remains that the majority of the scenes can be paralleled in Carolingian sources and the style points in this direction too. Whilst in some cases one might suppose the Anglo-Saxon artists could have had access to the same late antique models as the Carolingian artists, in certain scenes, for instance the tomb in the scene of the Maries at the Grave, they are quite clearly making use of Carolingian innovations.

Though the Metz school ivories have some stylistic features in common with the Benedictional, such as the ground pattern, the draperies are less involved and the figure proportions rather different. Moreover the most remarkable feature of the Benedictional, its rich and varied colour, is very different from that of Metz school manuscripts which retain the illusionistic palette of the late antique period. Nothing in Anglo-Saxon art preceding it has prepared us for this splendour, not even the New Minster Charter.[54] This manuscript, which has a *terminus post quem* of 966, is both unusual in form for a charter and very sumptuous; it is written in gold and the miniature page is stained purple. This technique, known from a small number of late antique manuscripts, and imitated in Carolingian and Ottonian codices, is very uncommon in Anglo-Saxon manuscripts. The miniature shows King Edgar in the centre flanked by St Peter and a female saint, perhaps the Virgin or possibly St Etheldreda. The king is adoring the Christ who is frontally enthroned, upheld in a mandorla by angels. Homburger has compared the iconography with an Ascension miniature and we are again reminded of the Athelstan Psalter. The similarity is not confined to the iconography. The large almond-shaped eyes, the oval heads and

    Frontispiece

    Plate IVa

the simpler drapery forms also recall the Psalter. At the same time the hems swirl and the fluttering edges are outlined in white to emphasise them. This can be seen as a transitional style between the Psalter and the Benedictional. The fact that the figure of the king seen from behind is repeated in the Entry to Jerusalem in the Benedictional is confirmation of their connection.

Plate XII

Both Homburger and Wormald have seen connections with the drapery style of the so-called 'Ada school', the group of Gospel books and ivories which are connected with the Emperor Charlemagne and which date just before and just after 800.[55] Boeckler also emphasised this connection and considered that the artist of the Benedictional combined this kind of linear agitated patterning with the more static style inherited from the Athelstan Psalter and the New Minster charter.[56] The contrast between the surface patterns of the drapery and the static poses of many of the figures in the Benedictional was emphasised by Homburger. This important observation may confirm that different models were used for the iconography, i.e. the Metz school ivories, and for the style.

Plate VIb

In considering the Benedictional's colouring Homburger drew attention to the swirling cloud patterns as evidence of the influence of the more illusionistic, naturalistic style of an earlier period, a style which was inherited by the Carolingian Reims school. There is no sign of those swirling cloud patterns in the Ada group nor of the chalky white pigment which is evident everywhere in the Benedictional. To find similar colours and painting we have to look at later Carolingian manuscripts, those associated with the reign of Charles the Bald. Both in the so-called Palace group and in some of the manuscripts of the Franco-Saxon group something more like the paler chalky shades of the Benedictional occur.[57] The ribbon-like clouds which come from late antique illusionistic painting via the Reims school are gradually transformed into pattern in these later Carolingian manuscripts, as they are in the Benedictional. It should not be forgotten that the Ada group Gospels continued to be copied and even in contemporary tenth-century Ottonian manuscripts, such as the Codex Wittekindeus from Fulda, a rather similar range of colour and richly varied drapery is found.[58] Further study of the iconography of Anglo-Saxon Evangelist portraits may help with this problem.

Whatever his sources the Anglo-Saxon artist is using colour to further the effect of all-over richness and variety achieved by the linear patterns of drapery and outline and by his crowded centripetal compositions. He goes far beyond any Carolingian artists in this. Colour is not illusionistic as in late antique art nor is it used to emphasise and separate plane and outlines as in Ottonian painting. The artist uses the same colours in his frames interweaving them so that the frame seems to coalesce with the miniatures, just as the figures themselves overlap and interlace with it. How far illusionism has been left behind can be seen for example in the miniature of the Entry to Jerusalem. The brilliant green ground from which the fantastic trees with their intertwining branches grow above, is not a setting suggesting space, but is used to add to the effect of surface pattern by its fretted edge which emphasises the outlines of the groups below.

Plate XII

In a later article Homburger suggested more specifically than he had in 1912, that the Anglo-Saxon artists had a Metz school Sacramentary before them.[59] There are difficulties in this view. Besides the differences in the style of the figures and the colouring, almost all the Drogo Sacramentary scenes are incorporated into historiated initials, and the historiated initial, though there are two examples in the Benedictional, remains surprisingly rare in Anglo-Saxon art.

Another problem is provided by the figures of prophets on the stole of St Cuthbert made for Bishop Frithestan between 909 and 916. Though their style, the faces particularly, connects them with some of the Athelstan manuscripts discussed earlier, they are much more classical in their rhythmical poses, being compared by Dr Freyhan with the Vatican Cosmas Indicopleustes, a Byzantine manuscript of the so-called Macedonian Renaissance of the late ninth century.[60] If some such model was available at Winchester, where the stoles are thought to have been made, could it have been known to the artists of the Benedictional? For example the classical motif of the elbow covered by the overmantle in the prefatory miniatures of the Benedictional can be compared with the Prophet Jonah of the stole. The humpy ground of the Benedictional is also represented in the stole. There is also the recent discovery of a piece of a presumably large scale wall-painting from Winchester of before 903 to warn us of how little we know about what models and artistic traditions were already available there in the early tenth century.[61]

Whatever the solutions to these difficult problems the conclusion suggested here is that the Benedictional's illumination is a conscious attempt to emulate Carolingian illumination. Some attempt had already been made to do this in the second quarter of the tenth century. But what distinguishes the Benedictional is its consistency. It rejects all features of the earlier native insular tradition more thoroughly than any other Anglo-Saxon manuscript, either earlier or later.[62] The manuscripts which succeed it in fact do not hesitate to re-introduce such features.

This is striking in the matter of the initials. The richness and splendour of their decorated initials are one of the most obvious distinguishing features of insular manuscripts and they had a great influence on Carolingian illumination. But in the Benedictional all the initials to the Benedictions are plain gold capitals. There is not a single snapping beast head, and only one small piece of interlace in one of the frames, which, as Professor Wormald has shown, derives from a Carolingian manuscript of the Franco-Saxon school, rather than from an insular source.[63] On fols. 6ᵛ and 8 there are a few blobs on the continuation capitals such as are found in insular manuscripts, though even here the colours, yellow, green and orange, are more like those used in Carolingian than in insular manuscripts. In the rest of the text even these features are avoided. The script too, of course, is one of the earliest and most splendid examples of the English version of Caroline minuscule with no features of the native script which continued to be *see p.108* used by other scribes, particularly in vernacular manuscripts.[64]

The frames, the *circos multos,* of the Benedictional which are perhaps its most remarkable feature and which were specially mentioned by Godeman himself, might at first sight seem to negate my thesis. Certainly the emphasis on the decorative features, the way frames and miniatures overlap and interlace so that the whole becomes a single patterned whole, recalls insular carpet pages. This is undeniable, but even so, as Homburger and Freyhan in their discussions have shown, the acanthus leaf forms are closer to Carolingian adaptations of classical vegetable ornament than are, for example, the plant scrolls of *Frontispiece* the Junius Psalter or even of the New Minster charter. The chalice-shaped leaves and the various fruit and flower forms used in both those manuscripts, forms which are already seen in the Cuthbert embroideries and whose Eastern derivation has been demonstrated by Freyhan, are consistently avoided in the Benedictional. Even in the frames it is Carolingian art which has provided both the forms of the arches and of the square frames with their corner rosettes and the type of acanthus used as filling. And if the artist has devoted as much thought and labour to them as he has to the scenes inside them, it should be remembered that there are Carolingian as well as insular precedents for that. There are Carolingian manuscripts of the Palace School of Charles the Bald, which also contain pages filled with ornament which almost over-whelms the scenes inside them. This is not to devalue the extraordinary brilliance and inventiveness of the artist or artists of the Benedictional.

There is not space to consider the further considerable debts of Anglo-Saxon art to Carolingian art in the period following the pro-duction of the Benedictional. One other manuscript may be considered,

firstly because it is a copy of *Regularis Concordia* itself with a
miniature as frontispiece, and secondly because it could perhaps reflect
an original of the reform period now lost. The miniature shows a king   *Plate XIII*
enthroned between two ecclesiastics under an arcade, St Dunstan with
the pallium on the right, King Edgar in the centre and St Aethelwold on
the left. A monk kneeling below signifies the acceptance of the Rule.
The manuscript, now in the Cotton collection in the British Museum,
comes probably from Christ Church, Canterbury.[65]

Another manuscript, now at Durham, contains an almost identical
miniature, except that this time the central figure of the king is not
included.[66] The reason for this is that the miniature precedes not the
Regularis Concordia but a copy of Aelfric's Grammar. The two
manuscripts are close in date, belonging to the middle or third quarter
of the eleventh century. The Durham manuscript is probably slightly
later in date and its miniature no doubt copies that in the Cotton
manuscript.

The scene is a variation of the 'Dialogue' picture of which there are a
number of late antique and Carolingian examples.[67] At the same
time it recalls the three seated figures in the miniature in the
Benedictional of St Aethelwold for the feast of the Circumcision (fol.   *Plate XIV*
22^v). Could it be that a contemporary copy of *Regularis Concordia,*
which must have existed, had a prefatory miniature from which the
Cotton miniature derives? The resemblance to the Benedictional
miniature cannot be used to confirm such a hypothesis. But it seems
not unlikely to me (note the staff held by the left hand figure in the
Benedictional), and if so, this is another example of the desire of the
leaders of the reform movement to make manifest, by their encouragement of a new art, the new spirit they aimed to bring to English
monasticism.[68]

Chapter 13

ANGLO-SAXON SCULPTURE OF THE REFORM PERIOD

by Rosemary Cramp

The relationship between the reformed rule of English monasteries in
the tenth century and sculpture is difficult to define largely because of
certain factors inherent in the nature of the material and its production.
In the first flowering of English monasticism in the late seventh and
early eighth centuries one can trace a relationship, in the North at least,
between the manuscripts produced in the monastic scriptoria, and the
carving on crosses and grave covers associated with monastic churches
and their cemeteries. In the post-Viking period, there is less certainty as
to how sculpture was produced and under what patronage. In the
Danelaw it seems clear that small local schools of carvers worked and
distributed within a limited area, and possibly these. were independent
lay workmen. Aelfric's account of the rebuilding of Abingdon and
Winchester[1] implies, that, as in the building of Hexham three
hundred years before, some monks worked on the buildings, although
there seems also to have been an influx of extra workmen who had to
be catered for. Nevertheless we have no record of the great monastic
figures of the century engaging in stone carving as for example Dunstan
did in metal working. Lawrence Stone states categorically that '. . . at
no time so far as we know was the sculptor in stone any other than a
professional layman. At first he was merely one of the members of
the mason's yard, who might be asked to turn his hand to anything
from the dressing of a wall to the carving of a tympanum . . .'[2]
Nevertheless only seven pages later he seems to imply that such
workmen would be closely associated with monasteries for in defining
the relative role of the monastery and nobility he says, '. . . It was the
former that provides the workmen, the models and the inspiration,
the latter whose piety or pride found expression in the payment of
the costs involved . . .'
All this is sheer surmise. The charter references to Egberht or Athelstan
raising crosses to mark boundaries of sanctuaries or to commemorate
councils are often of doubtful authenticity and we can hardly say as
some have that there was a court school of carvers. Certainly there is an

immense regional division between north and south for this period, with twice as much material from the north to reinforce the difference. W. G. Collingwood summarises his feelings by stating trenchantly that science and history '. . . have to remember the conditions of the stone

cutter's craft, the human circumstances which make it necessary to consider that craft on its own terms, distinct from the traditions of the book-painter and the metal worker. Otherwise there is no accounting for the taste or want of taste that hedged monumental art within such narrow lanes as we find it followed, while all the wealth of ornament in manuscripts and metal was open to any explorer who could have got his head above the fence.'[3]

By this he presumably means that the work of the sculptors was not under the control of, and thus constantly revitalised by, the contacts of the great religious centres, and for the Northumbrian Danelaw this is certainly true. In those areas of England for which we have documentary evidence for the rebuilding of churches and refounding of monasteries, one would not feel so happy with this judgment. We may set alongside it the apparently contradictory view of Professor Zarnecki: 'This art of stone or stucco reliefs and of sacred images in the

round, must have been produced by highly competent professional artists who were capable of carving in stone and ivory, working in metals, painting murals, and illuminating manuscripts . . . The ability to work in so many different media explains the close stylistic relationship that often exists between works in different materials and sizes'.[4]

Of course these statements are both valid. W. G. Collingwood had worked his way forward through the mass of Northumbrian stone carvings to the crude local works of the Viking Period, Professor Zarnecki was considering southern English art of the immediately pre-Conquest period, and comparing it, unfavourably, with continental ivories and three-dimensional metal-work. I hope I shall be able to show close relationships between southern English sculpture and other media, and also how works are translated in scale from one medium to another. We shall also see inherited traditions modified.

It would indeed be strange if the great religious ferment of the tenth century and the revitalisation provided by foreign contacts should not have produced some response in the sculpture of the period. However, even in such areas where the reform may be documented, it is not unreasonable to postulate a class structure in stone carving, whereby the friezes, capitals, and wall panels of renovated or rebuilt churches may reflect the new taste of the age, and grave markers, whether crosses or recumbent slabs, may be produced by more conservative schools of provincial stone masons. Sussex and Berkshire provide good examples of crude local grave stones of the tenth and eleventh centuries and the dreary assembly of repetitive patterns of the eleventh century plait panels of the grave covers of the East Midlands betray a workshop which operated over a wide area. In this case one need not think of itinerant craftsmen choosing their stones from the regions in which they travelled, but of the finished monuments travelling from some centre near a quarry, such as Barnack. Many of these grave stones appear to be of Barnack stone. However, until a total survey is done in the manner begun by E. M. Jope[5] nothing conclusive can be said. The localisation of centres of production for stone carvings is at least a possibilty less remote than trying to localise metal working centres from analysis of metal artifacts, but it has to be combined with a study of the ornament in a manner not attempted by Jope, or bizarre results can follow. For example, I see no reason to assign the same date to the sculptures at Colyton and Dalton on the basis that they are made of the same stone.

As the final preliminary to considering the monuments one must stress that there is practically no way of dating Anglo-Saxon sculpture except by stylistic criteria; and that the dating of styles, for this period, depends on the dating of manuscripts. However, there can be no certainty as to whether one should allow a time lag of months, or even years between the appearance of the style in manuscripts and in sculpture. Moreover there are certain independent local traditions in stone carving which confuse the issue, so that there is no one clear-cut line of development.

We must now consider what characteristics we should accept for the style of the tenth and early eleventh centuries, which if found on sculpture might lead one to place it within that extensive date bracket. At the risk of appearing to traverse the whole sequence of Wessex sculpture in an attempt to arrive at the tenth century I must mention some pieces which others have dated to the tenth or even eleventh, but which I would date earlier, so that it is clear that I have not disregarded them.

The earliest Wessex sculpture does not appear to have an independent tradition of stone carving motifs such as that of Northumbria or Mercia, but from its inception in c.800 is closely linked in iconography with the other arts — particularly manuscripts. Early pieces such as the door lining from Bradford on Avon, the jambs at Britford, or the Codford St Peter cross[6] are linked by interlace types, foliage details, and in the last case, figural styles, with the Canterbury groups of manuscripts of the late eighth to early ninth centuries.[7] This school is succeeded and partially overlapped by a series whose plant scrolls and animal ornament are derived from Mercian, notably West Midland models. Such are for example Rowberrow, West Camel, Tenbury, Frome, Steventon, Colerne and Dalton. These have been dated by Talbot Rice to the eleventh century[8] because of a supposed resemblance to Ringerike ornament. Cottrill[9] dated them to the eighth or ninth century because of their analogies with manuscripts such as Vatican Barbarini Lạt.570. I would prefer to see the styles beginning in the early ninth century on pieces such as a recumbent slab with an Agnus Dei at Ramsbury, and the rosettes from the earlier Ramsbury cross or the remarkable shaft at Dalton which is closely linked with the *Book of Cerne.*[10] Some characteristics of this group seem to continue into the early tenth and are slowly modified by the new ideas of the reform period.

The distinctive attributes of the official southern art of Winchester, which can be most convincingly seen in the manuscripts, are a lively narrative figure style, and the acceptance of the acanthus as the fashionable plant scroll. This ousts the earlier vine-scrolls, popular in England throughout the eighth century, and the combination of palmette and ivy scroll, which, in southern England at least, co-exists with the vine in the ninth century. The ascription of sculpture to the reform period is however complicated by the fact that, during the early ninth century, there is demonstrably a new wave of classicism in the sculpture of pre-Viking Northumbria and Mercia, which is comparable with, if not directly linked to, the Carolingian copying of antique models in schools. At Otley (Yorks.)[11] and in Mercia at Fletton (Hunts) not only are the figure styles directly comparable with Carolingian manuscripts, but also one finds the Carolingian acanthus, usually taken to be the hall-mark of later Winchester art.

In an attempt to show how difficult it is to be sure of the period of classical revival in sculpture I would like to discuss two monuments more fully. The first is the Wolverhampton column; the second, the cross-shaft from East Stour. The column which stands in St Peter's churchyard, Wolverhampton, still shows even in its present worn condition a quality of carving and distinction of iconography unmatched in cross sculpture in the Midlands. This column, which nearly all commentators seem to consider carried a cross head, was obviously put up to commemorate some major event, and it was suggested by Clapham that it was to be associated with the founding of a minster at Wolverhampton by the Lady Wulfruna in 994.[12] A similar date was proposed by Baldwin Brown.[13] However, Kendrick[14] dated it to the mid-ninth century and called it 'the noblest monument that has

Plates XVI, XVII

come down to us from the pre-Alfredian sculptures of the West-Saxon supremacy' and this view has been developed further recently by Michael Rix.[15] The classical appearance of this column is perhaps emphasised because it seems to be a Roman column re-used, but is mainly produced by the crisp zones of plant ornament. Rix makes the point that although acanthus ornament is rare in pre-Danish England it does appear in ninth-century English manuscripts of the Canterbury

Plate XVII   school, particularly the type of stiff leaf ornament shown in zone C. When he compares the mode of cutting with English metal work of the Trewhiddle period, as for example the rosette binding in the volutes of zone E, and the lozenge fields in zone B, he is less convincing, however. The pendant triangles can be found in metalwork and sculpture of the Viking period; altogether the Wolverhampton column is much more like Carolingian than English work. Rosette centerings are a commonplace in Carolingian stucco and ivories, and if one accepts the bronze screens from the palatine chapel at Aachen as a Carolingian copy of the antique[16] then we can parallel here the method of binding with rosettes the inhabited and plain running scrolls. Nevertheless the Palatine scroll is still partly a vinescroll, and the Wolverhampton foliage is more like the acanthus border on the mid-ninth century ivory from Metz.[17] The birds and beasts in the lozenges and roundels are, none the less, as Rix says, Anglian in type, and can be compared with Breedon, at least in their disposition. They are so worn that it is difficult to see any betraying minor detail, but certainly the manner in which they are left free of a camouflaging growth of plant scroll is more like English work of the ninth century than that of the later tenth as for example on the ivory penner from London or the Corpus Christi Bedè, CCCC 183. The detail that makes me uncertain as to whether one should firmly assume a ninth-century date is the attitude of the small birds in zone B who reach down and peck with exaggeratedly gaping

see pp.204-5   beaks. This attitude is common in tenth- to early eleventh-century manuscripts such as the Bosworth Psalter, and is found also on

Plate XXIIIb   metalwork such as the Canterbury censer cover. If the Wolverhampton column is to be dated a hundred years earlier it represents the first surviving instance of this trick. We have no evidence that crosses were set up at the foundation of monasteries save for those, usually with inscriptions, which are associated with monastic burial grounds and it could be that the Wolverhampton column was some form of an imitation of the continental carved column such as that at Trier, dated 958. Perhaps the Wolverhampton piece is a royal monument, which would be an exotic outlier from the main sphere of Wessex art. In whatever period, it has no obvious copies[18] in the area unless one derives the crude round shafts of the West Midlands from its form. Even with this group however the top of the shaft where it survives is finished differently.[19] There is among the fragments built into the south porch at Avebury a fragment of architectural sculpture with similar stiff acanthus as on zone C at Wolverhampton, but this is not datable. There are of course round shafts in Wessex, for example in the ninth-century round shaft from Winchester with palmette trees and stag, [20] or the possibly eleventh-century shaft from Yetminster (Dorset). I should feel happier to see this column as a revival of the antique in the tenth century rather than a precocious ninth-century copy of Carolingian work, but I think the case must rest as not proven.

A less debatable entry into tenth-century sculpture is however provided by the East Stour shaft. This is by far the most elaborate and well preserved carving of plant scrolls from Wessex. The faces of the cross are divided by arched bands enriched by pellets, circles or chevrons: a method of dividing up a field such as is also found on the ribbon animal group. The scheme is cleverly contrived so that on each face the plant scrolls and interlace panels change position. The cross has been described by N. Drinkwater,[21] who compares several features with ninth-century art, but dates the cross in the eleventh century. The account is accompanied by drawings which give a good idea of the whole although they are not accurate in detail. I shall follow his labelling of the faces, although now that this piece is in the British Museum the terms north, south, east and west are not meaningful.

Plate XVIII

The East face has a medallion plant scroll which springs from a stepped base, the stems bifurcate to fall into triple bunches below and to form a new medallion above. The grape bunches are naturalistically shaped but there are no leaves save the palmette type which cling to the inside of the top medallion and sprout from the junctions of the medallions. This feature may be compared with the Britford door jambs. The form of the tree scroll with stepped base can also be seen at Gloucester, Kelston and Winchester. Above is a ribbed bell-flower of the type seen on the famous Sassanian silver vase now in the Hermitage, Leningrad.

Plate XVIII, left

On the North face the lower panel has a tree scroll of distinctive southern English type. The flat central stem formed of scooped triangular segments, sprouts side tendrils, and terminates in a stiff berry bunch. This form of stem with swelling triangular sections can be traced in metalwork and manuscripts of the later ninth and early tenth centuries, for example the Hillesøy disc (which for no good reason has been placed in eighth-century Northumbria), the back of the Alfred Jewel, and the Corpus Christi Bede, CCCC 183. The form of leaf-flower is popular in late eighth-century continental manuscripts and is also

Fig.19, j, p.190

Fig.19, c-d, p.190

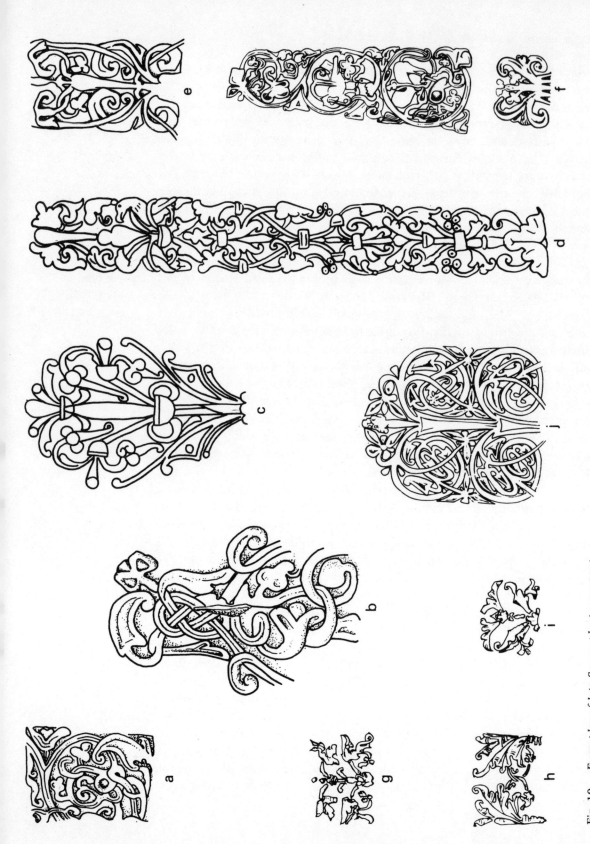

Fig. 19.   *Examples of late Saxon plant ornament*

a, b: Maperton cross, Somerset; c: Back of the Alfred Jewel; d: Border of CCCC 183, folio 1b; e: Littleton Drew cross, Wilts;
f: Colyton cross, Devon; g, h, i: Cuthbert vestments; j: Cross from East Stour, Dorset: detail of North face

Drawing: Robin Palmer

found on an unpublished cross from Gloucester Priory, and the
Lechmere headstone, both of which could be mid-ninth-century. The *Plate XIX*
triangular leaves with sunken centres and curling tips again are typically
southern. The first stage of such leaves is found at Britford, but this
type is also known at Gloucester and Chew Stoke. The idea of scooping
out the centre of the leaf could be derived from the painted shadows of
manuscripts such as the Luxeuil Sacramentary and an attenuated form
of them with a cruder form of linking and coil ending is to be seen at
Ramsbury on a grave cover. The cross has however been dated
according to what is apparently the latest ornament in it, the Sarmatian
type palmette or Byzantine blossom. The form of the flower with its *Plate XVIII,*
right
notched petals and ribbed sunken ornament is possibly derived from
metalwork, of which there are Hungarian examples in the ninth
century, such as the reliquary from Ketschemét, Pest.[22] The pelleted
and incised dividing bands on the cross could also be attributed to
metal work origins, although such bands and ornamental 'body patterns' are known on the animal style crosses. I would therefore like to
attribute this cross to the early tenth century and to see some
inspiration for it provided by imported metalwork, which transformed
earlier Wessex features of the plant scroll.

A curious link with the East Stour ornament is provided by an
unpublished trial piece or mould from the excavations at St Augustine's *Plate XXa*
Abbey, Canterbury. This was unfortunately discovered on the spoil heap
so is of little use for dating but one may observe the same deeply cut,
closely spaced ornament surrounded by a pelleted border. The six
petalled rosettes have gone slightly awry, but they may be compared
with a cross shaft and grave cover at Ramsbury,[23] but the open
flower with curling tips can be related to the East Stour blossom. It is
disappointing that Canterbury has provided so little sculpture from the
excavations of the monastery of St Peter and St Paul. Despite the fact
that there is little good stone available in the area, there are literary
references to an elaborately sculptured tomb over the body of Augustine. [24] However all the material so far recovered seems to be eleventh-
century. One would like to link the east Stour shaft to some important
centre but this is singularly difficult to achieve. In fact the great monastic
centres such as Glastonbury, Canterbury, Sherborne and even Winchester
itself have been so far rather unproductive in providing examples of sculpture which can plausibly be assigned to the tenth century.

From Winchester itself the round shaft with a palmette tree, fine *see p. 189*
interlace and a naturalistic stag has already been noted, and it seems
that in the ninth century the ribbon animal style with pelleted body
was known there. Part of a cross shaft with this animal ornament built

into a wall in St Thomas's Street possibly came from St Rumbold's cemetery and a similar ribbon animal is depicted on an impost from Martin Biddle's excavations of the Old Minster.[25] Some tantalising fragments such as part of a ram's head have emerged from the Old Minster excavations, but so far there are no extant examples of the type of ornament mentioned in the descriptions of the six-storied tower at Winchester each storey of which, according to R. N. Quirk's interpretation,[26] could have displayed elaborate figural carvings. It is obvious both in England and on the continent[27] that a great deal of important sculpture has been lost for this period, and in England at least the remains which survive indicate that the taste for decorative appliqués of stone carving, which manifested itself as early as the seventh century in Northumbria, was developed and found new inspiration in the tenth century. What survives gives some indication of what may be lost.

Fig. 20, p. 194   Pride of place, for external decorative sculpture *in situ,* must be given to the famous tower at Barnack, Northants. Here there is evidence for a cemetery, which the cross fragments seem to indicate spanned the late ninth to early tenth century. On the tower itself the north, west and south faces have inset panels each about five and a half feet tall and one and three-quarter feet wide, showing a stiff tree scroll surmounted by a bird. These scrolls are extremely difficult to place in the English series, nor is it easy to find parallels abroad. The impression is given of a transitional or conservative scheme in which, particularly on the south face, the new disposition of the acanthus scrolls has affected the older vine scroll. The sequence of thickening on the stems we have already noted as a trick which begins in the ninth century and continues in tenth-century work and the composition particularly of the south face reminds one of the tree on which a bird perches in BM Claudius B.iv, fol. 36v which Wormald postulates as based on a tenth-century copy of an early Christian manuscript.[28] On this panel and on the West the side tendrils are 'clipped' on to the frame in the manner of binding tendrils in filigree such as the Kirkoswald brooch found with a hoard of ninth-century coins and it may be that there is some metalwork prototype behind this panel. Baldwin Brown suggested that these looked like bronze or iron grilles and it could well be that they were copying some humbler grilles of the same type as the Aachen screen, *Fig. 19, d,* seen also in scrolls of manuscripts such as CCCC 183. The leaves with *p. 190* scooped centres seem to be a curious mixture of Midland trefoil type which finds its earliest expression at Breedon, and the small, stiff leaves of some Carolingian acanthus scrolls.

The schematic tree vine remains and prolongs its life in Northumbria and it is perhaps significant that the bird parallels for Barnack that

Baldwin Brown cites from Anglo-Saxon sculpture are from North-umbrian crosses of what could be the early tenth century. Nevertheless the single bird on top of a scroll, like the Yorkshire examples, may ultimately be traced back to some of the provincial continental schools of manuscripts of the ninth century where works like the Saint-Amand Gospels favour a fleshy upright plant and where one of the illustration of the comedies of Terence has two birds associated with a tree scroll.[29] Although there are some hints of ninth-century originals behind the Barnack panels I would more happily ascribe them to a rather old fashioned atelier of the early tenth century. This date too would fit the foliage on the sundial lower on the West face of the tower.

The effect of earlier fashions of plant ornament can be seen on other examples of acanthus ornament on southern crosses which seem to date to the tenth century. However one must be cautious in seeing this hybridisation as a distinctly sculptural phenomenon, since it is found on objects in other media that have some independent dating claims. The famous stole and maniple at Durham, embroidered between 909 and 916, are usually taken as proving the acceptance of acanthus ornament in the court art of Wessex.[30] Nevertheless R. Freyhan pointed out the differences between the plant from the embroideries and the acanthus scrolls and friezes on Carolingian ivories and manu-scripts.[31] He derived the plant from a Middle Eastern type of sheathed flower, specifically Sassanian. (The same origins, in fact, as I have postulated for the plant ornament on the East Stour cross). The form of tree scroll on maniple II which Freyhan compares with a Coptic silk clavus of the sixth-seventh century in which the plants spring alternately from rounded and triangular-shaped vases is found in a stylised form not only on the Alfred Jewel and maniple II at Durham, but also the borders of CCCC 183, and sculpture at Colyton (Devon), Chew Stoke (Somerset), and Littleton Drew (Wilts.). The Colyton inhabited scroll which Kendrick[32] compared with the Lambeth Psalter, is to my mind more like CCCC 183 in detail. The large double outlined leaf with curling tip, the small scooped ivy leaf and the trefoil are all, as previously indicated, developments of earlier features but the crumpled bell flowers and tightly massed energy of the main scroll are nearer to tenth-century types. Below at Colyton is a panel of upright acanthus tree which is matched on a rather larger scale at Littleton Drew, and both these pieces are obviously closely linked with Chew Stoke and Maperton (Somerset). The distribution of these acanthus scrolls on sculpture seems to indicate some centre in western Wessex for their production, and the resemblance in points of detail would imply

Fig.19, g-i,
p.190

Fig.19, e-f,
p.190

Fig.19, a-b,
p.190

Fig. 20.
Barnack, Northants, Church of St John the Baptist: carved panels in West tower. Left to right: West face; North face; South face.

Drawing: Robin Palmer

some limitation of date. They are certainly quite different from the eleventh-century essays in acanthus ornament such as are found on the Sompting friezes, and the earlier style seems to die out on crosses and grave covers, in favour of the pelleted plaits and scrolls which are found at Bibury[33] and Winchester.[34]

The elegant figural styles of the reform period are reflected largely in crucifixion scenes, in stone and ivory, and some wall panels. In the space at my disposal I shall have to discuss them rather selectively. Unlike the plant scrolls some pieces represent a complete break with earlier traditions as well as an obvious reflection of the manuscript styles. Three angels have by common consent been assigned to the tenth century: that at Deerhurst, the pair at Bradford on Avon, and the one at Winterbourne Steepleton:[35] worthy representatives in stone of the clouds of witnesses which throng the Winchester manuscripts. Angel figures are common enough in earlier sculpture: in Crucifixion, Annunciation and Apocalypse scenes on the heads of crosses, as guardians, or figures for adoration but they are usually shown as standing figures or frontal busts. The earliest flying examples of which I know in English sculpture, are the little figures on the Rothbury cross head, which are not only without haloes but also without wings. The earliest and in many ways the most impressive of the tenth-century group is the mutilated bust set in a panel in the apse at Deerhurst. Kendrick, to whom this is 'a gaunt and Celtic looking masterpiece', dates it to the reign of King Alfred.[36] But Baldwin Brown,[37] and Clapham,[38] who consider it to be in its original position, assign it to the tenth, and in this they are followed by Talbot Rice,[39] who wonders whether it were copied from an earlier manuscript. The figure is complete in itself and obviously not part of a composition, so it possibly represents an archangel. It has been suggested recently by T. Mackay that it could have been a symbol of St Matthew. Whether as part of a sequence of four archangels or four evangelist symbols it might parallel the supposed scheme in the Winchester New Minster. The angel's hair is arranged in two rows of scallops in the manner of some Carolingian ivories when copying classical curls, or more remotely like the angels in the Book of Kells. The eyes are delicately lidded, the chin prominent, and the lips slightly pursed. It has a gaunt, slightly disdainful appearance. The nearest type for this angel that I can find in tenth-century art is BM Harley 603, fol.1, but the expression is quite different, and I think that one should accept this as an early tenth-century precursor of the gayer later figures — hieratic and solemn in the manner of the prophets on the Cuthbert embroideries.

The Winterbourne Steepleton angel is also not complete. This panel two feet long is built into the south wall of the church and shows an angel in flight, but unfortunately without his hands which might have given a clue to his activity. His head is turned back over the body, and the feet are kicked almost at right angles into the air. The head is squarish with strongly modelled features: almond eyes and slightly pouting mouth and his drapery is tightly swathed round the body with one flying fold. The folds at the hem of the tunic are conveyed rather crudely, by sharp V-shaped incisions, but there can be little doubt that the artist is attempting to copy angels of the type found in the New

Frontispiece Minster Charter. The flat fillet which binds the hair smoothly back over the ears is typical of manuscripts of the late tenth/early eleventh century and is not known in the many earlier angels in English sculpture. The fact that this angel is looking back over his shoulder seems to indicate that he is an attendant figure at some scene in which Christ is supported in a mandorla. When angels attend at crucifixion they are usually concentrated on the drama enacted between them, and do not allow themselves to be distracted in this way. The grave pair of flying angels from Bradford on Avon have been universally accepted as part of a tenth-century crucifixion scene such as one finds for example in the Sherborne Pontifical.[40] If this were in the position where they were discovered — over the chancel arch — it must have been a **huge** composition filling almost the entire wall. However, as has often been pointed out, a feature of tenth- and eleventh-century roods is their increased scale. These figures do not suffer, as some sculptures do, in being enlarged. They are well proportioned and the drapery folds over the body are skilfully conveyed in a few lines contrasting with the elaborate crumpled folds of the napkins which drape their hands.[41] In fact the plain banded hem is more reminiscent of the drapery on earlier tenth-century manuscripts such as the Dunstan Grammar or the Corpus Christi Bede.

The manner in which the drapery types in sculpture develop alongside the manuscript styles is well illustrated by another angel, perhaps from an Annunciation scene on the west wall of the tower at

Plate XXb Stinsford (Dorset).[42] Even in its mutilated state this is a bustling active angel with a mission. The complicated layers of its drapery with kicked out hems remind one forcibly of the drawings of the mid-eleventh century such as the Psychomachia of Prudentius.[43] One other pair of angels must be mentioned to complement this group: the two soaring, yearning figures from the tiny plaque only seven and a half by five centimetres dug up in St Cross Street, Winchester.[44] They have usually been considered part of a group perhaps surrounding a central Majestas. They have no haloes and their hair is not bound but

falls in a soft loose roll. In these attributes and the kicked out drapery
at the hem, they are reminiscent of the Carolingian Metz school, but in
England this type of drapery, and the stiff leaf ornament such as is
found at their feet, is best paralleled in manuscripts of the period
1000-1120, one example of which is the New Minster Register. The
relationship between ivories and manuscripts is more intimate than
between manuscripts and stone carvings and there seems no doubt that
many of them were carved in monastic workshops and so could have
mirrored directly the style and iconography of the house. Only in the
crucifixion scenes does one find the parallel problem to those of stone
where new and old traditions combine. Other ivories may reflect the
excitements with new themes and formulas which we have seen as
animating the literate group in society in this period. An interesting
example is the seal matrix eight and a half centimetres high, found in a
garden at Wallingford. This piece was dated by Longhurst to the late
tenth century.[45] However, the seal has been restruck: the earlier seal
incribed *Godgyðe* closely copies a coin of c.990, but the later figure of
a man inscribed *Godwin* is mid-eleventh-century. It seems reasonable
therefore to assign the matrix of the earlier seal to the late tenth
century. The subject illustrates Psalm 109, 'The Lord said to my Lord:
sit thou at my right hand until I make thine enemies thy footstool.' As
it now is the scene is a Binity with the co-equal Father and Son seated
on a throne and deeply engaged in contemplation of one another. The
Father holds a rod of power and the Son seems to hold a scroll in his
left hand and to bless with his right.[46] This theme is popular in
manuscripts of the Winchester school and the positioning of the figures
is very close to the Canterbury Psalter fol.199^V although the round
beardless faces and attributes of the figures on the ivory cannot be
directly paralleled in manuscripts. The theme of the ivory has been
related to the Offices of the Holy Cross and Trinity for the New
Minster, Cotton D.xxvii fol.75^V and is a perfect example of how the
new liturgical ideas of the reform affected not only manuscript but
plastic iconography. The distribution of Winchester ideas in the newly
founded centres in the Danelaw is well illustrated by an ivory plaque
supposedly discovered at North Elmham, Norfolk, and now in the
Museum of Archaeology and Ethnology, Cambridge.[47] Christh in a   *Plate XXc*
mandorla above has his hand held up in blessing and, as the inscription
says, is exhibiting his wounds. Below are St Mary and St Peter with two
angels supporting a large cross around which are grouped tiny figures.

Also reflecting perhaps liturgical changes in the tenth and eleventh
centuries are the large-scale roods parts of which survive in significantly
large numbers in Hampshire[48] although the popularity of the

crucifixion scene both on wall panels and on crosses is widespread from Northumbria to Wessex in the tenth and eleventh centuries. Dr Taylor has illustrated some of these and discussed a possible liturgical use for the internal large roods, such as Romsey or Breamore, and clearly these mirror the Carolingian-derived art of the manuscripts. Nevertheless there are many small stone or ivory roods which seem to reflect earlier English or provincial models such as the smaller Romsey plaque or an ivory now in the Victoria and Albert Museum.[49]

Plate XXI   Something of the new learning of the Reform is perhaps reflected in some exotic animal ornament such as Cranbourne or Melbury Bubb. The latter is apparently a round-shafted cross converted into a font, and it provides a unique example of what may be early eleventh-century ornament. Four large beasts, a stag and three lions or panthers with frond-like tails, are solemnly disposed around the shaft. Their tails are knotted in loose loops and squeezed in between them are three small anonymous creatures, bipeds or quadrupeds, whose tails also are overwhelmingly looped and knotted. The strange lizard-like creature at whom the stag sniffs incredulously is remotely akin to the sprawling *Plate XXIIa* beast from Melbury Osmond, but is hardly reminiscent of the hound which by rights should be attacking the hart. On the other side of the stag however a small dog leaps ineffectively at a large panther-like creature. Obviously here there is some connection with the oriental lion hunt motif, such as is later adapted on Romanesque capitals,[50] but in the Melbury Bubb shaft there is no hint of savage combat. The staid procession of great beasts reminds one of late Saxon poems such as *The Panther* which adapting the *Physiologus* says admiringly of the panther *þæt is wrætlic deor!*   The panther was a type of Christ and if this is so at Melbury Bubb the powers of evil are shrunken, ineffectual little monsters.

The sculpture of the reform period is in many ways, as I have attempted to show, a natural development of what has gone before with no dramatic break. Nevertheless in the infusion of new ideas from the Winchester school of manuscripts new plant forms and a new iconography spread throughout southern and parts of Midland England. The utility of sculpture in stone is that even though it may have strayed from its exact location it usually does not leave the site. This enables one to have some concrete image of how far-reaching was the effect of the new ideas. One can plot the spread of acanthus ornament and improved figure carving, but there are large areas of England in Northumbria and East Anglia, where, and this is a sobering thought, there are over a thousand fragments of carvings which could date to the period of late ninth to late eleventh century which show no

sympathy with or ability to adopt the new art. The community of St
Cuthbert at Chester-le-Street and Durham may have possessed the
famous embroideries, and some southern English manuscripts, but they
did not use them as models. They seem to have been as irrelevant to the
beleagured Northern English cut off by the Danelaw, as were the many
Roman carvings which existed for any Anglo-Saxon to see in the sixth
century. These northern Christians may have reverted to building
wooden churches as they did at Chester-le-Street, but they still clung to
the tradition that it was fitting for a Christian to have a stone grave
marker which satisfied either traditional or secular Viking taste.

Professor Zarnecki remarked, in his review of late Saxon sculpture in
southern England, that one wondered why the English bothered to
carve such two dimensional work when painting would have done just
as well. Of course much of the sculpture must have been painted: we
have evidence for this from the earliest period in the balusters and
carved imposts at Monkwearmouth and this continues in the architectural sculpture such as Martin Biddle has excavated at Winchester,
and in stone crosses of varying dates. All the same the real answer to
this theory seems to be that while on the Continent there was an
unbroken tradition of stucco work and wall painting as alternatives to
stone carvings, the English adopted decorative stone carvings very early,
and maintained the tradition of using stone panels for the decoration of
their churches. While at Malles one finds wall paintings of figures in
niches surrounded by painted frames, at Breedon or Castor the figures
and their surrounding frames are carved as wall panels, and we have
seen this tradition continues into the eleventh century.

The transfusion of the reform ideas was to produce some dramatic
and individual pieces, even though it would seem that to some of the
intellectuals of the reform, the visual arts were of secondary importance. As Aelfric said 'In one way we look at a picture in quite
another way at writing' and certainly the result of the movement was
not to produce sculptural conformity. No doubt as in the age of Bede,
the wall paintings and stone carving in churches, and the sculpture of
crosses were for the enlightenment of the unlettered, but as for the
later Middle Ages this was the way in which the ordinary man and
woman in the countryside became aware, as a supplement to sermons
he may not have swiftly grasped, of the spread of new theological ideas.
Perhaps then it is fitting that we should not forget the evidence for the
popularisation, even vulgarisation, of the reform.

Chapter 14

TENTH-CENTURY METALWORK

by D. M. Wilson

In this chapter I shall examine the corpus of English metalwork of the tenth century. The number of surviving objects is small and the general standard of the material makes mockery of the fact that since the Middle Ages Dunstan has been the patron saint of the jeweller and silversmith. Only rarely does its quality rise to any considerable heights, and then only on minor and insignificant objects. From documentary sources it is clear that there were many grand treasures in the churches of England in the tenth century[1] but none of these survive in this country. In fact we have only the rather miserable mounts of a crozier in Cologne cathedral[2] and a small portable altar now in the Musée de Cluny in Paris[3] to give us any idea of the richness of ecclesiastical metalwork in the dying years of the Anglo-Saxon period. In this country three bronze censer-covers comprise the total surviving corpus of liturgical metalwork of the period of the *Regularis Concordia*.[4] For the rest we are dealing almost completely with secular material, often of a rather second-rate quality.

The material is, however, important in two entirely different ways. Firstly, it is of importance as archaeological evidence (for the occurrence of objects ornamented in this style in archaeological contexts may enable us to date that context); secondly, because in the metalwork lie clues to the origins of the Winchester style and of tenth-century English art, clues that are not present in the more photogenic material which gives a name to that style. It is my intention here to suggest that many features of the Winchester style were already present in English metalwork by about 900. I shall also touch on the relation of the English metalwork to continental material both in Scandinavia and in central Europe.

In order to examine the first of these two points we must look in some detail at the art of the ninth century. It is interesting that Otto Homburger, in his doctoral dissertation on the Winchester school as long ago as 1912, took as one of his starting points a piece of metalwork — the back of the Alfred Jewel.[5] He soon moved away

Fig. 19, c, p. 190

from this object to the art of the manuscripts which formed the main material of his study. Even if we ignore the Alfred Jewel — which might after all have been made to the order of another Alfred than the king of that name — we have a sufficiently reliable series of dates (which I have enumerated on two occasions[6]) to enable us to build up a fairly firm chronological sequence for the art of the metalworker in this period.

In the ninth century there are at least three objects — a finger-ring bearing the name of King Aethelwulf, another bearing the name of Queen Aethelswith and the seal of Bishop Aethilwald — which can be dated within the life-times of these people.[7] Another secondary, but important, method of dating provides a useful *terminus post quem* for many objects. This occurs when an object is found in a hoard of coins. For the ninth century, seven hoards are known to contain objects decorated with Anglo-Saxon ornament.[8] The most important is that from Trewhiddle (Cornwall), which was deposited in 872-5: the ornament of the objects in this hoard includes motifs of a specific type, executed in silver and niello. The two chief motifs are, firstly, animals with a speckled sub-triangular body;[9] and secondly, a foliate orna- *Fig. 21, a,* ment, each leaf of which has a double nick at the contour. This latter is *p. 203* related to a leaf ornament which goes back to the eighth century, but *Fig. 21, b* which in this form appears, for example, on a brooch in the hoard from Beeston Tor (Derbyshire), dated to c.875, and on that most splendid *Fig. 21, d* object, the Fuller brooch. On certain objects, such as a finger-ring from *Fig. 21, e* Poslingford in Suffolk, a balanced 'potted-plant' motif occurs — one of the traditions of which is undoubtedly the vine-scroll, but which conceivably has some reminiscence of the balanced acanthus motifs which had already appeared in continental metalwork in the first half of the ninth century.[10] I see these two motifs — the Poslingford 'potted plant' and the balanced continental acanthus — at the root of the ornament which occurs on the Sittingbourne scramasax. In one of *Fig. 22, p. 203* the panels of this object is leaf ornament of the Trewhiddle style — ornament which suggests a late ninth-century date for the object — while another panel depicts a distinct ragged leaf ornament, which is clearly at the root of the Winchester acanthus ornament and which is very close to that which occurs, for example, on the stole of St Cuthbert. Winchester acanthus rarely occurs by itself on metalwork. *Fig. 23, p. 203* The most remarkable departure from this tendency is the ornament on the back of the seal-die of Aelfric, found just outside the boundaries of *Fig. 24, p. 203* ancient Winchester, in the parish of Weeke. This object is dated to the late 970s because the seal is modelled on coins struck between March 978 and Michaelmas 979. It was consequently made a few years after the painting of the Benedictional of St Aethelwold. The ornament

Frontispiece

Plate XXIIb

Fig.25, p.203

Plate XXIIc

Fig.19, d,

p.190

Frontispiece

Plate XXIIIa

resembles the corner of one of the frames of a Winchester manuscript, perhaps a little less lush than the Benedictional and closer to the ornament of the Charter of the New Minster[11] with its more attenuated tendrils. Similar attenuated tendrils occur on such objects as the mount from Southampton and on a lost object — a strap-end from Buccombe Down (Isle of Wight).[12] A reasonably close parallel was found at Meols in Cheshire.[13]

This strap-end can serve to introduce a series of objects which demonstrate tenth-century metalwork as it really is. The finest piece is undoubtedly the strap-end from the excavations at Winchester itself, which is in practically mint condition. It is perhaps most closely related in design to the ornament of the borders of the dedication page of the Corpus Christi *Vita Cuthberti* (CCCC 183). For here the same birds, beasts and balanced foliate ornament are clearly seen.[14] The free voluted terminals of the foliage of the strap-end are, however, more closely paralleled to the borders of the New Minster Charter and I have dated the strap-end to the late tenth-century on this basis[15] — accepting Wormald's date for this manuscript.[16] The chunky quality of this moulded bronze is repeated on a fair number of objects of tenth-century date: objects like a small gilt-bronze jug, without provenance, which has ornament derived from a similar balanced vine-scroll; this would probably be dated to the late tenth century on the basis of the large shell spiral on the spout, which is a feature of a

Figs. 21-28 (opposite):   *all reproduced actual size.*

Fig. 21.   Details of late Saxon metalwork ornament.
            a: Sittingbourne scramasax;   *b*; Fetter Lane, London, sword-pommel;
            c: the Poslingford, Suffolk, ring;   *d*; a brooch from Beeston Tor, Derby-
            shire;   *e*; the Fuller brooch.

Fig. 22.   Panels from the Sittingbourne, Kent, scramasax.

Fig. 23.   Detail from the stole of St Cuthbert.

Fig. 24.   Ornament from back of a seal from Weeke, Hampshire.

Fig. 25.   Strap-end from Buccombe Down, Isle of Wight.

Fig. 26.   Niello ornament from the King's School, Canterbury, disc-brooch.

Fig. 27.   Strap-end from York.

Fig. 28.   Ornament of a strap-end from Winchester.

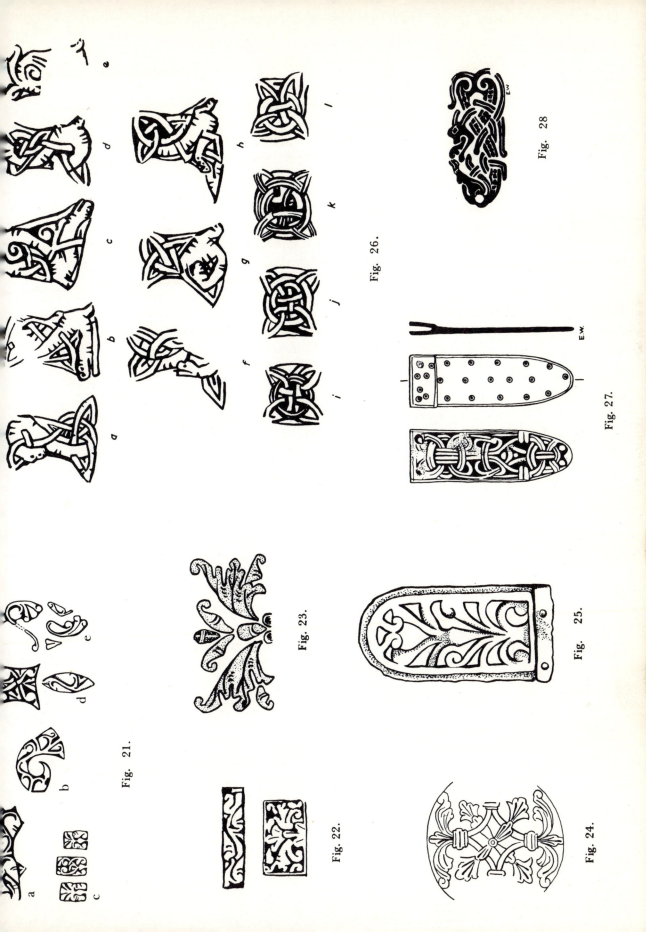

Fig. 21.

Fig. 22.

Fig. 23.

Fig. 24.

Fig. 25.

Fig. 26.

Fig. 27.

Fig. 28

tenth-century Scandinavian ornament introduced into England by the middle of that century.

By far the most important group of objects in this style comprises, however, the three censer-covers from Pershore, London and Canterbury, which take the form of church towers.[17] Of these, that from Canterbury is most interesting. The inlaid silver plates around its base bear classic ragged acanthus — executed in niello — which is not unlike that found on the Sittingbourne scramasax and is executed in the same material. It is impossible to date the ornament, but I would prefer to place it earlier in the tenth century than the Benedictional of St Aethelwold. The animals with their hips inlaid with silver plates have a clear origin in the menagerie of the inhabited vine scroll, as do the birds. The peculiar forward bent position of the neck is very often found in incidental ornament in the Winchester manuscripts. Both creatures can be seen, for example, at the head of the canon tables of the manuscript Trinity College, Cambridge, B.10.4, where even the stance of the bird is exactly the same as that on the Canterbury object.[18]

Plate XXIIIb

Fig. 22, p. 203

An even more contorted bird on a piece of metalwork leads us into realms of fascinating and justified speculation. It occurs in a roundel of a brooch found allegedly at Brasenose College, Oxford.[19] It undoubtedly belongs to the same ornamental tradition as similar birds in such tenth-century manuscripts as Bodleian Junius 27 and Tanner 10. (Unfortunately it is practically impossible to produce a photograph of this brooch as the enamel obscures the ornament.) It is, however, extremely interesting to note that champlevé enamel was being produced in an English idiom in this country in the tenth century. There is not a great deal of English enamel of this period — another piece also from Oxford I take to be rather later in date[20] — but two pieces, obviously made by the same hand (which come from opposite ends of the country) are of extreme interest. One is from Hyde Abbey, Winchester, and one from a Viking grave at Bedlington (Northumberland). I think that there can be little doubt that both objects were made in this country (the ornament is perhaps best paralleled in metalwork on a silver disc from Cuxton, Kent[21]) but there can be little doubt that they are modelled on a series of objects made on the Danube, and known, after the type site in Austria, as Kettlach enamels.[22] An example of this Kettlach type in the British Museum has no provenance. It is adequately paralleled in Austria and Hungary and certainly belongs to the class first discussed by Riegl at the turn of the century,[23] which is generally dated to the ninth century. The border of this object is made up of chunky animal ornament, so worn that it is

Plate XXIVa

Plate XXIVb

difficult for the untutored eye to sort it out. This same ornament is to be seen on other Austrian objects — the Kremsmünster candle-sticks.[24] Both Jenny[25] and Haseloff[26] have pointed out that this ornament is closely related to the style of the Canterbury censer-cover, and Arbman[27] (who has gone into this matter in some detail) could not come to any real conclusion as to the origin of the objects, but stressed both the English and Langobardic parallels. Particularly interesting is the presence of inlaid silver and niello on the bases of the candlesticks, techniques which are exactly paralleled on the Canterbury censer-cover. We have here a very distinct parallel between the ornament of England and central Europe in the tenth century, and it is hard to avoid the conclusion that there is some common tradition here although the cradle of the stylistic details is difficult to define. An interesting parallel is provided by the Henry II Gospel cover at Munich. *Plate XXIVc* The impressed gilt plates between the arms of the cross seem to bear animals and birds which are more closely paralleled in England than anywhere else in Europe.

In northern Europe two swords bear mounts which must be very closely related to the English series. They come from Vrångabäck and Dybäck in Skåne.[28] Brøndsted in 1923 implied that they were English,[29] and, although nobody has actually said that this was indeed their place of manufacture, this feeling has always remained at the backs of the minds of the people working on this material. The swords must be very closely modelled on English prototypes, as two of the panels on the Vrångabäck sword can be paralleled almost exactly in the ninth-century ornamental tradition, most clearly seen perhaps on an English brooch most interestingly found in Sweden at Stockholm.[30] In my opinion the swords are not English. I would suggest, however, that they were made in Scandinavia under strong English influence.[31] The ornament is very close to that found in the manuscripts, but is in some way slightly foreign. This may be a facet of that English influence in Scandinavia which can be seen on a number of objects — like the brooch from Austris on the island of Gotland[32] — which were made under strong influence of ninth-century English ornament with speckled animal ornament inlaid with niello. That English metalworkers were working in Scandinavia is further suggested by the presence of English moneyers there.[33]

English ornament had a great deal of influence on Scandinavian art of the late tenth and eleventh century. The rather ragged style of the later Winchester style lay at the roots of the full-blown Ringerike ornament with its elongated ragged tendrils, which appeared in Scandinavia in the eleventh century[34] and which makes itself felt in some of the major centres of English art — in London, for example, and at Winchester and Canterbury. In the tenth century Anglo-Saxon art was itself much affected by the art of the Viking peoples. This is particularly seen in the sculpture, not only of the areas under nominal Viking control, but also in the south of England — in places as remote from the Vikings, for example, as Bexhill.[35] Only rarely does Viking art appear on English metalwork. A few objects, like the rather splendid

Fig.26, p.203   brooch from the King's School, Canterbury, with its inlaid panels, bear an animal ornament akin to that seen on the annular brooch from Austris cited above. This ornament has its roots in the Trewhiddle creatures,[36] but the brooch bears other zoomorphic details which are clearly of Viking origin, as, for example, the double contour and the irregular ribbon interlace. This object seems to me to be the product of an English craftsman working in an unfamiliar idiom in a material with which he is completely at home.

A few fragments of insular metalwork are executed in motifs which belong to the Borre style — a strap-end from Canterbury and a mount

Fig.27, p.203   from York, for example.[37] But a rather surprising object is the strap-end found in the Winchester excavations which is decorated in the

Fig.28, p.203   Jellinge style. In many minor details this object departs from the classic Scandinavian Jellinge motif — these I have enumerated in the preliminary report on the object[38] — and it is rather surprising that the strap-end is the nearest approach by an English artist to the true Scandinavian style. It might even be said that this object was made in Winchester, but this is a pure guess.

It would not be proper to leave this rather summary discussion of the tenth-century metalworker's products without mentioning a most obtrusive and far-flung group of objects decorated in a technique already known in ninth-century England, but most popular in the tenth and eleventh centuries. These objects are all secular and are of iron encrusted with coarse foliate patterns executed in a yellowy copper wire or, more rarely, in a polychrome technique in which a number of wires of different materials (silver and bronze being the most usual) are inlaid in patterns. The technique most commonly occurs on riding equipment, particulary on stirrups.[39] But it also occurs on weapons — as, for example, on the hilt of a sword from the Thames at London.[40] The dating of such objects is obscure, and typological considerations would incline me to place them in both the tenth and eleventh centuries. Stylistically they tell us little, but they do demonstrate a lively use of a technique which has a long history and which was clearly described in technical terms by Theophilus in his treatise *De Diversis Artibus.*[41]

Little then can emerge from this study but certain suggestions can be made. Firstly, we can show that there was a fairly lively and easily recognisable style of ornament in metal in the tenth century; fine quality has been glimpsed in the large Winchester strap-end and such an object cannot have been unique. Secondly, we can show clearly that the tenth-century metalworker was using certain technical tricks — enamelling, niello, encrustation and filigree — in a thoroughly competent fashion. Thirdly, there is sufficient evidence to demonstrate a continuity of tradition between the ornament of the ninth century and that of the tenth century — and that this is more clearly demonstrated in metalwork than in any other medium. Fourthly, the English metalworker, while he drew on continental models, also influenced and worked in parallel with his continental contemporary — both in Scandinavia and in Central Europe. Lastly, it should be emphasised that the Scandinavian artist was also at work in this country and that, although we have much less material than the student of sculpture, we must seriously consider this influence as a factor in the total art of the tenth century.

NOTES AND REFERENCES

Chapter 2

1 The best general account of the reform is still that in *MO*, pp.31-82; see also *RC*, Introduction. The studies of E. John, mainly contained in *OB*, pp.154-264, are both stimulating and provocative; even those who cannot assent to all his conclusions recognise that he has brought a new dimension to the study of the reform.

2 Adam of Bremen, *Gesta Hannaburgensis Ecclesiae Pontificum* in *MGH* Scriptores, 7, ii, pp.319-27; see also C. J. A. Opperman, *The English Missionaries in Sweden and Finland* (London, 1937).

3 The date 940, which replaces the traditional 943, is due to a charter of King Edmund addressed in 940, to 'my faithful abbot Dunstan' (see *BCS*, no.752, *ASCh.*, no.466 and *MO*, p.xvi).

4 *ASC, s.a.* 964.

5 For these figures see *MO*, pp.697-701. This proportion of monastic bishops in England far exceeded those of later centuries.

6 M. Esposito, 'La vie de Sainte Wulfhilde par Goscelin de Cantorbéry', *Analecta Bollandiana*, 32 (1913), pp.10-26; I first drew attention to this Life in *Ampleforth J.*, 76 (1971), pp.51-3.

7 See *Fisher I.*

8 See *MO*, pp.80-1, for the evidence from both Domesday Book and the Abingdon Chronicle.

9 The argument is developed by R. W. Southern, *St Anselm and his Biographer* (Cambridge, 1965). With regard to the text of the Rule of St Benedict used by the reform, it is noteworthy that out of the 10 surviving examples no fewer than six are bilingual, some of which contain hesitant and inconsistent changes of gender for the use of nuns. The Old English version was the work of Aethelwold. Further study of these manuscripts would very likely shed light both on the place of origin of their archetype and on the standard of scholarship in the monasteries. For a hand-list of these manuscripts see *Rule*, p.27.

10 For the Lives of the saints, see select bibliography: for Dunstan, under *Adelard, B Life,* and in other matter contained in *Memorials;* for Aethelwold, under *Aelfric Life* and *Wulfstan Life*; for Oswald, under *Vita Oswaldi.* See also *Fisher II.* Biographies from the age of Bede include Eddius's Life of Wilfrid (ed. B. Colgrave, Cambridge 1927) and Bede's own Lives of the Abbots (*Baedae Opera Historia*, ed. C. Plummer, Oxford 1896).

11 For St Wulfstan of Worcester, see *Vita Wulfstani* and D. H. Farmer, 'Two Biographies by William of Malmesbury' in *Latin Biography*, ed. T. A. Dorey (London, 1967), pp.157-76.

12 The figures quoted below are taken from *MRH*.

13 A large number may have housed only ten or fewer monks from the start.

14 *ASC, s.a.* 971. Thurketil had no recorded contact, still less a 'novitiate', with the principal reformers.

15 See I. Atkins, 'An Investigation of Two Anglo-Saxon Kalendars', *Archaeologia*, 78 (1928), pp.219-40; A. J. Stacpoole, 'Regularis Concordia', *Ampleforth J.*, 76 (1971), pp.48-9; *Barlow*, passim.

16 *Gesta Pont.*, pp.431-2.

17 Eadmer, *Vita S. Dunstani* in *Memorials*, pp.237-8; *Gesta Reg.*, pp.304-6; *Gesta Pont.*, p.70.

Chapter 3

1 *Reginonis abbatis Prumiensis Chronicon,* ed. F. Kurze, Scriptores rerum Germanicarum (Hanover, 1890), p.129.

2 ibid., p.139, the date supplied by a later passage, p.147; *Vita S. Magnerici (archiep. Trev.),* MGH, Scriptores, 8, ed. G. F. Pertz, p.208; compare H. Sauerland, *Trierer Geschichtsquellen des 11. Jahrhunderts* (Trier, 1889), pp.46ff.

3 *Libri Confraternitatum Sancti Galli...,* ed. P. Piper, *MGH,* Libri Confraternitatum, 1 (Hanover, 1884), pp.136f., compare p.100: both entries conveniently reprinted in J. A. Robinson, *The Saxon Bishops of Wells,* Br. Acad. Suppl. Pap., 4 (London, 1918); *Gesta Pont.,* pp.399-400, English translation in *EHD,* pp.821-2.

4 *PL,* 132, cols.1075-7.

5 *RC,* p.2, §3.

6 *Notkeri Balbuli Gesta Karoli Magni Imperatoris,* ed. H. F. Haefele, *MGH,* Scriptores rerum Germanicarum, N.S., 12 (Berlin, 1959), and the review by J. M. Wallace-Hadrill in *EHR,* 76 (1961) pp.490-92.

7 Recorded in a letter from the Bishop of Brescia to the Bishop of Constance in 878: *Das Formelbuch des Bischofs Salomo von Konstanz,* ed. E. Dümmler (Leipzig, 1857), p.47.

8 For the two Burgundian kingdoms see esp. R. Poupardin, *Le Royaume de Provence sous les Carolingiens* (Paris, 1901), and *Le Royaume de Bourgogne* (Paris, 1907). For Wilfrid's Pyrenean 'principality' see R. d'Abadal i de Vinyals, *Els Primers Comtes Catalans* (Barcelona, 1958), pp.53-171, 233-47.

9 See E. Hlawitschka, *Lotharingien und das Reich an der Schwelle der deutschen Geschichte,* Schriften der *MGH,* 21 (Stuttgart, 1967), passim; also K. Hauck, 'Die Ottonen und Aachen', *KdG,* 4, pp.39-53.

10 J. Dhondt, *Études sur la Naissance des Principautés territoriales en France,* Rijksuniv. te Gent, Werken... Letteren, 102 (Bruges, 1948), esp. ch. 2 and appendices 1 and 3; K. F. Werner, 'Untersuchungen zur Frühzeit des französischen Fürstentums, I', *Welt als Geschichte,* 18 (1958), pp.256-89.

11 The immediate background to this situation is exhaustively analysed by H. Keller, 'Zum Sturz Karls III', *Deutsches Archiv,* 22 (1966), pp.333-84.

12 Regino's historical outlook and method have been well discussed by H. Löwe, 'Regino von Prüm und das historische Weltbild der Karolingerzeit', *Rheinische Vjbl.,* 17 (1952), pp.151-79, and K. F. Werner, 'Zur Arbeitsweise des Regino von Prüm', *Welt als Geschichte,* 19 (1959), pp.96-116; see also next note.

13 H. Löwe, 'Geschichtsschreibung der ausgehenden Karolingerzeit', *Deutsches Archiv,* 23 (1967), pp.1-30. For the similarities of the *Vita Alfredi* with Thegan's *Vita Hludovvici* rather than with the *Vita Karoli,* see my remarks in 'The educational tradition in England from Alfred to Aelfric: teaching *utriusque linguae*', *XIX^a SdS* (1972), p.455, n. 2. For Alfred's illness see C. N. L. Brooke, 'Historical writing in England between 850 and 1150', *XVII^a SdS* (1970), p.233, where a fuller study of the problem is announced.

14 For the concept of *respublica Christiana,* formulated in Louis's early years, see F. L. Ganshof, *The Carolingians and the Frankish Monarchy* (London, 1971), pp.261-72 ('Louis the Pious reconsidered' [1957]); J. Semmler, 'Reichsidee und kirchliche Gesetzgebung', *Zeitschr. f. Kirchengesch.,* 71 (1960), pp.37-65. From the enormous mass of recent literature on the idea of unity and its implications for the history of 9th-century Western Europe I select Ganshof, op. cit., pp.273-88 ('Some observations on the *Ordinatio Imperii* of 817' [1955]); W. Mohr, *Die karolingische*

Reichsidee (Münster, 1962). Disunity and its consequences are the central theme of Nithard's *Historiarum libri IV*, ed. Ph. Lauer (Paris, 1926): for the language of disunity see pp.4, 14, 28, 46, 82, etc.

15 Ermoldus Niger in his *Carmen in honorem Hludowici*, ed. E. Faral (Paris, 1932), lines 1092-7 (part of an account of the Imperial re-coronation of 816), links the expected *progenies* of Louis with the line of Abraham. But the 'Tree of Jesse' theme in art is not found until much later.

16 Hauck in *KdG*, 4; B. Bischoff, 'Hadoardus and the manuscripts of classical authors from Corbie' in *Didascaliae: Studies in honour of A.M. Albareda*, ed. S. Prete (New York, 1961), pp.41-57; Bischoff in *KdG*, 2, pp. 42-6.

17 R. Folz, *Le Souvenir et la Légende de Charlemagne dans l'Empire germanique médiévale* (Paris, 1950), pp.28-37, 47-68; H. Beumann, *Ideengeschichtliche Studien zu Einhard...* (Darmstadt, 1962), pp.15-39 ('Einhard und die karolingische Tradition im ottonischen Corvey' [1952]).

18 J. Fleckenstein, 'Königshof und Bischofsschule unter Otto dem Grossen', *Archiv f. Kulturgesch.*, 38 (1956), pp.38-62; E. Ewig, 'Kaiserliche und apostolische Tradition im mittelalterlichen Trier', *Trierer Zeitschr.*, 24-26 (1956-8), pp.147-86; *Die Urkunden Zwentibolds und Ludwigs des Kindes*, ed. Th. Schieffer, *MGH*, Diplomata (Berlin, 1960), pp.5ff., 84f., and my comments in *EHR*, 77 (1962), pp.131-3.

19 *MO*, p.25, but see the sharp comments of Christopher Hohler in *JEH*, 8 (1957), pp.224-5, on the limits of Carolingian 'liturgical uniformity'.

20 The reform decrees and related texts concerned with the monastic life have been critically and splendidly edited by J. Semmler in *Initia Consuetudinis Benedictinae: Consuetudines Saeculi octavi et noni*, ed. K. Hallinger, Corpus Consuetudinum Monasticarum, 1 (Siegburg, 1963), pp.423-582. For 9th-century St Martin's and Odo's activity there see E.-R. Vaucelle, *La Collégiale de St-Martin de Tours* (Paris, 1908), chs.2, 3; J. Wollasch in *Neue Forschungen über Cluny und die Cluniacenser*, ed. G. Tellenbach (Freiburg im Breisgau, 1959), pp.163-5 and passim; *Vita Odonis* (*PL*, 133, cols. 43-86), esp. chs. 11-22.

21 *MGH*, Scriptores, 15, pp.215-6; Semmler, op. cit. in n. 20, pp.457-68, 473-81. Ph. Schmitz, 'L'influence de St. Benoît d'Aniane', *IVa SdS* (1957), pp.401-15, is a useful summary.

22 *PL*, 103, cols. 423-702, 713-1380. The *Codex* exists only in the 9th-century MS Munich clm. 28118 and a 15th-century copy of it, the *Concordia* in four or five MSS: for the probable chronological priority of the latter see the references assembled by A. de Vogüé, *La Régle du Maître*, Sources Chrétiennes, 105-7, 3 vols. (Paris, 1964), 1, p.136, n. 1.

23 The expanded text of the 817 *Capitula* is that published by A. Boretius, *MGH*, Legum Sectio II, Capitularia regum Francorum, 1 (Hanover, 1883), pp.343-9.

24 The texts are in *PL*, 102, cols. 689-932, 593-690. The English MSS are Cambridge Univ. Ee.2.4 (with three leaves in the Bodleian Library, Oxford) and Ff.4.43: on these now see *ECM*, nos. 3, 8.

25 W. Hafner, *Der Basiliuskommentar zur Regula S. Benedicti*, Beitr. z. Gesch. d. Alten Mönchtums u. d. Benediktinerordens, 23 (Münster, 1959).

26 *MO*, p.28 (but the context of this judgement should be noted); Th. Kempf in *Handbook of Church History*, ed. H. Jedin and J. Dolan, 3 vols. (London-New York, 1965-9), 3, p.320.

27 But see *GK*, pp.798-819, and the literature cited by Semmler, op. cit. in n. 20, p.427, n.22.

28 *Analecta Monastica*, Studia Anselmiana, 20 (Rome, 1948), 1, pp.21-74. A link between Benedict's treatise and Court scholarship of the 790s is provided by the collection of creeds used by the author, which appears first in the supplementary material of the 'Dagulf Psalter', Vienna Nat. Bibl. lat. 1861, and shortly afterwards in a Lyons copy of a Court collection of texts, Rome, Casa Madre dei Padri Maristi, cod. s.n.: I am preparing a study of this collection.

29 Paris BN Lat. 7900: L. W. Jones and C. R. Morey, *The Miniatures in the Manuscripts of Terence*, 2 vols. (Princeton, 1931), pp.94ff., and Pls.; and BN catalogue [J. Porcher], *Manuscrits à peintures du VIIe au XIIe siècle* (1954), no. 104; Orleans, Bibliothèque de la ville, MS 233 (203). For Hisperic and other 'Celtic fringe' texts and manuscripts see P. Grosjean in *Celtica*, 3 (1956), pp.37ff., and my own remarks in *XIX^a SdS* (1972), pp.472ff. In the lecture as delivered I spoke of 'the Fleury library catalogue in Bern, Bürgerbibliothek cod. 4', having regrettably overlooked the fact that its Fleury origin has long been rejected and a connection with a reformed house in Lotharingia suggested: see Strecker in *Deutsches Archiv*, 5 (1942), p.24.

30 There is a voluminous recent literature on this subject, of which K. Schmid, 'Religiöses und sippengebundenes Gemeinschaftsbewusstsein in frühmittelalterlichen Gedenkbucheinträgen', *Deutsches Archiv*, 21 (1965), pp.18-81, may be taken as a representative example. It has been skilfully used and a proper note of caution introduced in K. Leyser's invaluable 'The German aristocracy from the ninth to the early twelfth century: a historical and cultural sketch', *Past and Present*, no. 41 (Dec. 1968), pp.25-53.

31 B. Bischoff, *Mittelalterliche Studien*, 2 vols. (Stuttgart, 1966-7), 2, pp.56-76 ('*Caritas*-Lieder').

32 Further examples are collected, for example, in J. Choux, 'Décadence et réforme monastique dans la province de Trèves, 855-959', *RB*, 70 (1960), pp.204-23, with extensive, if not always accurate, references to the literature.

33 *Recueil des Chartes de l'Abbaye de Cluny*, ed. A. Bernard and A. Bruel, 6 vols. (Paris, 1876-1903), 1, no. 112; an improved edition by J. de Valois in *Millénaire de Cluny*, Ann. de l'Acad. de Mâcon, 3rd series, 15 (1910), 1, p.210. For the interpretation of the 'protection' clauses see esp. J. Lemarignier, 'L'exemption monastique et les origines de la réforme grégorienne' in *A Cluny: congrès scientifique en l'honneur des Saints Abbés Odon et Odilon*, Soc. des Amis de Cluny, (Dijon, 1950), pp.288-340, esp. 291-301; H. Appelt, 'Die Anfänge des päpstlichen Schutzes', *Mitt. öst. Inst. GeschForsch.*, 62 (1954), pp.101-11; a good summary in H. E. J. Cowdrey, *The Cluniacs and the Gregorian Reform* (Oxford, 1970), pp.4ff., 22ff.

34 See esp. Wollasch, op. cit. in n. 20, pp.88ff. The Bishop of Mâcon (whose metropolitan was the Archbishop of Lyons) at that time is shown by other charters to have been a *Gerardus*.

35 *PL*, 133, cols. 854ff.; Wollasch, op. cit. in n. 20, pp.96ff., 120ff., compare 61-74.

36 Wollasch, op. cit. in n. 20, p. 112; *Vita Oswaldi*, pp.413ff. (Oswald), p.423 (Germanus, later at Westbury-on-Trym, Winchcombe and Ramsey); *Aelfric Life*, p.259 (Osgar).

37 *RB*, 70 (1960): pt. 1 is entirely devoted to Gerard of Brogne and the context

in which his work as a reformer took place; the contributions of J. M. de Smet, pp.5-61, and J. Wollasch, pp.62-82, 224-31, are particularly important.

38 *GK*, pp.79f. The contribution of St Peter's to the English reform movement is therefore somewhat misrepresented in P. Grierson's admirable study of 'The relations between England and Flanders before the Norman Conquest' [1940], repr. with revisions in *Essays in Medieval History*, ed. R. W. Southern (London, 1968), pp.74f.

39 H. Büttner, 'Verfassungsgeschichte und lotharingische Klosterreform', *Aus Mittelalter und Neuzeit: G. Kallen . . . dargebracht*, ed. J. Engel and H. M. Klinkenberg (Bonn, 1957), pp.17-28; F. Lotter, *Die 'Vita Brunonis' des Ruotger*, Bonner Hist. Forsch., 9 (Bonn, 1958), pp.65-109; compare *GK*, pp.51-62, and Fleckenstein, op. cit. in n. 18.

40 *Stenton*, p. 444. The relatives whom Bishop Theodred (fl. 926-51) names in his will have English names (D. Whitelock, *Anglo-Saxon Wills* (Cambridge, 1930), p. 4); and his visit (or visits) to Pavia is, if anything, evidence of an English rather than a German background since the city was not on any route that would have been used by German visitors in the pre-Ottonian period; but it was on the standard road to Rome for Englishmen, as we know from the itinerary of Sigeric (*Memorials*, pp.392ff.) and by implication from *ASC, s.a.* 888.

41 For this see T.A.M. Bishop, 'The Corpus Martianus Capella', *Trans. Cambr. Bibliogr. Soc.*, 4 (1964-8), pp.257-75; *Classbook*, esp. p.xv f.; Bullough, art cit. in n. 13, pp.475ff.

42 The account of the marriages of Edward's daughters in *Aethelweard*, p.2, and in Florence of Worcester's *Chronicle*, ed. B. Thorpe, 2 vols. (London, 1848-9), 1, p.117, are without chronological indications. Several cruces were convincingly solved by R. L. Poole, 'The Alpine son-in-law of Edward the Elder', in *Studies in Chronology and History*, ed. A. L. Poole (Oxford, 1934), pp.115-22, here esp. 115-7. For Eadgifu's marriages see further K. F. Werner in *KdG*, 4, p.457. The principal documentary and other references to *Hugo Magnus* are collected by Werner, op. cit. in n. 10, pp.283ff., and by W. Kienast, *Der Herzogstitel in Frankreich und Deutschland* (Munich-Vienna, 1968), pp.57-67.

43 But see K. Leyser, 'Henry I and the beginnings of the Saxon empire', *EHR*, 83 (1968), pp.1-32.

44 Poole, op. cit. in n. 42.

45 Veste Coburg MS 1: I. Hubay, *Die Handschriften der Landesbibliothek Coburg* (Coburg, 1962), pp.9ff., Pls. I, II; BM Cotton MS Tiberius A. ii: *Robinson II*, pp.59f.

46 F. M. Stenton, 'The historical bearing of place-name studies: the place of women in Anglo-Saxon society' [1943], in *Preparatory to Anglo-Saxon England*, ed. D. M. Stenton (Oxford, 1970), pp.314-24; W. Levison, *England and the Continent in the Eighth Century* (Oxford, 1946), pp.30, 251f.

47 *MGH*, Scriptores, 15, p.277.

48 *MGH*, Diplomata regum et imperatorum Germanorum, 1 (Hanover, 1879-84): *Dipl. Ottonis I*, nos. 3, 5, 7, 13, etc. Note that the title *consors (regni)* was not used in Germany at this time, as I myself previously wrongly thought, although it was standard usage in the *regnum Italiae*: see T. Vogelsang, *Die Frau als Herrscherin im hohen Mittelalter*, Göttinger Bausteine zur Geschichtswissenschaft, 7 (Göttingen, 1954), pp.17-22.

49 And not for Eadgyth at the beginning of Otto's reign, as I am reported as saying in *Ampleforth J.*, **76** (1971), p.35.

50 L. Scheffczyk, *Das Mariengeheimnis in Frömmigkeit und Lehre der Karolingerzeit,* Erfurter Theologische Studien, 5 (Leipzig, 1959), pp.461-96. *Adiutrix* occurs already in the *Homilia in assumptione b. Mariae, PL,* 95, col. 1569C, which is usually regarded as a composition of Paul the Deacon, and indeed in prayers in the 'Book of Nunnaminster': *An ancient manuscript of the eighth or ninth century . . .* , ed. W. de G. Birch, Hants. Record Soc. (London-Winchester, 1889), p.88. In view of the occasional later use of *(Maria) imperatrix* - but not, I think, before the 11th century - it is interesting to note that Alcuin declares in his *De Fide s. Trinitatis* III, 4 *(PL,* **101**, col.46) that as the purple-dyed woollen cloak *imperiali majestati tantummodo digna fiat, qua nullus alius induitur nisi augusta praeditus dignitate,* so the Holy Spirit descending on the Virgin brings it about that *lana fieret divinitate purpurata, solummodo aeterno imperatori indui dignissima.*

51 BM Add. MS 49598: *Roxb. Ben.* (complete fascimile with an excellent introduction); *Faber Ben.* The interest of the miniature on fol. 102ᵛ was pointed out at the conference by Dr Deshman. H. Barré, *Prières anciennes de l'occident à la Mère du Sauveur* (Paris, 1963), pp.132ff., uses quite other evidence to demonstrate that Winchester 'était un centre actif . . . de dévotion mariale; cette orientation lui venait sans nul doute de l'évêque Ethelwold . . . ' The provision of a benediction for the feast of St Etheldreda *(Roxb. Ben.,* p.37) is another noteworthy feature of the Benedictional; is it not more likely that the cult of this royal East Anglian abbess was brought to Winchester by Queen Aelfthryth (daughter of Athelstan, ealdorman of East Anglia) than by Bishop Aethelwold, as is usually supposed?

52 It will be obvious that the lecture is printed substantially as delivered. I have, however, abbreviated some sections and slightly expanded others to take account of the criticisms and suggestions of Prof. P. Sawyer, Mr C. Hohler, Fr Alberic Stacpoole and other participants: to all these I am grateful.

Chapter 4

1 The earliest Life of St Dunstan, that by the anonymous Saxon priest, B, and the slightly later Life by Adelard will be referred to as the *'B Life'* and *'Adelard'* respectively; they will be cited by page from *Memorials,* pp.3-52 and 53-68 (see bibliography). *Robinson II* discusses in more detail the careers of the three saints and much of the background to the reform movement.

2 *Stenton,* p.446.

3 The Life of St Aethelwold by his disciple Aelfric (the *'Aelfric Life'*) will be cited by page from *Chronicon monasterii de Abingdon,* ed. J. Stevenson, RS, 2, 2 vols. (London, 1858), 2, pp.253-66; that by Wulfstan (the *'Wulfstan Life'*) will be cited by column from *PL,* 137, cols.81-114.

4 The Anonymous Life of St Oswald (the *'Vita Oswaldi'*) will be cited by page from *Historians of the church of York,* ed. J Raine, RS, 71, 3 vols. (London, 1879), 1, pp.399-475.

5 *Stenton,* p.448.

6 *B Life,* p.46.

7 *Adelard,* p.56.

8 *Adelard,* p.61; see list of monastic bishops in *MO,* Appendix IV, pp.697ff.

9 *RC,* p.4, §7.

10 *Wulfstan Life,* col.98.

11 *Vita Oswaldi,* pp.457 and 462.

12 *EHD,* p.848.

13 *Vita Oswaldi,* p.434; see *Stenton,* p.447: 'Through the promotion of monks whom Dunstan had trained the example of his rule at Glastonbury influenced the whole course of the monastic revival, and it is for this reason above all that he is entitled to be regarded as its leader.'

14 *Aelfric Life,* p.262; *Wulfstan Life,* col. 93.

15 *EHD,* p.848.

16 See *ASC* (A) and (E), *s.a.* 964.

17 *RC,* pp.2-4, §§4-5.

18 *Stenton,* p.452.

19 *RC,* pp.2-3, §4.

20 For the foundation dates of monasteries see *MO,* pp.50f., and *MRH,* Appendix I, pp.466-87.

21 See *Stenton,* p.445.

22 *RC,* p.6, §9.

23 See *Robinson I,* p.37. For an earlier date see E. John in *JEH,* 9 (1958), pp.159-172, a shortened and revised version of which appears in *OB,* pp.234-48.

24 For monastic bishops see *MO,* Appendix IV, pp.697ff.

25 But see *Stenton,* p.449: 'At the decisive Council . . . Dunstan does not seem to have been present.'

26 *EHD,* p.848.

27 See *Stenton,* p.450; *RC,* pp.4-5, §7.

28 See *Stenton,* p.367: '. . . there are few parallels in any country to the enthusiasm with which Edgar brought the whole power of the English state to the furtherance of Dunstan's religious policy.'

29 *Compotus Rolls of the Obedientaries of St Swithun's Priory, Winchester,* ed. G. W. Kitchin, Hants. Record Soc. (London-Winchester, 1892), Appendix VII, pp.174ff.

30 *RC,* pp.5-6, §§8-9.

31 *RC,* Introduction, pp.liii ff.

32 Ep. 39: S. Anselmi, *Opera Omnia,* ed. F. S. Schmitt, 6 vols (Edinburgh, 1946-61), 3, p.151.

33 See T. Symons, 'Sources of the Regularis Concordia', *DR,* 54 (1941), pp.14-36, 143-70, 264-89.

34 i.e. the tax payable to the King on the death of persons of rank. *RC,* p.69, §69.

35 *RC,* p.3, §4.

36 *RC,* p.30, §32,

37 *RC,* p.12, §16; pp.13-14, §§ 18-19; p.16, §20; §24; p.21, §25; p.23, §27.

38 *RC,* p.7, §10.

39 *RC,* p.6, §9.

40 *RC,* p.19, §23.

41 *RC,* p.26, §29.

42 *RC,* p.20, §24.

43 *RC,* p.38, §40.

44 *RC,* p.33, §34.

45 *RC,* p67, §68.

46 *RC,* pp.43-4, §45.

47 *RC*, p.3, §5.

48 The basic treatment of this theme is *GK*.

49 *CM*, 3, pp.26ff.

50 *PL*, 105, col.815ff.

51 *CM*, 3, pp.115ff.

52 *PL*, 105, col.817: 'Ad quam etiam admonitionem sacer conventus intimo gaudio repletus, expansis in coelum manibus, creatori omnium gratias agens benedixit. Quippe qui talem tam pium, tamque benignum ecclesiae suae sanctae principem cunctisque eius necessitatibus sapientissimum ac devotissimum praetulerit procuratorem.'

RC, p.3, §4: 'Huius praecellentissimi regis sagaci monitu spiritualiter compuncti non tantum episcopi, verum etiam abbates ac abbatissae, quod talem ac tantum meruerunt habere doctorem erectis ad aethera palmis immensas celsithrono grates voti compotes referre non distulerunt.'

53 *RC*, pp.12-13, §§16-17; p.16, §20; p.53, §54; pp.23-4, §27.

54 *RC*, p.13, §17.

55 On customaries generally see U. Berlière, 'Coutumiers monastiques', *RB*, 29 (1912), pp.357-67, which lists editions up to that date.

56 *PL*, 133, cols.43ff.

57 *CM*, 2, pp.1ff.

58 *CM*, 1.

59 *CM*, 5, pp.137ff.

60 *CM*, 5, pp.73ff. (*Einsiedeln*); pp.7ff. (*Trèves*); pp.113ff. (*Verdun*).

61 *RC*, p.8, §11.

62 *PL*, 133, col.56.

63 *RC*, pp.15-16, §20.

64 *CM*, 2, pp.2, 31f.

65 *RC*, p.28, §31.

66 *CM*, 5, pp.138, 146.

67 *RC*, p.39, §41.

68 *CM*, 5, p.143.

69 *RC*, p.15, §19.

70 *CM*, 5, p.9.

71 *RC*, p.16, §20.

72 *CM*, 5, p.84.

73 *CM*, 5, p.53.

74 *RC*, p.17, §21.

75 *CM*, 5, p.107.

76 *RC*, p.19, §23.

77 *Trèves*: CM, 5, p.15; compare *Einsiedeln*: *CM*, 5, p.103.

78 *RC*, p.21, §25.

79 *CM*, 5, p.108.

80 *RC*, p.29, §31.

81 *CM*, 5, p.57.

82 *RC*, p.61, §62.

83 *CM*, 5, pp.23f.

84 *CM*, 5, pp.55f.

85 *RC*, p.66, §67.

86 *CM*, 5, p.132.

87 *RC*, p.67, §68.

88 *CM*, **5**, p.76; compare *Trèves: CM*, **5**, p.51.

89 *RC*, pp.36-7, §37.

90 *CM*, **5**, p.119.

91 There is in course of production, under the general editorship of Professor Kassius Hallinger, OSB, a new corpus of monastic documents which will furnish us not only with better texts of the customaries which have so far been available, but also with hitherto unknown - or at least unpublished - material. Some volumes of this corpus have, I understand, already been published, but I have not been able to consult them *(Corpus Consuetudinum Monasticarum* (Siegburg, 1963-)).

92 *RC*, Introduction, p.li.

Chapter 5

General bibliographical note

Most editions of English, including pre-Conquest, service books are publications of the Henry Bradshaw Society, cited as HBS with the volume number; except the third volume of the Westminster Missal (HBS 12), cited as WM III. In preparing this last Wickham Legg checked a large number of English, some French, and the Roman Missals, and those of several Orders, many of them otherwise unpublished; noted whether or not they agreed in the choice of prayers and chants with Westminster; printed or gave a reference when the prayer was different; and indexed the whole. The work is priceless. It has to be remembered when using it, however, that feasts not kept at Westminster, but which figure in the other books, are ignored, there is sometimes hesitancy when comparison is not straightforward, and the index is thus in varying degrees incomplete for texts and affectations in the other books.

For identifying prayers (no attempt has been made to distinguish slightly variant forms in this) reference is to some edition where the prayers are numbered, the number being preceded by an identifying abbreviation. This will normally be D for the wholly admirable: J. Deshusses, *Le Sacramentaire Grègorien,* Spicilegium Friburgense, 16 (Freiburg, Switz., 1971), which gives the variants of practically all 9th-century MSS of this text. For the other obvious early books the editions used, all by the late Dom C. Mohlberg, OSB, are in the *Rerum Ecclesiasticarum Documenta - Series maior: Fontes* (Rome, 1956-): L = the Leonine Sacramentary (exasperatingly called 'Veronense' by the editor); V = the Vatican Gelasian (*Liber Sacramentorum Romanae* Ecclesiae; and MF = *Missale Francorum*. There is an index verborum to the edition of the Leonine.

For prayers which survived into the Tridentine Roman Missal detailed collations from the published classic sacramentaries (and, for 8th-century Gelasians, the unpublished ones also) are given in P. Bruylants, *Les Oraisons du Missel Romain* (Louvain-Paris, 1952), cited as

Bruylants. This, like WM III, notes where the formulae are different (but does not print them) and indexes; and it has an index verborum.

V. Leroquais, *Les Sacramentaires et Missels manuscrits des Bibliothèques publiques de France* (Paris, 1924), will be cited as Leroquais, *Missels.*

I should like to draw attention to (and express my gratitude to the authors of) the following:
H. Bohatta, *Bibliographie der Breviere, 1501-1850* (Leipzig, 1937)
W. H. Frere, *The Hereford Breviary,* III, HBS, 46 (London, 1913)
L. Gjerløw, *Ordo Nidrosiensis Ecclesiae* (Oslo, 1968)
W. H. J. Weale, *Bibliographia Liturgica,* ed. H. Bohatta (London, 1928)
Frere and Gjerløw have exceptionally valuable indices; Bohatta and Weale, supplemented for breviaries by the relevant volume of the *Gesamtkatalog der Wiegendrücke* (Leipzig, 1925-), like those pre-Tridentine service books which were printed while still in use. These printed books are frequently the only surviving (or, in the greater libraries, the only accessible) witness to the use of a particular church. They are normally authoritative, being prepared for the chapter, order or monastery concerned, and of absolutely certain provenance. And, though MS confirmation is desirable, the use they give usually differs only in slight, more or less discountable, particulars from the use of the same church in the 13th century. They have, in any case, no less evidential value than 15th-century manuscripts.

It has been assumed that those likely to wish to check MSS will recognise such abbreviations as BM Cott., CCCC, BN Lat., etc.

Notes to the text

1 For details of these fragments and their editions see K. Gamber, Codices *Liturgici Latini Antiquiores,* of which there were two editions (with different serial numbers) in quick succession, both equally inconveniently arranged (Freiburg, Switz., 1963 and 1968).

2 An attempt to redress the Frankish bias has been offered by K. Gamber, most accessibly in his *Missa Romensis* (Regensburg, 1970). Unluckily, though he is often clearly right, he has chosen to oppose to a view, whose principal fault was that it was too simple, another view which is also too simple and involves even more numerous unlikely postulates. There are usually several other possible explanations of anomalies in fragments (on which his argument is too frequently based) besides his own and the one which would first occur to a more orthodox liturgist. No-one (or no-one else) can really assess probabilities until a few complete 'non-Roman' central Italian books are in print.

3 There is an immensely detailed study by A. Chavasse, *Le Sacramentaire Gélasien* (Tournai, 1958). England for him does not exist, a limitation which lessens the force of several of his arguments.

4 'Impression' because I have not even gone systematically through the relevant MSS in English libraries, and the obvious printed source, A. Ebner, *Quellen und*

Forschungen zur Geschichte und Kunstgeschichte des Missale Romanum... (Freiburg im Breisgau, 1896), is not systematically informative on the point either.

5 This emerges from comparing the evidence of Ebner (see previous note) and Leroquais, *Missels*. But since writing this I have learned of Nordenfalk's redating of the Sacramentary of Echternach to the late 9th century. I cannot take account of this book, since I do not directly know it.

6 For Ratoldus's book and this whole question see below, pp.64-67.

7 See Baumstark's well-known essay in *Die älteste erreichbare Gestalt des Liber Sacramentorum...*, ed. K. Mohlberg, Liturgiegeschichtliche Quellen, 11-12 (Münster, 1927), particularly pp.62ff. Baumstark raised the question: what books did St Birinus, whose mission was independent of that of St Augustine, bring with him to Wessex? I have not attempted to play this particular card, but it certainly cannot be cheerfully assumed that Canterbury and Dorchester used rigorously identical books.

8 *The Leofric Missal*, ed. F.E. Warren (Oxford, 1883), p.70; both feasts together preceded by a mass (the same as in the New Minster Missal, HBS, 93) for a vigil. *Rituale Ecclesiae Dunelmensis*, ed. U. Lindelöf, Surtees Soc., **140** (Durham, 1927), p.3: Candlemas only. The Durham Ritual has a collect for St Quentin's day, uses *Laetetur ecclesia* as the collect for St Denis (which I can parallel only in BM Add. 15419, to the best of my belief a missal of Saint-Quentin en Vermandois) and, with reservations about the separate sanctoral, should be a copy of a Saint-Quentin book. Both books begin the sanctoral with St Stephen, as do all Old English mass books (except the New Minster Missal, and that of Giso of Wells), the sacramentary BN Lat. 9533 from Echternach (datings vary c.900-1000), and the earliest sacramentaries in Leroquais, *Missels*: from Saint-Denis, Troyes (?), Corbie (local use), Saint-Maur-des-Fossèes, and Lagny (11th century), Marmoutier, Cambrai, Foicy, Saint-Aubin d'Angers, Saint-Benoît-sur-Loire, Arles-sur-Tech, Girona, Cîteaux and Saint-Rémi-de-Reims (12th century); and in Ebner (see n. 4) specimens from Bobbio (11th) and Monza (12th). The Troyes book (BN Lat. 818), at least, has Candlemas in the temporal. It is obvious, since so many of these are the earliest surviving from the churches named, that there is room for discussion about the proper interpretation of their evidence. There is, however, no point in starting any until more is known in detail about the text of all these books. They must all be related, directly or indirectly, since the removal of the saints of the three days following Christmas from the temporal is a piece of logic contrary both to tradition and to convenience: and the truly logical moved Christmas to the sanctoral as well (two examples, one in Ebner, c.1100, from Lorsch, and one in Leroquais, 12th century, from Souvigny). Leroquais lists four (should be three) 10th-century, eight (should be nine) 11th-century and 39 12th-century sanctoralia beginning like Giso and New Minster with St Silvester: Ebner has 12 of these, starting in the 11th; and sanctoralia beginning Vig. Andreae (none till the late 12th, Leroquais only) are normally a mere reorganisation of this quite illogical, but eventually standard, arrangement. Leroquais also has one 11th- and four 12th-century sanctoralia starting, like the Vatican Gelasian, with Felix, i.e. after the end of the Christmas season.

9 *Venerabilis Bedae Opera Historica*, ed C. Plummer, 2 vols (Oxford, 1896), 1, p.141 and notes.

10 There is no satisfactory list of this material. The complete books have mostly been known for some time, though the British Museum acquired an entirely

unknown 11th-century pontifical in 1971; insofar as they are listed, those outside
the British Museum can best be sought in W. H. Frere, *Bibliotheca Musico-Liturgica*
(London, 1894, lately repr.); if abroad, in private hands, or in the British Museum,
consult appropriate publications or the notes or introductions 'to appropriate
volumes of the HBS. For hymnals see now H. Gneuss, *Hymnar und Hymnen im
englischen Mittelalter* (Tübingen, 1968). Apropos of various details in this excellent
work, I remain convinced that D (with three hymns for St Augustine) is a St
Augustine's book (see pp.88ff.). The 'Burnt Breviary' of the Cathedral is 14th-
century and indeed burnt; but the only legible rubric about a hymn on St
Augustine's day there (for Second Vespers) prescribes the common. I should, on
the contrary, quibble about the precise sense in which BM Cott. Tib. A.iii is a Christ
Church book. The Lyre Psalter, BM Add. 16975, certainly has the litany, and
probably therefore the hymnal, of Bec (see pp.73, 82). I have never concerned
myself specially with hymns; but the Bec litany, with trifling alterations, is found in
the psalters or breviaries of so many English monasteries after the Conquest (for
obvious reasons), that it would probably clarify matters if the content of the Bec
hymnal were established and used as a standard for comparing later English
Benedictine ones. Reverting to pre-Conquest books, the best guide. to *disjecta
membra, ordines* buried in miscellaneous collections, translated into Anglo-Saxon,
etc., is *Ker Catalogue*; and several of the relevant texts are printed or summarised in
Aelfric Letters. But neither of these works sets out to list material in Latin, and it is
much to be hoped that the provision of such a list is on the future programme of
one of the obvious specialists.

11 See general bibliographical note.

12 See H. Ashworth in *Ephemerides Liturgicae*, **72** (1958), pp.39-43; G. G.
Willis, *Further Essays in early Roman Liturgy* (London, 1968), p.196; and
Deshusses, op. cit. in general bibliographical note. I should perhaps explain that I
accept nearly all Dom Ashworth's conclusions, but consider that accepting that the
book familiar from 9th-century Gregorians did not exist in the form we know until
some advanced date in the 7th century still leaves an immense number of other
possibilities open. Nobody would have guessed there was ever a book quite like the
Leonine if it had not survived.

13 Avignon, Musée Calvet, MS 176. Leroquais, for once nodding, overlooked
the mass in it for St Theodoret, patron of Uzès cathedral, and the fact that the two
SS Veredemius of Uzès and Avignon have feasts on different days, and assigned it
to Avignon. The prayers D Pad. 506 and Pad. 568 will be found in place in it on the
appropriate Sundays.

14 BN Lat. 12052, Leroquais, *Missels*, 1, no.31, of which an edition has for
some time been in preparation for HBS. Extensively used by Dom Ménard in the
notes to his edition of the Gregorian (*PL*, **78**), and by Dom Martène in his *De
antiquis Ecclesiae Ritibus* (Antwerp, 1736-8).

15 See D 55*-63* for masses for the Vigil (not in Ratoldus) and Feast in
February in the 9th century, and (for later use) HBS, **86**, pp.81ff. Ménard (*PL*, **87**
col.408) gives the cues for the mass given on 1 October in Ratoldus, commenting
that the prayers (D 59*-63*, omitting the preface) refer to the *dies natalicius*
although assigned to the Translation. They obviously belong to the *dies natalicius*,
where all other books put them; the mass used in February in Ratoldus in their
place is Gelasian for the Octave of St Andrew (V1085-87, with the preface D
1715), which all other books assign to the Octave for which it was manifestly
selected.

16 The prayers correspond broadly with D Pad. 823, D 112 and Pragen. 42/4.

17 The most convenient single reference, leading to most of the literature, is F. Lot, *Mélanges d'Histoire Bretonne*, 2 (Rennes, 1907), pp.188ff.

18 Not printed by Ménard.

19 This is characteristic of Gallican and Mozarabic books. Otherwise, and apart from Ratoldus, I have noticed it only in the Missel de Saint-Eloi (Ménard's MS *de base*) and, as a clearly secondary feature, since the blessings are frequently not entered at the right place in the formulary, in the Leofric Missal (see n. 8).

20 Both masses for St Samson were published, with the variants of most early MSS, by the Abbé F. Duine in his *Inventaire Liturgique de l'Hagiographie Bretonne* (Paris, 1922).

21 The masses for St Denis's vigil and feast are regularly D 253*-261*; for his octave they are as in HBS, 93, p.173. Anything else is unusual. The cues for the mass of St Cucufas are given in *PL*, 87, col.398.

22 BN Lat. 11589 (the Sacramentary of Saint-Méen) and BN Lat. 2297, with sanctoralia beginning respectively with St Silvester and St Felix.

23 Orleans, MS 127, Leroquais, *Missels*, 1, no.35. See *Millénaire Monastique du Mont Saint-Michel*, ed J. Laporte, 2 vols. (Paris, 1966-7), 1, pp.751ff. The book was used in WM III and drawn on by Marténe.

24 The error *adoneo* (for *admoneo*) in the first collect (Gallican *praefatio missae*) is in all copies except BM Add. 26655, allegedly from Evreux, 12th-century, which has *audoeno* and BN Lat. 14446, allegedly from Saint-Martin de Troarn, 12th-century, which has *a deo*, both emendations which make things much worse.

25 Both masses are found, usually at different centres, in Brittany, Normandy and England; in BN Lat. 2297 the 'new' mass is used for the vigil and the 'old' mass for the day. In Angers, MS 102 (from Saint-Aubin-d'Angers) the 'old' mass seems a 10th-century and the 'new' mass an 11th-century addition. The 'new' mass alone is attested for Orleans and Chartres and is found in the 12th-century Hungarian missal Zagreb, MR 123. Since this last (very interesting) book is likely to be known to few, it may be as well to say that when the late Abbé Bourque says it is copied from a book from Saint-Wandrille, he is to be heard — as so often — with patience but with disbelief.

26 The cues are given in *PL*, 87 col. 304.

27 *DS. qui. bm. A. aplm. per passionem . .* , to be found in any printed Anglo-Saxon pontifical or benedictional.

28 The date may be one or two years out; see J. A. Robinson, *The Saxon Bishops of Wells*, Br. Acad. Suppl. Pap., 4 (London, 1918).

29 HBS, 4, p.124.

30 Printed Warren, op. cit. in n. 8, p.302, and C. Wordsworth, *Pontificale Ecclesiae S. Andreae: the Pontifical Offices used by David de Bernham* (Edinburgh, 1885). p.69. The collect of this (Gelasian for St Gorgonius but adapted, if that actually is its source, with several changes) also calls St Cuthbert a martyr, and I think must once have been the true collect of the mass as used at Dol: the single collect in Ratoldus ought to have been chosen as a *praefatio missae*, paralleling the 'first collect' of the 'old' mass for St Samson. The secret and postcommunion are standard, as found at Fulda or later at Durham. The Sidney Sussex, or Cuthbert, Pontifical was long at Durham and T. A. M. Bishop now says (*ECM*, p.14) that the mass is entered by the same hand of c.1000 as that which made some additions to

facilitate the practical use of the totally different mass for St Cuthbert in CCCC 183. The latter is the copy of Bede's Two Lives of St Cuthbert normally held to have been presented by King Athelstan to the clergy of St Cuthbert on the occasion of the *Brunanburh* campaign. I cannot here go into all the complications caused by this revelation; but I can now only make sense of the evidence if the particular votary who took the Cuthbert Pontifical north was so distinguished that he was allowed to scribble in King Athelstan's book. Bishop Alfwold of Sherborne seems a possibility.

31 To the bibliography given by D. Turner, HBS, 97, p.xxx, add the convenient critical edition by P. L. Ward in *EHR*, 57 (1942), pp.345ff. The essential study is C. A. Bouman, *Sacring and Crowning* (Groningen, 1957), but he has dated both the Leofric Missal and the Ratoldus text far too late.

32 This, as is well known, seems actually to be the anniversary of St Parize of Nevers, taken from a copy of the Hieronimian Martyrology. The proper anniversary of the man buried, presumably under an inscribed tomb, beside the altar of the Old Church at Glastonbury ought, of course, to have been known (because kept) if the Glastonbury community had an unbroken existence. From which I should conclude that it did not have an unbroken existence.

33 The Paulinus who precedes Patrick in the litany should not be the Archbishop of Trier (who appears much higher up) and is most unlikely to be the saint of Nola. He could be either S. Pol de Léon or, in the light of the extraordinary later Glastonbury tale of his repairs to the Old Church, the Bishop of Rochester. As the latter is in the calendar, and there is no sign (other than the dedication of the church of Paul in Cornwall) of any veneration or relics of the Breton in England, I take it to be the Rochester saint.

34 See J. A. Robinson, *Somerset Historical Essays* (London, 1921), p.19, for the various references.

35 On this see the edition by myself and Dom Anselm Hughes in *Relics*, pp.155-91.

36 For the text of these, the widespread offices for the Invention of St Stephen and for the Trinity and that for St Lambert see R. Jonsson, *Historia: études sur la genèse des offices versifiés*, Stud. Lat. Stockholmensia, 15 (Stockholm, 1968), pp.214ff.

37 HBS, 45.

38 Calendar in HBS, 72, no. 8; masses for English saints in Warren, op. cit. in n. 8, pp.303ff.; used in WM III; but mainly unpublished.

39 J. A. Robinson, *Mediaeval Calendars of Somerset* (repr. from Somerset Rec. Soc., 42 (1927), pp.143ff.), p.7 (original pagination, p.148).

40 The Sherbroke Missal in the National Library of Wales.

41 *Chronicon Monasterii de Abingdon*, ed. J. Stevenson, RS, 2, 2 vols. (London, 1858), 2, p.279: . . . *propter austeritatem regulae . . . uix aliquis susciperet mona- chatum nisi pauper: et ideo ut divites attraheret instituit . . . et relaxauit quae non sunt in regula sancti Benedicti.* Others would render the *coop(er)toria* he intro- duced as 'cloaks' rather than 'bed covers'. His famous arrangements for bodily refreshment are listed on the same page and, in greater detail, in 1 p. 346.

42 ibid., 2 p.258.

43 *Frithegodi Monachi Breuiloquium* . . . , ed. A. Campbell, Thesaurus Mundi (Zurich, 1950), p.68.

44 There are two formulae in the Egbert Pontifical (ed. W. Greenwell, Surtees

Soc., **27** (Durham, 1853), pp.126-7), one of which reappears in the Durham Ritual (ed. cit. in n. 8, p. 116) and in the Red Book of Darley. That it should be these three particular books suggests that perhaps, even at the time, the formula was slightly outlandish. Unfortunately Egbert cannot be localised. The litany, with Cuthbert, Guthlac and Paulinus (emphasised because last) among the confessors, suggests some connection with Glastonbury, as does the usual blessing for St Andrew as patron of the diocese; and the presence of Vincent last among the martyrs suggests Abingdon which was, of course, a daughter of Glastonbury, and where there were relics. The puzzle is the invocation of St Felix, martyr, in the order for blessing a cross, but he may come from a distant model.

45 I had supposed, foolishly trusting a shortened concordance, that the objection must have been to blood (Acts XV, 20); but Mr Andrew Martindale has sternly reproved me for displaying such ignorance of the Bible. The source, in spite of Acts X, is Leviticus XI, 29ff., though the risks of crocodiles and chameleons falling into the beer have been unaccountably overlooked by the venerable Irishmen who revived these rules. The regulation as such is found first in the Penitential of Cummean, and in its qualified form, to which the blessing relates, in the Penitential of Theodore. There is considerable variation in the penances assigned to both server and consumer by the different authorities. Old-fashioned priests (see n. 47 below) probably continued to impose them for a long time, but reputable canonists of the 11th century and onwards do not mention the matter. See L. Bieler, *The Irish Penitentials* (Dublin, 1963), pp.130, 216; *Councils*, 3, pp.183, 428; C. Vogel, *Le Pontifical Romano-Germanique du dixi*eme siécle, 2 vols. (Vatican, 1963), 2, p.239.

46 The prophetical lesson *Scripsit Moyses canticum* (Deut. XXXI, 22-30) ends with the words which introduce the song, and to make sense the lesson should simply continue with the song itself, *Attende caelum*, set to music to be sung as a tract. But lessons and tracts in the 10th century were commonly in separate books, with inadequate cross-references. When providing for the guidance of their flocks, the eminent authors of the *Concordia*, MS *F*, (obediently followed by the Old English order for Whitsun Eve in the second, Exeter, part of CCCC 190 (printed in *Aelfric Letters*, Appendix II), by the Missal of Robert of Jumièges (HBS, 11), by the Nidaros Ordinal of the 13th century, and therefore by every church following the rubric in Norway, Iceland and the Isles) substituted the tract *Vinea* (Isa. V, 1), which should follow a quite different lesson. The inescapable implication is that those responsible did not know the Bible very well, and regarded chants as chants, without any special awareness of their Biblical context or meaning. The error has been partially corrected in MS *T* of the *Concordia* (which presumably means that the schoolmaster at Canterbury was told to alter his Winchester nonsense), and in the Latin order printed in *Aelfric Letters*, Appendix II, from the first part of CCCC 190, but this too would appear to have been wrong originally.

47 The pontificals are Egbert (BN Lat. 10575, once at Evreux Cathedral), Dunstan (BN Lat. 943, early at Sherborne, later at Notre Dame, Paris) and Lanalet (Rouen A 27, early at St Germans in Cornwall, later at Jumièges, HBS, 74). Bodl. 718, from Exeter, which has the Frankish *Jura quae sacerdotes debent tenere* between the preface and the text of Egbert's Penitential, must descend, even if indirectly, from the MS in which the trouble arose. The Worcester miscellany 'C' (CCCC 265) has the *Jura* as a distinct, anonymous item. But what, textually, is a later stage in this process is found in the older Worcester MS BM Cott. Nero A.i

('G'), where the *Jura* have not merely been included in the *Excerptiones de libris canonicis;* but they (and not, as earlier editors have imagined, the *Excerptiones*) have had added on the margin, clearly under the influence of the pontificals, a shortened form of the title of the Pentitential as the proper title for themselves. Barlow 37 is a latish 12th-century copy of the same collection as 'C', with most of the same items in the same order; but here the *Jura* again appear between the preface and the text of Egbert's Penitential. I imagine this is where they stood in the book in the library of the place (I suspect Winchester) from which this collection ultimately stems; but whereas the instructor at the time the archetype of 'C' was prepared knew what they were and dictated them, or had them copied, separately, his successors did not know. Incidentally, the Penitential in Barlow 37 shews St Egbert's rule about weasels in beer was still being at least copied out in the latter part of the 12th century.

48 CCCC 422: calendar in HBS, 72, no.14; extracts in Warren, op. cit. in n. 8, pp.271ff., *Ker Catalogue,* no.70, for further reference. It is beautifully written, and its contents carry with them the implication that it was anticipated it might be the only book some priest had, not just to say but to sing his services for the year. The question, very difficult to settle, is whether this was because the man was a missionary on the move, or whether this is all the parishioners of St Helen's, Darley, could expect. I am hoping to edit it in conjunction with Dr. R. I. Page.

49 CCCC 41.

50 Durham Ritual, ed. cit. in n. 8, p.129. It is ultimately L 205 incorporating a text resembling Vogel, op. cit. in n. 45, *ordo XL,* paras. 100-101 (2, pp.158-9).

51 *Aelfric Letters,* p.68. Fehr's idea, p.XLII, that Archbishop Wulfstan suffered from some kind of psychological disability, which rendered him incapable of using three words when 30 would do, does not seem much of an excuse.

52 This seems certain for the services of St Aethelwold in the libellus Rouen, V. 107.

53 CCCC 391. This book has been unlucky: a good deal of it is in HBS, 56, the best print of the calendar is in HBS, 72, no.17, and most of the rest, apart from the psalter, is in HBS, 89-90, where the index (in 90) indexes only 89.

54 CCCC 146: unpublished, but used in the notes to HBS, 24. Its Benedictional, however, is closer to that published in HBS, 51 (for which it was not used) and that of St Aethelwold.

55 Worcester Chapter MS F 173. See the communication by F. E. Warren, 'An Anglo-Saxon Missal at Worcester', *The Academy,* 28 (July-Dec. 1885), pp.394-5. It is possible to differ about the particular Winchester house for which it was intended. I agree with Mr Ker that it was the cathedral; Swithun is in capitals in the litany and Grimbald absent from it; the body reaches the cathedral (prayer invoking SS Birin, Swithun and Aethelwold) before it reaches the New Minster (prayer invoking SS Peter, Paul, Judoc and Grimbald); and the latter prayer is rubricated specifically for the New Minster, a detail which suggests to me that it was not the writer's own house.

56 BM Add. 28188, a Pontifical with a Benedictional providing for Aethelwold, Birin, and Swithun as patron, and with Sativola (of Exeter) in the litany. The other distinctive saints in the litany (as Mr Ker points out, those of Ramsey) come from the model or partial model, BM Cott. Vit. A.vii. On the latter see now *ECM,* p. 24, note.

57 *Liturgische Reimoffizien des Mittelalters,* Analecta Hymnica Medii Aevi, 13,

ed. G. M. Dreves et al. (Leipzig, 1892), no.7, from the breviary of Odense in Denmark. The best MS, formerly at Philadelphia, is now in the Pierpont Morgan Library.

58 Thomas of Walsingham, *Gesta Abbatum Monasterii Sancti Albani*, ed. H. T. Riley, RS, **28** (IV), 3 vols. (London, 1867-9), 1, p.28. The editor did not properly collate Matthew Paris's text, which should have been his basis; but Paris is himself answerable for reproducing the account of a certainly non-existent Leofric, Archbishop of Canterbury, brother of an almost certainly non-existent Aelfric II, Abbot of St Albans. See under Aelfric, Archbishop of Canterbury, in *DNB*, and *The Heads of Religious Houses, England and Wales, 940-1216*, ed. D. Knowles, C. N. L. Brooke and V. C. M. London (Cambridge, 1972), p. 65. There have been several brisk attempts to cut the Gordian knot, but all seem quite arbitrary, since they fail to explain how the tangle can ever have come into being.

59 This subject has received no detailed treatment in print since Miss Bateson's solid article in *EHR*, **10** (1895). Several new documents related to those previously known have indeed been brought to light, but they have been used to produce a picture of Archbishop Wulfstan which is not credible. I have given some indication of what I think and why in n. 47, but there is far more work to do than I have done. Briefly, I do not believe that the Archbishop himself did, could have, or conceivably would have, prepared a commonplace book of the kind attributed to him. I do not believe the handwriting said to be his is his. And I think the content of BM Cott. Tib. A.i (Aelfric Batte's miscellany from Canterbury) creates a presumption that all this material, including the Archbishop's rhythmical compositions in English, was available at Winchester; which I suspect was, with interruptions, Aelfric the Homilist's home for much of his life. As for the Archbishop, the man who asked Aelfric for his Pastoral Letters can hardly himself have been a canonist; and most of his life must in any case have been spent not in a library, but in the saddle. He could easily have whiled away the time on horseback putting into rhythmical prose matter fed to him by a secretary. As for Worcester, although William of Malmesbury seems to have misunderstood the story, we know at least that there was a German monk Winrich there, who reckoned he knew about ecclesiastical law (*Vita Wulfstani*, p.14). I cannot imagine what the man was doing at Worcester, unless he was specially imported to teach it.

60 See the *MGH* edition of Alcuin's letters (by Dümmler) for the relationship between the various collections; and *Memorials*, pp.355ff., for the English correspondence included in this MS.

61 L. Gjerløw, *Adoratio Crucis* ... (Oslo, 1961), pp.54ff.

62 L. Gjerløw, *Ordo Nidrosiensis Ecclesiae* (Oslo, 1968), p. 258.

63 The mass is Gelasian for the day, except for the super populum which is D 161, not V 103.

64 See Jumièges: *Congrès... du XIIIe Centenaire*, 1 (Rouen, 1955), pp.295ff.

65 On the Saturday before Palm Sunday, where Robert is Hadrianic, the Bede has a completely different mass made up from the Frankish Gelasian and Saint-Amand prayers for the day. It ought, therefore, to go back to a pre-Hadrianic Gregorian without any mass on this day. So, probably, does Robert; and some textual ancestor no doubt read like the Bede; but its peculiarities have been normalised in transmission.

66 Westminster Abbey CA (MS) 36/17-19, and Bodl. Lat. Lit. c. 38/9. The identification of these as parts of the same MS is due to Mr Ker.

67 HBS, **93**.

68 T. Schmidt, 'Problemata', *Fornvännen*, **58** (1963), and 'Smärre liturgiska bidrag VIII', *Nordisk Tidskrift för Bok- och Biblioteksväsen*, **31** (1944). The fragments, so far, are all from the sanctoral, which does not normally on its own offer reliable evidence about the Roman basis of a book.

69 HBS, **72** nos. 4, 5.

70 The Drummond Missal is now in the Pierpont Morgan Library. It was edited by G. H. Forbes, *Missale Drummondiense* (Burntisland, 1882), but his edition is scarce. See similarly *The manuscript Irish Missal . . . of Corpus Christi College, Oxford*, ed. F. E. Warren (London, 1879), and HBS, **15**. Further F. Henry and G. L. Marsh-Micheli, *A Century of Irish Illumination 1070-1170*, Proc. R. Irish Acad., **62**, Sec. C, no.5 (Dublin, 1962), and A. Gwynn in *Studies in Church History . . .*, ed. C. W. Dugmore and C. Duggan (London, 1964-),1, p.47. In company with Wickham Legg I am doubtful if the Rosslyn Missal can be older than the 13th century, whatever palaeographers may say.

71 They are L 309 and 466.

72 What establishes that the Sarum Missal cannot be Carolingian (although it may easily be under Caroligian influence) is the number of prayers it contains which are in the Leonine Sacramentary but which searches to date have failed to discover in any French book. The list of those found in the Sarum Missal, for which no possible intermediary, even Ambrosian, has so far been found, is: L 10, 14, 28, 91, 123, 174, 466, 637, 647, 744, 851, 865, 928, 1256. A source for Leonine prayers available in France is needed to account for those used in the local masses in the Phillips Gelasian (printed in the appendix to L); but the distribution of these masses does not spread far from the Channel in northern France, and the source could have come from England. For example, the very rare mass for St Maurice (who has some sort of mass in nearly every book) has left traces I have noticed only at Barking, as an addition to Angers 102, and in Bodl. Can. Lit. 345 (from Pistoia!). The term 'Roman Libellus' often used in this connection is best avoided, as different writers have used it in different senses, and we do not know, in fact, what the vehicle which transmitted these texts in any given case was like.

73 The identification was. made by Warren in his edition of the Corpus Christi missal, see n. 69, but until the publication of Leroquais, *Les Pontificaux manuscrits des Bibliothèques publiques de France*, 4 vols. (Paris, 1937), and Andrieu, *Les Ordines Romani du haut Moyen Age* (Louvain, 1931-6), there was no way to tell how distinctive the Besançon rubric was. On the liturgy of Besançon see A. de Vrégille in *Revue du moyen-âge latin*, **5** (1949). It is best known through excerpts published by Martène from a pontifical in his time at Tours but now untraceable.

74 The *ordines* are those for Maundy Thursday (Reconciliation of Penitents and Blessing of Oils, the officiant at the second being *archipraesul*) and are identical with those printed by Martène from his book at Tours. The formal Reconciliation of Penitents seems not to have been English usage (Theodore's Penitential XIII, 4 in *Councils*, **3**, p.187), which would acccount for the great variety of foreign orders for it found in 10th- and 11th-century service books. That beginning *Secundum morem orientalium . . .* as in the Worcester Miscellanies 'O' and 'G' (*Aelfric Letters*, p.248) is one of two different ones in BM Cott. Vit. A.vii mentioned in n. 55 above (it is on fols. 65-8), but it does not seem to be in any other pontifical.

75 Rouen, MS A. 313.

76 This identification, though 'official', was clearly still a matter for discussion

in William of Malmesbury's day, and he makes it as clear as he could in his position that he did not himself accept it.

77 J. Hunter, *Ecclesiastical Documents*, Camden Soc., **8** (London, 1840), p.16.

78 By letter, for which and for many other kindnesses I am most gratefully indebted to him.

79 He is normally on 25 April. The calendars which place him on 18 May are, I think, all English; they include HBS, **72**, nos. 1, 4, 5, 7, and the Metrical Martyrology of York, published by A. Wilmart in *RB*, **46** (1934), pp.41-69.

80 *DS. qui beatissimum . . . propitius,* also in the Leofric Collectar (and therefore perhaps from Liège) but not among the numerous collects published by Laporte, op. cit. in n. 23, pp.473ff.

81 D 848, 718, 708, 247. The Tours book I used was BN Lat. 10504.

82 L 282a.

83 When this paper was originally delivered I had accepted, without checking, the 'negative' variant in Bruylants for the Reichenau palimpsest; this proves, however, to have the standard Hadrianic text.

84 MF 36-44. I have not, however, searched foreign MSS for these prayers.

85 L 1010, 1011 (mass at the ordering of a priest or deacon) and L 950 (for the making of a deacon).

86 *Pater sancte omnipotens deus* . . . also in HBS, **24** (Robert), p.127, HBS, **39** (Magd. Coll.), p.75, etc.

87 *Missa Romensis,* see n. 2 above, p.141 and refs. The text of the Trento book is published in D.

88 I cannot find my note on the Reims book I used, I think an incunable in the Bibliothèque Nationale.

89 The much rarer Trento mass for the Thursday of the First Week is known to me complete only from Reims, Cambrai and Saint-Quentin; Saint-Méen; and the eccentric Paris missal Ste. Geneviève, MS 93. With the Hadrianic postcommunion and super populum it occurs in England, in Normandy, and at Carcassonne. In the same way, the distinctive super populum for the Thursday in the Second Week (the other three prayers are Gelasian for the day) is found at Reims, Cambrai and Saint-Quentin; Carcassonne; and Saragossa. This seems to be decisive for Reims being the place in the North where these masses were truly native. But the area over which their influence can be detected is given by the common combination, on the Third Thursday, of the first three Trento prayers with the (unexceptionable) Hadrianic super populum. This duly appears at Saint-Quentin and Carcassonne, which one might have expected in the shorter list; and I know it also from: Saint-Méen; Normandy and post-Conquest England; Lund; Gniezno and Plock; Prague; Esztergom; Aquileia; Salzburg, Freising, Passau and Brixen; Bamberg; Eichstedt and Würzburg (suffragans of Mainz); Lübeck (suffragan of Bremen); and the abbey of Stablo (dioc. Liège, prov. Cologne). The appearance of an early book of this kind at Trento (prov. Aquileia) is not, therefore, particularly surprising or necessarily very significant; its significance lies in its being early, since this stops the mouths of those who, without it, would certainly have said disdainfully that these prayers were 'late'. On this point I ask all liturgists to search their consciences.

Chapter 6

1 All Anglo-Saxon charters are listed, with references to manuscripts, editions and comments in *ASCh.* (see bibliography). Charters will be referred to here by their numbers in this list.

2 F. E. Harmer, *Anglo-Saxon Writs* (Manchester, 1952), pp.38-41.

3 Pierre Chaplais, 'The Anglo-Saxon chancery: from the diploma to the writ', *J. Soc. Archivists*, 3 (4) (October, 1966), p.174.

4 M. P. Parsons, 'Some scribal memoranda for Anglo-Saxon charters of the 8th and 9th centuries', *Mitt. öst. Inst. GeschForsch.*, ErgänzBd. 14 (1939), pp.13-32.

5 For the references see Harmer, n. 2 above.

6 Chaplais, op. cit. in n. 3, p.166.

7 Chaplais, op. cit. in n. 3, pp.162-3; see also pp.163-6 and his article 'The origins and authenticity of the royal Anglo-Saxon diploma', *J. Soc. Archivists*, 3 (2) (October, 1965), pp.59-61.

8 G. R. C. Davis, *Medieval Cartularies of Great Britain* (London, 1958), nos.1068-9.

9 H. P. R. Finberg, *The Early Charters of the West Midlands* (Leicester, 1961), pp.11-12.

10 Listed in *ASCh.*, p.55, under MS Harley 4660.

11 Listed in *ASCh.*, p.68.

12 *ASCh.*, no.731.

13 For example *ASCh.*, no.906.

14 E. John, *Land Tenure in Early England* (Leicester, 1960), pp.80-139. The text is given as Appendix I, pp.162-7.

15 *ASCh.*, no.788, based on no.786.

16 *ASCh.*, nos. 520, 726, 773.

17 *ASCh.*, nos. 401, 402, 428, 633.

18 *ASCh.*, nos. 361 (compare no.402), 751.

19 *ASCh.*, no.913.

20 See A. Campbell's forthcoming edition of the charters of Rochester.

21 This point is discussed in *OB*, pp.245-7.

22 See also the subscription of Leofstan in the two versions of *ASCh.*, no.1360.

23 I. Atkins, 'The church at Worcester from the eighth to the twelfth century', part ii, *Antiq. J.*, 20 (1940), pp.7-8.

24 *OB*, pp.234-48.

25 A. J. Robertson, *Anglo-Saxon Charters* (Cambridge, 1956), pp.360-1.

26 *Robinson I*.

27 *OB*, pp.247-8.

28 ibid.

29 *ASCh.*, no.1333; see *Robinson I*, pp.19-20.

30 Apart from *ASCh.*, no.1333, on which see previous note, there are two leases, *ASCh.*, nos. 1321, 1329, discussed in *Robinson I*, pp.34-6.

31 *ASCh.*, no.1336.

32 *OB*, p.245.

33 Wulfheah *preost* in *ASCh.*, no.1374; Wulfgar *clericus* or *preost* in *ASCh.*, nos. 1327, 1342, 1352 and 1372.

34 *ASCh.*, no.1369.

35 *Hemingi Chartularium Ecclesiae Wigorniensis*, ed. T. Hearne (Oxford, 1723), p.265.

Chapter 7

1 *MGH*, Legum Sectio II, Capitula Regum Francorum, **1**, ed. A. Boretius (Hanover, 1883), pp.105-7; Legum, **1**, ed. G. H. Pertz (Hanover, 1835), p.87.

2 *RC*, pp.13-14, §18.

3 *King Alfred's West Saxon Version of Gregory's Pastoral Care*, ed. H. Sweet, EETS, **45 & 50** (London, 1871), pp.2-3.

4 Good examples are to be found in Alfred's laws, 4-6, Athelstan's Grately decrees, 24-26, and Edgar's *Wihtbordesstan* code, IV Edgar, 1-1.8: *Liebermann*, **1**, pp.50-56, 164-5, and 206-9.

5 *Barlow*, pp.255-76, especially pp.273ff.

6 *Liebermann*, **1**, p.196: II Edgar 1.1-3 on tithes, and 3.1 on other payments. The King's *gerefa* was to act as the disciplinary agent.

7 *Liebermann*, **1**, p.198: II Edgar 4-4.3. Dorothy Bethurum (Mrs Loomis), in an important article 'Regnum and sacerdotium in the early eleventh century', *Whitelock Festschrift*, p.134, has recently pointed out that these penalties are modified half a century later in the time of Wulfstan to the point where only vague penalties are decreed — *lahslit* among the Danes, a fine (*wite*) among the English: the so-called Laws of Edward and Guthrum, 6.1 (*Liebermann*, **1**, p.130). The main legal stream, directed of course by Wulfstan, maintains the initial penalty of 30 pence extra payment and 120s. fine to the King (VIII Aethelred 10 and 10.1, I Cnut 9 and 9.1: *Liebermann*, **1**, pp.265 and 292). Later in the 11th century, possibly after the Norman Conquest, a modified penalty of a 60s. fine and a twelvefold payment was attempted (*Romscot* 2: *Liebermann*, **1**, p.474). The King's disciplinary sanction remains a constant feature.

8 K. Sisam, *Studies in the History of Old English Literature* (Oxford, 1953), pp.278-87, 'The relationship of Aethelred's Codes V and VI', argues powerfully that Aethelred V was the document enacted at King's Enham, that Aethelred VI was a version of the decrees directed to the clergy at York, and that the Latin paraphrase was intented for the upper clergy.

9 *Liebermann*, **1**, p.240: V Aethelred 10.2. The language of the decrees is strong — *cyrican ne ðeowige, ne cyricmagunge mid unriht ne macie, ne cyricþen ne utige.*

10 Wulfstan was Bishop of London from 966 to 1002, when he was translated to Worcester and York. He remained in possession of the sees until his death in 1023, though an assistant bishop was appointed to Worcester in 1016. D. Whitelock, *Sermo Lupi ad Anglos*, 3rd edition (London, 1963), Introduction.

11 *Stenton*, p.468.

12 M. Bateson, 'A Worcester Cathedral Book of Ecclesiastical Collections made c.1000 AD', *EHR*, **10** (1895), pp.712-31. *A Wulfstan Manuscript*, ed. H. R. Loyn, EEMF, **17** (Copenhagen, 1971), pp.49-52.

13 K. Jost, *Die 'Institutes of Polity, Civil and Ecclesiastical'* (Bern, 1959), especially pp.39-77; the eight virtues are described on p.52, the seven attributes on pp.53-4 and three supports to the kingdom on p.55.

14 ibid., pp.75-77. Dorothy Bethurum in the article referred to in n. 7 above takes a rather different view of Wulfstan's attitude to the *regnum* from my own. Stressing the Archbishop's disenchantment with kingship in the person of Aethelred, Miss Bethurum draws a contrast between the Carolingians, who made the health of the state depend upon the health of the king, and Wulfstan, who made it rather depend upon the strength of the Church. She emphasises therefore

Wulfstan's conscious building up of the power of the Church, his constant efforts to improve the status of the clergy, to claim that celibate priests were worthy of the rank of thegn, to equate efficacy of sacraments with the character of the priest. I agree with Miss Bethurum that it is unlikely that Wulfstan accepted the ideal of clerical withdrawal, but am more inclined myself to read Wulfstan's recognition of his involvement in the world as part of the essence of the Carolingian compromise.

15 Z. N. Brooke, *The English Church and the Papacy* (Cambridge, 1931), pp.127-31 and 137.

16 *Stenton*, p.469.

Chapter 8

1 ' "Remember the words we often spoke over the mead when we boasted about hard strife, heroes on the bench in the hall: now it can be tested who is brave. I mean to make known my lineage to all, that I have belonged to a great family in Mercia; my grandfather was called Ealhelm, a wise ealdorman, a wealthy man. Thegns in that people shall not reproach me for leaving this army, making for home, now my lord lies cut down in battle. That is the heaviest of blows to me: he was both my kinsman and my lord." Then he advanced, his mind set on revenge, until he pierced one of the seamen in that army with his spear, so that that man lay on the ground killed with his weapon' (lines 212-28a). The poem is readily available in *Sweet* and elsewhere.

2 Text H in *Bischof Wærferths von Worcester Übersetzung der Dialoge Gregors des Grossen*, ed. H. Hecht, Bibliothek der angelsächsischen Prosa, 5 (repr. Darmstadt, 1965).

3 *Aelfric Homilies*, 1, p.2; *Aethelweard*, p.51.

4 See the facsimile, *The Pastoral Care*, ed. N. R. Ker, EEMF, 6 (Copenhagen, 1956), fol.1^r-2^v, and Ker's account in his introduction, pp.24-5. See further N. Ker, 'The handwriting of Archbishop Wulfstan', *Whitelock Festschrift*, pp.315-31.

5 See M. R. Godden, 'The sources for Aelfric's homily on St Gregory', *Anglia*, 86 (1968), pp.79-88.

6 ed. by S. J. Crawford in *The Old English Version of the Heptateuch . . .*, EETS, O.S., 160 (London, 1922, repr. 1969); the Laud manuscript also contains Aelfric's summary of Judges.

7 ed. by (among others) W. W. Skeat in *The Holy Gospels in Anglo-Saxon, Northumbrian, and Old Mercian Versions* (Cambridge, 1871-87); the Northumbrian and Mercian versions are continuous glosses.

8 The West Saxon Gospels were still being copied in the south-east at the end of the 12th century or the beginning of the 13th, and much annotation in the Claudius manuscript testifies to an active interest in its text of the Old Testament books in the south-east during the 12th century.

9 See the facsimile of this manuscript, *A Wulfstan Manuscript*, ed. H. R. Loyn, EEMF, 17 (Copenhagen, 1971).

10 A facsimile of this manuscript is planned for the EEMF series.

11 See the facsimile of this manuscript, *The Old English Illustrated Hexateuch*, ed. C. R. Dodwell and P. Clemoes, EEMF, 18 (Copenhagen, 1974).

12 A full account of the surviving evidence for the circulation of Aelfric's *Catholic Homilies* will be included in my forthcoming edition of the first series and M. R. Godden's of the second. For an example of the Exeter use of text by Aelfric

see P. E. Szarmach, 'Three versions of the Jonah story: an investigation of narrative technique in Old English homilies', *Anglo-Saxon England*, 1 (1972), pp.183-92.

13 *Aelfric Homilies*, 1, p.304, lines 9-15. For a discussion see 'Postscript' (pp.77-8) to J. E. Cross, 'More sources for two of Aelfric's *Catholic Homilies*', *Anglia*, 86 (1968), pp.59-78.

14 *Early English Homilies from the twelfth-century Manuscript Vespasian D.xiv*, ed. R. D.-N. Warner, EETS, O.S., 152, no. XXV.

15 *Aelfric Letters*, Brief I, sect. 73.

16 *Aelfric Homilies*, 1, p.218, lines 30-31.

17 J. E. Cross, 'Aelfric — mainly on memory and creative method in two *Catholic Homilies*', *Studia Neophilologica*, 41 (1969), pp.135-55, esp. 139-40 and 150-51.

18 See G. E. Maclean, 'Aelfric's version of Alcuini Interrogationes Sigeuulfi in Genesin', *Anglia*, 6 (1883), pp.425-73, and 7 (1884), pp.1-59.

19 See M. W. Bloomfield, *The Seven Deadly Sins* (repr. Michigan, 1967), p.113.

20 *Sweet*, no. XVI, lines 179-86.

21 For his 'Sermo de sacrificio in die Pascae' see *Aelfric Homilies*, 2, no. XV.

22 For his 'Sermo de Cena Domini' see *Bethurum*, no. XV.

23 *Bethurum*, nos. Ia, Ib, IV and V.

24 *Medicine in Medieval England* (London, 1967), ch. 1, esp. pp.18-23.

25 A text close to, but slightly better than, the one in BM Egerton 2797, which was written in the Low Countries in the 11th century. Compare pp.188 and 191 in D. Whitelock, 'The numismatic interst of an Old English version of the legend of the Seven Sleepers', *Anglo-Saxon Coins*, ed. R. H. M. Dolley (London, 1961), pp.188-94.

26 C. L. Smetana, 'Aelfric and the early medieval homiliary', *Traditio*, 15 (1959), pp.163-204.

27 *Aelfric Homilies*, 1, p.3, lines 4-8.

28 'No Christian shall practise divination by the moon; if he does, his faith is worth nothing' (*Aelfric's De Temporibus Anni*, ed. H. Henel, EETS, O.S., 213 (1942), VIII.7).

29 'Now some people say . . . that the moon turns according to what the weather is going to be like that month, but neither good weather nor bad alters it from what its nature is' (ibid., VIII.11).

30 *Aelfric Homilies*, 1, p.304, line 9.

31 ibid., p.172, lines 24-7.

32 See, for example, ibid., p.3, lines 2-4, and p.8, lines 9-16.

33 H. Gneuss, 'The origin of standard Old English and Aethelwold's school at Winchester', *Anglo-Saxon England*, 1 (1972), pp.68-83.

34 See pp.32-3 of the introduction to the facsimile, *Aelfric's First Series of Catholic Homilies*, ed. N. Eliason and P. Clemoes, EEMF, 13 (Copenhagen, 1966).

35 'He said once to the Bishop Timothy that there will be dangerous times in the last days of this world on account of men's sins, and, he said, men will then love all too much this deceitful world and will be too covetous of worldly riches, and too many will become too proud and all too overbearing and too arrogant, and some will become terribly derisive of divine services and scornful of learning and approving of injustice, and some will become deceitful and plausibly cunning and without bonds of good faith damned in sins' (*Bethurum*, no. V, lines 16-23).

36 'This is a description of the nature of a human being, how he becomes man

in his mother's womb. First the person's brain is formed in his mother's womb. Then the brain is covered with membrane in the sixth week. In the second month the veins are formed. They are divided into 365 shorter and longer ones and the blood then flows into the feet and up into the hands, and he is then separated into limbs and grows in all his parts. In the third month he is a being without a soul. In the fourth month he is firm in his limbs. In the fifth month he is alive and grows and the mother [?] faints, and then the ribs are formed. She has various pains when the body of the foetus is taking shape in her womb. In the sixth month he gets a skin and his bones are growing. In the seventh month the toes and fingers are growing. In the eighth month the organs in his breast are growing, and heart and blood, and he is all firmly made. In the ninth month women really know whether they will be able to give birth. In the tenth month the woman will not escape with her life if the child has not been born, because it will become a fatal illness in her belly — very often on a Monday night[!]' (*Leechdoms, Wortcunning and Starcraft of Early England*, ed. O. Cockayne, RS, 35, 3 vols. (London, 1864-6), 3, p.146).

37 *ASC, s.a.* 1048; *Sweet*, no. XVIII, lines 1-24. See further C. Clark, 'The narrative mode of *The Anglo-Saxon Chronicle* before the conquest', *Whitelock Festschrift*, pp.215-35, esp. 231-3.

38 'While the King was speaking these words, by chance his young daughter came in and kissed her father and those sitting near. When she came to Apollonius she returned to her father and said: "Oh good King and my dearest father what young man is this who sits near you in a seat of such honour with a sad expression? I don't know what he's grieving about." Then the King said: "Dear daughter, this young man's been shipwrecked, and he's pleased me more than anyone else in the games, and that's why I've invited him to this feast of ours. I don't know what sort of a person he is or where he's from; but if you want to know who he is, ask him, for it's fitting for you that you should know." Then the girl approached Apollonius and said courteously: "Although you're quiet and unhappy, I can see your noble birth in you. If it doesn't seem too grievous to you, now tell me your name and tell me what's happened to you." Then Apollonius said: "If you must ask about my name, let me tell you I've lost it in the sea. If you want to know about my ancestry, know that I've left it in Tarsus." The girl said: "Tell me more clearly so that I may understand it" ' (G. L. Brook, *An Introduction to Old English* (Manchester, 1955), text 4, lines 1-20).

39 *Sweet*, no. XV, lines 70-83.

40 'And nevertheless, for all this truce and treaty and tribute, they went about in bands wherever they liked and harried our wretched people and plundered and killed them' (*ASC* (C), *s.a.* 1011). See further C. Clark, op. cit. in n. 37, esp. pp.225-30.

41 'Here in this land, as is plain to see, too many are grievously injured through the injuries of sin. Here are killers of men and killers of relatives and slayers of priests and persecutors of monasteries, and here are perjurers and murderers, and here are prostitutes and murderers of children and many foul perjured fornicators, and here are witches and sorceresses, and here are thieves and robbers and plunderers, and, in short, countless crimes and wicked acts of every kind. And we are not ashamed of them at all, but we are very ashamed of beginning atonement as books teach, and that is plain to see in this wretched people corrupted by sin' (*Sweet*, no. XVI, lines 159-68).

42 'The head of the household is our Creator, who governs those he has created,

and possesses his chosen in this world, as a lord does his household in his hall' (*Sweet*, no. XIII, lines 39-42).

43 'This vineyard sprouts God's chosen, from the righteous Abel until the last saint who will be born at the end of this world, as though it were propagating so many vine-shoots' (*Sweet*, no. XIII lines 47-50).

44 See P. Clemoes, *Rhythm and Cosmic Order in Old English Christian Literature* (Cambridge, 1970), esp. pp.15-25.

45 'The eighth age is the one eternal day after our resurrection when we shall reign with God in soul and in body in eternal happiness, and there will be no end to that single day when the saints will shine as the sun does now' (Crawford, op. cit. in n. 6, 'Aelfric: on the Old and New Testament', lines 1191-4).

Chapter 9

1 This chapter is a summary rather than a transcript of the paper read at the conference in view of the author's proposed publication *Style in Dramatic Art* in which extended essays on Romanesque and Gothic drama will appear.

2 See H. C. Gardiner, *Mysteries' End* (New Haven, 1946); G. W. G. Wickham, *Early English Stages,* 2 vols. (London, 1959-63), 1, pp.307-22; O. B. Hardison, Jr., *Christian Rite and Christian Drama in the Middle Ages* (Baltimore, 1965), pp.1-34; V. A. Kolve, *The Play called Corpus Christi* (Stanford, 1966).

3 See Sandro Sticca, *The Latin Passion Play: its Origins and Development* (New York, 1969).

4 The Latin text is printed in E. K. Chambers, *The Medieval Stage,* 2 vols. (Oxford, 1903), 2, pp.306-9; also in J. M. Manly, *Specimens of the Pre-Shakespearean Drama,* 2 vols. (Boston, 1897-8), 1, pp.xix-xxi. The Latin text also appears with an English translation in *RC*, pp.49-50, §§51-2. The translation given here is one made by the late Professor William Beare and Glynne Wickham. For bibliographical details and further comment see Karl Young, *The Drama of the Medieval Church,* 2 vols. (Oxford, 1933), 1, pp.582-3, and 2, p.410, and William Smolden, 'The origins of the *Quem Quaeritis* and the Easter sepulchre music-drama, as demonstrated by their musical settings,' *The Medieval Drama*, ed. Sandro Sticca (New York, 1972), pp.121-54.

Chapter 10

1 S. Frere, *Britannia* (London, 1967), pp.350-9.

2 P. Corder, 'The reorganisation of the defences of Romano-British towns in the fourth century', *Arch. J.,* 112 (1955), pp.20-42; S. Frere, 'The end of towns in Roman Britain' in *The Civitas Capitals of Roman Britain*, ed. J. S. Wacher (Leicester, 1966), pp.87-100, esp. 88-9.

3 S. C. Hawkes and G. C. Dunning, 'Soldiers and settlers in Britain, fourth to fifth century', *Med. Arch.,* 5 (1961), pp.1-70, revised in *Ber. d. Römisch-Germanischen Komm.,* 43-44 (1962-3), pp.155-231.

4 G. Clarke in *Winch. Exc. 8*, pp.292-8, and 9, pp.94-8.

5 See E. Keller, *Die spätrömischen Grabfunde in Südbayern,* Münchener Beitr. z. Vor- u. Frühgesch., 14 (Munich, 1971).

6 *Winch. Exc. 9*, pp. 101-102, fig. 3.

7 J. N. L. Myres, *Anglo-Saxon Pottery and the Settlement of England* (Oxford, 1969).

8 ibid., p.78; Frere, op. cit. in n. 2, pp.90-3, fig. 18.

9 S. Frere, 'Excavations at Dorchester on Thames, 1962', *Arch. J.*, 119 (1962), pp.147-9, fig. 21, esp. nos. 6,7.

10 *Antiq. J.*, 50 (1970), pp.68-70, fig. 2.

11 Myres, op. cit. in n. 7, pp.62-83, with maps 3, 4A.

12 P. Schmid, 'Bemerkungen zur Datierung der jüngsten Siedlungsphase auf der Dorfwurt Feddersen Wierde, Kreis Wesermünde', *Neue Ausgrabungen u. Forschungen in Niedersachsen*, 4 (1969), pp.158-69.

13 P. Schmid and M. Biddle in *Probleme der Küstenforschung* (forthcoming).

14 A. L. Meaney and S. C. Hawkes, *Two Anglo-Saxon Cemeteries at Winnall*, Soc. for Medieval Arch., Monograph 4 (London, 1970), pp.1-6, fig. 2.

15 *Med. Arch.*, 6-7 (1962-3), p.307; 8 (1964), p.233; A. Meaney, *Gazetteer of early Anglo-Saxon Burial Sites* (London, 1964), pp.102-103.

16 *ASC* (F), *s.a.* 648; Bede, *HE*, III, 7.

17 Bede, loc. cit.; *Stenton*, p.122.

18 Among those buried in Old Minster were Cynegils (d. 643), Cenwalh (d. 674), Cynewulf (d. 786), Egbert (d. 839), Aethelwulf (d. 858), Alfred (d. 899, translated to New Minster c.903), Edmund (d. 946), Eadred (d. 955) and Cnut (d. 1035); Egbert (acc. 802) is said to have been consecrated there and Edward the Confessor (acc. 1042) was crowned there on 3 April 1043.

19 M. Biddle, 'Archaeology and the beginnings of English society' in *Whitelock Festschrift*, pp.391-408, esp. 393-6.

20 *Winch. Exc. 10.*

21 By analogy with such names as Aldermanbury, Bucklersbury and Lothbury in the City of London; E. Ekwall, *Street-Names of the City of London* (Oxford, 1965), pp.194-7.

22 P. V. Addyman and D. H. Hill, 'Saxon Southampton: a review of the evidence', *Proc. Hants. Field Club*, 25 (1968), pp.61-93, and 26 (1969), pp.61-96.

23 Winchester: *urbs*, 947 (*BCS*, no.824; *ASCh.*, no.526); *civitas*, c.730 (Bede, *HE*, III, 7), 877 (*BCS*, no.544; *ASCh.*, no.1277). Southampton: see O. G. S. Crawford in *Antiquity*, 16 (1942), pp.36-50, esp. 39-40; Addyman and Hill, op. cit. in n. 22, 25 (1968), pp.62-5; *mercimonium*, c. 720 (*Vita . . . Sancti Willibaldi*, ed. T. Tobler (Leipzig, 1874), pp.14, 308, 321); *wic*, in the form (*Ham-*)*uuih*, c.720 (ibid.), *wic*, 1045 (Kemble, no.776; *ASCh.*, no.1012).

24 M. Biddle and D. Hill, 'Late Saxon planned towns', *Antiq. J.*, 51 (1971), pp.82-3.

25 ibid., pp.70-85.

26 *BCS*, no.605; *ASCh.*, no.1443. This matter will be fully discussed in M. Biddle and B. Kjølbye-Biddle, *The Old and New Minsters in Winchester*, Winchester Studies, 4 (Oxford, forthcoming).

27 *BCS*, no.630; *ASCh.*, no.1560; W. de G. Birch, *An Ancient Manuscript*, Hants. Record Soc. (London-Winchester, 1889), pp.32-33, 96.

28 ibid., pp.3-6.

29 *Winch. Exc. 8*, pp.314-5, 317-21, fig. 13.

30 I follow here P. Grierson, 'Grimbald of St Bertin's', *EHR*, 55 (1940), pp.529-61, with some additional material relating to the developing topography of the site which will be discussed in Biddle and Kjølbye-Biddle, op. cit in n. 26.

31 The earliest reference to the *monasteriolum*, from which all later references appear to derive, is in the *Vita prima* of St Grimbald in *The Monastic Breviary of*

Hyde Abbey, 4, ed. J. B. L. Tolhurst, HBS, 88 (London, 1939), fol. 289 (*lectio* VI).

32 Grierson, op. cit. in n. 30, p.550.

33 ibid., pp.554-5.

34 ibid., pp.556-7. For the earliest reference to the two years occupied by the building of the monastery (*infra biennium totam fabricam miranda celeritate cosummae*) see op. cit. in n. 31, fol. 290 (*lectio* IX).

35 BCS, no.602. *ASCh.*, no.370; and *BCS*, no.605, *ASCh.*, no.1443. Although spurious in its present form, *BCS*, no. 602, contains material on record in other pre-conquest sources.

36 *LV*, pp.5-6.

37 *Regesta Henrici Primi, 1100-35*, ed. C. Johnson and H. A. Cronne, Regesta Regum Anglo-Normannorum, 2 (Oxford, 1956), no.1070; for the best text see *Registrum Johannis de Pontissara*, ed. C. Deedes, Canterbury and York Soc., 30 (London, 1924), pp.439-41. For a 14th-century statement as to the rights of the Cathedral Priory (the successor of Old Minster) over burial in the city and suburbs, see Winchester Cathedral Library, *Records*, 1, fol. 38. I am grateful to Mr D. J. Keene for help with this matter.

38 *LV*, pp.4, 215.

39 BCS, no.1302, *ASCh.*, no.807, reflects the pressure of town life on the monasteries. The content of this somewhat doubtful charter seems acceptable.

40 *(to) flæs[c]mangere stræte*, 996 (Kemble, no.1291; *ASCh.*, no.889); *(to, andlang) scyldwyrhtana stræte* (ibid.); *(on) Tænnere stret*, 990 (Kemble, no. 673; *ASCh.*, no.874).

41 *Catalogue of English Coins in the British Museum: Anglo-Saxon Series*, 2 vols. (London, 1887-93), no. XXI.

42 M. Dolley, 'The location of the pre-Aelfredian mint(s) of Wessex', *Proc. Hants. Field Club*, 27 (1970), 57-61. I am grateful to Mr Dolley for allowing me to see in advance of publication a typescript of this article, which arose from the delivery of my present paper at the *Regularis Concordia* conference in 1970.

43 The market is first mentioned c.900, *(on) þa ceap stræt, (andlanges) þære ceap stræte* (BCS, no. 630, ASCh., no.1560; see n. 27), referring to the east end of High Street.

44 *BCS*, no.1302; *ASCh.*, no.807.

45 Only an outline can be given here; for a full discussion see Biddle and Kjølbye-Biddle, op. cit. in n. 26. A summary related particularly to the 11th and 12th centuries will be found in F. Barlow, M. Biddle, O. von Feilitzen and D. Keene, *Winchester in the Early Middle Ages: an edition and discussion of the Winton Domesday*, Winchester Studies, 1 (Oxford, 1974), part IV, forthcoming.

46 *BCS*, no.474; *ASCh.*, no.307. A suspicious charter.

47 Lantfred, prose account of the miracles and translation of St Swithun written before c.998, BM Royal MS 15 C.vii, fol. 26^V printed from a Vatican MS in the excerpt from Lantfred in *Acta Sanctorum, Julii*, 1 (Antwerp, 1746), pp.331-7, and therefore omitted by E. P. Sauvage, *Analecta Bollandiana*, 4 (Brussels, 1885), p.33, where it would have been Bk. II, cap. X, according to Sauvage's division. See also Wulfstan, *Narratio metrica de Sancto Swithuno* in *Frithegodi Monachi Breuiloquium . . .*, ed. A. Campbell, Thesaurus Mundi (Zurich, 1950), Bk. I, cap. XIII, line 1393.

48 *LV*, pp.2, 163-4, 291.

49 *Winch. Exc. 8*, pp.315-7, figs. 12, 13.

50 The chapel *might* be the otherwise unrecorded church of St George known

from the route followed by funeral processions c.1000 to lie in this general area; Worcester Cathedral Library, MS F 173, fol. 21, printed and discussed by C. H. Turner in *J. Theol. Stud.*, **17** (1916), pp.65-8. For the controversial question of the *haligdom*, the treasury, and the royal archives, see now C. Hart, 'The *Codex Wintoniensis* and the king's *haligdom*', *Agric. Hist. Rev.*, **18** (1970), pp.7-38.

51 M. Biddle, 'Wolvesey: the *domus quasi palatium* of Henry de Blois in Winchester' in *Château Gaillard III*, ed. A. J. Taylor (Chichester, 1969), pp.28-36.

52 *Winch. Exc. 3*, pp.258-60, fig 6; *4*, pp.326-7; *5*, p.273; *6*, pp.282-3; *7*, p.324; *10*, forthcoming.

53 For the chapel, *Winch. Exc. 3*, fig. 6.

54 See n. 47.

55 A. J. Robertson, *Anglo-Saxon Charters* (Cambridge, 1939), no.53; *ASCh.*, no.1376. The interpretation of this charter will be discussed in Biddle and Kjølbye-Biddle, op. cit. in n. 26.

56 *Annales de Wintonia, s.a.* 1042, in *Annales monastici*, ed. H. R. Luard, RS, 36, 5 vols. (London, 1865), 2, p.19.

57 ibid., p.51.

58 *BCS*, nos. 1163, 1302, *ASCh.*, nos. 1449, 807; Robertson, no.53, *ASCh.*, no.1376; *LV*, p.8.

59 *ASC* (E), *s.a.* 963 for Nunnaminster; cf. *ASC* (A), *s.a.* 964 for New Minster.

60 *BCS*, nos. 1163, 1302; *ASCh.*, nos. 1449, 807. Compare Birch, op. cit. in n. 27, pp.129-32.

61 *LV*, pp. x, 5-6.

62 *LV*, pp. lxiii-lxvi, 147-53, 159-63. For the translation and relics of St Grimbald see Grierson, op. cit. in n. 30, pp.557-9.

63 *LV*, p.8, compare *BCS*, no.1302; *ASCh.*, no.807.

64 *BCS*, no.1163; *ASCh.*, no.1449.

65 *LV*, p.8.

66 *BCS*, no.1190; *ASCh.*, no.745; compare *LV*, pp.232-46. Probably a record of what happened in 966, the charter itself need only be dated 966 x 984.

67 *Winch. Exc. 9*, pp.116-23, figs. 6,7,8.

68 This is suggested by the location of the church or chapel of the Virgin and all Holy Virgins on the route followed by Winchester funeral processions c.1000, since this was the dedication of the lowest storey of the New Minster tower; see Turner, op. cit. in n. 50.

69 *LV*, pp.9-10; *Quirk II*.

70 Two certain and three possible graves were found inside the 7th-century church during the excavations of 1962-9, but the original stone flooring had been almost entirely removed in demolition, and burials in stone coffins placed on, or cut into, such a floor would not have been recognisable.

71 *Winch. Exc. 7*, pp.321-2.

72 *Quirk I*, esp. pp.38-41.

73 *MO*, pp.40-41.

74 Robertson, op. cit. in n.55, no.53; *ASCh.*, no.1376.

75 *Quirk I*, pp.43-4.

76 ibid., pp.41-3, 56-9.

77 *Winch. Exc. 7*, pp.316-7, Pls. LXIII*b*-LXVI.

78 *Quirk I*, pp.48-56.

79 *Winch. Exc. 8*, pp.315-7, 320-21, figs. 12,13.

80 *Quirk I*, p.59.

81 C. Heitz, *Recherches sur les Rapports entre Architecture et Liturgie à l'Époque Carolingienne* (Paris, 1963), pp.77-82, 165-7.

82 *Winch. Exc. 7*, pp.320-21, Pl LXVI*b*; *8*, pp.318-21.

83 *Quirk I*, p.53.

84 F. Kreusch, *Beobachtungen an der Westanlage der Klosterkirche zu Corvey*, Beih. d. Bonner Jb., 9 (Kölin-Graz, 1963), pp.60-70, Bild 20; idem, *Über Pfalzkapelle und Atrium zur Zeit Karls des Grossen*, Dom zu Aachen: Beitr. z. Baugesch., 4 (Aachen, 1958), pp.85-100, Bild 38; idem, 'Kirche, Atrium und Portikus der Aachener Pfalz' in *KdG*, 3, pp.501-505, fig. 5; Heitz, op. cit. in n. 81, pp.145-61.

85 After the demolition of 1093-4 the stone coffins of some burials in the westwork were carefully preserved in position in a special courtyard centred on the site of St Swithun's original burial; *Winch. Exc. 8*, p.317. No other graves within Old Minster were preserved in this way.

86 D. Whitelock, *The Beginnings of English Society*, Pelican History of England, 2 (Harmondsworth, 1968), p.50.

87 *Quirk I*, p.62.

88 ibid., pp.59-62.

89 The remarks relating to the difficulty of identifying burials within the 7th-century church (n. 70) are equally applicable here.

90 Aelfric, Life of Swithun in *Lives of Three English Saints*, ed. G.I. Needham (London, 1966), lines 359-61 and passim; Wulfstan (ed. cit. in n. 47), Bk. II, passim.

91 *BCS*, no.1302; *ASCh.*, no.807.

92 Thomas Rudborne, *Historia maior Wintoniensis* in *Anglia Sacra*, ed. H. Wharton, 2 pts. (London, 1691), 1, Bk. I, VI (p.185), Bk. II, I (pp.187, 189).

93 Unum Beati Swithuni Miraculum, lines 29-32 in BM Royal MS 15 C.vii, fol. 125^v; printed by A. A. Locke, *In Praise of Winchester* (London, 1912), pp.124-5.

Chapter 11

1 An exhaustive bibliography, both historical and architectural, is given by F. Oswald, L. Schaefer and H. R. Sennhauser, *Vorromanische Kirchenbauten* (Munich, 1966-71), p.100. Details of the original western gallery are still disputed, and my reconstruction follows that of F. Oswald, *Kunstchronik*, 18 (1965), pp.29-37. Oswald describes and illustrates the conflicting theories and gives evidence which, after careful inspection of the building, I regard as establishing the reconstruction shown here in Fig. 8, p.144.

2 K. H. Schäfer, *Die Kanonissenstifter im deutschen Mittelalter* (Stuttgart, 1907), pp.188-91.

3 ibid., pp.76-95; Gernrode, p.82. There were 24 canonesses (p.130); and 8 canons, of whom 4 were priests (p.100, n. 4).

4 *Hariulf: Chronique de l'abbaye de Saint-Riquier*, ed. F. Lot (Paris, 1894). Lot gives reasons for believing that the manuscript which perished by fire in 1719 was Hariulf's original text, substantially completed in 1088 and in part revised about 1105 (p.LXVI). He also records the copying and publication of the text before the manuscript was destroyed (pp.LVII-LXIX).

5 J. Mabillon, *Acta Sanctorum . . .*, 4(1) (Paris, 1677), pp.123-30.

6 This fragment, commonly called Libellus Angilberti, was published by Lot as Appendix VI to his *Hariulf*. It was also published independently by E. Bishop in

DR, **14** (1895), pp.84-98, and reprinted in *LH*, pp.314-32, with many useful comments.

7 In *Spicilegium*, ed. L. d'Achery (Paris, 1661); and, from an independent copying of the original, in de la Barre's edition of the same work (Paris, 1723); see *Hariulf*, p.LXV.

8 The drawing was first published by P. Petau, *De Nithardo* (Paris, 1613), and secondly by Mabillon, op. cit. in n. 5, p.111. The drawing shows the church before the Romanesque reconstruction of Abbot Gervin II (1075-96), and equally certainly after the addition by Abbot Gervin I (1045-75) of the eastern exterior crypt which it shows. The church represented in the drawing is therefore that of the time of Hariulf.

9 *LH*, p.315, gives reasons for believing that Hariulf and another scribe independently copied this material from a much earlier document which they had difficulty in reading.

10 A detailed reconstruction of the church is given by W. Effmann, *Centula: St Riquier* (Münster, 1912). An independent study on more cautious lines was given by G. Durand, *La Picardie historique et monumentale*, 4 (Amiens-Paris, 1911), pp.180ff. For a brief modern survey see J. Hubert, *Saint Riquier et la Monachisme Bénédictine en Gaule à l'époque Carolingienne* (St Riquier, 1959). For a study of the altars see E. Lehmann, 'Die Anordnung der Altäre in der karolingischen Klosterkirche zu Centula', *KdG*, 3, pp.373-84. For the excavation of St Mary's church, see H. Bernard, 'Premières fouilles à Saint-Riquier', *KdG*, 3, pp.369-73.

11 H. Reinhardt, *La Cathédrale de Reims* (Paris, 1963), pp.23-36, also fig. 3 and Pl. 3. The evidence from Reims is particularly important because the surviving foundations settle beyond doubt the great size of the western gallery-church.

12 J. Hubert, op. cit in n. 10; also in *IVa SdS* (1957), pp.300-303.

13 Mabillon, op. cit. in n. 5, p.127.

14 *Hariulf*, pp.70-1.

15 *Hariulf*, p.308.

16 *Hariulf*, p.298. The service on Saturday of Easter Week provided for the monks to go down to the font from St Richar and then up from it to St Saviour.

17 *Hariulf*, p.299.

18 *Hariulf*, pp.305-6; also Lehmann, op. cit. in n. 10, pp.376-80, where in line 10 of p.379 St Stephan should read St Laurentius as specified in the statutes of Angilbert.

19 *Hariulf*, pp.299-302.

20 The credit for interpreting the great 9th-century church at Corvey belongs to W. Effmann, whose posthumous *Die Kirche der Abtei Corvey* (Paderborn, 1929) is still the greatest source book for the church. The most complete and convincing modern study is H. Busen, 'Kloster und Klosterkirche zu Corvey' in *Kunst und Kultur im Weserraum*, ed. H. Eichler (Corvey, 1967), 1, pp.19-42, with exhaustive bibliography. The liturgical arrangements were first considered in detail by F. Kreusch, *Beobachtungen an der Westanlage der Klosterkirche zu Corvey*, Beih. d. Bonner Jb., 9 (Köln-Graz, 1963), pp.49-73.

21 Kreusch, op. cit. in n. 20, pp.49-51.

22 Busen, op. cit. in n. 20, pp.35-6.

23 The full text from Letzner is given by Kreusch, op. cit. in n. 20, p.55.

24 C. R. Peers and A. W. Clapham, 'St Augustine's Abbey church, Canterbury', *Archaeologia*, 77 (1927), pp.201-18. The rededication by St Dunstan is recorded in

William of Thorne's Chronicle of St Augustine's, Canterbury, ed. A. H. Davis (Oxford, 1934), p.38.

25 For plans of the abbey churches and monastic buildings see *ASArchit.*, p.136.

26 *MO*, p.35.

27 A. W. Clapham, 'Note on the pre-Conquest Cloisters', *Archaeologia Cantiana*, **46** (1934), pp.191-4.

28 M. Biddle, 'Archaeology and the beginnings of English society' in *Whitelock Festschrift*, p.406, n. 2.

29 R. Krautheimer, 'Iconography of Medieval Architecture', *JWCI*, **5** (1942), pp.1-33.

30 H.M. Taylor, 'The Anglo-Saxon Cathedral Church at Canterbury', *Arch. J.*, **126** (1969), pp.101-30. This gives the sources in the original Latin and in translation. D. Parsons, 'The Pre-Conquest Cathedral at Canterbury', *Archaeologia Cantiana*, **84** (1969), pp.175-84. R. D. H. Gem, 'The Anglo-Saxon Cathedral Church at Canterbury: a further contribution', *Arch. J.*, **127** (1970), pp.196-201. E. C. Gilbert, 'The date of the Late Saxon Cathedral at Canterbury', *ibid.*, pp.202-10.

31 It is of course possible that Canterbury originally had a west entrance, which was later blocked, as was suggested by Gem, op. cit. in n. 30, p.196.

32 Gem, op. cit. in n. 30, p.196, n. 5. Steps at this point need not suggest a crypt beneath the oratory as is implied by Gilbert, op. cit. in n. 30, p.207.

33 Taylor, op. cit. in n. 30, p.112.

34 Gilbert, op. cit. in n. 30, p.207.

35 J. B. Ward Perkins and R. G. Goodchild, 'The early Christian Antiquities of Tripolitania', *Archaeologia*, **95** (1953), pp.1-82, especially pp.67-70.

36 For a discussion of the historical and archaeological evidence see *ASArchit.*, pp.250-7, and for the further evidence from William of Malmesbury see Joan and Harold Taylor, 'Pre-Norman Churches of the Border', in *Celt and Saxon . . .*, ed. N. K. Chadwick (Cambridge, 1963), pp.252-7.

37 Peers, Clapham and Horne in *Proc. Somerset Arch. Soc.*, **74** (1928), pp.1-9.

38 For an example at Werden on the Ruhr see H. M. Taylor, 'Corridor Crypts . . . ', *N. Staffs. J. Field Stud.*, **9** (1968), pp.19-23. For Great Britain it must suffice to name three examples, of which the first lies in Scotland and the others in England: at Ardwall Island, an early shrine in the open was later enclosed in a wooden oratory, and still later in a stone church (C. Thomas in *Med. Arch.*, **11** (1967), pp.127-188); at Hexham, the Anglo-Saxon cemetery clustering round the contemporary sanctuary was later partially enclosed below the Norman sanctuary and still later wholly covered by that of the 13th century (*ASArchit.*, fig. 130); and at Repton a freestanding 8th-century royal mausoleum within the grounds of the earlier abbey was later built over to become a crypt beneath the sanctuary of the enlarged abbey church (H. M. Taylor, 'Repton Reconsidered', in *Whitelock Festschrift*, pp.351-89).

39 *EHD*, p.472.

40 H. P. R. Finberg, *The Early Charters of the West Midlands* (Leicester, 1961), p.76.

41 *Gesta Pont.*, p.169

42 It is only fair to add that the evidence from the sources named in notes 39 and 41 appeared not to convince Professor Knowles that a monastery existed at Deerhurst

before Oswald's bishopric at Worcester. For that view see *MO*, p.52; but for an indication that he later accepted this as a *refoundation* see D. Knowles, C.N.L. Brooke and V.C.M. London (ed.), *The Heads of Religious Houses, England and Wales 940-1216* (Cambridge, 1972), p.102.

43 See, for example, W. H. Knowles, 'Deerhurst Priory Church', *Archaeologia*, 77 (1927), pp.141-64; E. C. Gilbert, 'Deerhurst Priory Church', *Trans. Bristol and Gloucs. Arch. Soc.*, 61 (1939), pp.294-307, and 'Deerhurst Priory Church Revisited', *ibid.*, 73 (1954), pp.73-114; *ASArchit.*, pp.193-209; E. D. C. Jackson and E. G. M. Fletcher, 'The Anglo-Saxon Priory Church at Deerhurst' in *Studies in Building History*, ed. E. M. Jope (London, 1962), pp.64-77.

44 Excavations to settle this and other questions were carried out in 1971 and 1972 under the direction of Mr P. A. Rahtz. See *Current Archaeology*, 3 (1971), pp.135-9, and 'Deerhurst Church, interim note on 1971 excavation', *Trans. Bristol and Gloucs. Arch. Soc.*, 90 (1971), pp.129-35.

45 See an article by J. C. Buckler, edited by A. E. Hudd, and with footnotes by G. Butterworth, in *Trans. Bristol and Gloucs. Arch. Soc.*, 11 (1886-7), p.17, n., for the foundations, and p.30, n., for the marks which were seen on the side walls from floor to roof when the plaster was removed.

46 Doubt has been raised about the original position of this carving. It is very difficult to settle whether features in rubble walls are original or later insertions; but I can see no evidence to suggest that this is a later insertion. The carving seems to have been left unfinished or to have been given a smooth surface for painting. The representation seems to be the type in which the Virgin holds a medallion which carries an image of the Holy Child. See A. Grabar, *Byzantium* (London, 1966), figs. 180 and 193 for examples of this iconography in the 6th and 7th century in Egypt and Rome. I am indebted to Miss B. Raw for this reference.

47 The doorway H in this wall is square-headed both on the east and also on the west.

48 The existence of the doorway H proves that when the wall was first built the floor was still in existence.

49 *ASArchit.*, fig. 316.

50 A picture of the ceremony at Aachen in 1664 is reproduced in *Berichte des Karlsvereins*, 121 (Aachen, 1968), p.18. Notes on the history of this ceremony at Aachen from 881 onward and of its survival there and at Kornelimünster to the present day are given by L. Hugot, *Kornelimünster*, Rheinische Ausgrabungen, 2 (Köln-Graz, 1968), p.18, with a picture of the modern ceremony Pl. 3,2.

51 Doubts might be felt whether it would be safe to span a 21ft.-wide nave at a height of 40ft. with a floor carried on wooden beams. My doubts on this score were set at rest when I noted that the dining hall of Clare College, Cambridge, is 30ft. wide and since 1668 has carried at about the same height two ranges of student rooms opening from a central corridor and all supported on wooden beams across the full span of the hall, which is about 60ft. in length without any cross-walls.

52 At Repton there is evidence of a wide doorway that led at a similar height and position from above the choir to a room above the sanctuary; and at Norton there survive four doorways, at a similar height, formerly leading from the central tower into upper chambers above the nave, sanctuary and transepts.

53 A. G. Hill, 'Some post-Visigothic churches of Spain', *Archaeologia*, 59 (1904), p.42.

54 Mr Biddle's excavations at Winchester, reported elsewhere in this volume, pp.136-139, seem to show a like conservatism at the Old Minster, where the core of

King Kenwalh's church begun about 642 survived until after the Conquest.

55 See, for example, L. Hugot, op. cit. in n. 50, and H. Borger, *Beiträge zur Frühgeschichte des Xantener Viktorstiftes*, Rheinische Ausgrabungen, **6** (Köln-Graz, 1969).

Chapter 12

1 BM Add. MS 49598. See *Faber Ben.* for the quotation.

2 I regret that I have not been able to take into account Dr. R. Deshman's Princeton Ph.D. dissertation 'The iconography of the full-page miniatures of the Benedictional of St Aethelwold' (1969). I am grateful to him for discussing the Benedictional with me. When his work is published we shall have new and important evidence for the contribution made to the art of the reform period by the Anglo-Saxon royal house.

3 Boulogne-sur-Mer, Bibliothèque municipale, MS 10. Briefly mentioned in *Homburger*, pp.4, 47; F. Wormald, 'Decorated initials in English manuscripts from AD 900 to 1100', *Archaeologia*, **91** (1945), pp.120, 133; *Rice*, p.206.

4 BM Add. MS 47967. *The Tollemache Orosius*, ed. A. Campbell, EEMF, **3** (Copenhagen-London-Baltimore, 1953); Wormald, op. cit. in n. 3, pp.118ff.

5 E. H. Zimmermann, *Vorkarolingische Miniaturen* (Berlin, 1916), Taf. 227, 254a, 270.

6 Oxford, Bodleian Library, MS Junius 27 (*Summary Catalogue*, no.5139). *Ker Catalogue*, pp.408-9; J. J. G. Alexander, *Anglo-Saxon Illumination in Oxford Libraries*, Bodleian Library Picture Books, Special series, 1 (Oxford, 1971), Pls. 2a-c. Many initials have been cut out.

7 M. Schapiro, 'The initials of the Leningrad manuscript of Bede', *Scriptorium*, **12** (1958), pp.191-207.

8 *The Vespasian Psalter*, ed. D. H. Wright, EEMF, **14** (Copenhagen, 1967).

9 BM, Cotton MS Galba A.xviii. Miniatures reproduced by E. G. Millar, *English Illuminated Manuscripts from the Xth to the XIIIth Century* (Paris-Brussels, 1926), pp.2-3, Pl. 2.

10 *LH*, p.141, n.

11 *The Rabbula Gospels*, ed. C. Cecchelli, J. Furlani, M. Salmi (Olten-Lausanne, 1959); A. Grabar, *Les Ampoules de Terre Sainte* (Paris, 1958).

12 W. F. Volbach, *Elfenbeinarbeiten der Spätantike und des frühen Mittelalters* (Mainz, 1952), no.110, Taf. 33.

13 MS Rawl. B. 484, fol. 85. Alexander, op. cit. in n. 6, Pl. 1c.

14 K. Weitzmann, *The Fresco Cycle of S. Maria di Castelseprio* (Princeton, 1951), pp.54-5, fig. 5, discusses the iconography which is based on the classical scene of the birth of Dionysus. The woman pouring water into the bath is found at Castelseprio and in earlier examples, but not in the Utrecht Psalter, see E.T. De Wald, *The Illustrations of the Utrecht Psalter* (Princeton, 1933) on fols. 42^r, 50^v and 88^v. It is not clear if the figure on the left in the Rawlinson MS is the doubting midwife, Salome. For a 6th-century Byzantine example see J. Beckwith, 'Some early Byzantine rock crystals', in a memorial volume for David Talbot Rice (Edinburgh University Press, forthcoming).

15 Volbach, op. cit. in n. 12, no.56, Taf. 14.

16 CCCC MS 286. F. Wormald, *The Miniatures in the Gospels of St Augustine* (Cambridge, 1954).

17 L. H. Loomis, 'The Holy Relics of Charlemagne and King Athelstan. The Lances of Longinus and St Mauricius', *Speculum*, 25 (1950), pp.447ff.

18 For an insular Last Judgment in which Christ holds the Cross see St Gallen, Stiftsbibliothek, Cod. 51, second half of the 8th century. J. Duft and P. Meyer, *The Irish Miniatures in the Abbey Library of St Gall* (Olten, 1954), p.101, Pl. XIV.

19 MS Junius 11 (*Summary Catalogue*, no.5123). *Drawings*, p.76. I. Gollancz, *The Caedmon Manuscript of Anglo-Saxon Biblical Poetry: Junius XI in the Bodleian Library* (Oxford, 1927).

20 O. Pächt, *The Rise of Pictorial Narrative in Twelfth-Century England* (Oxford, 1962), p.5. G. Henderson, 'Late-antique influences in some English medieval illustrations of Genesis', *JWCI*, 25 (1962), pp.172ff., and 'The sources of the Genesis cycle at Saint-Savin-sur-Gartempe', *JBAA*, 3rd series, 26 (1963), pp.11ff. It is possible to suggest that the inclusion of Abel is due to Gregory the Great's homily for Septuagesima (*PL*, 76, col.1154), which was translated into Old English by Aelfric (*Sweet*, p.62), and in which he speaks of the saints from Abel the Just to the last elect: *ab Abel justo usque ad ultimum electum.* I owe this reference to the kindness of Prof. P. Clemoes. Abel's offering is represented at Ravenna in the mid-6th century in the mosaics of San Vitale. Ravenna, where eastern and western iconographies occur in conjunction, might well be the source behind the Psalter pictures, I feel. For the saints making their offerings in rows one also thinks of a 6th-century Ravenna monument, Sant'Apollinare Nuovo.

21 Cambridge, Trinity College, MS B.16.3. *Rickert*, Pl. 19.

22 MS 223. J. Prochno, *Das Schreiber- und Dedikationsbild in der deutschen Buchmalerei*, I Teil: *800-1100* (Leipzig-Berlin, 1929), pp.11-16.

23 *Schriftquellen*, 1, p.502, no. 1854.

24 Oxford, St John's College, MS 194. *Drawings*, p.77, Pl. 40*b*. Alexander, op. cit. in n. 6, Pl. 5.

25 Cotton MS Tiberius A.ii. *Drawings*, Pl. 40*a*; *LH*, p.141, n.; *Ker Catalogue*, pp.239-40. For the inscriptions in the Gandersheim Gospels which may have been given to Otto the Great in exchange, see I. Hubay, *Die Handschriften der Landesbibliothek Coburg* (Coburg, 1962), MS 1. I am indebted to Mr Michael Woods for this reference. There is a useful discussion of MSS associated with Athelstan in *Robinson II*, pp.51-71.

26 MS 183. *Rickert*, Pl. 20*a*; *Ker Catalogue*, pp.64-5.

27 St Gallen, Stiftsbibliothek, Cod. 23. Prochno, op. cit. in n. 22, p. 18, Taf. 18*.

28 Cotton MS Otho B.ix. *Ker Catalogue*, pp.223-4, with references.

29 Oxford, Bodleian Library, MS Auct. F.4.32; *Classbook; Drawings*, p.74, Pl. 1.

30 F. Saxl and R. Wittkower, *British Art and the Mediterranean* (Oxford, 1948), Pl. 21.1; that the kneeling figure is an addition is stated by M. W. Evans, *Medieval Drawings* (London, 1969), p.24, Pl. 24; *Drawings*, p.74, leaves the question open; against this view, see *Classbook*, pp.vi-vii.

31 *Drawings*, nos. 51, 54, comparing a Carolingian drawing of the Trinity, Vatican Pal. lat. 834: A. Goldschmidt, *German Illumination*, 2 vols. (Florence-New York-Paris, 1928), 1, Pl. 61.

32 *Elfenbeinsk.*, 1, nos. 13, 14.

33 *Rickert*, p.32, compares the monks in the frontispiece of the Trinity College, Cambridge, Hrabanus with the kneeling Dunstan. The main figure of Christ cannot

be derived from such a model, however. The type of the kneeling abbot is repeated in a number of later Anglo-Saxon manuscripts.

34 *ECM*, p.xx, Pl. I.1.

35 *Artem scribendi necnon citharizandi pariterque pingendi peritiam diligenter excoluit: B Life*, pp.20-21.

36 Oxford, Bodleian Library, MS Bodley 579 (*Summary Catalogue*, no.2675); F. E. Warren, *The Leofric Missal* (Oxford, 1883); *Drawings*, no.49; Alexander, op. cit. in n. 6, Pls. 9, 10; *English Kalendars before AD 1100*, ed. F. Wormald, HBS, 72 (London, 1934), pp.43-55; A. Heimann, 'Three illustrations from the Bury St Edmunds Psalter and their prototypes', *JWCI*, 29 (1966), pp.39-59.

37 *Drawings*, pp.29-35, 69-70.

38 *Roxb. Ben.; Faber Ben.*

39 *Faber Ben.*, p.12. All 12 Apostles are shown on fols. 2^v-4, however. It seems more likely to me that the Majesty was on the first verso, and that there were three, not two, Choirs of Angels each with three angels, ie. nine orders. Then came, on facing versos and rectos, Patriarchs, Prophets, Martyrs, Confessors, Virgins and Apostles, as in the Athelstan Psalter, where the inscriptions have got misplaced, however, the inscription for the Patriarchs being placed below the Prophets.

40 Paris, BN Lat. 1141. A. Boinet, *La Miniature Carolingienne* (Paris, 1913), Pl. CXXXIII. It should not be forgotten that standing saints are represented in the calendar of the Athelstan Psalter. Aethelwold himself made for Abingdon a gold retable on which the 12 Apostles were represented, see *Chronicon monasterii de Abingdon*, ed. J. Stevenson, RS, 2 ,2 vols. (London, 1858), 2, p.278.

41 *Homburger*, p. 8; *Elfenbeinsk.*, 1, no.96.

42 An iconography probably deriving from Reims. See F. Oppenheimer, *The Legend of the Ste. Ampoule* (London, 1953), pp.37, 140ff., 276-7, Pls. 2-3.

43 *Elfenbeinsk.*, 1, nos. 74, 66.

44 *Elfenbeinsk.*, 1, no.118.

45 Paris, BN Lat. 9428. W. Köhler, *Die karolingischen Miniaturen*, 3, Zweiter Teil: *Metzer Handschriften* (Berlin, 1960), p. 161, Taf. 88*b*.

46 Elfenbeinsk., 1, no. 31.

47 Elfenbeinsk., 1, nos. 86, 89.

48 Benedict Biscop had Apocalypse scenes painted in the church at Monkwearmouth. An Apocalypse at Valenciennes, Bibliothèque municipale, MS 99, probably copies an insular MS, see M. R. James, *The Apocalypse in Art* (London, 1931), pp. 22, 33. It was exhibited at the 10th Council of Europe Exhibition at Aachen in 1965; see exhibition catalogue: *Karl der Grosse . . . /Charlemagne . . .* (Aachen/Aix-la-Chapelle, 1965), no.444 (pp.267-8), where it is ascribed to the Middle Rhine (?Mainz), c. 800.

49 Paris, BN Gr. 510, fol. 301, Gregory Nazianzus. S. Seeliger, *Pfingsten* (Düsseldorf, 1958).

50 Rouen, Bibliothèque municipale, MS Y.7 (369), fol. 29^v. V. Leroquais, *Les Pontificaux manuscrits des Bibliothèques publiques de France*, 4 vols. (Paris, 1937), 2, no.189, Pl. V.

51 H. Feldbusch, *Die Himmelfahrt Mariae* (Düsseldorf, 1951), Taf. 2.

52 BM Harley MS 2904. *Drawings*, no. 36, frontispiece, Pls. 8,9. C. Niver, 'The Psalter in the British Museum, Harley 2904' in *Medieval Studies in Memory of A. Kingsley Porter*, ed. W. R. W. Koehler, 2 vols. (Cambridge, Mass., 1939), 2, pp.667ff. There is, however, no evidence that this is in fact the 'Psalterium Sancti

Oswaldi' mentioned in a 14th-century Ramsey inventory. For its probable Winchester origin see *Rickert*, p.34, and *ECM*, p.14.

53 G. Zarnecki, 'The Coronation of the Virgin on a capital from Reading Abbey', *JWCI*, 13 (1950), pp.1-12.

54 BM Cotton MS Vespasian A.viii. *Rickert*, Pl. 25; D. Whitelock, 'The authorship of the account of King Edgar's establishment of the monasteries' in *Philological Essays in honour of Herbert Dean Merritt*, ed. J. L. Rosier, (Mouton, 1970), p.131, says that the charter was probably drawn up by Aethelwold himself. For the date see F. Wormald, 'Late Saxon art: some questions and suggestions', *Studies in Western Art: Acts of the 20th International Congress of the History of Art*, ed. M. Meiss, 4 vols. (Princeton, 1963), 1: *Romanesque and Gothic Art*, pp. 23-6.

55 W. Köhler, *Die karolingischen Miniaturen*, 2: *Die Hofschule Karls des Grossen* (Berlin, 1958). Exhibition catalogue (see no. 48) nos. 412-9 (pp.244-53) and 517-33 (pp.332-44).

56 A. Boeckler, *Abendländische Miniaturen bis zum Ausgang der romanischen Zeit* (Berlin-Leipzig, 1930), pp.53-4.

57 Nordenfalk in *Early Medieval Painting*, A. Grabar and C. Nordenfalk (New York, 1957), pp.151ff. Boinet, op. cit. in n. 40, Pls. CXIII-CXXXV. For the use of Corbie liturgical manuscripts as a model for the reformed English Caroline minuscule, see *ECM*, pp.xi, n. 1, and 12.

58 East Berlin, Deutsche Staatsbibliothek, Cod. theol. lat. fol. 1. Boeckler, op. cit. in n. 56, Taf. 35; E. Rothe, *Medieval Book Illumination in Europe* (London, 1968), p. 237, Pl. 15.

59 O. Homburger, 'L'art carolingien de Metz et l'"Ecole de Winchester" ', in *Essais en l'honneur de Jean Porcher*, ed. O. Pächt, *Gazette des Beaux Arts*, 62 (1963), p.42.

60 R. Freyhan, 'The place of the stole and maniple in Anglo-Saxon art of the tenth century', *Relics*, pp.409-32.

61 F. Wormald, 'Anniversary address', *Antiq. J.*, 47 (1967), pp.159-65, colour plate; *Winch. Exc. 5*, p.277, Pl. XXII.

62 For the possible connection of the Eagle symbol of St John blowing a trumpet (fol. 19v) with the Lindisfarne Gospels (or perhaps its Cassiodoran model) see R. L. S. Bruce-Mitford in *Evangeliorum Quattuor Codex Lindisfarnensis*, ed. T. D. Kendrick et al. (Olten-Lausanne, 1960), p.159, n. 9, Pl. 28d.

63 *Faber Ben.*, p.13. See also F. Wormald, 'A fragment of a tenth-century English Gospel Lectionary' in *Calligraphy and Palaeography: Essays presented to Alfred Fairbank*, ed. A. S. Osley (London, 1965), pp.43-6.

64 *ECM*.

65 BM Cotton MS Tiberius A.iii. *Drawings*, no. 31, Pl. 23; C. R. Dodwell, *The Canterbury School of Illumination* (Cambridge, 1954), pp.3ff., 37, 120, Pls. 2b, 3a, dating the manuscript c.1040-70; *RC*, pp.lv-lix, frontispiece.

66 Durham, Cathedral Library, MS B.III.32. *Drawings*, no. 20, Pl. 29; R. A. B. Mynors, *Durham Cathedral Manuscripts* (Durham, 1939), pp.28-9, Pl. 15a; F. Wormald, 'Two Anglo-Saxon miniatures compared', *Br. Mus. Quarterly*, 9 (1934-5), pp.113-5, Pl. XXXV; Dodwell, op. cit. in n. 65, pp. 5, 120, Pl. 3b, dates it c.1050-80. The manuscript only reached Durham in the late 17th or early 18th century and is probably of Canterbury origin.

67 J. J. G. Alexander, *Norman Illumination at Mont St. Michel c.966-1100* (Oxford, 1970), pp.100-102.

68 I should like to thank Prof. C. R. Dodwell for reading and commenting on this paper. Unfortunately Prof. Wormald's paper 'The Winchester School before St Aethelwold', in *Whitelock Festschrift*, pp.305-13, appeared too late for me to make use of it.

Chapter 13

1 *Aelfric Life*, p.264.

2 L. Stone, *Sculpture in Britain: the Middle Ages* (Harmondsworth, 1955), p.3.

3 W. G. Collingwood, *Northumbrian Sculpture of the Pre-Norman Age* (London, 1927), p.184.

4 G. Zarnecki, '1066 and architectural sculpture', *Proc. Br. Acad.*, **52** (1966), p.90.

5 E. M. Jope, 'The Saxon building stone industry in southern and midland England', *Med. Arch.*, **8** (1964), pp.91-118.

6 I do not regard these as 10th-century pieces. It is beyond the scope of this paper to discuss them, but I do so in *Kolloquium über spätantike und frühmittelalterliche Skulptur*, 3 (Mainz, forthcoming). For illustrations see *Kendrick I*, Pls. LXXV, LXXVI.

7 This point is made by Stone, op. cit. in n. 2, pp.21-22. I would modify his view, however, by seeing closer resemblances between these three fragments and the Vespasian Psalter dated early 8th century, than with the later Canterbury MSS such as the *Codex Aureus*, Royal IE.6., or Vatican Barbarini Lat. 570 — whose influence can be detected on a later Saxo-Mercian group of sculptures.

8 *Rice*, p.128.

9 F. Cotrill, 'Some pre-conquest stone carvings in Wessex', *Antiq. J.*, **15** (1935), pp.144-151.

10 This can be seen in the mask with animal terminal moustaches and the type of winged biped with speckled body.

11 R. Cramp, 'The position of the Otley crosses in English sculpture of the eighth to ninth centuries', *Kolloquium über spätantike und frühmittelalterliche Skulptur*, 2, ed. V. Milojčić (Mainz, 1971), pp.55-63.

12 The charter which records this event is however discredited, see *ASCh.*, no.1380.

13 G. Baldwin Brown, *The Arts in early England*, **6**(2) (London, 1937), pp.272-3, Pl. 102.

14 *Kendrick I*, pp. 192-3, Pl. LXXXVI.

15 M. Rix, 'The Wolverhampton cross-shaft', *Arch. J.*, **117** (1960), pp.71-81.

16 *KdG*, 3, p.177, Pls. 10, 11.

17 *Emp. Carol.*, p.237, Pl. 216.

18 The bindings of the triangular panels could however be copied on the smaller shaft at Sandbach, Cheshire.

19 Rix's reconstruction with a square-sectioned shaft above the collar is no more certain than that the shaft was simply capped by a cross head in the manner of the Trier shaft.

20 *Kendrick I*, Pl. LXXXV.

21 N. Drinkwater, 'A pre-conquest cross-shaft, formerly at East Stour in Dorset', *Arch. J.*, **117** (1960), pp. 82-7.

22 Burlington Fine Arts Club, *Catalogue of an exhibition of art in the Dark*

Ages in Europe, c.400-1100 AD (London, 1930), pp.105-6, Pl. 33.

23 *Kendrick I*, Pl. XCIX. The scooped petal often grouped in a rosette may, like the 'Byzantine blossom', be derived from East Christian art. See [M. C. Ross] *Catalogue of Byzantine and Early Christian Antiquities in the Dumbarton Oaks Collection*, (Washington D.C., 1965), no.33, Pl. 26, p. 32.

24 See *Historia translationis sancti Augustini episcopi... auctore Goscelino ... (PL*, 155); relevant extract quoted in *Schriftquellen*, 1, pp.189-90, no.700.

25 I am grateful to Mr Biddle for allowing me to see this material in advance of publication and also for drawing my attention to the account of the Winchester carved tower.

26 *Quirk II*.

27 See C. Beutler, *Bildwerke zwischen Antike und Mittelalter*, (Düsseldorf, 1964).

28 *Drawings*, no.28, Pl. 19(*a*).

29 *Emp. Carol.*, fig. 173.

30 I stress both the region and the social milieu for the production of these works since we obviously have no proof of how swiftly and how widely this style was disseminated.

31 R. Freyhan, 'The place of the stole and maniple in Anglo-Saxon art of the tenth century' in *Relics*, pp.412-3.

32 *Kendrick II*, p.40, Pl. XXXIV.

33 Mentioned in *Trans. Bristol and Gloucs. Arch. Soc.*, 41 (1918-19), p.188, and illustrated fig. 49.

34 The material from the excavations at the Old Minster, Winchester, includes many examples of pelleted plait-work.

35 *Rice*, Pls. 7*a*, 7*b*, 8*a* and 8*b*.

36 *Kendrick I*, p.217.

37 G. Baldwin Brown, *The Arts in early England*, 2, 2nd edition (London, 1925), fig. 87, facing p.219.

38 *Clapham*, p.137.

39 *Rice*, pp.92-3.

40 Zarnecki, op. cit. in n. 4, p. 90, n. 1.

41 It is usually accepted that this iconography, like the fillet which binds flat the hair, is derived from a Byzantine prototype.

42 *Rice*, Pl 10*b*.

43 CCCC 23. *Rice*, Pl. 71*b*.

44 *Rice*, Pl. 33.

45 M. H. Longhurst, *English Ivories* (London, 1926), pp. 10, 74, 75, and Pl. XVII; O. M. Dalton, *Catalogue of the Ivory Carvings of the Christian Era... in the... British Museum* (London, 1909), no.31; J. Beckwith, *Ivory Carvings in Early Medieval England* (London, 1972), no.41, pp.53, 126, illustr. 78, 79. Longhurst, Dalton and Beckwith consider this to be Trinitarian scene with the figure of the Dove broken off between them. Certainly something is broken between the figures, but one must accept Kantorowicz's view that we do not know what was there, so this piece cannot be claimed as the earliest English example of Trinitarian iconography: see E. H. Kantorowicz, 'The Quinity of Winchester', *Art Bulletin*, 29 (1947), pp.73-85 (p.74, n. 6). Beckwith implies that both carvings are of the same late 10th- or early 11th-century date.

46 It could be that he is pointing to the Father with his right hand, but the

gesture looks more like a blessing. In some 11th-century manuscripts the figures hold books, see for example Kantorowicz, op. cit. in n. 45, Fig. 1. Kantorowicz, Longhurst, Dalton and Beckwith all draw attention to the relationship between the scene on the seal and that in the Winchester Offices, of which this figure is an illustration.

47 Longhurst, op. cit. in n. 45, Pl. VII, p.6.

48 A. R. and P. M. Green, *Saxon Architecture and sculpture in Hampshire* (Winchester, 1951).

49 The examples associated with buildings have been listed by *Quirk II*, pp.29-30, and more fully described by Joan and Harold Taylor, 'Architectural sculpture in pre-Norman England', *JBAA*, 3rd. series, 29 (1966), pp.4-17, but until more work is done on their iconography little more can be said. Miss B. Raw and Miss E. Coatsworth are engaged in complementary research on this material.

50 For a discussion of the oriental origins of these beasts see R. Bernheimer, *Romanische Tierplastik und die Ursprünge ihrer Motive* (Munich, 1931).

Chapter 14

1 See, for example, the treasures of Ely listed in *Schriftquellen*, 1, pp.410ff.

2 *Elfenbeinsk.*, 4, Pl. II, 10.

3 D. M. Wilson, *The Anglo-Saxons*, 2nd edition (Harmondsworth, 1971), Pl. 16.

4 *Metalwork*, Pls. XII-XIV, XXIV and XXVII.

5 *Homburger.*

6 Wilson, op. cit. in n. 3, p.19, and *Metalwork*, pp.5-9.

7 *Metalwork*, pp.117-8, 131.

8 Listed in *Metalwork*, p.7.

9 *Metalwork*, fig. 40.

10 Compare the capitals of the Soissons Gospels, see C. R. Dodwell, *Painting in Europe, 800-1200* (Harmondsworth, 1971), Pl. 20.

11 *Kendrick II*, Pl. II.

12 See *JBAA*, 11 (1855), p.36.

13 J. D. Bu'lock, 'The Celtic, Saxon and Scandinavian settlement in Wirral', *Trans. Hist. Soc. Lancs. and Cheshire*, 112 (1960), fig. 4*f*.

14 *Kendrick II*, Pl. XXXIII, 1.

15 *Winch. Exc. 7*, pp.326-8.

16 F. Wormald, 'Late Anglo-Saxon art: some questions and suggestions' in *Studies in Western Art: Acts of the 20th International Congress of the History of Art*, ed. M. Meiss, 4 vols. (Princeton, 1963), 1: *Romanesque and Gothic Art*, pp.19-26.

17 *Metalwork*, Pls. XII-XIV, XXIV and XXVII.

18 *Metalwork*, Pl. VIII*a*.

19 *Metalwork*, fig. 5, and M. Chamot, *English Medieval Enamels* (London, 1930), Pl. 3*b*.

20 Chamot, op. cit. in n. 19, Pl. 1*e*.

21 *Metalwork*, Pl. XVII, 14.

22 A number of these brooches are illustrated by K. Dinklage, 'Karolingischer Schmuck aus dem Speyer- und Wormsgau', *Pfälzer Heimat*, 6 (1955), pp.1-4, 41-6.

23 A. Riegel, *Die spätrömische Kunstindustrie*, 2 parts (Vienna, 1901-23), 2, pp.70ff.

24 H. Arbman, 'Die Kremsmünsterer Leuchter', *Medd. Lunds Univ. hist. Mus.* (1958), pp.170-92.

25 W. von Jenny, 'Ein Leuchterpaar der ottonischen Zeit aus Stift Kremsmünster' in *Forschungen zur Kunstgeschichte und christlichen Archäologie*, 1: *Neue Beiträge zur Kunstgeschichte des 1. Jahrtausends*, (Baden-Baden, 1952), pp.285ff.

26 G. Haseloff, *Der Tassilokelch* (Munich, 1951), pp.66-7.

27 Arbman, op. cit. in n. 24.

28 M. Strömberg, *Untersuchungen zur jüngeren Eisenzeit in Schonen, Völkerwanderungszeit − Wikingerzeit*, Acta Archaeologica Lundensia, 4to series, 4, 2 vols. (Lund, 1961), 2, Pl. 65.

29 J. Brøndsted, *Early English Ornament* (London-Copenhagen, 1924), p.267

30 R. L. S. Bruce-Mitford, 'Late Saxon disc-brooches' in *Dark-Age Britain*, ed. D. B. Harden (London, 1956), Pl. XXXIa.

31 A recent find of a buckle from Winchester has made me question this judgment. Its ornament is closely related to that on these two swords. See *Winch. Exc. 10*.

32 D. M. Wilson and O. Klindt-Jensen, *Viking Art* (London, 1966), Pl. XLVI.

33 Information from Mr R. H. M. Dolley.

34 See, for example, the Velds stirrup mounts, which may equally well be English or Scandinavian (*Metalwork*, Pl. IXa).

35 *Kendrick II*.

36 *Metalwork*, fig. 40.

37 D. M. Wilson, 'Two tenth-century bronze objects', *Med. Arch.*, 9 (1965), pp.154-6.

38 *Winch. Exc. 3*, pp.263-4.

39 eg. *Metalwork*, Pls. XXI, XLI,

40 D. M. Wilson, 'Some neglected late Anglo-Saxon swords', *Med. Arch.*, 9 (1965), Pl. IIA. Since this was published another sword has been published by V. I. Evison, 'A sword from the Thames at Wallingford Bridge', *Arch. J.*, 124 (1967), pp.160-89.

41 Theophilus, *De Diversis Artibus*, ed. C. R. Dodwell, Nelson's Medieval Classics (London, 1961), pp.162ff.

ABBREVIATIONS

The abbreviations are mainly those referring to journals and serial publications most frequently quoted in the notes. In all other cases where shortened forms of periodical titles are used, British Standard 4148 (1967), *Recommendations for the Abbreviation of Titles of Periodicals,* has been followed as far as possible.

Antiq. J.	*Antiquaries' Journal*
Arch. J.	*Archaeological Journal*
BM	British Museum, London
BN	Bibliothèque Nationale, Paris
CCCC	Corpus Christi College, Cambridge
DR	*Downside Review*
EEMF	Early English Manuscripts in Facsimile
EETS	Early English Text Society
EHR	*English Historical Review*
HBS	Henry Bradshaw Society
JBAA	*Journal of the British Archaeological Association*
JEH	*Journal of Ecclesiastical History*
JWCI	*Journal of the Warburg and Courtauld Institutes*
Med. Arch.	*Medieval Archaeology*
MGH	*Monumenta Germaniae Historica*
SdS	*Settimana di Studio del Centro Italiano di Studi sull'Alto Medioevo* (Spoleto)
RB	*Revue Bénédictine*
RS	Rolls Series

SELECT BIBLIOGRAPHY

This bibliography is not intended to be a balanced selection of works referring to the late Anglo-Saxon period. It is simply a list of the titles most frequently quoted by the contributors to this volume, gathered together for the convenience of the reader. The criteria for selection, applied with a little modification, were that a work should be referred to by more than one author or frequently by any one author. The left-hand column is a key to the abbreviations which appear in the notes to the chapters.

ASArchit.   H. M. and Joan Taylor, *Anglo-Saxon architecture*, 2 vols. (Cambridge, 1965)

ASC   *Anglo-Saxon Chronicle*, various editions, most conveniently in *EHD* (see below)

ASCh.   P. H. Sawyer, *Anglo-Saxon charters: an annotated list and bibliography*, R. Hist. Soc. Guides and Handbooks, *8* (London, 1968)

Adelard   *Epistola Adelardi . . . de vita S. Dunstani* in *Memorials* (see below), pp.53-68

Aelfric Homilies   *The homilies of the Anglo-Saxon church . . . the sermones catholici, or homilies of Aelfric*, ed. B. Thorpe, 2 vols. (London, 1844-6)

Aelfric Letters   *Die Hirtenbriefe Aelfrics*, ed. B. Fehr, Bibliothek der angelsächsischen Prosa, *9*, repr. with a supplement to the introduction by P. Clemoes (Darmstadt, 1966)

Aelfric Life   *Vita S. Aethelwoldi . . . auctore Aelfrico* in *Chronicon monasterii de Abingdon*, ed. J. Stevenson, RS, *2*, 2 vols. (London, 1858), 2, pp.253-66

Aethelweard   *The chronicle of Aethelweard*, ed. A. Campbell, Nelson's Medieval Classics, (London, 1962)

BCS   W. de G. Birch, *Cartularium Saxonicum . . .*, 4 vols. (London, 1885-99)

B Life   *S. Dunstani vita auctore B* in *Memorials* (see below), pp.3-52

Barlow   F. Barlow, *The English church, 1000-1066* (London, 1963)

Bethurum   D. Bethurum, *The Homilies of Wulfstan* (Oxford, 1957)

CM	*Consuetudines monasticae*, ed. P. B. Albers, 5 vols. (Stuttgart and Vienna, 1900-12)
Clapham	A. W. Clapham, *English romanesque architecture: before the conquest* (Oxford, 1930, repr. 1964)
Classbook	*Saint Dunstan's classbook from Glastonbury*, intro. by R. W. Hunt, Umbrae codicum occidentalium, 4 (Amsterdam, 1961)
Councils	*Councils and ecclesiastical documents relating to Great Britain and Ireland*, ed. A. W. Haddon and W. Stubbs, 3 vols. (Oxford, 1869-78)
Drawings	F. Wormald, *English drawings of the tenth and eleventh centuries* (London, 1952)
ECM	T. A. M. Bishop, *English caroline minuscule* (Oxford, 1971)
EHD	*English historical documents, c.500-1042*, ed. D. Whitelock (London, 1955)
Elfenbeinsk., 1, etc.	A. Goldschmidt, *Die Elfenbeinskulpturen . . .*, 4 vols. (Berlin-Oxford, 1914-26)
	1, 2: *. . . aus der Zeit der karolingischen und sächsischen Kaiser, VIII-XI Jahrhundert* (1914, repr. 1969)
	3, 4: *. . . aus der romanischen Zeit, XI-XIII Jahrhundert* (1923, 1926)
Emp. Carol.	*L'empire carolingien*, ed. J. Hubert, J. Porcher, W. F. Volbach (Paris, 1968)
Faber Ben.	*The Benedictional of St Ethelwold*, with an introduction and notes by F. Wormald, Faber Library of Illuminated Manuscripts (London, 1959)
Fisher I	D. J. V. Fisher, The Anti-Monastic Reaction in the Reign of Edward the Martyr, *Cambridge Hist. J.*, 10 (1952), pp.254-70
Fisher II	D. J. V. Fisher, The Early Biographers of St Ethelwold, *EHR*, 67 (1952), pp.381-91
GK	K. Hallinger, *Gorze-Kluny: Studien zu den monastischen Lebensformen und Gegensätzen im Hochmittelalter*, Studia Anselmiana, 22-3, 24-5, 2 vols. (Rome, 1950-1)
Gesta Pont.	William of Malmesbury, *De gestis pontificum anglorum libri quinque*, ed. N. E. S. A. Hamilton, RS, 52 (London, 1870)

Gesta Reg.	William of Malmesbury, *De gestis regum anglorum libri quinque*, ed. W. Stubbs, RS, 90, 2 vols. (London, 1887-9)
Hariulf	*Hariulf: chronique de l'abbaye de Saint-Riquier*, ed. F. Lot (Paris, 1894)
Homburger	O. Homburger, *Die Anfänge der Malschule von Winchester im X. Jahrhundert* (Leipzig, 1912)
KDG, 2, etc.	*Karl der Grosse: Lebenswerk und Nachleben*, ed. W. Braunfels, 5 vols. (Düsseldorf, 1965-8)
	2: *Das geistige Leben,* ed. B. Bischoff (1965)
	3: *Karolingische Kunst,* ed. W. Braunfels and H. Schnitzler (1965)
	4: *Das Nachleben*, ed. W. Braunfels and P. E. Schramm (1967)
Kendrick I	T. D. Kendrick, *Anglo-Saxon art to AD 900* (London, 1938, repr. 1972)
Kendrick II	T. D. Kendrick, *Late Saxon and Viking art* (London, 1949)
Ker Catalogue	N. R. Ker, *Catalogue of manuscripts containing Anglo-Saxon* (Oxford, 1957)
LH	E. Bishop, *Liturgica Historica* (Oxford, 1918 repr. 1962)
LV	*Liber Vitae: register and martyrology of New Minster and Hyde Abbey*, ed. W. de G. Birch, Hants. Record Soc. (London-Winchester, 1892)
Liebermann	F. Liebermann, *Die Gesetze der Angelsachsen*, 3 vols. (Halle, 1898-1916)
MO	D. Knowles, *The monastic order in England*, 2nd edition (Cambridge, 1963)
MRH	D. Knowles and R. N. Hadcock, *Medieval religious houses: England and Wales*, 2nd edition (London, 1972)
Memorials	*Memorials of St Dunstan, archbishop of Canterbury*, ed. W. Stubbs, RS, 63 (London, 1874)
Metalwork	D. M. Wilson, *Anglo-Saxon ornamental metalwork, 700-1100, in the British Museum* (London, 1964)
OB	E. John, *Orbis Britanniae, and other studies* (Leicester, 1966)
PL	J.-P. Migne, *Patrologiae cursus completus . . . series latina*, 221 vols. (Paris, 1844-1900)
Quirk I	R. N. Quirk, Winchester cathedral in the tenth

century, *Arch. J.*, 114 (1957), pp.28-68

Quirk II   R. N. Quirk, Winchester New Minster and its tenth-century tower, *JBAA*, 3rd series, 24 (1961), pp.16-54

RC   *Regularis concordia . . .* , ed. T. Symons, Nelson's Medieval Classics (London, 1953)

Relics   *The Relics of St Cuthbert*, ed. C. F. Battiscombe (Oxford, 1956)

Rice   D. Talbot Rice, *English art, 871-1100*, Oxford History of English Art, 2 (Oxford, 1952)

Rickert   M. Rickert, *Painting in Britain: the middle ages*, Pelican History of Art, 2nd edition (Harmondsworth, 1965)

Robinson I   J. A. Robinson, *St Oswald and the church of Worcester*, Br. Acad. Suppl. Pap., 5 (London, 1919)

Robinson II   J. A. Robinson, *The times of St Dunstan* (Oxford, 1923, repr. 1969)

Roxb. Ben.   *The Benedictional of St Aethelwold*, ed. G. F. Warner and H. A. Wilson, Roxburghe Club (Oxford, 1910)

Rule   *The rule of St Benedict*, ed. D. H. Farmer, EEMF, 15 (Copenhagen, 1968)

Schriftquellen   O. Lehmann-Brockhaus, *Lateinische Schriftquellen zur Kunst in England, Wales und Schottland vom Jahre 901 bis zum Jahre 1307*, 5 vols. (Munich, 1955-61)

Stenton   F. M. Stenton, *Anglo-Saxon England*, Oxford History of England, 2, 3rd edition (Oxford, 1971)

Sweet   *Sweet's Anglo-Saxon reader*, revised by D. Whitelock (Oxford, 1967)

Vita Oswaldi   *Vita Oswaldi auctore anonymo* in *Historians of the church of York and its archbishops*, ed. J. Raine, RS, 71, 3 vols. (London, 1879), 1, pp.399-475

Vita Wulfstani   William of Malmesbury, *Vita Wulfstani*, ed. R. R. Darlington, Camden Soc. Publs., 3rd series, 40 (London, 1928)

Whitelock Festschrift   *England before the conquest: studies in primary sources presented to Dorothy Whitelock*, ed. P. Clemoes and K. Hughes (Cambridge, 1971)

Winch. Exc. 1   M. Biddle and R. N. Quirk, Excavations near
                       Winchester Cathedral, 1961, *Arch. J.*, 119 (1962),
                       pp. 150-94;

Winch. Exc. 2, 3, etc. thereafter, M. Biddle, Excavations at Winchester,
                       19—, annually in *Antiq. J.* as follows:

      1962-3, 2nd interim report: 44 (1964),
            pp. 188-219

      1964, 3rd interim report: 45 (1965),
            pp. 230-264

      1965, 4th interim report: 46 (1966),
            pp. 308-332

      1966, 5th interim report: 47 (1967),
            pp. 251-279

      1967, 6th interim report: 48 (1968),
            pp. 250-284

      1968, 7th interim report: 49 (1969),
            pp. 295-329

      1969, 8th interim report: 50 (1970),
            pp. 277-326

      1970, 9th interim report: 52 (1972),
            pp. 93-131

      1971, 10th interim report: 55 (1975),
            forthcoming

Wulfstan Life   *Vita S. Ethelwoldi auctore . . . Wolstano* in *PL*,
                       137, cols. 81-114

ADDITIONAL READING
not referred to in the text

R. R. Darlington   Ecclesiastical reform in the late Old English
                    period, *EHR*, (1936), pp.385-428

                    Aethelwig, abbot of Evesham, *EHR*, 48 (1933),
                    pp.1-22, 177-98

M. Deanesly   *The pre-conquest church in England* (London,
                   1961)

                   Sidelights on the Anglo-Saxon church (London,
                   1962)

C. J. Godfrey   *The church in Anglo-Saxon England* (Cam-
                   bridge, 1962)

D. Whitelock   Archbishop Wulfstan, homilist and statesman,
                   Trans. R. Hist. Soc., 4th series, 24 (1942),
                   pp.25-46

INDEX

Preliminary Note

Śaints' names are entered thus: 'Blank, saint'. Entries in the form 'St Blank' indicate place names or church dedications.